LUTHER'S WORKS

LUTHER'S WORKS

VOLUME 4

LECTURES ON GENESIS
Chapters 21—25

JAROSLAV PELIKAN
Editor

WALTER A. HANSEN
Associate Editor

CONCORDIA PUBLISHING HOUSE · SAINT LOUIS

Contents

General Introduction

THE first editions of Luther's collected works appeared in the sixteenth century, and so did the first efforts to make him "speak English." In America serious attempts in these directions were made for the first time in the nineteenth century. The Saint Louis edition of Luther was the first endeavor on American soil to publish a collected edition of his works, and the Henkel Press in Newmarket, Virginia, was the first to publish some of Luther's writings in an English translation. During the first decade of the twentieth century, J. N. Lenker produced translations of Luther's sermons and commentaries in thirteen volumes. A few years later the first of the six volumes in the Philadelphia (or Holman) edition of the *Works of Martin Luther* appeared. Miscellaneous other works were published at one time or another. But a growing recognition of the need for more of Luther's works in English has resulted in this American edition of Luther's works.

The edition is intended primarily for the reader whose knowledge of late medieval Latin and sixteenth-century German is too small to permit him to work with Luther in the original languages. Those who can, will continue to read Luther in his original words as these have been assembled in the monumental Weimar edition (*D. Martin Luthers Werke*. Kritische Gesamtausgabe; Weimar, 1883 ff.). Its texts and helps have formed a basis for this edition, though in certain places we have felt constrained to depart from its readings and findings. We have tried throughout to translate Luther as he thought translating should be done. That is, we have striven for faithfulness on the basis of the best lexicographical materials available. But where literal accuracy and clarity have conflicted, it is clarity that we have preferred, so that sometimes paraphrase seemed more faithful than literal fidelity. We have proceeded in a similar way in the matter of Bible versions, translating Luther's translations. Where this could be done by the use of an existing English version — King James, Douay, or Revised Standard — we have done so. Where it could not, we have supplied our own. To indicate this in each specific instance would have been pedantic; to adopt a uniform procedure would have been artificial — especially in view of Luther's own inconsistency in this regard. In each volume the translator will be responsible primarily for matters of text and language, while the responsibility of the editor will extend principally to the historical and theological matters reflected in the introductions and notes.

Although the edition as planned will include fifty-five volumes, Luther's writings are not being translated in their entirety. Nor should they be. As he was the first to insist, much of what he wrote and said was not that important. Thus the edition is a selection of works that have proved their importance for the faith, life, and history of the Christian Church. The first thirty volumes contain Luther's expositions of various Biblical books, while the remaining volumes include what are usually called his "Reformation writings" and other occasional pieces. The final volume of the set will be an index volume; in addition to an index of quotations, proper names, and topics, and a list of corrections and changes, it will contain a glossary of many of the technical terms that recur in Luther's works and that cannot be defined each time they appear. Obviously Luther cannot be forced into any neat set of rubrics. He can provide his reader with bits of autobiography or with political observations as he expounds a psalm, and he can speak tenderly about the meaning of the faith in the midst of polemics against his opponents. It is the hope of publishers, editors, and translators that through this edition the message of Luther's faith will speak more clearly to the modern church.

J. P.
H. L.

Introduction to Volume 4

WITH the lectures in this volume (Weimar, XLIII, 137–430; St. Louis, I, 1368–1765) Luther brought to a close his exposition of the life of Abraham. For sheer length as well as theological scope, this was the most extensive "biography" he ever produced. Beginning midway in Volume 2 (pp. 236 ff.) and continuing through all of Volume 3 of *Luther's Works,* the biography of Abraham has come to a conclusion here in Volume 4, and "we have buried the saintly patriarch Abraham" (p. 318). There follow the opening chapters of the succeeding patriarchal narratives, which will conclude with the life of Joseph, at the end of the Book of Genesis and the end of Luther's *Lectures on Genesis* in Volume 8 of *Luther's Works.*

Once again the lectures on chapters 21–25 leave us largely uninformed about their chronology and the circumstances under which they were delivered. In the Introduction to Volume 3 we surmised that Luther was lecturing on chapter 19 of Genesis about March or April 1539. For the lectures in the present volume we have two dates that are more definite — only two dates, but both extremely helpful. During the autumn of 1539 Wittenberg suffered one of its periodic visitations of plague. One of the victims was Luther's friend and colleague on the university faculty, Dr. Sebald Münsterer, who was buried on October 26, 1539. From a marginal note, whose authenticity we have no reason to question, we learn that Luther began his lectures on chapter 22 of Genesis on the day after Münsterer's burial. He counseled those who feared the plague to take flight without feeling guilty or ashamed; for himself, however, he believed that the greatest menace was fear itself, and he chose to go on with his lectures. Thus the exposition of chapters 20 and 21 probably fell into the six months between April and October 1539.

There is one other reference in this commentary that provides information about the progress of Luther's lectures: Luther's statement (p. 266) that Philip Melanchthon had taken seriously ill while in Weimar and that Luther and his colleagues were praying for his recovery for the sake of the work of the church and of the university. From a letter addressed to Luther by Melanchthon on June 14, 1540, and from Luther's reply of June 18, we may conclude that Luther's statement, spoken in connection with his exposition of Gen. 24:15, came at about this time. It would seem to follow from this that chapters 22 and 23 of Genesis had been the subject of Luther's lectures during the last two months of 1539 and the first four or five months of 1540, and that he began lecturing on chapter 24 perhaps in May of the latter year. A few pages later, in his comments on Gen. 24:29 (p. 281) Luther refers to outbreaks of arson; as our note on this passage indicates, we have succeeded in finding parallel references to arson in two letters written by Luther on June 12, 1541, and on July 8, 1541. But this parallel, while illuminating and rather intriguing, is certainly not sufficient evidence to warrant any hypothesis that it took Luther an entire year to move from Gen. 24:15 to Gen 24:29, a total of only 15 pages in our edition.

In this volume, as in all of its predecessors, we have based our translation on the Weimar edition of Luther's works. But we have had even more occasion than before to discover a large number of typographical errors in the Weimar text. So many are there, in fact, that we have not called attention to each of them in a separate footnote but have documented our corrections or emendations only where the errors were egregious or where they have actually confused two Latin words. Similarly, we have not annotated our corrections of the identification of references, chiefly Biblical references, in marginal notes or footnotes by the Weimar editors. On the other hand, where the original text itself contains a faulty citation (e. g., p. 281, note 55), we have corrected it in our translation and explained the correction in a footnote. The one exception to this latter procedure has been the numbering in the Book of Psalms. As we have mentioned in other volumes (cf. *Luther's Works*, 13, pp. ix–x), Luther often followed the numbering of the psalms in the Vulgate even late in his life. Apparently unaware of this, the Weimar editors of the *Lectures on Genesis* have inserted an exclamation point in brackets where Luther numbered a psalm according to the Vulgate; we have not followed the Weimar edition in this gratuitous editorial practice, nor have we made specific references to our adaptation of Luther's numbering to that of the Hebrew Bible and the Authorized Version.

As has been the case in previous volumes, the editing of the English translation of Luther has provided an opportunity for tracing many quotations and allusions that have remained unidentified in all previous editions. For example, Luther refers explicitly to Josephus and Pliny in his discussion of "red earth"; but as far as we can tell, no edition of Luther has identified the references before (p. 331, note 30). We have also tried to locate the sources of Luther's references to the Christian and Jewish exegetical traditions. Most of his information about the latter came from Lyra, whose commentary we have continued to consult throughout. But we have discovered that at least one datum was supplied to Luther by the pioneering work of Johannes Reuchlin (cf. p. 393, note 79) rather than by Nicholas of Lyra (cf. also *Luther's Works,* 14, p. 335, note 54). Most of the other Biblical, classical, patristic, and medieval quotations and allusions have been duly noted; but our researches have also led once more to occasional and total frustration (e. g., p. 219, note 2). Finally, we have also adverted once or twice to the editorial problem that affects all of Luther's *Lectures on Genesis,* the question of authenticity and reliability (cf. *Luther's Works,* 1, pp. x–xii), and we have found reason to change neither our conclusion that Luther's editors have taken liberties with individual passages of his work nor our conviction that the result of their editing as a whole is nevertheless fundamentally reliable.   J. P.

LECTURES ON GENESIS

Chapters 21–25

Translated by
GEORGE V. SCHICK

CHAPTER TWENTY-ONE

I HAVE often cautioned against disregarding the chronology in the sacred accounts. We must keep in mind which patriarchs lived at the same time, for in this way extraordinary light is thrown on the history. Thus Abraham saw all the men mentioned in the genealogy that is recorded in Gen. 11. He was a contemporary of Noah for 58 years and of Shem for 31. Moreover, Arphaxad was a contemporary of Abraham for 84 years. Shelah lived three years after Abraham, and Eber 64 years. Peleg was a contemporary of Abraham for 48 years; Reu, for 78 years; Serug, for 101; Nahor, for 49; Terah, for 135. Was this not a most glorious age? During this time the Word was spread abroad by so many teachers of whom some, like Shem, saw the first world, that is, the fathers before the Flood, like Methuselah, who saw Adam, the first human being. And yet Satan prevailed among the children of iniquity. Therefore Sodom was destroyed, and the kingdoms of the world were troubled in various ways by wars. Yes, even Abraham himself was led astray by the showy religion of the Chaldeans; but he was called back by Shem and the other fathers.[1] It was Noah's son Ham who brought this bane into the world. Accordingly, Japheth, too, degenerated, and the Messianic line remained in the house of Shem alone, by whom the promise was passed on to Abraham. Thus the chronology throws light on the account if one takes into consideration the entire character of the times.

1. *The Lord visited Sarah as He had said, and the Lord did to Sarah as He had promised.*

2. *And Sarah conceived, and bore Abraham a son in his old age at the time of which God had spoken to him.*

3. *Abraham called the name of his son who was born to him, whom Sarah bore him, Isaac.*

[1] On the basis of Joshua 24:2 Luther concluded that Abraham had been an idolater before his call; cf. *Luther's Works*, 2, pp. 239—240.

Moses is very wordy in this passage. He repeats nearly all statements twice. Evidently it is his purpose to commend to us that most exuberant joy of the saintly patriarch. After awful misfortunes Abraham has not only found a safe place and a favorably disposed king, but Sarah becomes pregnant and bears him the son who is the heir of the promise. But if the joy of parents is genuine when children are born to them in the usual manner without a promise, how much more Abraham rejoiced over this his son for whom he had now waited so many years after he had been promised! Accordingly, what thus far has been an object of hope, and what he has believed, this is now a reality; and, if I may express it in this way, the promise has now been made flesh.

We cannot come close to feeling this joy; for the things which thus far had been invisible and impossible, which Abraham had believed, are now visible and altogether possible — an example for us, that we may learn that there is no real joy in this world except that which the Word brings when it is believed.

When Moses mentions the definite and established time, this has the purpose of emphasizing the promise and of making us pay greater attention to the Word of creation than to the work itself. Thus Isaac was born on approximately the same day on which Sodom was destroyed a year earlier, evidently in order that the godly parents might have a joy to counterbalance the vastness of their grief. For God does both: He brings down to hell, and He brings back; He afflicts, and He makes glad.

Therefore the fact that Moses frequently brings God's Word or promise into this account does not imply that our ordinary way of giving birth takes place without the Word. For when God once said (Gen. 1:28): "Be fruitful," that Word is effective to this day and preserves nature in a miraculous way. But how few there are who believe this or are aware of it!

Hence just as Augustine says about the five loaves that He who fed the five thousand people feeds the entire world to this day by the same miracle,[2] so we can correctly state about the birth of a human being that it is just as miraculous today as was the birth of Isaac.

But because of their frequent occurrence these great miracles

---

[2] Augustine, *In Joannis Evangelium Tractatus*, Tr. XXIV, 1, *Patrologia, Series Latina*, XXXV, 1593.

have become commonplace. Therefore God sometimes puts forth a new work, not that it may be a greater one but to show that those common and ordinary works which happen among us are similar to those extraordinary ones and are derived from the same source, that is, from the almighty Word of God. For the growth of the fruits of the field and the preservation of various kinds, this is something just as great as the multiplication of the loaves in the wilderness. Nor is it in vain that everywhere in the Gospel Christ employs images or analogies drawn from creatures. But we are deaf, blind, and stupid; nor do we marvel at anything except at those things that appear to be extraordinary.

The passage through the Red Sea and through the Jordan were grand miracles; but who regards it with wonder that we, too, cross the ocean itself every day? For what else is this, that although it is the nature of water to flow and to cover the earth, nevertheless by virtue of the Word which God spoke — "Let the waters be gathered together" (Gen. 1:9) — the earth continues to stand, and both the lower and the upper waters hang suspended, as it were, and we actually dwell among the very waters round about?

One may make the same statement about the birth of a human being. Nobody comprehends what a great thing it is, and yet it is regarded lightly, in accordance with the ancient saying: "What happens every day becomes commonplace." [3] But the cause of this is original sin, from which have sprung hideous lust, depravity, troubles, sicknesses, and other evils. When one becomes aware of these, God's work, together with the Word, is put out of sight, and men begin to shrink from this saintly kind of life which has such a wonderful blessing from God. But it is the common lot of all God's works that they are covered up in this manner and polluted, so to speak, by many vexations and misfortunes.

What troubles are experienced by someone who governs a state! The citizens are disobedient. Discipline cannot be maintained even by means of severe punishments. Moreover, the hatred and enmity resulting from punishment are an unbearable burden. Furthermore, in addition to this there is Satan, the enemy who throws empires into turmoil by means of offenses. Do you suppose that one who gives proper consideration to all these facts will assume a public office? Therefore he who wants to rule in such a manner as to keep a tranquil

---

[3] Rufus Festus Avienus, *Arati Phenomena*, ed. A. Breysig (Leipzig, 1889), 318.

heart will put these annoyances out of sight and will look at the Word and the will of God. There he will see that whatever other kinds of life there may be, he is leading the kind that pleases God, and that he has entered upon it at God's command.

The whole world has nothing better, more precious, or nobler than the church, in which the voice of God is heard and God is worshiped with true forms of worship, that is, with faith, invocation, patience, obedience, etc. Yet the church is so hidden from view by the cross, by afflictions, by dishonor, and by contempt that the world concludes that nothing is more detestable and baneful.

Indeed, look at Christ Himself. What is more wretched than He? "We saw Him full of scabs," says Isaiah (cf. 53:2-3), "so that we turned our faces away from Him." Yet He is the Son of God, the King of glory, and the salvation of all men. Why, then, is it strange if few are aware of the dignity of marriage and of the miracle of birth? For this is the source of those familiar sayings that a wife is a necessary evil and that she is an irksome blessing.[4] But if we were mindful of the Word, we would judge differently. Now, since we are blinded by original sin, we pay no attention to the Word, and we take into account solely those things which we find offensive.

Therefore let us learn to look at the Word and the will of God; then we shall bear everything calmly, no matter how bitter it is. Moses distinguishes the sin of lust from the work of God in an excellent way, inasmuch as he emphasizes so many times that Sarah conceived and gave birth, just as the Lord had said, and that this took place at the age when the passion of sexual desire had subsided. In this manner we, too, should distinguish vices, which original sin brought on, from the creation and works of God. I am sure that I was created a male.[5]

Moreover, marriage is God's institution. "It is not good," He says, "that the man should be alone" (Gen. 2:18). But inconveniences, vexations, and sundry crosses are encountered in marriage. What does it matter? Is it not better that I please God in this manner, that God hears me when I call upon Him, that He delivers me in misfortunes, and that He benefits me in various ways through my life's companion, the pious wife whom I have joined to myself?

---

[4] Cf. *Luther's Works*, 1, pp. 118—119.

[5] Luther seems to mean that it was by the creating will of God rather than by the Fall that the difference between male and female came about.

He who reasons thus puts himself into the purity of Paradise. For just as the prophet says (cf. Hab. 3:15): "Your horses were in the mud of many waters, and yet your chariots were salvation," so it also happens in the household, in the government, and in the church. All have a very great abundance of annoyances, and yet those who regard the Word keep an even temper and experience deliverance. For God often puts on a beggar's mantle, as is wont to happen on the stage, although He is King of kings and Lord of lords.[6]

Therefore the prophet (Is. 45:15) calls Him "a God who hides Himself."[7] For under the curse a blessing lies hidden; under the consciousness of sin, righteousness; under death, life; and under affliction, comfort. But one must look at the Word, for those who do not have the Word follow their own feeling and remain without comfort in their tears and sorrow. Why do the monks withdraw into monasteries? Doubtless to be free from the inconveniences which, as they see, abound in the whole world. With the same intent the pope chose celibacy, although he sought to obtain a reputation for saintliness in this manner. But the inconveniences which God inflicted on the human nature because of sin should not be shunned.

Moreover, consideration should be given to the brilliant rays of the Word of God with which God has adorned the household, the state, and the church. Thus it will come about that we shall not be offended by the inconveniences and adversities, none of which were in Paradise and which are necessary in the world to keep nature in check. And indeed what the monks flee from in the world they find in twofold measure in the monasteries. For the devil dwells even in the desert.[8] Therefore let it be your concern to be in a state about which you can maintain with certainty that it has been instituted by God. This no monk can say about his monastic life, and no papist can say it about his celibate life.

Moses praises and exalts the birth of Isaac at such length because he wants to remind us that nothing should be given so much consideration as the Word itself. Those who do this see that the entire

---

[6] Cf. the Epilog to *All's Well That Ends Well:* "The king's a beggar, now the play is done."

[7] This is the origin of Luther's well-known term *Deus absconditus.*

[8] Apparently a monastic proverb, which may have originated with the words of *The Life of St. Antony,* by Athanasius (ch. 11): "So he at once set out for the mountain by himself. But there was the Enemy again!"

world is full of miracles. But clear eyes are needed; otherwise the most excellent works of God become ordinary because of their frequent occurrence, and the glory of the Word and the works of God is obscured.

Physicians see neither the Word nor the glory in the marvelous work of the birth of a human being. Though they do not know its real cause, they are nevertheless forced to admire and praise the result. For they set aside the filth and the sweat or excrement, that is, the lust, and look upon the work of birth purely by itself. They consider the arrangement of the members, their characteristics, their uses, etc. This they do even though they lack the spiritual wisdom which the Word shows.

But we go beyond their wisdom and also contemplate God's will and Word, namely, the spiritual crown with which God adorned marriage: "Male and female He created them" (Gen. 1:27). "It is not good that the man should be alone; let Us make a help for him" (Gen. 2:18); and "He blessed them, saying: 'Be fruitful and multiply' " (Gen. 1:28). This is the golden crown which all godly spouses wear on their heads; and in spite of it the unclean world, like swine, directs its mouth and eyes toward the mud and filth, and values only the inconveniences. As for ourselves, let us learn to understand our own blessings — true blessings indeed — and the desert will become for us a Paradise. Then we shall be able at least to suffer and endure all adversities with moderation, or patiently bear them. For this reason Moses inculcates the Word of God and His promises so earnestly.

4. *And Abraham circumcised his son Isaac when he was eight days old, as God had commanded him.*

Abraham assigns the name to his son by divine authority, for the angel of the Lord had stated that this name should be given to him. He also circumcises his son on the eighth day, and Moses adds that this was done in accordance with the Lord's command. Therefore just as Abraham does everything in accordance with the Word and his call, so we, too, should see to it that we undertake nothing without the Word and are not found in a state or work about which we have doubts.

The papists reproach us severely because we do not accept their self-chosen works and forms of worship. This, however, is a theological issue for us,[9] lest we enter upon a kind of life or work concerning which we do not have God's express command.

But I am speaking of such works as have to do with worship; for reason has its own particular course in civil affairs, which it manages on its own without the Word. But nobody can boast of his worship unless it has the Word, is enveloped by the Word as by cloths, and is enclosed, so to speak, by it. Then no trial or vexation of the world can come through which we cannot pass. Even if we have to walk through water and mud, we shall nevertheless overcome, according to the prophet (Hab. 3:15), who promises that the chariots of the Lord are salvation though stuck fast in mud.

Therefore we, too, have the most excellent treasure which the holy patriarchs had, namely, the Word. Let us take pains to guard it properly, and let us not allow our adversaries to draw us away from the level road into the desert that is full of thorns and to adopt self-chosen forms of worship. First let them prove their claims with the Word, and then we shall follow them. But when they extol the authority of the fathers, of Augustine, of Gregory, and likewise of the councils, our answer is: "Those things have no claim on us. We demand the Word. Augustine and the councils are not the Word." Therefore we shall not walk in their ways, in accordance with Christ's saying (Matt. 10:5): "Do not turn aside into the ways of the Gentiles."

5. *Abraham was a hundred years old when his son Isaac was born to him.*

Moses records this not only because of the number of the years but rather to praise the miracle that God so blessed that old man that in his hundredth year he begot a son when his body was already exhausted because of age. But here, too, Moses separates the pure work of God from the uncleanness and hideousness with which original sin has bespattered the work of God. For because Abraham is a hundred years old, who does not realize that he would not [10] have approached Sarah if God had not commanded him to do so?

On the debate about the years of Abraham — whether he was the first-born or not — we have touched above, and it is certain that the computation of the Jews as well as that of Lyra is wrong; for it

[9] Luther's phrase is *caput doctrinae nostrae.*

[10] At the suggestions of the Erlangen and Weimar editors we have accepted the conjectural addition of a *non* here.

eliminates sixty years.[11] But we shall deal with these matters in another place.

6. *And Sarah said: God has made laughter for me; every one who hears will laugh over me.*

7. *And she said: Who would have said to Abraham that Sarah would suckle children? Yet I have borne him a son in his old age.*

At this point the philologians wrangle much among themselves; for although the verb צָחַק properly denotes "to play," "to laugh," "to joke," they assign a variety of meanings to it. In Ex. 32:6 Moses states: "The people sat down and rose up to play." In the Books of the Kings (2 Sam. 2:14) we read: "Let the young men arise and play"; that is, let them fight with weapons, and let them perish by wounding one another; and below (Gen. 26:8) it is stated concerning Isaac: "The king saw Isaac fondling Rebecca." Here, as the Jews explain, Moses is speaking of sexual intercourse.[12] Thus there are many grammarians and countless grammatists.[13] Yet among these you would find no one whom you could call a learned Hebraist. For because the subject matter has been lost, the language or the words have also been lost.

We shall take the meaning from the subject matter itself and disregard the disputes of the philologians. Accordingly, the proper meaning of the verb is "to laugh." Therefore when Sarah says: "God made laughter for me," this means that she rejoiced in earnest and was glad about the son whom she had borne, not only with a carnal gladness — like that of other mothers of whom Christ says that they do not remember their former anguish after giving birth (John 16:21) — but with a gladness of the Holy Spirit, because she had actually become a mother as a result of God's blessing.

On account of her barrenness Sarah had so far been regarded as a woman under a curse, because God was begrudging her the usual blessing. Consequently, she undoubtedly concluded that a great injury was being inflicted on her. But now, after the birth of her son, she, too, boasts of the divine blessing, leaps with joy, and says: "Now God causes me, too, to laugh and be glad of heart because of this His unhoped-for favor."

---

[11] See *Luther's Works* 2, p. 238, note 34, and p. 276.

[12] The source of this information is Lyra *ad locum.*

[13] Luther distinguishes between *grammatici* and *grammatistae.*

The opinions current at that time support this understanding; and if some do not take note of them, why is it surprising if they are in doubt about the words? Throughout that entire time before the birth of Christ the blessing of matrimony was considered a most important matter among the Jewish people, just as, on the other hand, barrenness was considered a curse.

Today this blessing is not esteemed so highly, because the pope has introduced celibacy as a holy kind of life. Moreover, even though those who live in the married state lack this blessing, nevertheless they do not for this reason fear the wrath of God or the contempt of men. They are tormented only by their desire for children, but they do not feel God's wrath in their conscience. Thus the change of opinion has changed the world.

But at that time this most saintly woman lived in deepest sorrow; and the more she was aware of having been deprived of the blessing, the more troubled she was. Now, therefore, when the Lord has regard for her with the great boon that she not only gives birth to a son but to a son who will be the ancestor of Christ, there is exuberant joy in the Holy Spirit in addition to the joy of the flesh. Therefore she is carried away by her joy in this manner and speaks words which are sobs, as it were, of exuberant joy. For she knows that from this son of hers there will be born the One who will deliver the entire human race from the everlasting curse.

Yet these are words not only of joy but also of shamefacedness, as though Sarah meant to say: "Not only has the Lord made me laugh and rejoice most exuberantly in the Holy Spirit, but also among men all who hear of it will laugh at me. For childbearing is the function of young women whose age is suited for giving birth. But that I, an old woman whose vigor is exhausted, that I, who am all but a corpse, give birth to a child, does this not deserve to be laughed at?" Accordingly, just as she leaps with the utmost joy before God, so she feels ashamed before men.

Besides, it is common in every language for words to have their proper meaning at one time and a figurative meaning at another time. And so the verb צָחַק, which properly means "to laugh," is used by antiphrasis (which is very common among the Hebrews) for "to laugh at." Similarly, in German we call a worthless fellow by antiphrasis *ein fromm kind, ein edles kreutlein*.[14] Thus I explain the verb "to laugh" in this passage by antiphrasis.

[14] A usage analogous to the English "You little darling!"

"The Lord has made laughter for me" is spoken in its strict sense, for laughter denotes joy. But when Sarah adds: "And men will laugh at me," this is spoken figuratively; that is: "They will condemn me as a lustful old woman. But blessed be the Lord, who caused this laughter for me. Men laugh; I, too, laugh. And I know that the Lord has made this laughter for me." Thus these are words of one who rejoices with a sincere joy and yet is mindful of the ridicule of the world.

The following words — "Who would have said to Abraham?" — are also explained in various ways. Here again I see many philologians but no Hebrews. Therefore we have every right to take it upon ourselves to give instruction and, as we do so, to go beyond all the rabbis. For the subject matter does not have its origin in the words. No, the words have their origin in the subject matter, just as Demosthenes answered someone who asked how one should speak properly: "Say nothing unless you know it well." [15] When the subject matter is well considered in advance and properly understood, then the appropriate words for setting forth the subject matter will also present themselves.

Hence here, too, the meaning must be sought from what the circumstances require. Accordingly, Sarah is very glad and full of wonder. This makes it impossible for her to give adequate expression to the joy she has experienced in her heart. She says: "If my Isaac were not lying in his cradle, who would ever have the audacity to say that a son was born to my husband Abraham?" In German it is expressed more clearly: *Wer durffts Abraham ansagen so ein gross herrlich Wunderwerck?*

But the name "Abraham" is interpreted more correctly in accordance with the subject matter. It signifies the house or family of Abraham, as though Sarah meant to say: "Who would ever believe or have the audacity to say that a son was born to Abraham in his hundredth year when his wife was in her ninetieth? Who could consider it possible for a son to be born to these two?" Therefore they are words of spiritual and physical joy. For when the heart is joyful in the true God, the flesh also exults, just as, on the other hand, we also see that the flesh [16] is affected when the heart is sad. This latter sense I consider to be more appropriate.

[15] Cf. also *Luther's Works* 3, pp. 67 ff.

[16] We have followed the suggestion of the Erlangen editors and have substituted *carnem* for *corda*.

At this point the Jews also ask why Moses states in the plural number that Sarah suckles children, when she did not have any except the one son Isaac; and they invent the story that Sarah said these words at the feast, about which something follows a little later. They say that when the other women could not be convinced that Sarah had actually given birth to a child but thought she had bought a boy from some poor woman and pretended that this was her son, she suckled many infants at the feast in the sight of all the women and in this way removed the suspicion that her statement about having borne a son was false.[17]

Such are the fabrications of the Jews. How much simpler it is to say that the plural is used in place of the singular! We say that he who has found only one coin has found money. And a man is called a father because of his children, even though he has only one offspring. This way of speaking is very common in all languages; but because the Jews do not understand what is being discussed, they deal properly neither with the words nor with the grammar. Our sophists do likewise. Since they have lost the things that pertain to theology, they have groped around in the darkness like blind men. For it is everlastingly true that lack of knowledge of the subject matter results in lack of knowledge of the words, and those who afterwards want to debate about the subject matter on the basis of the words inevitably talk nonsense. One must have a familiarity with and a knowledge of the subject matter. But for those who do not have the subject matter it is impossible to speak properly.

8. *And the child grew and was weaned; and Abraham made a great feast on the day that Isaac was weaned.*

Here Augustine asks why Abraham made a feast, and a great one at that, not on the day of birth or circumcision but on the day of weaning, since the day of birth appears more suited for a feast, just as it is the custom of nearly all people to celebrate a birthday.[18] The day of circumcision had also been commanded by God, but none of these things can be said about the day of weaning.

Augustine concludes that there is no answer to this question unless that joy — the joy one also feels because of the birth of Christ —

---

[17] This information comes from Lyra *ad* Gen. 21:7.

[18] Augustine, *Quaestiones in Heptateuchum Libri VII*, I, 50, *Corpus Christianorum*, XXXIII, p. 19.

is understood spiritually. Then one needs solid food, not milk. I am not relating this opinion of Augustine for the purpose of scoffing at the saintly man, who is the only one to touch on this passage, but because it is good and necessary that these saintly fathers sometimes are found to be like ourselves, that is, that they are human beings, so that the glory of our God, who is strong in our weakness and wise in our foolishness and errors, may stand firm.

This the papists do not know. Out of the individual statements and words of the saintly fathers they make articles of faith which one may not oppose even in the least. But God is wonderful in His saints, and so wonderful that through their failings and errors He manifests His wisdom to us. Therefore one must believe the one and only Word of God, not the canons, and not the statements of the saintly fathers except insofar as they are in agreement with the Word, just as Augustine himself says about himself and his books.[19] For no one has the authority to burden the church with new doctrines.

Therefore so far as the question that has been submitted is concerned, I will let St. Augustine have his own opinion. Nevertheless, this is not to be tolerated, that he deals with a historical account only from a spiritual point of view. For the historical accounts should be explained by themselves, inasmuch as they are not without meaning, no matter how unimportant they may seem.

Therefore our opinion about the very saintly man Abraham can be as follows: that he was unwilling to imitate the customs of the heathen, because he had been warned either by the Holy Spirit or by the saintly fathers and his ancestors who were still living at that time. Moses similarly prohibits the religious customs of the heathen, and especially those of the Egyptians.[20]

Furthermore, this, too, is true, that the time of weaning was very suitable for a feast. Ishmael was thirteen years old when he was circumcised, and because of his age he could bear the pain of circumcision; but Isaac was an infant eight days old when he was circumcised. At that age, therefore, he needed more attentive care from his parents. For circumcision brought on great pain, as we see in the Book of Joshua (5:8) that the people tarried and rested until they were healed from their circumcision.

And below (Gen. 34:25) it is related of Simeon and Levi that

---

[19] Cf. Augustine, *Reply to Faustus the Manichaean*, XI, 5.

[20] Luther is evidently thinking of passages like Lev. 18:3.

they attacked the Shechemites on the third day, when the pain of the wound is at its worst. We can say the same thing about the day of birth; for often not only the infant but also the mother is endangered by the birth. Therefore these two days — of the birth and of the circumcision — were not suitable for a feast. Accordingly, they postponed this until the time of weaning, when the infant had grown well in strength. This would be my reason if it were necessary to give an answer to this question.

But here one must also note that it was common practice for the saintly fathers to feast together; for Abraham undoubtedly invited to this feast Shem — that is, Melchizedek [21] — the king and priest, with his household, likewise other fathers, and provided rather sumptuous fare. For Moses does not state without a purpose that Abraham provided a great feast. Therefore the saints may also refresh themselves physically, especially when they are burdened by sadness and misfortune, just as Scripture states (Prov. 31:6): "Give wine to those in bitter distress." Likewise Ps. 104:15: "Wine gladdens the heart." It should be the purpose of feasts to gladden hearts and to refresh them after sadness. For God dislikes sadness. When hearts are burdened with it, they cannot praise or give thanks.

Accordingly, this was not a feast of frivolous men. No, it was a feast of the saintliest fathers, who thanked God for having confirmed and fulfilled His divine promise; and they not only refreshed their bodies with rather sumptuous food but also refreshed their hearts with sacred discourses, just as Paul states in Acts 14:17 that hearts are satisfied with food and gladness as a result of the Lord's kindness.

Therefore this passage should be taken note of against the gloomy hypocrites who all but kill their bodies with their unnatural fasts and do not give the flesh the necessary care which God has given it but are so exhausted by tormenting themselves that they become altogether useless. One must keep to the middle of the road, for it is safest. "Not in reveling," says Paul (Rom. 13:13-14); "but make provision for the flesh, yet not in its lusts," [22] lest there happen what is written in Ex. 32:6: "The people sat down and rose up to play."

Of such a nature are the excessively bountiful German feasts;

[21] Luther identified Melchizedek with Shem, the son of Noah; cf. *Luther's Works*, 2, p. 382.

[22] Luther interpreted both Rom. 13:13-14 and Eph. 4:26 in a way that attached the negative only to the second part of the prohibition; cf. *Luther's Works*, 27, p. 69, note 54.

but godly people feast to gladden the heart and to give thanks to God, as Moses says (Deut. 16:11): "And you shall feast before your God."

Here it should also be noted that in this way God gives Abraham a palpable demonstration of His grace. He had promised him a son, but He delays the fulfillment of the promise. Meanwhile Abraham, who is satisfied with the Word alone, believes the promise and simply clings to the invisible things. But it happens in due time that the invisible things become visible. We, too, should imitate this and set it before our eyes. We believe that our flesh will rise again on the Last Day. This should be as sure for us as if it had already happened; for we, too, have the Word and the same spiritual comforts that Abraham had.

Therefore just as a hundred years ago we were nothing, so when death will have destroyed our flesh, our flesh will come forth again from nothing and will live. Thus the things we have at the present time instruct us clearly about the things we shall have in the future. Let no one say by way of objection that Abraham had the promises; for do we, too, not have the promises in Baptism and in the Eucharist?

The only difference between us and Abraham is this, that Abraham believed the promises, but we do not believe them. Through faith Abraham made visible things out of invisible things, but we cling solely to the visible things and do not feel God palpably in ourselves, as Paul says in Acts 14:17 that He has left in us sure evidences of His presence and goodness.

Nevertheless, Abraham had an advantage that was unique and not to be regarded lightly. We do not have that advantage. He was sure of descendants, because both sons would live. Above, when he was reminded by the Word of God, he learned that twelve princes would spring from Ishmael. He also knew about Isaac that Christ would be born from him. This example we observe in Abraham alone and his family, for no one of us can be sure about the life of his descendants during a single year.[23] But this is merely a physical benefit. We, however, so far as spiritual promises are concerned, are either on a par with or even above Abraham; and if we could only believe as Abraham believed, we would be in

[23] Luther had personal reasons for this thought when his daughter Elizabeth died in 1528 and again when Magdalene died in 1542.

Paradise, yes, even in heaven itself. For we are baptized, not into the house of Crassus or of Caesar but into the kingdom of heaven. Besides, we have received absolution and the Lord's Supper. Yet even though we have more promises than Abraham had, we snore in our sluggishness and neither thank God nor rejoice in the spirit.

Hence we do not lack promises, but we lack the faith that Abraham had. Among the papists, however, even doctrine itself has perished; for they teach nothing about faith, nothing about the Word of God, which absolves from sins and gives comfort, and nothing about the promises. They teach only the merits of one's own works. Baptism is altogether dead among them; they absolve only those who are contrite and have confessed; and they teach those who use the Lord's Supper that they are doing a work of obedience toward the church. About the remission of sins and about the way of approaching it by faith they teach nothing. But it behooves us to open our eyes, to consider the blessings we have, to give thanks for them, and to rejoice like Abraham, who is glad not only in the spirit but also in the body.

9. *But Sarah saw the son of Hagar the Egyptian, whom she had borne to Abraham, that he was a mocker.*

Some are of the opinion that this happened on the very day of the feast; for they think that Ishmael and Hagar were offended by the sumptuousness of the feast and made some insulting remark. But the circumstances show that these events took place some years after the weaning and that the quarrel went on, not for one day but even for several years. Paul indicates this (Gal. 4:29) when he speaks of the time of the persecution. Nor was it a quarrel about an insignificant matter. Ishmael wanted to have the prerogative of primogeniture, and his mother Hagar was proud in a boastful manner because Abraham became a father through her. These things the brother threw up to the boy Isaac, who now, because of his age, was susceptible to insult and persecution; and perhaps, as is wont to happen, he brought the greater part of the domestics over to his side, as though he were the sole heir of the promise. For what he had heard about the twelve princes who would be born of him, this undoubtedly caused his youthful mind to become puffed up. Therefore he dreamed of a kingdom for himself and despised Isaac in comparison with himself. His mother acted the same way toward Sarah, who, although she was a very saintly woman, nevertheless, in accordance with the rule,[24] was weak. For the saints, as I have repeatedly stated, should be praised in such a manner that they nevertheless remain for us examples of patience and of weakness.

Finally Sarah became impatient of the contempt and the insults. When she saw that there was no remedy except to expel Hagar and her son from the house, she reported the matter to Abraham. This quarrel did not last only one day, as I have also stated above; but Sarah concealed the insults for a number of years. Moreover, Hagar appears to have stirred up her son and to have fomented quarrels in the household. For this reason Sarah attacked her rather severely, as follows.

10. *So she said to Abraham: Cast out this slave woman with her son; for the son of this slave woman shall not be heir with my son Isaac.*

11. *And the thing was very displeasing to Abraham on account of his son.*

Sarah mentions the mother first, evidently because Hagar was the main cause of those quarrels. She does not mention Ishmael by name, and thus she shows her contempt by calling him the son of the slave woman. But above we praised the saintly Sarah because she was obedient to her husband and called him lord; and it is surely a very outstanding virtue in a wife if she is subject to her husband, holds him in honor, and fears him.

"Where, then," you say, "is now[25] this reverence toward her husband? Sarah says to Abraham: 'Cast out the slave woman.' This is rather dictatorial; and because this quarrel, as the circumstances prove, lasted a long time, Sarah undoubtedly was often irksome to her husband, since she continued to demand that the mother be cast out with her son." Both were stubborn, and they skillfully embellished their cause against Sarah before Abraham and the whole household. For it has always been a very common practice in the world for instigators of wrongs to defend themselves and to put the blame on those who have been hurt.

Therefore when Abraham was either too ready to believe or too slow and too easygoing to punish, Sarah seems to have for-

[24] Some editions have *carnem* ("flesh") rather than *canonem* ("rule").

[25] We have followed the suggestion of the Erlangen and Weimar editors and substituted *nunc* for *nobis*.

gotten her former humility and modesty, and to be giving her husband an order, as it were, and making him her servant.

But the saintly woman by no means forgets her duty. Therefore her words must not be understood as though they were spoken haughtily and imperiously. Very important and very just reasons prompt Sarah to accuse the mother and her son, for they were stubborn in their pride and unbearable in their presumptuousness, since they wanted to rule and to be the heirs of Abraham. Therefore they despised Sarah and ridiculed her son Isaac in various ways.

Accordingly, Sarah's words should be understood as those of a suppliant and of one who is imploring her husband's help with the utmost reverence and humility: "Alas, my husband, we shall certainly have no peace unless you interpose your authority and cast Hagar and Ishmael out of the house; for it is their desire that I and my son, who alone is your true heir, be completely subdued."

In this manner Sarah implores the help of her husband. But she does not command him. Even though she was the mistress of the household, she nevertheless does not arrogate to herself so much power that she would cast out Hagar without seeking Abraham's advice. But first she submits the matter to the master of the house with reverence and humility, and she points out what in her own judgment is the way to achieve harmony. Moreover, what she says about the inheritance should not be understood as though she wanted Ishmael to be excluded from the inheritance; she simply says that he should not be made an heir together with Isaac, but that Isaac should keep his portion for himself.

But this plan made by his wife displeases Abraham very much. For he, like any human being, was preoccupied with love for his first offspring. Nor did he consider the promise as carefully as Sarah did. His fatherly affection evidently prevented him from doing so. For the saints, too, are unsettled and carried away by their affections. Accordingly, Abraham considered it unfair to exclude his natural and lawful son from the inheritance. Sarah, on the other hand, makes fundamental distinctions between the son of the slave woman and her own, and, as Augustine says, she is not excited like a woman; but she is speaking under the influence of the Holy Spirit, and she relies on the sure promise which she had heard concerning her son.[26]

[26] Augustine, *Quaestiones in Heptateuchum Libri VII*, I, 51, *Corpus Christianorum*, XXXIII, p. 19.

Ishmael, too, had his promise; for the Lord said to Abraham (Gen. 17:20): "I have heard you praying for Ishmael, for of him shall be born twelve princes." But Sarah noted more carefully that an additional statement was made about her son with these words: "But I will establish My covenant with Isaac."

Abraham, evidently preoccupied with love for his first-born, did not consider these words as carefully as Sarah did. She makes a very fine distinction between her own son and Hagar's. In the first place, she knows that Ishmael is the son of a slave woman. But she considers herself the mistress, as she actually was. In the second place, she knows that Hagar, as a slave woman, is not independent, but that she herself is free, that it is intolerable for the son of the slave woman to be regarded as the equal of the son of the free woman, and that therefore it is improper for the slave woman to try to oppress the free woman and mistress and for the son of the slave woman to want to treat the son of the free woman with contempt.

These considerations give the saintly mother the heart boldly to implore her husband's help; but Abraham, constrained by his fatherly affection, turns a deaf ear. Not once or twice, therefore, but more frequently than this a violent outburst occurred between the godly spouses, since the father kept on excusing Ishmael. Accordingly, Sarah, spurred on by so many injustices and affronts, had reason to look more carefully at the promise. For the statement of Isaiah (28:19) is true: "Trouble gives understanding"; likewise, hunger is the best condiment. For those who are afflicted have a better understanding of the Holy Scriptures; the smug and prosperous read them as if they were some poem written by Ovid.

But in the fourth chapter of the Epistle to the Galatians Paul points out why these events are recorded, and we have carefully explained this passage in our commentary.[27] For it is not without reason that the saintly mother opposes her husband's will in this manner. It is her purpose to prevent Ishmael from coming into the inheritance together with Isaac. Above she even called Ishmael her son, for this is what she said about Hagar (16:2): "That I shall obtain children by her." And when Abraham instructed him to do so, Ishmael called Sarah his mother. For she was his lawful though not his natural mother.

---

[27] Cf. Luther's discussion in the *Lectures on Galatians, Luther's Works*, 26, pp. 433 ff.

The Saracens have made use of this name because Ishmael was the lawful son of Sarah, and they boast of their right of primogeniture.[28] But Sarah maintains that there is a difference as a result of the promise. She neither wants Ishmael to be made the equal of her son in the inheritance, nor does she invent this difference because of a womanly affection. The promise points it out, inasmuch as God plainly speaks of "My covenant with Isaac."

Abraham did not consider this exclusive promise as carefully as Sarah did. Therefore he is greatly displeased by Sarah's request and opinion. He thinks that Ishmael is not being treated fairly, and he is unwilling to let Sarah change his yes to a no.

All the domestics, you see, were already of the opinion that Ishmael would be a joint heir with Isaac and that he ranked higher than Isaac because he was born earlier. Therefore Hagar and her son Ishmael behaved in a haughty manner and despised Sarah and her Isaac. Later on this state of affairs gave rise to much disagreement between the saintly spouses.

Yet it should be noted that this disagreement did not arise over trifling matters and that Sarah was not carried away by her womanly affection. She had very weighty and very just reasons, namely, God's promise. It is about this that she is contending, and she does not want it taken away from her son.

On the other hand, Abraham is also motivated by just reasons for not excluding Ishmael; for he knows that Ishmael is bone of his bone and flesh of his flesh. How, then, could he tolerate it that Sarah wanted him cast out of the house?

For these reasons a division arose in Abraham's household, and without a doubt, as happens, each side had its applauders and instigators. Accordingly, those who declare that managing a household is a vulgar kind of life can learn from these examples that in wedlock there is far severer training in faith, hope, love, patience, and prayer than there is in all the monasteries. For the monks neither see nor undergo trials as grievous as these; they cultivate swinish emotions and are envious of the better bread and wine of others.

These spouses, however, are fighting about the promises, and they are doing so in the fear and obedience of God and in true humility. But these very excellent virtues are obscured when they are dismissed as works done by the laity and common to all spouses, while it is

[28] Cf. *Luther's Works*, 22, p. 17, note 14, on his knowledge of Islam.

said to be an outstanding virtue to shut oneself up in a monastery, to torture oneself with fasts, to be sad, etc.

This account is useful for comforting spouses, in order that they may not think it strange if disputes arise among even the most affectionate and the saintliest people. One should rather consider that in marriage there are such varied exercises in godliness and love, while, on the other hand, the self-chosen forms of worship of the monks are nothing but dung. For what saintliness can it be to do nothing except what pleases yourself? And yet they boast that they have renounced themselves and their possessions.

But it is a true renunciation when we voluntarily give up those things which we could claim for ourselves with the greatest right, that is, when our natural feeling is given support by a command of God. Thus Abraham is the natural and lawful father of Ishmael; he is also one flesh with Hagar.

Such sentiments are very deep. Therefore Abraham feels his innermost heart assailed. Added to this there is God's command that he should defend his wife and care for and support his son. Nevertheless, Sarah maintains that the mother should be cast out together with her son, not because they displeased Abraham, toward whom they undoubtedly were very respectful, but because they ridiculed Isaac.

Accordingly, these are torments of which the entire papacy, because of its abominable celibacy, has no knowledge.

Therefore they call the life of married people a "secular" life, but it surely has a place among the highest levels of spiritual life. For the loftiest sentiments of married people toward God and man are being cultivated.

In this passage Abraham is an instance. He is compelled by a twofold right, the natural and the divine, to defend his lawful wife and son. Because of this feeling he is unable to see the promise clearly. On this account a violent outburst of anger occurs, and there is a very sharp quarrel — to give us an example and to comfort us, in order that when slight offenses arise, we may be mindful of the life and the lot that are common to all men.

One should derive another consolation from this. We are to know that those who live a godly life — in the household, in the state, or in the church — will not be without crosses and troubles.

Abraham, a high priest in the house of God, undoubtedly worshiped God devoutly. But what happens? At this point he is being tested by God Himself and is commanded to obey Sarah. For Moses continues as follows:

12. *But God said to Abraham: Be not displeased because of the lad and your slave woman; whatever Sarah says to you, do as she tells you; for through Isaac shall your descendants be named.*

13. *And I will make a nation of the son of the slave woman also, because he is your offspring.*

Here Abraham is forced simply to give up his opinion and to cast out his son, whom he loved very much, together with the wife, of whom he was very fond. Who does not see that this is a far heavier burden than when a monk wears a cowl and girds himself with a rope? Likewise those who have a position in the government and are godly have as many devils to plague them as there are citizens; and those who teach in the church make the whole world hostile to them. Therefore those who long either for marriage or for a magistracy in order that they may be able to live in leisure and sumptuously are foolish.

Accordingly, the three celestial hierarchies about which the asinine sophists prattle so much [29] are nothing else than the life in the household, in the state, and in the church. Those who live outside these three orders live in a self-elected kind of life which, throughout the prophets, God rejects and condemns.[30]

Abraham has very saintly thoughts, and his will is very upright; for he realizes that by divine and human right he is under obligation to his wife and son yet is compelled to cast out both; and there would have been no end to this conflict if God had not intervened.

Furthermore, by His own testimony God proves that Sarah did not speak out of carnal affection and did not command her husband in a haughty manner, but that she begged him humbly and reverently, even though she had a very just cause. The entire account bears witness that Sarah treated her husband with reverence. But at this point she is compelled by God's command to undertake something contrary to her husband's will.

Nor does Sarah do this under the impulse of the emotion she feels as a woman. But she has been submissive for a long time, and on the

[29] Luther is referring to Pseudo-Dionysius the Areopagite, *De caelesti hierarchia.*

[30] Luther is referring to passages like Jer. 7:31.

occasion of this outburst of anger she has been well trained by humility, faith, hope, and love. Finally she overcomes herself and puts the Word of the promise ahead of her duty toward her husband. This is how everyone should remain in his own calling. By no means should he do anything contrary to the Word for the purpose of pleasing someone.

Today we, too, do our duty and pray for the emperor and the other princes, who nevertheless hate our doctrine exceedingly. But we see that our prayers are in vain, inasmuch as the emperor and the princes do not want to be converted to the Word. Then our faith is put into practice, so that in the end we decide that if one or the other must perish, it is better that the world rather than God and the church of God should perish.

Abraham had not given such careful consideration to the promise. Therefore God repeats it and once more expressly states: "Through Isaac shall your descendants be named." Accordingly, He does not condemn the saintly will and the just sentiment that Abraham loves his wife and son; but He merely reminds him of the promise which gave to Ishmael the hope of becoming a great nation. The covenant, however, He reserved for Isaac alone.

The godly mother takes note of this difference, but because of his love for his son Abraham does not take such careful note of it. Therefore he is commanded by God's voice to yield to Sarah, who relied on a definite statement.

Without a doubt, however, these things were done either through Shem or through another of the patriarchs to whom Sarah submitted this case. He pronounced this verdict against Abraham; and because it is in agreement with the Word of God, Moses is right in stating that God Himself settled this dispute with His verdict.

The promises were twofold. The temporal one had concerned Ishmael; the eternal and spiritual one had concerned Isaac. Therefore when Ishmael wanted to have the ascendancy, it was easy to decide that this must not be tolerated and that, as is recorded later (Gen. 25:23) about Jacob and Esau, the older should serve the younger in the eyes of the world.

Thus Abraham heard from the fathers who were living at that time the intrepretation of the promise made in chapter seventeen, namely, that an eternal covenant was made with Isaac, who not only

was born as the result of the promise but would also produce a blessing, namely, Christ, who blesses all believers.

On the other hand, since Ishmael had only a temporal promise,
by which he was puffed up when he despised Isaac, he deserved to
be driven out. These facts have been recorded for our instruction,
in order that we may learn that we can serve God in the saintliest
obedience even though we are only married people, or, as the papists
call us, laymen.

Through Isaac shall your descendants be named.

This little sentence should be most carefully noted, in order to
refute the Jews, whose arguments against us Christians run as follows:
"All the descendants of Abraham are also the heirs of Abraham. We
circumcised Jews are descendants of Abraham. Therefore we are also
heirs. On the other hand, those who are not Abraham's descendants
cannot be Abraham's heirs. You Christians are Gentiles and are not
descendants of Abraham. Therefore you boast in vain that you are
the church. For this is what it means to be the heir of Abraham."

Relying on these arguments as on battering-rams, they glory against
us and subvert many of our people, as I hear is happening under ungodly princes.[31] This, of course, is their reward for driving out godly
pastors far and wide and leaving the people defenseless and unin-
structed in religion. For because they are deprived of the Word, they
are unable to resist the reasoning of the Jews. For neither fact can
be denied: the title that they are the descendants of Abraham must
be conceded to the Jews, and we cannot deny that we are Gentiles
and do not belong to the family of Abraham.

But St. Paul, assuredly a well-versed master, refutes these arguments of the Jews superbly in Rom. 9 and Gal. 3. He maintains that
the major premise in the first syllogism is false, namely, that the
universal proposition, that all who are the descendants of Abraham
are his heirs, is not true. And against this he adduces an instance
which no Jew can deny: Ishmael is a true descendant of Abraham —
a descendant born of Abraham's own flesh; nevertheless, he is driven
out and does not share the true inheritance with Isaac.

Accordingly, Paul's response to the major premise is this, that he
postulates a threefold progeny of Abraham. The first is physical and

[31] Cf. Luther's letter to Anton Lauterbach, February 9, 1544 (W, *Briefe*, X,
526).

without the promise concerning Christ. Ishmael, who was born of
the flesh of Abraham, was an offspring of this kind.

The second progeny, says Paul, is physical, but with the promise
concerning Christ. Thus Isaac, too, was born of the flesh of Abraham; but he had the promise: "I shall establish My covenant with
Isaac."

The third progeny, says Paul, is not physical but is the offspring
only of the promise. Although it certainly does not belong to the
flesh of Abraham, still it holds fast to faith and embraces the promise
made to Abraham.

Therefore the major premise in the first syllogism — that all who
are descendants of Abraham are his heirs — is false, for this is not
true in Ishmael's case. Therefore the historical account forces us
to change the universal proposition into a particular one if the argument is to be valid at all: "Some descendants of Abraham are the
heirs of Abraham."

But if the Jews add the minor premise that they are those descendants of Abraham, they must prove that claim; for we can prove
that they are descendants of Abraham just as Ishmael was. But
Ishmael was excluded from the promise. Hence the Jews, too, are
excluded.

Therefore it is necessary to determine who are the true descendants of Abraham — the descendants who share in the promise. Here
again the historical account is illuminating for us, just as Paul proves
from the books of Moses that only those who result from the promise
are heirs, whether they are physical descendants of Abraham or not.

At this point it is clear how the second argument is to be refuted;
for in it, too, the major premise is faulty. For it is not altogether
true that those who are not physical descendants of Abraham cannot
be heirs of Abraham. The promise makes true heirs of Abraham, as
is clear in the case of Isaac. Therefore those who accept the promise
in faith are true sons of the promise and heirs of Abraham, as Christ
says (Matt. 3:9): "God is able from stones to raise up children to
Abraham." But if they come from stones, then they do not come
from the flesh and bones of Abraham.

Therefore the text is clear. Ishmael is a descendant of Abraham,
born most truly of his flesh. Consequently, he called Abraham his
father; and he, in turn, was addressed by his father as son. Yet he
is cast out of the house. But Isaac remains in the house as the sole

heir. He was born as the result of the promise, actively and passively, so to speak: passively, because the Blessed Seed is promised to him; actively, because he believes the promise.

This the Jews do not consider, for they have lost the true doctrine concerning the promise and faith; and they cling simply to the physical birth, which by itself alone is nothing unless the promise and faith are added.

Thus Absalom is the son of David according to the flesh; but because he does not believe, he perishes. Similarly, the people who died in the desert were also children of Abraham; but because they did not believe, they were destroyed. It is impossible, however, for the son of the promise, the heir of Abraham and the people of God, to perish.

Hence the essential quality [32] of the heirs is the promise itself, for by it alone those who are not children of the flesh are made heirs. But physical birth is only a material cause so weak and useless that even if you are really born of the flesh of Abraham, you are not for this reason an heir of Abraham.

Therefore Paul is right in stating that those are heirs who are of the promise, that is, who hear the promise and believe the promise, whether they were born of the flesh of Abraham or not. For the promise, which is the Word of God, is so effective and powerful that it calls into existence the things that do not exist (Rom. 4:17). Christ says (Matt. 3:9) that children are raised up for Abraham from stones.

This power the flesh or physical birth does not have. Only the Word has it, because it is omnipotent.

A little while ago, however, I stated that the promise is twofold: a passive one, which happens to us; and an active one, which we accept by faith. But it is the latter which makes us, too, who are by nature Gentiles, heirs of Abraham, yes, brothers and fellow heirs of Christ (Rom. 8:17).

Therefore the Jews boast in vain against us that they are the descendants of Abraham. For it does not follow from this that they are also the heirs of Abraham, unless they apprehend the promise and believe in Christ.

The Jews are indeed descendants of Abraham, born of his own flesh and blood. But that physical birth does not make children of

[32] The technical scholastic term is *forma substantialis.*

God, as John (1:13) says: "Who are not of blood"; that is, who have the physical birth and according to the flesh are children of Abraham. "Nor of the will of the flesh"; that is, who are legitimate children or children by adoption. "Nor of the will of man"; that is, who are of the prophets who ruled and taught, as the papists in our time boast of their apostolic succession. "But who are born of God"; that is, who believe the promise and accept it with firm faith. For it is not enough to be born of the flesh of Abraham; and Isaac himself would not have been the heir of the promise unless, in addition, there had been faith.

Therefore you should note that there is a threefold progeny. One is the natural progeny, without the promise; another is the natural one, with the promise; and still another is of the promise only, without being natural. Of these three only that one is cast out which is physical, without the promise, as is clear in the instance of Ishmael; and the final cause of his being cast out is, as we learn from Paul (Gal. 4:21-31), that this distinction between children and heirs might be maintained, lest we fall into the error of the Jews, who think that it is enough to have Abraham as their father.

The glutton in Luke 16:24 also calls Abraham his father, but in vain. For only those who cling to the promise are considered children of Abraham, whether they are born of the flesh of Abraham, as Isaac was, or not. Thus Christ tells the Jews in John 8:39 ff.: "If you are Abraham's children, do the works of Abraham; but you are doing the works of your father, the devil." Let this be enough to check the stubborn Jews, who boast so much about the blood and flesh of Abraham.

Furthermore, the same game is going on at the present time and, if one may put it this way, has been going on among all nations ever since the beginning of the world. The Jews are stubborn and obstinate because of their birth according to the flesh, and they boast that they alone are the people of God.

But look at the Turks, and you will see that they rely on the same trust in the flesh. For because they fight successfully against the Christians and have increased their power through many great victories, especially in these latter times,[33] they first take from us with the utmost smugness the title that we are the people of God, espe-

[33] In 1526 the Turks had won the Battle of Mohács in Hungary, and in 1529 they had captured Buda; Luther may be thinking of such events as these.

cially since we are being plagued by so many defeats. But they arrogate to themselves the glory that they are the people of God, because they are so successful from day to day, especially against the Christians; for the Turks are by no means so fortunate when they fight against the Tartars and the Persians.[34]

Therefore since the Turks are elated by their success and are crammed, as it were, with victories, they regard us as dogs and swine. Sennacherib did the same thing at Jerusalem, and his success made him a blasphemer, so that he boasted that his idols were stronger than God, whose abode was in Jerusalem (2 Chron. 32:13-15).

Thus later on the gods of the Romans made the entire world subject to Rome. Consequently, the Romans were sure that their religion was the best, and the most pleasing to God. Therefore just as the Jews take pride in their birth according to the flesh, so the Turks in our time believe that they are the only people of God under the sun.

If you ask for the reason and how they prove this, they cite their victories, success, power, and wealth. They attach no importance to God's promise; nor do they have any knowledge of it. They are unaware of God's majesty, which bestows the kingdoms of the world even on the unworthy and ungodly; for the Turkish empire, whatever its extent, is nothing but a morsel of bread which a rich head of a household throws to his dogs.

This the Turks do not know. But Christians know it, and they regard the entire world with all its wealth as nothing; for they are waiting for another, better life in which one star will be more beautiful and more magnificent than this entire world. Moreover, for this conviction of theirs they have a firm foundation, namely, the promise of God which has been set before them in the Son of God, while the Turks have their stinking Koran, their victories, and the temporal power on which they rely. I readily believe, however, that in places which are close to the Turk many Christians lose courage because of this stumbling block and fall away from the faith, because they see that they are unlucky, but that the Turks are very prosperous.

Such Christians need faithful teachers to remind them that God's favor should not be gauged from things that will perish, such as wealth, power, and victories, but from eternal benefits. For to bestow kingdoms and the wealth of the world is a small token of the

[34] A century earlier, in 1402, the Ottoman sultan Bayezid I had been defeated by Timur.

majesty of God. These things God gave for the use of all when He created the world, but that gift reveals the nature of the Divine Majesty when we shall rise from the dead and live in the new world, and forever at that. Therefore it serves no purpose to say: "God is granting kingdoms. He is granting wealth. Consequently, I have a propitious God."

One should rather say: "God gives a promise, and it deals with eternal life. Consequently, He is truly propitious." Therefore the text before us should be used as a proverb: "Through Isaac shall your decendants be named"; that is, he who has the promise and believes shall be the heir.

Where there is no promise, or where the existing promise is not believed, there, in spite of wealth and kingdoms of the world, prestige and power, no church is to be found and no people of God. It is Ishmael who is cast out of the house, not Isaac, the heir.

Thus the pope and his followers arrogate to themselves the name "church," but we should be fully convinced that they cannot be the church. The reason is that they are not the children of the promise; that is, they do not believe the Gospel but persecute it. Therefore although they boast of their apostolic succession, their office, and their legitimate authority, nevertheless, if they do not believe the promise, they are nothing except Ishmael in the house of Abraham; that is, they are children of perdition, not heirs.

As is clear from what has been said, Moses, Christ Himself, John, and Paul make this distinction; yes, the Second Commandment itself, when it forbids taking the name of God in vain, proves clearly enough that this is a false church — a church which does not want to refrain from using the name of God and yet misuses it.

But this serves to comfort us, for the name of God is awesome and should be feared. Because the false church uses it against the members of the true church, it must inevitably terrify them. When the pope excommunicates us, he does so by making use of the name of God. Therefore one should know from the Second Commandment that these very people who claim to be the only ones who are the church are misusing the name of God.

Accordingly, one must make a distinction in dealing with the church and with the name of God. God's name is worthy of reverence and is holy, but it is very frequently misused. Then we should not be afraid; but we should be despisers, not indeed of the name of God but of those who misuse it and want to frighten us.

You must have the same opinion about the church. It is saddening to hear the papists lie and say that we are reprobate and dead members of the church; but let us distinguish between the true use of the name "church" and its misuse. Ishmael also calls Abraham father, but the situation is far different from what it is in the case of Isaac. Thus the papists call themselves the church; but if it is true — as cannot be denied, not even by Satan — that the church is made up of those who have the promise and believe it, it follows that the pope with his followers is not the church, but that he misuses the name "church," because he is an enemy of the promise and persecutes those who believe the promise.

Therefore it is certain that the name "church" is very often grossly misused, for not only heretics but even Turks and Jews call themselves the church. Therefore he who simply says that he is the church says nothing at all. He must prove this. Otherwise we shall have every right to hold the name "church" in contempt, because it is being misused.

But the Second Commandment compels us to make a distinction; for just as the name of God is being misused, so the name "church" is also being misused. For the church exists only where the Word is and where there are people who believe the Word, in accordance with this text: "Through Isaac shall your descendants be named."

But the pope persecutes the Word and takes the name of the Lord in vain. Therefore he is the Antichrist and that loathsome beast (Rev. 13:1) which has blasphemous names on its forehead, that is, which teaches nothing but real blasphemies and profanes the name of God through constant misuse.

In the Gospel of John (14:23) Christ says: "If a man loves Me, he will keep My Word." Therefore those who want to be the people of God or the church must have the Word of Christ, that is, the promises of God; and they must keep them, that is, believe them. These are the people whom the Father loves and to whom He comes to make His home in them (John 14:23). But so far are the pope and his followers from keeping the Word of Christ that they alone most tenaciously hate and persecute it.

Because they frighten us with the name "church" and the name "God," let us make the distinction which the Holy Spirit makes in the Second Commandment, namely, that some use the name of God properly, but that others misuse the name of God. The proper use of the name of God is where the Word and the promise are. On the other hand, where the Word is blasphemed, there the name of God is being misused.

Therefore we should not be frightened; for we know that among such people the Father and the Son and the Holy Spirit do not make their home, but that the devil himself lives there, as is recognized from their forehead, on which there are blasphemous names.

In short, there is no people of God unless it has the promises and believes them. Those who, like the Jews and the Turks, trust in works, laws, and other gifts are not the church, because works, laws, etc., are not the promise.

But in our churches we retain the confession, accept the promises, and keep the Word of Christ. As a result, up to this time many have been killed and are still being killed solely on account of the Word, because they refuse to give up the confession of the Gospel. These are the sure signs which prove that we are the true church, but that the pope and his followers are the church of Satan.

But what shall we say to this? The papists baptize, they administer the sacraments, and they absolve from sins; therefore they are the church. And we cannot deny that we ourselves, through their ministry — because we were baptized by them — came into the fellowship of the true church.

My usual answer to this objection is as follows: The external sacraments and also the Word can be transmitted or administered even by the ungodly. Judas, for his person, did not belong to the church; yet he was in the ministry of the church, and those who were baptized by him were rightly baptized.

We may say the same thing about the papists, who, so far as they themselves are concerned, are blasphemers and ungodly. Yet when they baptize, administer Communion, and absolve — provided that they retain the essentials — their ministry is valid. For even though they are blasphemers, still I, who make use of their ministry and believe, am not a blasphemer; but through faith I truly obtain what God's promise offers, no matter how wicked he who recites the promise to me may be.

Therefore it is not enough to have the name "church," to be called a bishop, a cardinal, a priest. "All these things," as Paul says, "are carnal and pertain to the person." But God does not regard the person;[35] nor should we regard those masks of the flesh. We should look at the Word and on the basis of this account devise a proverb against the papists in the following manner: Abraham has two sons. One of them is a son according to the flesh and does not have the promise of Christ. He persecutes the other son, who is the heir of the promise. The same thing still happens today, will always happen, and has happened from the beginning; for Cain, the first-born, demanded the promise for himself and killed his brother Abel.

Accordingly, just as the sons of Abraham are of two kinds, so the church is of two kinds. One is killed and suffers persecutions; the other kills and persecutes the brethren, just as Cain and Ishmael did. But each of the two has its own sure fruits. The false church blasphemes and persecutes the Word; but the true church retains the confession and patiently bears persecutions, just as today we stand before the emperor and the entire world and confess the Word.

On the other hand, the papists deny the Word of Christ and try to suppress it by means of their ungodly decrees. These fruits of praise and of blasphemy, of confession and of denial, are manifest. Therefore we cannot doubt that the church of the pope is the church of Satan, even though godly people can make proper use of their ministry when they retain the essentials.

Therefore let us carefully note this text, which prevails against all who glory in the flesh. The Jews glory in their blood and say that they are the descendants of Abraham; the Turks, in their victories and power; the pope, in the apostolic succession. But we reject the conclusion when they say: "We are the successors of the apostles in our office; therefore we are the church." For in this passage it is written: "Through Isaac shall your descendants be named," not through Ishmael; that is, the people of God are not those who have the physical succession but those who have the promise and believe it.

For a twofold use is made of the name of God: a blasphemous one and a holy one. In the true church it is holy and to be feared, but in the false church it is not to be feared. For one must boldly hold on to and constantly inculcate this comfort which the Second

[35] Luther has in mind such New Testament passages as Acts 10:34; Rom. 2:11; Eph. 6:9; Col. 3:25.

Commandment teaches, namely, that the name of God is subject to very gross misuse.

It is a common statement in the schools that equivocal terms are not valid for teaching,[36] for those who employ equivocal terms start out from confused words with several meanings. Therefore they teach nothing. Thus the name "God," and also the name "church," are being used in an equivocal sense; for some make proper use of it, but others use it in an improper way.

Thus when the pope declares that all who do not approve of his decrees incur the wrath of Almighty God, this in itself is a terrible statement; but it is equivocal and improperly used. Therefore I do not care a straw about those threats and thunderbolts. Likewise, the name "church of God" has no meaning in logical argumentation; for a dialectician does not accept a word unless it has only one meaning.

Therefore the true church of God is the one which does not misuse the name of God but hears and keeps the Word of Christ, that is, believes the promises. When I hear its name, I prostrate myself in true humility and worship it, for I am sure that the Father, the Son, and the Holy Spirit dwell in it. But when those who do not keep the Word of Christ but persecute it and walk in their self-chosen forms of worship adorn themselves with the name "church," then the word which by its nature has only one meaning becomes equivocal.

Therefore just as it would be folly to be afraid of a painting of a man drawing a sword, so it is folly to be frightened by the name "church" when it is used in a blasphemous manner; for it is merely the picture or mask of the church. But the true church is where Isaac, the son of the promise, is. There the name of God should be feared. There is our salvation and our strength, as the psalm says (Prov. 18:10): "The name of the Lord is a strong tower; the righteous man runs into it."

In short, where the Word of Christ is and is kept — that is, believed — do not be in doubt about the church, even if he who either administers the sacraments or teaches is godless and a blasphemer. "For the Word of the Lord, like rain, does not return empty" (Is. 55:10-11).

This is why we say in the Creed: I believe in the holy church; that is, the church which has the Word by which all things are consecrated (1 Tim. 4:5). But this church puts up with Ishmael, its

---

[36] Cf. Aristotle, *Topics*, 1, 15.

persecutor, until the words and prayer of Sarah and Isaac begin, that is, until the true church, by its persistent prayer and crying, brings it about that Ishmael is cast out. Yet Ishmael does not believe this until he experiences it in very fact.

13. *And I will make a nation of the son of the slave woman also, because he is your offspring.*

The Lord commanded that Ishmael should be cast out. Lest He appear to have forgotten His former promise about the twelve princes (Gen. 17:20) and to repent of His plan, He repeats the promise and adds that He will do this for the sake of Abraham, whose descendant Ishmael is. Thus the natural son is indeed cast out. Nevertheless, he is established as a very powerful king of the world.

Accordingly, someone will say: "Establishing him king of a very large people is not casting him out, is it?" For Ishmael's descendants occupied the entire southern region, and today the Saracens are still a great people.

Thus this account serves to teach us that God allots kingdoms and governments even to reprobate and evil men, not because of their merit — which is nil — but for the sake of Abraham, that is, the church, which alone in the world prays for kings and governments, in order that it may be able to have a quiet lodging place in this life and to propagate the Word of God in peace.

Just as the Turk persecutes the church, so he does not believe that he is aided by the prayers of the church, which prays for all governments (1 Tim. 2:1-2). He attributes it to his Koran and to his righteousness; for he boasts of his true religion and true worship of God, inasmuch as he is an enemy of images and statues. But us he hates and persecutes as idolaters.

Nor did King Alexander realize that it was the help of the church of God that made him so successful. Nevertheless, it is true that only the prayer of the true church preserves all kingdoms for the sake of the little band of the godly, who are in need of a lodging place in this life.

Similarly, what Emperor Charles has in this world, he has because of the service and prayers of the church of Christ. Therefore one should note well the clause "because he is your offspring" in what God says to Abraham. For on Abraham's account, that is, on account of Abraham's meritorious conduct, Ishmael is established as emperor and monarch.

But since all kingdoms are preserved and flourish because of the prayers of the church, how unfair it is that it is being oppressed and trodden underfoot by those very people whom it so faithfully aids! For to the church alone God has given the command to concern itself with praying for kings (1 Tim. 2:2); and this because peace, good order, and security are needed for propagating the Word and gathering a church through the Word, as the historical accounts of the first empires, the Babylonian and the Assyrian, show.

Therefore so far as the present account is concerned, Abraham is compelled to change his mind. But Sarah has her way and accomplishes what she had undertaken, for she looked more closely at the promise and understood it more clearly than Abraham did. For God also reveals some things to the lowly. He does so in order that the great may be humbled. Now there follows another struggle; it has to do with the Second Table, just as the former struggle had to do with the First Table.

14. *So Abraham rose early in the morning, and took bread and a skin of water, and gave it to Hagar, putting it on her shoulder, and he sent her away along with the boy. And she departed and wandered in the wilderness of Beer-sheba.*

This is surely a sad story if you consider it carefully, although Moses relates it very briefly. After Abraham is sure about God's will, he hastens to obey. He rises early in the morning, does not count any money, and gets ready no garments for an unknown and long journey. He simply sends away his very dear wife, who was the first to make him a father, and his first-born son, and gives them nothing but bread and a bottle of water.[37] These are the treasures which his son Ishmael and his wife Hagar receive from the father.

But does it not seem to be cruelty for a mother who is burdened with a child to be sent away so wretchedly, and to an unfamiliar place at that, yes, into a vast and arid desert? Abraham does not send a young male slave along. He does not send a female slave along. The destitute mother and her destitute son are cast out from the true father's estate, and of all his possessions they carry away nothing except a little bread and water, which no doubt was food and drink for only a few days. If he had either given them wine or had provided them with money, their misfortune would have been more bearable.

[37] In the original these final phrases are in German rather than in Latin.

Now, however, in the judgment of reason Abraham seems to be acting cruelly; but in this instance he actually sacrificed conjugal and paternal love, which are two most powerful attachments. For we should not suppose that Abraham was a Wendish boor.[38] No, he was a truly godly, saintly, gentle, humble, and compassionate man who actually loved even his enemies.

Why, then, does Abraham send his wife and son away in such destitution, as though they were his enemies? Where is his fatherly heart? When the angels came, he set before them butter, a calf, and bread baked in ashes, although he did not yet recognize them (Gen. 18:8). But here he thrusts his own first-born son out of his inheritance into exile, as though his fatherly affection had suddenly become entirely extinct and dead.

Let every one of us consult his own heart. If you had a female partner in an honorable marriage and a natural offspring were born to you and you were not hard and stern by nature, would you be able either to overcome or to cast aside your fatherly affection to such an extent that you would not provide at least a servant to be their guide on the way?

Therefore Abraham did not do this without a very great struggle and very heavy sorrow, for he was not a stone or a rock. But he sent his very dear wife away with loud sobs and many tears. God does not change nature in the saints, nor does He destroy their affections. Thus it is altogether likely that neither Hagar nor her son Ishmael laughed, but that they were utterly dejected by this unheard-of announcement of their exile.

Accordingly, this expulsion is described as a tragedy, although the words are few. If Abraham had not heard the promise and had not comforted both the mother and her son with it, he could have feared for their life because of the wolves, bears, and lions in the desert. In short, Abraham would not have treated the Sodomites, who were very wicked people, so harshly; for he continued to pray for them and came near dying in his prayers (Gen. 18:23-33).

Assume, then, that the monks who are living in the monasteries are saintly. What will you find in them that is similar to this one painful and difficult work, namely, that Abraham overcomes two

[38] The Wends, who call themselves "Sorbs," were a Slavic tribe surrounded by Germans; thence they had a reputation for outlandish customs.

very great attachments, toward his wife and toward his son, when he yields because of the obedience he owes the command of God?

Therefore this is an outstanding example of obedience, faith, and all good conduct, but especially of true obedience toward God; for these events did not happen in as brief a time as the words make it sound. Nevertheless, they had to be described in this manner, in order that we might learn from Abraham's example that God must be loved above all things, and loved so perfectly that you love nothing in the entire world in the same way, neither your wife nor your children nor your own life. But if Moses had wanted to record everything as it happened, he would have needed a large volume for this one account. For who could describe the tears and sighs of the mother as well as of the son?

Accordingly, they moved Abraham, Sarah, and finally the entire household to pity and tears. But especially Abraham and Sarah urged both to bear this expulsion patiently; for, as they said, it was God's will expressed by a definite word that Ishmael should leave his home and his native country and should wait for God's blessing in another place than in the land of Canaan. Moreover, they said that God is unchanging and truthful and would not forsake them but would bountifully give them what He had promised, namely, a most powerful kingdom.

I am not inventing these things, but the very situation and Moses' earlier narrative clearly suggest these circumstances. For the history of the Sodomites shows how godly and how gentle and compassionate Abraham was even toward his enemies. How, then, could he refrain from tears in this instance, when he sent away his wife and his first-born son in this manner with meager provisions?

He said: "My dear Hagar, I have not forgotten what I owe you and your son, my own flesh, and I would gladly keep both of you with me and perform the duties of love which I owe you; but God's command demands and directs something else. For the sake of God, therefore, bear calmly the fact that you two are being cast out in a state of such destitution. God does not want to make you rich through my wealth; He wants you to experience His blessing in a different place."

What, then, can be set before us that is more profitable than this account for instructing us regarding most important matters? For it warns us by the example of Abraham that when God gives an order, one must not delay or argue. God wants obedience, but delay displeases Him. His innate affections confused Abraham too, so that he thought: "Where will my poor wife stay with her son? Where will she find an abode? Who will defend her against harm?"

But his faith, strengthened by a trustworthy assurance, smothers all these thoughts of the flesh, though not without difficulty and great grief, and simply clings to this hope: "God will look out for them. God will take care of them, for He loves them more than I do and will be more able to help them."

Accordingly, this example is suitable for us to learn to do quickly and without argument whatever we know has been commanded by the Word of God. When Christ said to Peter (John 21:21-22): "Follow Me," Peter, oblivious, as it were, of the command but concerned about John, said: "What about this man?" But the Lord rebukes him and says: "What is that to you? Follow Me!"

Therefore Abraham's conduct is proper. He does not argue about where Hagar will go with her son; he simply turns his attention to the command of God, who had ordered him to cast out the mother with her son. That is what the examples or exercises of saintly men are like.

The monks, as I have said before, boast of their self-denial, their purifications, and their mortifications; but for them it is a mortification if they see that a brother who is sitting near them gets better or finer bread or fish. But in Abraham we see that the flesh is truly crucified, and that his inclination, even when it is just and saintly and also strengthened by a divine command, is mortified. For it is God's command that one should love one's wife, defend one's children, lay up treasures for one's children, etc.

Abraham is commanded to smother this natural inclination and saintly affection, and to send away his wife as well as his son in such a manner that they take with them not even a penny from his vast possessions. If this is not an example of mortification, I do not know what can be called mortification. He loves both his wife and his son; but when he is commanded to cast them out, he obeys without delay when God summons him, and he cuts short all arguments, no matter what fortune may eventually overtake the exiles.

This is the description of the expulsion or departure. As you see, it is pitiful enough; for neither side was able to hold back its tears. It was hard for Ishmael and his mother to leave the wealthy, kindly, saintly father and his entire church. For the father it was hard to send them away in such destitution and in the future not to have the companionship of the two. This also brought sorrow to Sarah herself and to Isaac. But both sides obey the will of God and kill their innate feelings, even those feelings that are strongest, namely, toward children and wife — feelings which cause us to undergo and bear even the greatest hardships.

But this is a proper observance of the vow of continence, of which the lazy crowd of monks — yes, even those among them who want to be the saintliest — have no knowledge.

The final little statement which Moses adds, namely, that "she wandered in the wilderness," tends even to increase our sympathy, since there was no one to guide the way. Because they did not know where they were going, they wandered in the wilderness. Furthermore, the word "to wander" indicates that they were in a very confused state of mind, with the result that they did not know where they were going, as happens to those who are bewildered because of fear and grief. We know that by nature the female sex is weak in spirit and is gravely upset even by slight inconveniences. What, then, shall we think about Hagar as she wanders so pitifully in the desert, without a guide, without provisions for the way, and without any human help? But another misfortune happens, one that is greater and sadder. This is described next.

15. *When the water in the skin was gone, she cast the child under one of the bushes.*

16. *Then she went, and sat down over against him a good way off, about the distance of a bowshot; for she said: Let me not look upon the death of the child. And as she sat over against him, she lifted up her voice and wept.*

The account could not have been written in a more horrifying way, even though Moses, in his customary manner, employs very few words. The mother and her son had water for three or four days, and with it they refresh themselves in the wilderness; but after this there is no more water. Therefore death is imminent for both, and from thirst at that, which is unbearable for our nature.

If someone wanted to rant against Abraham at this point, he could make him the murderer of his son and wife. The responsibility for this outcome lies in him who, as it seems, is cruelly casting out his own flesh. And Moses himself employs rather horrifying words; he states that Ishmael, now almost dead from thirst, was laid under a bush by his mother, and that her motherly affection constrained her to withdraw from him, lest she see her son breathe his last.

Who would believe this if Moses had not recorded it? Clearly one misfortune follows on the heels of the other. The first-born son was cast out from his father's house and was deprived of all of his father's wealth. In addition to this, in the desert he is now in peril of his life because of hunger and thirst.

Moreover, it is a tragic misfortune that the mother lays the lad in the grass under a bush; for she is so heartbroken through grief that she cannot bear the sight of her dying son. Someone will say: "Abraham should have thought of these misfortunes beforehand and should not have acted so hastily, especially in a matter altogether contrary to natural love or affection."

I have stated above that we should take very careful note of this example, in order that we may not argue when God commands something but may obey Him without delay. It will certainly not be easy for us to imitate this obedience which Abraham showed here, but what the monks are doing — wearing cowls and abstaining from meat and the handling of money — this will be very easy for us to imitate.

Therefore Abraham was no ordinary Christian or confessor, if I may express myself in this way. No, he was a martyr of martyrs. For who is there who does not know how intense a father's affection toward his children and wife is? It is easier for a parent to suffer death than to forsake his own or to permit great harm to be done to them. But everything must yield to a command of God; and if you want to be a Christian, this is not a matter of wearing a black or gray garment. No, everything must be risked, not only wife and children but your own life.

For Christ teaches clearly (Matt. 10:37) that "he who loves father and mother more than Me is not worthy of Me." This means: "When I come with My Word and command, then you must forget everything you have and possess in this whole world."

What, I ask you, have you ever heard or read about this denial in the writings of any monk? To be sure, they inscribe "Deny yourself" on the doors of their dwellings.[39] But if you judge the matter

[39] Drawings of the entrances to monasteries of the sixteenth century still show the motto *Nega teipsum* inscribed on the door.

on the basis of their actions, this means nothing else to them than "Forsake a poor kitchen, and enter a rich one; shun the inconveniences and hardships of the world, that is, of the household and of the government; enjoy a life of ease, and fatten yourself like a pig, and begrudge everybody whatever he has." Oh, what an easy and pleasant mortification of the flesh!

But the more patient and the more compassionate Abraham was, the more laudable his obedience is; for he puts God's command above everything else and loves God above all things, and to such an extent that he casts his most dearly beloved son and his very winsome wife out of his house like enemies.

To be sure, this expulsion is described in a manner that expresses grief, because the lad is weeping as he lies dying of thirst and his mother is unable to aid him in the desert; and if you judge the outward appearance, you will conclude that this is cruel, and you will blame Abraham. But what else was he to do, since God had given him the order?

But even though Ishmael is cast out of the house and the church of Abraham, nevertheless, as I have stated more than once above, undoubtedly many of the Canaanites were converted to the church.[40] Thus I do not doubt that Ishmael and many of his descendants were converted to the true church of Abraham. For the expulsion does not mean that Ishmael should be utterly excluded from the kingdom of God. No, the purpose is to let him know that the kingdom of God is not owed to him by reason of a natural right but comes out of pure grace.

For God gives nothing to anyone as the result of a right, in accordance with the statement (Rom. 11:35): "Who has first given to Him?" Nor is God anyone's debtor, for we would fare badly if He were our debtor. Indeed, we are all indebted to God. Therefore if He gives us something, He gives it, not because of a right but out of grace, which He lavishly and richly offers to all who believe His promise.

Ishmael and his mother must learn this lesson, since both wanted to proceed against Isaac on the strength of a right. Accordingly, I have no doubt that after this presumption of a right was destroyed

40 Cf. *Luther's Works*, 3, p. 40, on the conversion of the Canaanites.

by so harsh an expulsion, Ishmael and his mother returned to Abraham. For the opinion of the Jews that Keturah is Hagar pleases me.[41]

Therefore this account serves to teach us that we have nothing by reason of a right, but that everything comes as a result of the grace of God. The Jews want to be Abraham's heirs and to have possession of the blessing on the strength of a right, because they were born of the flesh of Abraham. Yet if they surrendered that right and sought refuge in grace, they would in this way become sharers in the promise.

Thus the pope boasts of his succession and on the strength of this right lays claim to the primacy for himself, but we in no wise concede this to him in the church. If he wanted to be first out of grace, we would put up with him; but when he insists on a right, we do not put up with him.

We say the same thing about the canons. If they left them optional, we would tolerate them; but because they make them binding, we utterly reject them and are harder than an anvil and a diamond. We would be softer than wax if our freedom were left to us.

Concerning monastic life our opinion is the same. The monks have their rules and exercises. They insist on these as a right, and they maintain that eternal life is their due. But who has commanded them to do this?

When God freely promises and gives all things abundantly for His Son's sake, is it not great ungodliness that we, thrusting aside His promise, presume to lay claim to eternal life for ourselves on the strength of a right?

Accordingly, by this example of Ishmael, God makes it clear that He owes nobody anything. Before Him, therefore, let no one boast of or glory in his righteousness and merit; but let the whole world be subject to God, prostrate itself, invoke His grace and mercy, and with one accord say (Ps. 143:2): "Enter not into judgment with Thy servant."

This is what Ishmael teaches every one of us. After he had been crushed in this manner, he simply renounced his right. Later on he came into the inheritance of the promise as a guest, as Paul says about the Gentiles in the Epistle to the Ephesians [42] (2:11-12).

For I believe that the descendants of Ishmael also joined the

---

[41] This comes from Lyra *ad* Gen. 21:15-16.

[42] In all editions the original has "Philippians" rather than "Ephesians" here.

church of Abraham and became heirs of the promise, not by reason of a right but because of irregular grace, just as we have stated above about the Cainites.[43]

This is the reason why the destitute son, along with his destitute mother — he alone along with her alone — was cast out of his father's house into the desert and into death from thirst and hunger, namely, in order that the exceedingly destructive beast called the notion of one's righteousness, right, and merit before God might be slain.

For before God nothing except grace has any value. If the Turks, the Jews, and the pope apprehended it through Christ, they would be saved; but since they are utterly blinded, they reject grace and rely on right and merit. Therefore they perish eternally.

Accordingly, this passage concerning the trials of Abraham and Hagar is wholly theological. For, as I have said, it was a great trial for Abraham to cast out his natural son along with his lawful wife in so brutal a manner, without making any provision whatever either for the wife or for the child but delivering both to what seemed to be certain death. For Abraham was not a hard stone; he was full of the Holy Spirit, who makes men gentle, humble, kindly, and beneficent.

Therefore this account is astonishing; but it is recorded about the saintly patriarch as an example for us, in order that we may learn that we should love and revere God above all things. Similarly, in chapter twelve Abraham is commanded to leave his country; and in Ps. 45:10 the church which has been gathered from the Jews is told: "O daughter, forget your father's house." And Christ says (Matt. 10:37): "He who loves father and mother more than Me is not worthy of Me."

Thus the Second Table contains the commandments dealing with love toward the brethren; but when a new commandment is added, as when Saul is commanded to kill the Amalekites, then we must be filled with wrath, persecute and kill them. Then we, like Abraham, must forget all love, even if a son has to be sacrificed. For the statement "I am the Lord your God" annuls that other commandment about loving one's neighbor and honoring one's parents.

Hence we observe a twofold mortification in the case of Abraham. The first has to do with the First Table. For in that case the conflict concerns God's promise. Contrary to the Word, Abraham wants it to be common to both his sons. This loyal affection is mortified, and

43 Cf. Luther's Works, 1, p. 301, note 58.

Abraham is forced to learn from his wife what the true understanding of the promise is.

The second mortification has to do with the Second Table, for Abraham is compelled to forget his loyalty toward his wife and son.

These examples should be diligently taught in the church; for they are in harmony with the Gospel, which teaches that the Word should be given preference above everything human. Since Abraham was taught by these [44] exercises, he had no hope that he would attain the fulfillment of the promise in this life; but he understood it to refer to other things — things greater than those that have to do with this life — since he is troubled by great trials and misfortunes even after the heir of the promise has been given to him.

The knowledge of eternal life, faith in the coming Christ, and the hope of the resurrection from the dead are the real blessings. These Abraham looked for because of the promise. He was not at all disturbed by these adversities — that he was compelled to wander about in this manner, to have no permanent abode, to cast out his wife and his first-born son. To the carnal man all these things seem to conflict with the promise. In reality, however, they are exercises of faith that are indispensable to us. But they are extraordinarily burdensome to the flesh, yes, altogether impossible.

These words — that Abraham gave Hagar a skin of water and bread — are few; but they, too, show what a pitiful misfortune this was. For consider the circumstances, and you will see that they are so horrible that they cannot be expressed in words. Not Sarah, not some servant, but Abraham himself, the father, equips his wife and son for the way. He puts bread and water on their shoulders and commands them to leave.

The account is almost like what is related about the sacrifice of Isaac. The grief would have been less heavy if Abraham had assigned this duty to a servant and if at that time he himself had gone to another place. But he is compelled to equip both of them for the way and to watch them in person as they leave. Therefore he must divest himself completely of his fatherly affection toward his wife and his son, like a hard and cruel man, as though he had never known them.

Moses considered this immeasurable fear and love of God worthy of being extolled in writing, inasmuch as Abraham is not only an

---

[44] The original has *hic*, but we have read *his* instead.

onlooker but also the cause of this misfortune. But if someone else had done this and had cast out of his house his wife with whom he had been closely associated for twenty years, more or less, what do you suppose Abraham would have done? But now, when God commands him to do this, he himself is the perpetrator, as it were, of this cruelty.

Abraham teaches us by his example that everything indeed should be done for the sake of one's neighbor, but that when we are ordered by a command of God to do something different, nothing in this entire life should be so dear and pleasing to us that we must not hate it, even our own life, as Christ says: "He who hates his life will find it" (cf. Matt. 10:39).

This, then, is forgetting one's father's house, as the psalm (45:10) expresses it. It is surely a piteous description, which I can hardly read with dry eyes, that the mother and her son bear their expulsion with such patience and go away into exile. Therefore Father Abraham either stood there with tears in his eyes and followed them with his blessings and prayers as they went away, or he hid himself somewhere in a nook, where he wept in solitude over his own misfortune and that of the exiles.

For, as I have stated repeatedly, Abraham was not a log or a stone; but he had a heart brimful of compassion and of love for his neighbors, and far more for the people of his household, namely, his wife and his first-born son. Where in this way trial follows upon trial and tears force out other tears, the mortification is real; and real are the exercises of the faith which mortifies even innate love. Therefore one may say that the instances of mortification of the monks and nuns, of which they boast, are trifles.

Beer-sheba, of which the text makes mention, is close to Egypt, and perhaps there were herds of sheep and cattle in the neighborhood. For the people of that region supported themselves by means of herds of cattle and lived in tents. There Ishmael and Hagar [45] encounter a new danger — a danger which stuns the mother and renders her almost cruelly unfeeling, just as Abraham, too, can appear to have acted cruelly, although for another reason; for he obeyed God's command.

Ishmael is being tortured to death by thirst. Since his mother

[45] The original has "Sarah," but we have followed the suggestion of the Erlangen editors and have read "Hagar."

could not watch this sad spectacle, she lays him down on the grass among the shrubs and goes away a short distance, as though she intended to abondon him when he was about to die. Nevertheless, she sits down nearby. From here she can hear the groans of the dying boy.

We know that it is great misery and a misfortune if an exile without a fixed abode wanders about among strange people; but the misfortune which the circumstances in this place reveal is greater. For Hagar is both a mother and a woman, and is alone and in the desert at that, after being cast out so suddenly from a spacious house. And now there is a lack of all provisions, and her son is dying.

Hagar could have had water from Beer-sheba, for undoubtedly the tents of shepherds were there. But the woman wanders about, not only afflicted in her body but also so disquieted in mind that she does not know what to do.

But it is a theological rule that Satan adds affliction to the afflicted and causes those who go astray physically also to go astray mentally. As we say in the German proverb, he is in the habit of climbing over a hedge where it is low and of pushing in the direction in which a wagon leans, in order to overturn it completely.

Accordingly, very sad thoughts, which Satan has outstanding ability to stir up, were added to these misfortunes. "Where shall I go now," thought Hagar, "a woman who has been pitifully cast out? There is neither a God in heaven nor a human being on earth who takes pity on us. God hates us. Therefore He will let us die here and perish in the desert from thirst and hunger."

This is that destructive addition from which Satan has his name when he is called Leviathan.[46] Out of a physical misfortune he makes a spiritual one, and to a burden he adds a burden that is greater. Moreover, Job (40:24) states that he cannot be caught with a hook; that is, he cannot be driven off by human strength. He is Leviathan, or the one who always adds something to the other pan of the scale and forces it down; he overturns the leaning wagon.

Accordingly, this was a severe trial and one that was far more serious than hunger or thirst. Therefore Hagar falls into a stupor so deep that she does not know what she is doing. Otherwise she would have seen the well and would have thought of the people of that

[46] Cf. *Luther's Works*, 1, p. 51, note 84.

place. But after she has become involved in those additions and exaggerations of Leviathan, she thinks that there are several hundredweights of affliction where there is but an ounce.

Thus the author of Revelation calls Satan "the accuser of our brethren" (12:10). For Satan makes those who are smug altogether adamantine, just as our antinomians are. But those who have a feeble and timid heart he dashes to the ground with his terrors as with the force of a thunderbolt.

Accordingly, Hagar is being tried not only by her physical expulsion but also by her spiritual one; and she is despairing to the point of death. The water had been used up, but there was a whole well in the neighborhood. Hagar does not think of this, for she is sunk in those lying thoughts which Satan has suggested: "Behold, Abraham is a man of God and His prophet; in his house alone is the true church, and he it is who is casting out you and your son. What other, surer proof can there be that you do not belong to that church?"

I would not like to have my heart attacked with such darts, for I have experienced how dangerous a wound this inflicts. If some minister of a church were to deny me absolution and keep me from Holy Communion, even though it were done for some trivial reason, I nevertheless believe that I would run away in despair with Judas and hang myself.

But Hagar does not hear this verdict of expulsion from some ordinary minister. No, she hears it from the foremost patriarch, who is the father of the promise. In what frame of mind, then, do you suppose she was?

About Lot we have heard above that he was so crushed and stunned by misfortunes that even though he saw, he did not see, and even though he did something, he was not aware of it. For his mind is preoccupied to such an extent with great grief and perils that all the senses in his body are virtually dead. Therefore this is called an ἔκστασις [47] and a trance, which is so powerful that Lot was completely without any knowledge of what he had done with his daughters.

Here good Hagar is also in such a state of violent emotion, and Moses indicates this by the word "to wander"; for her exceedingly

[47] Cf., for example, Gregory of Nyssa, *Fifteen Homilies on the Song of Songs, Patrologia, Series Graeca,* XLIV, 873.

great sorrow prevents her from seeing anything. Despair makes her deaf, dumb, blind, and thoughtless. Indeed, it simply kills her so far as all her senses are concerned.

Moreover, you see that here, in opposition to our antinomians, the Law is considered before the solace is mentioned. Ishmael and his mother Hagar acted proudly toward Isaac because they themselves were also the seed of Abraham; and they were hoping to get the inheritance because of their relationship according to the flesh.

First it was necessary that this state of mind be overcome by knowledge of the Law and by mortification. Those who have been mortified through the agency of the Law must then be buoyed up in turn and comforted by the Word of God. For they are contrite; they are not smug and proud, as Ishmael was.

Hence the passage before us gives us instruction concerning the exercise and function of the Law. Therefore Paul (Gal. 4:30) calls these words of Sarah, "Cast out the slave woman," words of the Law. He does not say: "What does Sarah say?" No, he says: "What does Scripture say?" If, then, Moses, with his written Law, was not yet in existence, still the Law was there in its use and exercise, because "to cast out" is a word of the Law.

Therefore let us utterly reject the antinomians, who cast the Law out of the church and want to teach repentance by means of the Gospel.[48] It is correct, of course, to say that people should be buoyed up and comforted; but a definition should be added — a definition stating who such people are, namely, that they are those who are wasting away from hunger and thirst in the desert after they have been cast out of their home and country, who sigh and cry to the Lord and are now at the point of despair. People of this kind are fit hearers of the Gospel.

But those who feel that they are in the state of grace because of some physical prerogative, who vaunt their own righteousness and sanctity, do not think they are in the desert. No, they think they are in Paradise. They do not know what it means to wander in the desert. They are not humbled. They are not killed. They must be struck with the hammer of the Law and broken to pieces. Yes, they must be reduced to nothing.

This is done through the Law, which says: "Cast out the slave

[48] Cf. *Luther's Works*, 22, p. 39, note 36.

woman with her son; for he shall not be the heir" (Gal. 4:30); that is, by nature we are all outside God's grace. For so far as our nature is concerned, we are children of perdition; nor is it of any benefit that the Jews are the descendants of Abraham, that at birth we bring with us the judgment of reason and the Law, and that in some measure we can adjust our will to the Law. All this contributes nothing to salvation.

But whatever there is of the Law, whatever there is of the will of the flesh and of man — of this it is said: "Cast it out!" For God cannot bear the presumption of Ishmael; that is, He does not want us to glory in our physical birth, in our strength, in the freedom of our will, in our wisdom and righteousness. All this must be mortified; all this must be despaired of, just as Hagar despairs in this place.

When this has happened and we have been thrust down into hell, this is the time to call us back by means of the sweet voice of the Gospel, which does not say: "Cast out!" No, it says (Matt. 9:2): "Take heart, my son, your sins are forgiven." For this reason Scripture says (1 Sam. 2:6) that it is God's work "to bring down to Sheol and to raise up, to kill and to bring to life."

This is the reason why Ishmael and his mother are cast out, namely, that the horrible and ungovernable evil of presumption of their own righteousness may be killed. For this is what he thought: "I am in the house of Abraham; therefore I am the heir." This self-confidence is such a poisonous evil and such a pernicious pest that it cannot be killed except through utter despair, so that a man, divested of everything he possesses, all but despairs of God and His grace and feels himself cast away by God. This the Father and the true Abraham, that is, God Himself, is compelled to bring about in us. For neither the church nor Christ nor righteousness concerns us at all unless harmful presumption is first completely overcome and mortified.

Therefore the antinomians, who defend themselves with our example, deserve to be hated by all, even though it is manifest why in the beginning we taught as we did concerning the grace of God. The pope had pitiably burdened the consciences with his traditions and had taken away all true means of help with which despondent hearts could be protected against despair. What else, then, could we do than encourage the disheartened people and hold out true solace to them?

We know, however, that one must speak differently to those who are sated, addicted to pleasure, and fat. At that time we were all cast out and exceedingly miserable. The water in the bottle had been consumed; that is, there was no comfort available. We were lying there dying, like Ishmael under the tree. Therefore we needed such teachers as would present to us the grace of God and teach us to breathe freely again.

The antinomians, on the other hand, want the doctrine of repentance to begin directly from grace. But I myself did not proceed in this manner, for I knew that Ishmael was cast out and in despair before he heard the comfort from the angel. Accordingly, I followed this example and comforted only those who were first contrite and despairing, whom the Law had thoroughly frightened and Leviathan had crushed and stunned. For Christ came into the world for their sake, and He does not want the smoking flax (Matt. 12:20) to be completely extinguished. Therefore He cries (Matt. 11:28): "Come to Me, all who labor and are heavy-laden."

Ishmael was not that kind of person before he was cast out of the house. He was proud and smug, and an antinomian Epicurean. "I," he said, "am the lord and the heir; Isaac and Sarah should yield to me." Should this pride have been fostered, or should it have been corrected? But by what other method could it have been corrected than by letting him be cast out together with his mother and letting him carry away with him nothing from the house of Abraham except that reward of the Law, namely, bread and water? For this is what the Law is wont to do. It leads the bound thief to the gallows; but before he is strangled, it refreshes him with a drink of water. Finally, however, the water gives out, and death remains. More than this the Law does not do.

Therefore let us learn that God hates all proud people; but those who have been humbled and have felt the power of the Law He comforts, if not through men, at least through an angel from heaven. For He does not permit such people to perish, just as He does not permit those who are smug to remain in Abraham's house.

Moreover, a teacher in the church must be well informed and experienced in both respects, in order that he may be able to refute and crush the gainsayers and to comfort again those who have been refuted and crushed, lest they be devoured. If our nature had not been corrupted by sin to such an extent, there would be no need for the preaching of the Law. But now, because of our hardness and extreme smugness, God cannot accomplish anything among us through His grace unless He has first broken and crushed our adamantine hearts.

Therefore in Gal. 4:22 ff. Paul also gives the following literal explanation of the passage before us. He says: "All who are of the synagog are people of this kind." Moreover, we learn by experience that not only the Jews but all men are people of this kind, just as I related above about the Turks, who take for granted that they are the people of God because they are distinguished by victories, and about the pope and his church, who appropriate the name "church" because they have the honor and the office.

In short, this account portrays all such people. They cannot be saved unless they are reduced to death and despair; for all of them, because of their physical birth and the powers this brings with it, take grace and the forgiveness of sins for granted.

I recall that an ungodly and very bitter enemy of the Gospel fell from a scaffold while he was inspecting a building that was under construction. Since he felt no ill effect from his fall — for not a single member had been injured — he cried out: "Now I know that I have a gracious God." [49] Thus the world is wont to do. Because of physical blessings it takes for granted that God is gracious. Such is its nature. Therefore its nature must be mortified, which is done through the Law.

Consequently, he who wants to be an heir of the promises must exclude everything that is not a promise, as St. Paul does in his Epistle to the Philippians (3:8), when he calls the righteousness of the Law refuse; for before God nothing is of any avail except the promise and grace set forth in Christ.

The flesh has its gifts, but nothing is owed them except bread and water. But eternal life does not come to the children of the flesh; it comes to the children of the promises, that is, to those who believe.

It is worthy of special note that God added a blessing for married people when He said (Gen. 1:28): "Increase and multiply." But this is a physical blessing and is restricted to the filling of the earth. No matter how saintly a father and a mother are, this is nevertheless of no advantage to the children who are born to them. Nor are the children saved on this account. If they are to be saved, they must become children of the promise, and they themselves must believe

[49] Cf., among other anecdotes, *Luther's Works*, 13, pp. 159—160.

the promise. For this reason the individuals must be baptized. It is of no benefit to me that you were baptized; I, too, must be baptized and believe.

Thus the expulsion of Ishmael is a matter that includes all men and unites the church of the past up to the end of the world; it points out that the first birth does not concern the kingdom of God and that without faith in the promise concerning Christ nobody can be saved. Therefore it is foolish for the papists to proclaim that they are the church. For the church is not a people that should be judged on the basis of a large number, of size, of wisdom, of power, of wealth, of prestige, of succession, of office, etc. Far less is it to be judged on the basis of self-chosen forms of worship. No, it is the people of the promise, that is, the people which believes the promise.

Therefore when they say: "The pope is the head of the church; hence whatever he commands is of God," you must say that this is not a logical conclusion, because the pope has neither any knowledge nor any understanding of Holy Scripture and believes it far less. He is a sort of mask of the church and not the church. Indeed, he attacks and persecutes the church, just as Cain attacked and persecuted Abel. This he does on account of the promise which he claims for himself, even though he does not believe it. Therefore let no one permit himself to be frightened by the magnificent terms "succession," "call," and "office."

The Turks also boast that they are creatures of God; and they swear by God, the Creator of heaven and earth. The pope boasts that he believes in Christ, namely, that He is the Son of God and the Redeemer of the world. Meanwhile he establishes monasteries and institutes Masses, fasts, the worship of saints, and the like, but in vain. For these are works of your own creation — of you who are made of flesh — and they are fruits of an evil tree. But if the tree is to become good, you must become a person of the promise; that is, you must accept grace and rely on mercy alone, something which cannot happen unless you apprehend the Word of the promise by faith. Ishmael is Abraham's natural son. Nevertheless, he is not the heir.

This is the argument of St. Paul, and no man will be able to invalidate it. We see plainly that the papists are persecuting the children of the promise, just as Ishmael persecuted Isaac. Therefore unless the groundless self-confidence they have acquired is mortified and reduced to nothing, together with all their fine gifts from the flesh, they will never be saved. Observe how the Turks are adorned with power and wisdom. The pope, too, and the cardinals are very wise men. Similarly, Plato, Cicero, and Socrates are also very great men. But they are not the church on this account; for they do not have this essential difference by which the church is set apart from the world, namely, the promise. Consequently, we concede to the pope and his followers their wisdom and prestige. And I add even the succession and office. But they are not the church on this account. For there is lacking that essential difference, which is faith in the Gospel. But those who do not believe the Gospel are not the church; nor do they belong to the kingdom of Christ.

Therefore, O pope, your papacy must first be killed, and you must be reduced to nothing before God. Otherwise you will never be even the smallest part of the church. This is something harsh, and to the papists it is unbearable. But it grieved Ishmael, too, to be cast out and separated from the church, and to be regarded as a member cut away from the church. Nor can anything more painful happen to all of us who are private individuals than to be deprived in this manner of all hope and confidence.

I, too, am very frequently troubled by this trial, that I look about for works in which I may be able to put my trust, because I have taught much, have benefited many, and have borne many more indignities than I deserved. But I realize that in real conflicts all these are nothing, and I am driven to the well-known confession of David, who said: "Lord, I am nothing but a sinner" (cf. Ps. 32:5); and (Ps. 116:11): "I said in my consternation: 'All men are a vain hope' "; that is, every man who deceives and is deceived is useless. Likewise (Ps. 143:2): "Enter not into judgment with Thy servant."

But I encourage myself with this hope alone, that in the Gospel I see that solace has been promised to the contrite, hope to the despairing, and heaven to those who have been put into hell; and the fact that the Son of God, without our knowledge, offered Himself for us to God the Father, His Father, on the altar of the cross, is sure proof of this hope.

If those who have first been humbled in this manner and have been driven to despair begin to be of good cheer because of Christ to the same extent that they despair of themselves, they become children of God and heirs. Yet you may find many who do not want to be humbled but plan vengeance and grumble. These people are doubly obdurate.

Therefore when you feel that you are being humbled, cast yourself at the feet of your heavenly Father and say: "O Lord, if Thou dealest with me in this manner, I shall bear it patiently, and I confess that I have deserved something more terrible. Therefore be merciful to me. If Thou dost not want me to be an heir, see to it that I remain a servant (Luke 15:19). Indeed, as the Canaanite woman says, I do not refuse to be a dog in Thy house so that I can at least eat the crumbs which chance to fall to the ground and otherwise are wasted (Matt. 15:27). Thou dost not owe me a thing by any right. Therefore I cling to Thy mercy."

This is the true way by which we come to grace and salvation. But few listen, and fewer obey and believe. The Jews recite these words daily in their prayers: "Blessed be God, who sanctifies us before all the people of the earth." [50] But this is not a prayer. No, it is the height of blasphemy against God, as the psalm (109:7) says: "Let their prayer be counted as sin!" For God is not one to show partiality. He sets forth His Word to all and wants all to believe and be saved. He makes no distinction between Jews and Gentiles; He wants to be the God of all. Therefore let no one be as arrogant as the ungodly Jews are. Let us all humble ourselves and acknowledge that we are nothing, but that whatever we are, we are by the free grace of God.

Paul, too, was puffed up by his own righteousness; but when, as he was near Damascus, he heard the voice of Christ, whom he had previously so smugly despised, he said with fear and trembling: "Lord, what dost Thou want me to do?" (Cf. Acts 9:6.) Where on this occasion was his boast that he was a son of Abraham, of the tribe of Benjamin, a Pharisee, and a student of the Law? Just as Ishmael came from the Law to the promise, from death to life, and from hell to heaven, so this happened to Paul too. This is why later on he manifests such ardor and such a spirit of power when he deals with this very discussion concerning the promise and merits, concerning grace and works, namely, that the promise alone and nothing else makes heirs — not physical birth, not circumcision, not other works of the Law.

[50] Luther is referring to the daily recitation of the *Shema,* with its accompanying prayers.

17. *And God heard the voice of the lad; and the angel of God called to Hagar from heaven, and said to her: What troubles you, Hagar? Fear not; for God has heard the voice of the lad where he is.*

The angel does not call Ishmael Abraham's son; he simply calls him a lad, which is a designation common among all men. And he says that the lad's cry has been heard. Undoubtedly the dying Ishmael did not mention that Abraham was his father; for, overwhelmed as he is by misfortune and grief, he forgets about it, and Leviathan, of whom we have spoken before — that is, Satan — makes his appearance and kills him spiritually with the power of the Law.

Therefore nothing else was left than the indescribable groan of a despairing heart. Ishmael confesses that he is unworthy of his father's house and inheritance, just as the prodigal son in the Gospel (Luke 15:21) says: "I am not worthy to be called your son." This groan God sees and hears. To be sure, Ishmael cried with his voice; but it was chiefly the distress of his heart and his contrition that led him to groan from the throat and to heave deep sighs. This music, which seems to us very sad and mournful, pleases God more than any other form of worship, as He says in Isaiah (57:15): "I shall dwell with a contrite spirit." For smugness is offensive to God.

The following story is told about the hermit Anthony, who was the originator of the monastic way of life.[51] He wanted to know with whom he would share his honor and glory in eternal life, for he was exceedingly pleased with himself because of this solitary kind of life. Accordingly, he hears in a dream that in Alexandria there is a certain cobbler or tanner who would share with him the same glory. Anthony is amazed at the comparison and goes to Alexandria with the intention of seeing the man who is his equal in sanctity. I do not know what grand things he promises himself from that cobbler; but when he came to him, he found that he gained his livelihood by working with his hands and in this manner supported himself, his wife, and his children. So he said: "Please, my dear cobbler, I know that you worship God faithfully and serve Him truly. Tell me, therefore, what you do, what you eat, what you drink, how or when you pray. You do not spend entire nights without sleep when you devote yourself to prayer, do you?" "Not at all," said the cobbler. "In the morning and in the evening I give thanks to God for His faithful protection and guidance. I ask for forgiveness of all my sins for

---

[51] On the source of this anecdote cf. *Luther's Works,* 3, p. 217, note 46.

Christ's sake, and I humbly pray that He would guide me with His Spirit and not lead me into temptation. After this prayer I get busy with my leather and provide sustenance for myself and those who are mine. Besides this I do nothing except to beware lest anywhere I do something against my conscience."

When Anthony hears this, he is amazed, and he realizes that self-chosen forms of worship are no worship and that therefore no trust at all should be put in them. This blessing not only happened to Anthony himself but is also a warning to all posterity — a warning by which God wanted to help His church, lest it indulge in self-chosen forms of worship, which always bring with them this pernicious pest of self-reliance, which must be crushed.

Poor clothing, coarse food, fasts, long prayers, vigils, or any works cannot be of benefit to us for eternal life. Only trust in mercy, only the promise, saves. If this is lacking, confess freely, and say: "I am nothing. The inheritance does not concern me; I have been cast out of my father's house."

This is the voice of the lad Ishmael, which God hears; and to those who cry in this manner He sends His angels from heaven itself.

Therefore this is a very great comfort for all those who feel that they have been cast out, that is, acknowledge their sins and tremble before the judgment of God. For He does not want to cast such people aside, nor can He do so; and if such people were without solace from men, it would sooner be necessary for an angel to descend from heaven to bring them comfort. Accordingly, God is called the God of the humble and afflicted who does not quench a smoldering wick (Matt. 12:20). But after the self-reliance of the flesh has been mortified in Ishmael, he becomes a true son of the promise; and what he first demanded on the basis of right, but did not obtain, he now, in his utmost need and despair, receives by grace.

It is a remarkable situation and one most worthy of noting that when Ishmael feels himself utterly cast away, he has God at his side and is very dear to God. And God cannot disregard the voice and the groaning of the afflicted lad. But if God had not heard him here, he would have perished eternally. But to God this is impossible. "For He is merciful and does not want the death of the sinner" (cf. Ezek. 33:11).

Accordingly, let us learn this rule: Only those who are contrite become children of Abraham, and this takes place out of extraordinary and pure grace. Therefore one should not be presumptuous about anything, just as one should not despair either. But our nature is such that it is presumptuous when there is peace and despairs when there is war, although one should steer a middle course and not lose heart in dangers but should trust in God's mercy and call upon His name, according to what is stated in Ps. 50:15: "Call upon Me in the day of trouble." Likewise Ps. 91:16: "I will show them My salvation."

Nevertheless, everyone must be cautioned not to suppose that contrition, about which we have already said a great deal, is deserving of grace, as the sophists falsely teach.[52] For many do not hear the Word, and many who hear the Word do not believe. The Word is offered to all, and "I am the Lord your God" is a general statement which applies equally to all. But presumptuous persons despise it, and those who despair do not believe that it applies to them. Therefore one should keep to the middle of the road, in accordance with this little line: "In the middle you will walk in greatest safety." [53]

It may be surprising that Hagar did not become frightened and flee when she heard the angel's voice in the desert. But I have stated that her mind was benumbed by such a great stupor that she did not think about who was speaking. Similarly, when Peter, who is in prison, is awakened by the angel and led out of the prison, he does not know that this is really taking place but thinks that something like it is happening to him in a dream (Acts 12:9). But the angel undoubtedly appeared in human form.

Moreover, because the Word of God is never proclaimed in vain, Hagar, too, is first awakened from death, as it were, by the angel's voice. Then she is enlightened with a new light of the Holy Spirit, and from a slave woman she also becomes a mother of the church, who later on instructed her descendants and warned them by her own example not to act proudly; for, as she said, she had been a lawful wife of Abraham, the very saintly patriarch, and had borne him his first-born son. But this physical prerogative had been of no benefit to her. Indeed, this prestige had given rise to her pride. But after she had been cast out on account of her pride and had been humbled, she finally attained grace.

Similarly, we who have lived in monasteries today tell others about

---

[52] Cf. the passages cited in Heiko A. Oberman, *The Harvest of Medieval Theology* (Cambridge, 1963), p. 148.

[53] Ovid, *Metamorphoses*, II, 137, cf. also p. 15 and p. 68.

our crosses and sufferings. Because we put our trust in them, we believed that we were sitting on the lap of God. Now, however, after we have been enlightened by the Word, we call all those righteousnesses on which we used to rely "refuse and loss," as Paul does (Phil. 3:8).

After Hagar had been instructed in the Lord's school in this manner, she gave excellent instruction to many pupils concerning the foremost doctrine taught in the church of God, namely, that no glorying according to the flesh is of any avail. She said that she had been in the same bed with Abraham and yet had been cast out of his house. Therefore he who boasts, let him boast that he knows the Lord (cf. 1 Cor. 1:31), that is, that he has the promise and believes it, and that without this faith everything else is useless.

In the Hebrew the angel's words are very brief. "What troubles you, Hagar?" he asks. But one should not suppose that these words were spoken in a harsh manner, as though he were rebuking her; for they are words of comfort. "Ah," says the angel, "why are you weeping? Why are you sobbing? What do you desire? There is no reason why you should be afraid. Dry your tears. God cares for you and your son. He wanted to crush you. Since this has been achieved, He wants you to be of good hope with regard to His mercy. Before this you, with your son, also prayed in the house of Abraham. But there God was unwilling to hear you, for your prayer was associated with pride and with contempt for your brother. But here He has heard you. Therefore believe that His church is here. For where God hears prayers, there His sanctuary is, there the church is, and there the unutterable sighing (Rom. 8:26) of those who despair of themselves is." Thus one must understand definitely that he is speaking specifically of the place where Ishmael is.

So the angel is sent from heaven to comfort the dying Ishmael and his mother. But since the remedy is so costly, the seriousness of the sickness with which both were afflicted is also evident; for an angel is sent to those who are overwhelmed by misfortune, not a human being. And here we are also reminded of the final cause, namely, that God does not let Ishmael and Hagar be cast out so pitifully because He hates them.

This false cause is the invention of Leviathan; but it is God's plan that they should be humbled and learn to put their trust in God's grace alone, not in merits or some carnal prestige.

Moreover, these things were recorded in writing through the Holy Spirit in order that the entire world and all posterity might learn that it is a universal and indisputable proposition that we are saved by grace, not by merits and works. There was no other remedy for crushing the pride in merits and prestige unless Ishmael, together with his mother, were cast out of the holy church of God, which was in the house of Abraham. But if this did not take place without great grief and many tears, yet the fruit which resulted was far greater; for in this way they attain grace and are saved.

This is the purpose of such a pitiful expulsion: God wants to teach us that we are saved by grace alone or by faith alone. Faith takes hold of the grace that is set before us in the promise. For the natural children are to be regarded as equal with those who are not natural children and yet believe. So there is one God of the Jews and of the Gentiles. The Jews should not boast of their prerogative according to the flesh, and the Gentiles should not despair because of their sins.

This is the chief article of our faith; and if you either do away with it, as the Jews do, or corrupt it, as the papists do, the church cannot exist. Nor can God keep His glory, which consists in this, that He is compassionate and wants to forgive sins and to save for the sake of His Son.

Thus the seemingly pitiful account serves to comfort us, who are wretched sinners and come into the church without worthiness and merits. But we have a place on a par with that of those who are natural children. For with God there is no respect of persons (Acts 10:34), and the promise alone avails; for it is the Word of God that abides forever (1 Peter 1:25).

But what can be the reason for doubting? Why do our opponents attack that proposition so vehemently when we say that we are saved by grace and not by merits? What moves them to do so? For our situation is far surer if we maintain that we are adopted as children through grace rather than through merits. If our situation depends on merits, we can never be sure when we have enough merits. Thus we can never be without the danger of damnation. What, then, prompts the papists to rely on works and merits rather than on the promise and grace?

The first reason is this, that they do not believe that God is the Creator of heaven and earth. If they believed that they are God's creatures and that God is their Creator, they would never confront Him with their merits or works; nor would they be presumptuous about anything. For how can one compare the Creator to the creature? The creature comes into being from nothing. Hence all things of which the creature is capable are nothing, that is, if they are opposed to the Creator, who gave it being.

For this reason Job says (4:17-19): "Can man be more righteous than God? Or will man be purer than his Maker? Even in His servants He puts no trust, and His angels He charges with error; how much more those who dwell in houses of clay, whose foundation is in the dust, who are crushed before the moth!" It follows, therefore, that the papists do not believe either that God is the Creator or that they are creatures, since they confront God with merits and works and trust in their works rather than in grace. But what does it mean that what is nothing wants to contend with God, its Creator?

The second reason for the doubting is that God does not deal with us in accordance with His majesty but assumes human form and speaks with us throughout all Scripture as man speaks with man. In Paradise He asks Adam (Gen. 3:9): "Adam, where are you?" as though He did not know unless Adam told Him. The saints cry out everywhere (Ps. 44:23): "Arise, Lord, why art Thou sleeping? Hear me, O Lord." Yes, Christ Himself says in the Gospel (Luke 6:38): "Give, and it will be given to you." He establishes a kind of exchange with us. Indeed, He tells us everything without majesty and, if I may use this expression, from the emptied form of God. But the result, as the proverb puts it, is that excessive familiarity breeds contempt.[54]

But God condescends in this manner because of our weakness, for we cannot bear it when He speaks in His majesty. Words of majesty are "Who has given a gift to Him that He might be repaid?" (Rom. 11:35), "He hardens the heart of whomever He wills" (Rom. 9:18), and "Before Him no one is blameless" (cf. Job 4:18). Who can bear these words? And yet, when He condescends in this way on our account, so that He speaks with us as the head of a household speaks with his servants, He is despised by us, and we conclude that He needs our money, our fasts, our prayers, our vigils, etc.

Thus the familiarity which should urge us to welcome God's kindness makes us presumptuous. He speaks with us about Himself

[54] Publilius Syrus, *Sententiae*, ed. J. Wight Duff and A. M. Duff (*Minor Latin Poets;* Cambridge, 1935), maxim 640; it was probably known to Luther through its incorporation in Aesop's fable of the fox and the lion.

as though He were a human being like ourselves. He pretends not to know where Adam is. He pretends to be sleeping. He lets a vineyard and promises the laborers rewards. We abuse this familiarity and humility of His and conclude that He is a shoemaker or craftsman who gives nothing by grace but does everything on the basis of merit. This is unbearable presumption, deserving of eternal death.

"Nevertheless," they say, "there is the promise (Luke 6:38): 'Give, and it will be given to you.'" What is this to you? You are not for this reason going to deny that you are a creature, are you? But if you are a creature, you are nothing over against your Creator, and you confront Him in vain with your merits and works. Do you not see that Ishmael, who is proud of his physical birth, is cast out of the house and is all but killed in the desert? But this is profitable to him, for in this manner he is freed from presumption and attains grace.

The psalm (100:3) states: "The Lord made us, and not we ourselves." Why does the Holy Spirit put us in mind of this, as though no one actually knew it? Truly, the entire world has need of this teaching. For all who are presumptuous about their works do not know that they were made by the Lord; and they need to be reminded that they were made by the Lord. Otherwise they would humble themselves before their Creator and not be presumptuous about their own powers, because whatever they have, they have from God. Thus ignorance of the act of creation makes us presumptuous. So does God's exceedingly great friendliness toward us.

Therefore it is necessary for God to put a lawgiver over us, as Ps. 9:20 expresses it, and to kill us along with Ishmael, in order that Paul's statement (cf. Eph. 2:8-9) may stand firm: "Through faith and not by works, through grace and not through our merits" we are what we are, even naturally and according to the body and the flesh, and to a far greater extent supernaturally and according to the spirit, so that we should simply say: "O God, have mercy on me!" This is what Ishmael and Hagar learned in the desert.

Ishmael's expulsion from the house shows how intensely God hates pride and presumption. On the other hand, however, learn here how God deals with those who have been humbled. Hagar is sitting there weeping very bitterly and in utter despair. For she sees that she has been cast out together with her son and has been excommunicated by Abraham, the father of the church. This is certainly a dreadful situation. For the Law does not jest. No, it truly humbles hearts, in order that they may realize that with all their powers and works they have merited nothing but eternal damnation.

Therefore the angel comes as a comforter and brings nothing but solace from God Himself. But Hagar is silent; for she is unable to answer, since she is prevented from doing so by her weeping. In the sorrow and sighs of a troubled heart the voice and tongue die, as it were. Therefore since she is silent when the angel addresses her, the angel absolves her from her sins and tells her not to fear.

Accordingly, you should note the difference between the Law and the Gospel. First Hagar had heard the sad statement that God wanted her to be cast out along with the boy. This voice of the Law depresses her proud spirit, especially when this trial in the desert had been added. When a heart is held in distress of this kind, it cries out with continual sighing (Ps. 51:12): "Lord, cast me not away from Thy presence." But what it means to be cast away from God's presence only the saints understand, that is, those who have been well humbled. Those who quarrel about merits and works do not understand it. Therefore the true voice of the Gospel comes. "Do not fear," it says; that is: "Hope for deliverance, you who up to this time have been crushed through the Law, rejected, and excommunicated. Your expulsion, the lack of water, the vast desert, and your dying son perturb and all but kill you; but God tells you not to fear. Just as the other things force you to fear, so God's kindness should encourage you."

Moreover, the contrast shows that Hagar feared and trembled very much; for what purpose would it serve to command her not to fear unless she had been perturbed by exceedingly great fear? The antinomians and the Epicureans stuff themselves. They play and dance. Therefore it would be futile to command them not to fear. But Hagar, along with her son, is in a state of utmost despair, not only because the water in the bottle was gone, but rather because spiritual water was lacking and because she felt that she had been excommunicated. She had come to the realization that up to this time she had cried out and prayed in vain, for she had been proud. Now, however, her prayer is being heard, because she is contrite and has been mortified along with her son. But God is the God of the humble, not only of the Jews but also of the Gentiles; but He resists the proud (cf. 1 Peter 5:5).

But observe how beautifully the angel tempers his speech. He does not say that Hagar's voice has been heard. No, he says that her son's voice has been heard. Yet he is not speaking with her son; he is speaking with Hagar. She herself, as the mother, was very greatly perturbed because of her dying son. Therefore when she hears that he is in grace and that a large kingdom or a great nation is promised to him, she is again completely cheered; nor does the fact that she is not at once restored or called back to the place from which she had been cast out stand in the way of this joy. "God," said the angel, "has heard the voice of the lad where he is." It is as though he were saying: "Before God you must make no distinction between Abraham's house and that tree under which your son is lying. Even though you are not in Abraham's house, nevertheless beware of doubting that you and your son belong to the same church.

"Abraham is indeed the father of the promise, and in his house is the true church. To be expelled from it seems to be a calamity. Therefore you think that you would be glad to be a slave maid in Abraham's house and that your son would be glad to be a slave. But this is not necessary; it is enough that you have been humbled. Indeed, so far as the nature of the place is concerned, this place in which you now are is not inferior to Abraham's house. For here God is speaking with you; here He hears the prayers of your son. Therefore He has a sanctuary here."

Paul does the same thing everywhere. He makes Gentiles and Jews equal and makes no other distinction except that the oracles of God were entrusted to the natural sons of Abraham (Rom. 3:2). This prerogative — that Christ would come from their descendants — the Gentiles did not have. Nevertheless, so far as the grace of salvation is concerned, the Gentiles are made the equals of the Jews, provided that they believe in Christ. Similarly, in this passage we see that God has an open ear for the voice of Ishmael, who is crying out in the desert under the tree outside Abraham's house. God hears Ishmael in order that this proposition may stand sure and firm, that God is the God of the humble and that "the Lord takes pleasure in those who fear Him" (Ps. 147:11). Peter says (Acts 10:34-35): "God shows no partiality, but in every nation anyone who fears Him and does what is right is acceptable to Him," whether he is circumcised or not; for the circumstances surely bring out this principle of exclusion.[55]

Therefore it is fitting and necessary for us to linger over this

[55] Luther sometimes uses the substantive *exclusiva* to refer to negative prefixes like *in-* or *a-*, but in this context the translation "principle of exclusion" seems more appropriate.

passage. For it is as true as anything can be that if our worthiness and merit have any value, we are lost. Therefore the papacy deserves the hatred of all men; for there all things are done with respect for persons and station — monk, nun, priest, or celibate. They all think: "We are poor; we are celibates; we fast; we pray. Hence the kingdom of heaven will surely be ours." But this is the pride of Ishmael, which God cannot bear. And we should give thanks to God when He shakes this reliance on merit out of us through sundry trials and teaches us that we are freely justified by faith and not because of the merits of works.

Accordingly, the fact that He seems to be so harsh and appears to be treating Ishmael so cruelly — this is profitable and necessary harshness, first, because of Ishmael, who could not be humbled in any other manner, and, secondly, because of ourselves, in order that we may have the hope and confidence in Him that we are saved solely through His grace and mercy, just as the Jews themselves are (Acts 15:9-11).

God hears those who cry out not only in the house of Abraham where the church is, but also under a tree, provided that you humble yourself and hope for grace through Christ. Thus the foremost article of our faith and our highest wisdom are confirmed — that not those born of blood, of the will of man, or of the will of the flesh are children of God, but those born of God (John 1:13), that is, those who believe the promise; for it is through this promise alone that He wants to save those who are not presumptuous because of birth or merit but believe in Christ. This is the angel's message. But he adds a command.

18. *Arise, lift up the lad, and hold him fast with your hand; for I will make him a great nation.*

Hagar could have thought: "What shall I do now, after God has again become gracious to me? Shall I return to Abraham's house?" "I am not commanding you to do this," says the angel. "I am not restricting you to any place. Go wherever you please. But lift up the lad, and hold him fast with your hand; that is, care for him, instruct him, and guide him." Thus he absolves the troubled woman from all excommunication and fear. He receives her again into grace and into participation in the promise of Isaaac, and at the same time he leaves her the freedom of going where she wishes. He does not restrict her to Abraham's house or to any other place. It is as though he were saying: "It is of little importance where you will be, provided that you fear and worship God and guide and care for your son. Do not be concerned at all about the place, the time, and the persons with whom you will be. Do the duty of a mother, and know that you are in God's care."

Accordingly, he has now restored Christian liberty to the woman who previously had been excommunicated and had been made a prisoner, as it were. God could have spoken with her as He does on Mt. Sinai, but the woman who had already been frightened previously could not have borne the voice of His majesty.

God shows the same kindness toward us. He speaks with us through the ministry of men and in this manner conceals His majesty, which is dreadful and unbearable for us. But because the ministry is too lowly and familiar, the pastors themselves, in the first place, and then God Himself, are despised in the ministry and all but trodden underfoot. But there will come a time when God, who humbles Himself in this manner for the sake of our salvation, will display His majesty and crush the smug scorners. Therefore let us recognize His exceedingly great and incalculable gift: that He emptied Himself in this manner and took on human form. Let us not on this account despise the Word; but let us fall on our knees and honor and prize the holy ministry through which God deigns to speak to us.

For we are truly that people. As Moses says about his Jews (Deut. 4:7), we have a God who draws near to us and dwells with us, since through your mouth He speaks with me and through my mouth He speaks with you. Yes, the Son of God Himself came down into the flesh and was made man for the sole purpose of drawing us unto Himself and in order that we might acquire hope in His mercy and not be afraid of Him as we shall be afraid of His majesty, which our nature cannot bear, as is written (Ex. 33:20): "Man shall not see Me and live," and also (Deut. 4:24): "God is a devouring fire." Therefore He assumed a weak form — a form like our own and for this reason completely human. We should not be afraid of it, just as we are not afraid of ourselves.

But all this is directed against the incurable failing of our nature, namely, that we all look at our works and merits and thus forget that we are the creatures, but that God is the Creator. We disregard grace, by which alone one must be saved. To counteract this evil,

God sent His Son into the world to show us the Father. But the Son sent the Holy Spirit to make it known that the Son was made man and became a sacrifice for us.

Because of such a stern excommunication it was altogether necessary for the angel to repeat the promise about the great nation. For Hagar had to think as follows: "Behold, I have been cast out along with my sons. Therefore even though God made a promise concerning twelve princes, nevertheless, because the excommunication came later, He regrets His kindness, and the promise is lost. For the excommunication does away with everything." Accordingly, the angel comforts her and gives the assurance that the promise will be sure. "You were cast out solely that you might be humbled and learn that what you have you do not have by some right because Abraham was your husband, but that you have it out of pure grace. This had to be taught and made known to the entire world by your example." This is the absolution. A physical comfort follows.

19. *Then God opened her eyes, and she saw a well of water; and she went, and filled the skin with water, and gave the lad a drink.*

Moses describes everything in a very simple manner. I have stated above about the stupor and ἔκστασις in which Hagar was that it was so great that she did not notice the well close at hand. But now, awakened by the Word of God as from a deep sleep and cheered up, she opens her eyes and sees the well. And her feet, which had previously been weakened because of the sadness of her heart, now perform their function. She runs to the well and draws water. With it she refreshes the dying lad.

Therefore Moses' statement that God opened her eyes means nothing else than that God dispelled the stupor of her heart with His Word, as the psalm says (119:25[?]): "My soul is changed through the Word"; that is, I have refreshed my soul and restored it, so to speak. Indeed, in trials that are rather severe hearts are deprived of reason, so that they perceive and understand nothing. A certain character in a comedy says that he is so angry that he cannot apply his mind to thinking.[56] But if anger upsets the mind to this extent, what would be the effect of the stupor and the distractions which an awareness of God's anger and of eternal damnation brings with it?

"The heart," says Augustine, "is where it loves rather than where

56 Terence, *Phormio*, II, 3, 10.

it lives." [57] One sees this in the case of lovers. Thus in great grief the heart is overwhelmed, and all the senses die, as it were. But such is the power of the Word of God that it restores to life the hearts that have died in this manner; the word of men cannot do this.

The fact that Hagar gives the lad a drink also serves to inform us how great the trial was. For sad thoughts usually deprive the body of its moisture, so that the tongue becomes dry and the entire human body experiences a weakening. When grief strongly affects and excites the heart, loss of consciousness and other distressing mishaps result.

20. *And God was with the lad, and he grew up; he lived in the wilderness and became an expert with the bow.*

21. *He lived in the wilderness of Paran; and his mother took a wife for him from the land of Egypt.*

So far we have heard how Ishmael, after he had been killed and mortified in the desert, was again received into grace and learned that not those who are born of the flesh of Abraham but those who believe the promise are children. For over and above physical birth God demands one's own or personal righteousness, which comes solely by grace, through faith alone, obviously in order that all glory before God may cease (Rom. 4:2).

Moreover, this is intended to comfort and teach us, in order that we may neither be presumptuous with regard to our gifts nor despair because of our sins but may follow a middle course. For those [58] who are presumptuous sin against the First Commandment and nourish in their hearts this satanically blasphemous statement: "I am my own God." But those who despair also sin against the First Commandment and blaspheme God; for they maintain that He is not compassionate, and they deprive Him of the foremost glory of His divinity.

Therefore the middle course is to confess and to believe that, as is stated in the First Commandment, He is our God, and that we are His creatures and work. So let us not despair, for we have a God.

[57] With the play on "loves" and "lives" we have sought to reproduce the play on "amat" and "animat" in Augustine's epigram, which had become proverbial by Luther's day.

[58] We have followed the suggestion of the Erlangen editors and have read *qui* instead of *quia*.

Nor let us be so presumptuous about anything; for we are creatures and, as Isaiah (cf. 40:6) says, nothing and dust.

When the text states that God was with Ishmael, this is rich comfort, which shows that God opens heaven to us when we have been humbled, and that He abundantly pours forth Himself and all things. For Ishmael is not only led back to the right way in order that he may not continue to be presumptuous; but after he has been humbled, he is brought back into the church from which he had been cast out because of his presumption, and God Himself appoints Himself as his Protector, directs him, blesses him, and now regards with favor everything he does.

Thus Ishmael undoubtedly developed into a well-informed and learned preacher who, after he had been taught by his own example, preached that God is the God of those who have been humbled; for it is God's custom to humble His own, not because He wants to crush them, but in order that He may break down blasphemous presumption, and that we may be fit for His grace.

After Ishmael had become a husband, he availed himself of this opportunity to bring his wife and her relatives and parents to the knowledge of God. Among the uncircumcised heathen he established a church like Abraham's church, different indeed with respect to persons and places but one that acknowledged and preached the same God and the same Offspring that was promised to the house of Abraham.

The verb "he grew up" is to be understood not only of Ishmael's natural growth (for at the time of his excommunication he was twenty years old, more or less) but with regard to the fact that God caused him to become great, in the first place, in the Word and spiritual gifts; for, says Moses, God was with him. In the second place, God also blessed him temporally, so that he begot twelve princes. And Ishmael undoubtedly became richer than Abraham, for he himself saw that twelve princes were descended from him. But Abraham's descendants did not increase in number so suddenly, although later on twelve tribes had their origin from his grandson Jacob.

Thus we learn how powerful a sacrifice a contrite heart is, and how pleasing a smoke or incense humiliation is to God. For the statement of the psalm (145:19) is true, that God fulfills the desire of those who fear Him; for they offer a holy sacrifice to God. But

God abhors those who are presumptuous, for He does not find un-utterable sighing (Rom. 8:26) among them.

It happens nearly always, however, that descendants degenerate. This is terrible. The many disasters and captivities show to what extent the people of Israel deteriorated. For Ishmaelitish presumption troubled them. Because they had the Word and the temple, they were smug and did not fear ruin. They not only gave free rein to sins, but they even devised new forms of worship. The same thing happened to Ishmael's descendants, who, as we see, were completely absorbed in the glory of their physical birth. For this reason they called themselves Saracens, not Hagarenes.[59]

But it is impossible for such ruin not to follow where the doctrine that we are children solely by grace and not by nature has been discarded. For from this antecedent there follows with perfect consistency the consequent that by nature we are all children of wrath (Eph. 2:3), and that, as Ps. 51:5 asserts, we were conceived in sin, that is, that the mass of semen from which we originate is tainted with sin.[60]

There are indeed excellent gifts in our nature, both of the body and of the mind. But what is God's pronouncement? "All flesh is grass, and all its beauty is like the flower of the field" (Is. 40:6). Where this doctrine does not exist, there minds are puffed up and dream up merits for themselves. They boast of their blood, their flesh, and their will, just as the pope does. Because he has the office, baptizes, distributes the Eucharist, and absolves by virtue of the Keys, he boasts that he is the head of the church. But his boast is vain. For in whatever manner he may pride himself on being the successor of the apostles, he does not hold fast to the faith of the apostles. Consequently, he is no part of the church; for not those who are born of the flesh but those who believe are children. I grant that the pope has the name "church," the Keys, and other gifts; but he does not for this reason have the Spirit of God.

Moses states that Ishmael was a rabbi [61] or master of the bow;

---

[59] For the origins of this mistaken etymology of the name "Saracen" cf. John of Damascus, *De haeresibus compendium*, 101, *Patrologia, Series Graeca*, XCIV, 764.

[60] See the passages on *massa peccati, massa damnabilis*, etc., collected in Francis Moriones (ed.), *Enchiridion Theologicum Sancti Augustini* (Madrid, 1961), No. 934—940.

[61] Luther uses the word "rabbi" because of the Hebrew text.

that is, he was skilled in shooting arrows. This is not to be understood to mean that he was able to aim [62] well; it means that he was an energetic warrior. For the bow was not used for exhibitions and games, as now; it was used against the enemy. The Arabs are still a warlike people and use bows, and they have never been completely subjugated by any monarch. Therefore the angel said above (Gen. 16:12): "His hand shall be against every man and every man's hand against him." For just as he has not subdued them all, so he has not been subdued. Perhaps his early training and first experience was the shooting of hares, deer, and birds in the desert; but the text refers to the extension of his empire. Accordingly, the descendants of Ishmael fell back into the error of their father after they had forgotten his humiliation.

The same thing will also happen to our descendants. In Acts 20:29 Paul says: "From among yourselves fierce wolves will arise." Thus in our day the Sacramentarians and the Anabaptists have arisen. At first they accepted our doctrine, but later they turned their madness and rage against us; for the wiles of Satan are the same at all times. The Saracens, as I have said, boast of Ishmael, and they do not see that their pride was reduced to nothing by his excommunication. Like the Jews, they want to have the glory from their ancestors, but not the spirit of their ancestors.

But it has been demonstrated that the descendants must have the same spirit, the same faith and promise. Otherwise they are not children of God. I must have faith and hold fast to the confession which Peter made. Otherwise I am nothing, even if I am the pope. Thus the church has diverse gifts; but the same faith, hope, and love firmly bind together all believers in Christ, the one Head.

At the end Moses mentions the wilderness of Paran to indicate that the expulsion was not imposed to destroy Ishmael. For Paran is near Beer-sheba and Gerar in the territory of the Holy Land, and borders on the tribe of Judah, as is clear from the Book of Numbers (10:12; 13:3, 26). Thus Ishmael did not live far from the house of Abraham.

Accordingly, the nearness also indicates that Ishmael was reconciled with his father Abraham and his church, although his descendants, as usually happens, gradually deteriorated.

[62] Here the Weimar text has *colimare*, which is meaningless; the Erlangen editors suggest *collimare*, which lexicographers call a "false reading" for *collineare* in classical authors.

It should also be noted that Moses expressly points out that Ishmael took a wife and that he did not follow his own inclination but heeded the authority of his mother, as an example for all young men and girls that they should accept the authority of their parents, especially in contracting a marriage, and not yield to their own sentiments and desires, contrary to the will of their parents.[63] The angel had commanded Hagar herself to take care of her son, to teach and guide him. Therefore Ishmael is commanded by the voice of God to obey his mother, who takes a wife for him from the land of Egypt; and the son, as is fitting, complies with his mother's decision and wish.

This piety is commended in this passage by the Holy Spirit, and God blesses Ishmael in accordance with the promise of the Fourth Commandment: "That your days may be long in the land" (Ex. 20:12). Therefore let us, too, remember our duty, and let us not despise the services of the men whom God uses as intermediaries. He wants children to be ruled by the authority of their parents. When you obey them, you are sure that you have obeyed God. Similarly, pastors have been appointed in the church. When you hear them, you hear God. Likewise an officer of the state is in charge by divine authority. Therefore it is Satan's trickery when these outward services are brought into contempt.

It is indeed true that the Holy Spirit alone enlightens hearts and kindles faith, but He does not do this without the outward ministry and without the outward use of the sacraments. Therefore when Paul is approaching Damascus, he is commanded to hear Ananias (Acts 9:12). But just as the Word is committed to us in the church, so in the household there should be no doubt that when you hear your parents giving some order, you are hearing God and are sure about God's will. On the other hand, if you deviate from the ministry and follow your own opinions, you will not only gain nothing, but you will take hold of Satan as God, and will be uncertain about your thoughts, whether they are of God or of the devil.

Thus Ishmael is most amply rewarded for his obedience, because he follows the advice of his mother when he takes a wife; for God blesses him abundantly. On the other hand, God curses those who

---

[63] Luther's treatise, *That Parents Should Neither Compel nor Hinder the Marriage of Their Children, and that Children Should Not Become Engaged Without Their Parents' Consent, Luther's Works,* 45, pp. 385—393.

are disobedient, as the examples show, namely, that the marriages which they contract contrary to their parents' will are unhappy.

22. *At that time Abimelech and Phicol, the commander of his army, said to Abraham: God is with you in all that you do;*

23. *now therefore swear to me here by God that you will not deal falsely with me or with my offspring or with my posterity, but as I have dealt loyally with you, you will deal with me and with the land where you have sojourned.*

This is a new trial. I have repeatedly stated that God leads His saints in this life in a manner so wonderful that one trial immediately follows another. But just as misfortunes impel to prayer and faith, so, when the saints are delivered, they are impelled to give thanks and to praise God's mercy. Nevertheless, a distinction must be made between those exercises of faith and faith itself, just as works always differ of necessity from the promise itself and from faith.

The trial which overtakes Abraham here is a very pretty and very specious virtue of the devil, namely, that untamable evil of envy, which has always caused the godly the most trouble in the world. The cause of the envy is that God had prepared a lodging place for Isaac in Gerar and the king had granted Abraham the freedom of living where he wanted. Therefore when everything is quiet and peaceful, and Abraham is prospering because of the Lord's blessing, the Palestinians envy him, as an exile, this good fortune. For Moses excuses the king, who, still mindful of his dream, converses with Abraham in a most friendly manner and respects him as a prophet of God.

Furthermore, the name "Abraham" increased the envy; for the Palestinians knew from the king's disclosure [64] that the land of Canaan and Christ, the Blessed Seed, had been promised to him. Then indeed, after this report had reached the entire court and the neighboring cities of the Palestinians, Abraham was an unbearable person to the Palestinians. When a son was born to the old man by his aged wife through an extraordinary miracle, they concluded that this foreigner had in mind to be the sole ruler in the land of Canaan.

For the devil this was an important enough reason for hating Abraham and inciting the Palestinians to envy against him. The

---

[64] We have followed the suggestion of the Weimar editors and have read *indicio* for *iudicio*.

rabble generally reacts in this manner: it is envious of increasing power and prestige. And since they knew from the promise that Abraham would inherit the land, they feared for themselves and their people; and they were considering plans either to suppress the foreigner or to hold him in check. Those who held the highest position at the royal court were the originators of this purpose. For although princes and kings are very pious, it is nevertheless not unusual nowadays for courtiers — or counselors, as we call them — to be fraudulent, envious, unjust, greedy, and full of deceit and lies. Therefore the commands and wishes of pious rulers are not always carried out.

Today our own princes are supporting the churches and are kindly disposed toward the ministers of the churches. But what are the nobles, the burghers, and the peasants doing? Are they not plotting, as it were, to stir up hatred against the ministry? In this way the devil incites his members against the godly. In Paradise he began to do this immediately.

Here, therefore, Abraham is contending against envy, and he displays a courageous heart; for he knows that Satan hates and disturbs every kind of life that is of God. Those who have no experience suppose that marriage is a kind of life in which there is nothing but pleasure and joy. But the countless inconveniences and annoyances that are incident to it demand a brave and patient heart. Somewhere you may find a godly peasant, but he is vexed by the envy of his neighbors. Foxes and wolves lie in wait for his cattle; the domestics are negligent, lazy, and thievish. In this situation, such a peasant has not only abundant occasion for good works but also an opportunity to learn patience.

The same thing happens to the patriarch Abraham. He rejoices that a son is born to him, and he seeks to procure convenient quarters for him. God blesses him and greatly increases his wealth; He adorns him with priestly glory, and the report concerning the promise of the land of Canaan is spread abroad throughout all Palestine. Consequently, envy is stirred up, and, as will follow below, daily quarrels arise because of the water he had to have (vv. 25 ff.). But who could enumerate all the troubles that arose anew every day? For envy is the most prolific of all evils. Therefore he leaves Gerar. Evidently it is his purpose to get away from the envy. Accordingly, this kind of life is most pleasing to God: doing good to everybody and nevertheless enduring envy, hatred, and the injustices of the devil and of men.

So far as the account is concerned, it does not seem to me that the king addressed Abraham voluntarily or of his own accord. But the leading men at court dinned into the very pious king's ears day and night that he should not snore in the danger at hand and should not permit the exile to deprive him of the kingdom; for, as they said, he was thriving and was aspiring to a kingdom because of some promise. Therefore King Abimelech should make the kingdom secure for himself and for his descendants, but this could not be done more properly than by exacting an oath.

The author of this advice was Phicol, the king's commander in chief; and with high-sounding words, such as are characteristic of courtiers, he urged the king not to appear to be slighting himself and his people. For this is the practice of courtiers: when they seem to be paying special attention to the interests of their rulers, they are serving their own advantage, in order that they may gain power for themselves.[65] Because the king does not believe that deceit is involved and that this advice springs from envy and hatred, he talks to Abraham with a guileless heart. "I see," he said, "that you are prospering and that the promise given to you is being fulfilled. Therefore I beg you not to be too harsh toward me and my people. You came to us as an exile, and we have been as kind to you as we could. I demand the same thing from you when the Lord exalts you, namely, that you do not drive out me, my son, and my grandson, and that you confirm this with an oath." The pious king is aware that he cannot resist the promise, but he fears that the promise will be fulfilled at once, because Isaac had already been born. Moreover, the thought that his descendants would deteriorate and that for this reason God would curse the ungrateful despisers of the Word and would transfer the royal honor to others troubled the godly king. Therefore he is satisfied if Abraham spares his son and his grandson.

This account also serves to give comfort and instruction. For today we, too, have our Phicol-like courtiers, who burn with envy and hate against the ministers of the churches and block all ways by which they suppose we are able to prosper. For they say that food and raiment are enough and that for many reasons one must take care that the ministers of the churches do not become rich. But it will surely come to pass that what they are afraid of will happen against their will. Now they want to save the crumbs when they

[65] *Luther's Works,* 13, p. 180.

support poor Lazarus, although formerly they poured out all their wealth on him who feasted; for they gave the bishops castles and cities and maintained them in excessive splendor and magnificence. Now, when those who teach truly and faithfully must be supported, they barely grant them the crumbs which otherwise would go to waste.[66]

This is the perverse wisdom of the world, because of which it not only brings a curse upon itself but also provides the opportunity that, just as the wealth of the papists grew in former times, so it may still happen today. For the papacy prospered when those two causes coincided: (1) that those who held ministerial offices in the churches were by nature ambitious and involved themselves in managing secular affairs; (2) that the nobles and the officers of the state were indolent, shunned exertions, indulged in pleasures, and left the care of the government to the ministers of the churches.

Today this will continue to increase the power of the priests. For while the princes hunt, feast, play, dance, and do not want to settle cases, discipline must eventually be in the care of the parish priests. But if they have been burdened with a variety of secular affairs, they of necessity put aside the Bible and the study of sacred matters; for they cannot serve the state and the church at the same time.

Meanwhile, to be sure, we diligently teach that those two offices, the civil and the ecclesiastical, should be kept separate; but we do so to no avail. Therefore the fact that priests are exalted and thrive is the fault not only of the ambitious bishops but also of the lazy magistrates, who indeed want to have glory and honor, as is proper, but do not want to work. Accordingly, when the very men who have been called for this purpose are unwilling to do their duty, and failures or diseases are perpetual in governments and require a physician, if the pastors of the churches then undertake the care of governmental affairs, they will eventually arrive at pontifical honor by this road.

Therefore the officials of the state should have been exhorted to bear the trouble and inconveniences which a careful way of governing brings with it, for the world wants to be governed. One is treated unfairly, another is beaten, and still another is subjected to shameful abuse. Therefore the world needs a medicine, as in a sickness. But if the people in the government are remiss, the task devolves upon

[66] This is a frequent complaint; cf., for example, *Luther's Works*, 2, p. 224.

those who are in the church. In this way their activities and the troubles to which they are subjected have raised them to the highest ecclesiastical offices. This not only weakened the churches but caused them to collapse completely. "The Phrygians," they say, "are wise behind the time." [67] The same thing is happening to our people. Formerly they spent too much on churches and bishops; now they begrudge Lazarus even the crumbs.

This wickedness will not cease without extraordinary punishment. Pious Abraham does not demand possession of the cities in Palestine; he leaves them to his king and is satisfied with grass and water for himself and his cattle. Indeed, he even gives way to the envy and dwells in nearby Beer-sheba. But even this the envy of the courtiers cannot tolerate; it wants him crushed and the blessing obstructed. They do not see that the more Abraham helps everybody, the more he is blessed. On the other hand, the more sparingly the courtiers give, the more they are cursed.

For thus it has been ordained: those who do not give to Christ, the beggar, give a superabundance to a glutton; and those who do not feed a hungry man will themselves perish from hunger. I would not readily impose the administration of the state on our necks again; but because the magistrates are sleeping soundly and put their obligation into the hands of others — therefore "If these were silent, the very stones would cry out" (Luke 19:40). They fill the world with many wrongs and injustices. Accordingly, treatment by a diligent physician is necessary to drive out these ailments.

Therefore I praise King Abimelech and excuse him for not dealing with Abraham voluntarily or of his own accord. He was urged to do so by the commander in chief at his court. It is an indication of his uprightness that he so humbly entreats the foreigner to show kindness to his people. He does not order him to leave the country but respects him as a priest of God.

24. *And Abraham said: I will swear.* [68]

The fact that Moses states clearly that Abraham swore seems to be contrary to the meaning of the Gospel and Christ's command (Matt. 5:34-37). But this example is necessary. Abraham does not refuse to take the oath, and by his action he teaches that these moral

---

[67] Where the Weimar text has *friges,* we have read *Phyrges.*

[68] This verse from the Bible does not appear in the original text of Luther.

[W, XLIII, 191]

and civil matters should neither be looked down upon nor neglected by the saints under the pretense of their religion. And we should give thanks to the Holy Spirit for recording the accounts of the saintly fathers in such a way that they are patterns not only of faith and of superior virtues but in civic life also over against the senseless monkish clods, who divest themselves of all friendliness and civility, manifestly because in this manner they are dead to the world and nevertheless very much alive in all kinds of vices. Therefore Abraham bears living witness against such people, namely, that civic life and actions are not displeasing to God.

But so far as Christ's command is concerned — "Do not swear at all" (Matt. 5:34) — the reply to this question is very easy if one takes into consideration the causes which Moses points out well in this account. One can truthfully give the simple answer that a righteous man does not sin even when he swears, but that he is rendering a service that is pleasing to God and men. But it is easier to explain the causes. The efficient cause is that Abraham is not swearing thoughtlessly, but because the king ordered him to do so. For here the authority of the civil government must not be lowered in our estimation, as the foolish mob of the Anabaptists raves. Therefore an oath which is imposed by the government is in agreement with the command of God, who has commanded us to obey the government.

The other, final cause is also indicated here, namely, that in this way peace is established between the domestics of the king and those of Abraham. For Holy Scripture says (Heb. 6:16): "An oath is the end of all controversies"; that is, it puts an end to controversies and quarrels. Who would deny that this is a holy and good work?

But this concerns the Second Commandment. For those who swear a true oath to the government honor God's name and adorn the truth. Moreover, they remove suspicions. Accordingly, the godly do a good thing when they bear witness to the truth by means of an oath. On the other hand, the ungodly do nothing right, because they always have this label attached to themselves: "These people err in heart" (Ps. 95:10).

Therefore our answer to the question is as follows: "The oath of those who swear thoughtlessly and do not defend the truth is beyond what is required and evil; but where the oath serves the truth and is useful for preserving goodwill and concord, there proper swearing does not abuse God's name but gives it honor, namely, that God may be feared and peace and quiet may remain."

Thus the Lord guides the patriarch even in his civic relations and defends him against envy by permitting him to take advantage of the laws and civic customs, and to conform to the common practices of men in order to maintain public peace. For in this matter Holy Scripture does not oppose philosophy and the laws but strengthens them and makes an oath a kind of sacrament, inasmuch as it is connected with the name of God and serves to reconcile hearts and to put an end to strife and suspicions.

25. *When Abraham complained to Abimelech about a well of water which Abimelech's servants had seized,*

26. *Abimelech said: I do not know who has done this thing; you did not tell me, and I have not heard of it until today.*

Here another example of civic life is presented. About the government and its authority we have written extensively enough,[69] for it is certain that the Gospel does not do away with civil laws and the obedience one owes to the government. Therefore not only the brazenness of our opponents but also their vicious spite is great when they accuse us of sedition, although our writings say the opposite.

How, then, shall we excuse Abraham, who in this passage appears not to be treating the king in accordance with his rank, inasmuch as he charges him with having violated their agreement, although the godly king, persevering in his godliness, solemnly asserts that he has no knowledge of all the misfortunes that have happened to Abraham? It is possible to say that Abraham implored the king's help, and without any cupidity at that. But this is a weak excuse. Indeed, these are examples from everyday life, in which, although we all stumble in various ways, nevertheless such failings are forgiven the godly. Abraham is deceived by his suspicious thought that, contrary to the agreement, the well had been taken away from him with the king's knowledge and at his command. Thus he also stumbles on a previous occasion, when he says that Sarah is not his wife but his sister. Yet he does not resort to such a plan with the intention of sinning; he does so out of anxiety and fear. It would indeed have been better not to chide the king; but since he is in the clutches of suspicion, he cannot think otherwise than that the king has knowledge of this deed. And certainly a government should not be so neglectful of its duty that it has no knowledge of the wrongdoings of its people.

[69] Cf. the treatises collected in *Luther's Works,* 45.

For although even a godly government cannot find out everything its people do but is bound to lack knowledge of many things, it nevertheless is not without fault.

"Therefore," you say, "should both be blamed — Abraham, because of his suspicion and because of his rather harsh behavior toward the king; and the king, because of his neglect of duty?" Yes indeed; for God wants us to consider ourselves sinners, so that we do not become proud but sing with David (Ps. 19:12): "Clear Thou me of my hidden faults, O Lord," and "Who can discern his errors?" And it is profitable for you to know that you have an office whose requirements it is impossible to meet everywhere. Those who think otherwise become proud, and because of their pride they stumble very seriously. Ordinarily, however, those who are novices at governing do this; for, like inexperienced archers, they miss the mark by very much. Thus it is not the intention of a pious government to do harm, but all its counsels are directed toward benefiting its people. The servants and councillors, however, whose services it is forced to use because it cannot adequately take care of so many affairs, do many things in the name of princes who would not tolerate them if they knew about them. Similarly, domestics make many mistakes of which the master of the house has no knowledge.

The same thing happens to the saints. They are not only plagued by punishments and many tribulations, but they are also often involved in the offenses of falling and making mistakes. But what one should learn is that they do not perish for this reason, provided that their will is sincere and pure, and that there is no indolence. For if private individuals cannot live without sin, those who are in the government can do so far less. Nevertheless, let everyone see to it that there is no wicked inclination and that there is no pretended lack of knowledge.

Accordingly, Abraham calls upon the government for help, but with a reprimand; for these are his thoughts: "This king should rule in such a manner that he has obedient servants to watch over his agreements." Here there surely was no wicked intention. Moreover, we ourselves experience today that the same thing happens at the courts of the princes. It has frequently happened to me that when I had procured something from a prince by his kind favor, the Phicols at the court interfered and prevented the execution of what the prince had commanded.[70] Therefore if we private individuals are unable to

---

[70] Cf. *Luther's Works,* 13, p. 183.

avoid all sins, we must pray all the more diligently for the government; for it has a large body, and the members of this body are rebellious and unsound in many ways.

Furthermore, in addition to this little sin which Abraham commits by wrongly suspecting the king, this passage should also be taken note of against the Anabaptists, namely, that one may appeal to the government for help against wrongs.[71] It would indeed be fine if the government did its duty of its own accord and did not wait until its aid is implored; but few do this, and not even by repeated entreaties can they be impelled to put an end to wrongs.

Such men are of the number of those of whom I have stated above that they desire glory, respect, and obedience. They delight in being called gods (Ps. 82:6); but if you appraise their morals and life, they are devils and tyrants, who have sins that concern not only the administration of the state but also their persons. Abimelech was not the kind of man who sins out of ignorance. Sins of this kind should be excused, and they should be mitigated through prayer before God. They should not be severely criticized. Far less should insurrections be stirred up because of them. Abimelech sins not only as a man but also as a ruler. He cannot know what is being done everywhere by his people. Nevertheless, this is a sin before God, evidently in order that no one may be haughty. Accordingly, I am in the habit of comparing this sin to the sins against the Law, or rather the Ceremonial Law.

But this is intended to comfort us, lest we think that the saintly men were monkish clods, dumb and without feeling; for these offenses prove that they were men and had passions like those we have. They were spiritual, to be sure, yet they lived in the flesh.

Accordingly, the fact that Abraham implores the king's help because of the well of which he had been deprived is a clear example that we, too, may implore the help of the government and avail ourselves of its protection, namely, the protection which the laws and the practice of the court allow. But if the government withholds its help from us, the wrong must be borne. Nevertheless, one should know that even pious officials of the state often sin; for even though the will may not be wanting, yet the knowledge is often lacking, although in many the will, too, is weak. Nevertheless, they should be held in honor, and the inconveniences should be borne. But in

[71] Cf. *Luther's Works*, 40, pp. 51—52.

the case of those whose will is evil spitefulness should be loathed, and they should be reproved.

Abimelech excuses himself very well. "I did not know," he says, "I did not hear of it, and you did not tell me." A godly government is not offended by an admonition but demands that it be informed by its subjects if there is any fault anywhere. For how can it know what is being done everywhere? But those who are proud and are offended by the disclosures [72] and admonitions of their subjects — as though lack of knowledge about something were a disgrace — are too little mindful of their situation; they never humble themselves before God or call upon God to pardon such sins.

But the government's lack of knowledge, as I have said, is an unavoidable sin — a sin just as inherent in the government as lust is inherent in everybody, without which certainly no one can live. Therefore let everyone acknowledge his shortcoming, for in this way it will happen that they will humble themselves and will not only implore God's help but will also beg for forgiveness of their hidden sins.

Therefore Bernard writes admirably to Pope Eugenius: "Of necescity you have no knowledge of many things, and of necessity you pretend not to know many things you do know." [73] Ignorance is a fault in the will. Because of it we tolerate the things we do not want. To be sure, Abimelech is a king; but he does not know everything his subjects are doing. For this is not man's glory; it belongs to God alone, who knows everything and cannot be deceived. Proud tyrants who do not want to be admonished arrogate this glory to themselves.

Therefore one should know that God Himself and then also the Law itself has demanded that we inform the government if any fault has been committed on the part of the state; for just as the government sins through its ignorance, so the subjects sin by withholding information. Accordingly, Abimelech flings back upon Abraham the guilt of not having reported the wrongs of the courtiers to him sooner; and to some extent Abraham is really at fault. Nevertheless, his agitation is not altogether unjustifiable. He saw that the minds of kings are peculiar and changeable; for they are in an extraordinary

[72] We have followed the suggestion of the Erlangen editors and have read *indiciis* for *iuditiis*.

[73] Cf., for example, Bernard to Eugene, Ep. 270, *Patrologia, Series Latina,* CLXXXII, 473—474.

office, and the things they govern are changeable. Therefore since the courtiers had harmed him, he could not be free from the suspicion that the king was aware of this.

Thus both are properly humbled: Abraham, for being suspicious and not informing the king; Abimelech, for not knowing. Abraham should have admonished the king, to prevent him from being in error. This was a duty of love. Therefore Abimelech is right when he complains that Abraham had told him nothing and that he himself had heard nothing from anybody. How evil, therefore, the situation is today, when almost everybody refuses to render this necessary service to the government! If you report somebody's wrongdoing to the government, everybody calls you a traitor. Consequently, this sin of giving the government no information is praised as a noble virtue. For what, should a king do in this situation if you refuse to tell him what it is impossible for him to know? Does he not seem to be innocent and excused?

Nevertheless, God wants him to be involved in the sin of ignorance in order that he may acknowledge that he does not have a universal government — which is an impossibility for a human being because of the sin of ignorance — but only a partial one, and in order that he may acknowledge that God is at the head of the universal government; for it is He who has universal vision and sees and knows everything, while a government, however good it may be, has only partial vision.

Therefore the government must be assisted; and when any public wrong is committed, all people should come running as though to put out a fire that affects all; for everyone should help the community to the extent that he is able to do so.

In this manner the Holy Spirit describes the saints with both active and passive predicates:[74] They have conformed to the civil practice of men by swearing an oath to the government and by seeking its help; and they have borne not only wrongs done by others but also, if I may express myself in this way, their own guilt and ignorance. Consequently, there is no lack of opportunity for them to pray: "Hallowed be Thy name. O God, why dost Thou make me an officer of the state, why a preacher, even though Thou knowest that I cannot satisfy Thy will? But Thou art with me as my Helper, and Thy angels

---

[74] On the predicates of activity and passivity cf. Aristotle, *Topics*, Book I, ch. 9.

are also with me. Moreover, Thou desirest in this manner to humble my proud stubbornness, in order that I may not make myself equal with Thee, who art just and knowest all things."

This passage, which deals with appealing to the government and informing it of dishonesty, is noteworthy, although few people do the latter. For nobody wants to incur the hatred of neighbors, nobles, and powerful men. Yet one should keep in mind that the government is very much in need of this service from us. Otherwise it cannot do its duty. But if you have reported a wrong and nevertheless are not given any assistance by the government, you should bear the inconvenience and know that you are blameless and have done your duty. However, an indifferent government will not go unpunished.

27. *So Abraham took sheep and oxen and gave them to Abimelech, and the two men made a covenant.*

28. *Abraham set seven ewe lambs of the flock apart.*

29. *And Abimelech said to Abraham: What is the meaning of these seven ewe lambs which you have set apart?*

30. *He said: These seven ewe lambs you will take from my hand, that you may be a witness for me that I dug this well.*

31. *Therefore that place was called Beer-sheba, because there both of them swore an oath.*

32. *So they made a covenant at Beer-sheba. Then Abimelech and Phicol, the commander of his army, rose up and returned to the land of the Philistines.*

The Holy Spirit proceeds with His description of the character of the saintly patriarch. Covenants and pacts are not works toward God — works that He needs. No, they have to do with temporal and human activities, in which the saints also participate. Therefore if anybody desires to know how Abraham conducted himself in civic affairs, he should carefully consider the account. Abraham does not shun any civic duties, does not refuse to take an oath, honors the king, implores his help, etc. Because of his affection for the prophet of God the king, too, takes an oath. Eventually both confirm the oath as though by a seal. Abraham presents the king with sheep and oxen, and the king does not disdain his gift. In this way the pact is confirmed as with a seal. No wordy documents are drawn up, as is the custom today. Both are satisfied to swear to what they have expressed in words. Afterwards the gift is added as a tangible sign.

This artlessness of the ancients in making agreements is very delightful. It reminds us how much the morals of our unfeeling age have deteriorated — our age, in which no confidence in compacts, no written agreements, and no seals are adequate. All agreements are eluded by deceit and confused by violence.

But Abraham does two things. In the first place, he presents sheep and oxen. In the second place, he gives as a separate present seven ewe lambs, not because the king needed such a gift, but in this way Abraham wants to bear public testimony among all the king's subjects that this well was produced by his effort.

In the Law such gifts are forbidden, for its text states: "You shall take no gift" (Ex. 23:8) and also "Gifts blind and corrupt judges" (Deut. 16:19). Indeed, even the writings of the heathen condemn gifts as an extraordinary bane of governments.[75] How, then, shall we excuse Abraham, who offers them, and the king, who accepts them?

My answer is the same as the one I gave above. Whatever a godly man does, he does rightly, even if he makes a mistake; for he has a heart that is right, and God looks mainly at this. On the other hand, an ungodly man, even if the work he does is good in itself, nevertheless does not please God, because he errs in his heart; that is, he does not know God, does not believe God, and does not fear God.

But here, too, one must consider the final cause. If gifts are given for the purpose of removing suspicions, hatred, and discord, and in order to gain goodwill and peace, they are properly counted among good works. Of what evil can the king suspect Abraham when he gives him such generous gifts? He who is generous toward another person surely does not want to harm him. Therefore it is honorable to accept a gift from a pious man. For he gives with a pure heart, not in order to put you under obligation to him and not to win an unjust cause through you but in order to foster mutual goodwill in this manner. Thus a bridegroom gives gifts to the bride to show his love and to promote goodwill. Therefore to bestow and accept gifts in this manner — these are the greatest acts of kindness and very necessary for this life. But those who kindle discord in this way or corrupt a judge and pervert the courts misuse gifts. Therefore one

---

[75] Cf. Aristotle, *Politics*, Book V, ch. 8.

should follow the rule which the proverb suggests: "Not all, not from all, and not always." For just as it is rude to refuse a friend's gift, so it is honorable not to accept gifts in an evil cause.

It happens for a definite purpose that the text tells about the seven ewe lambs and gives a detailed description of this ceremony. The king is a saintly man. But Phicol and the rest of the crowd of courtiers are wicked, envious, greedy, thievish, rapacious, etc. For all courts are always contaminated by this unfortunate appendage that they have Doeglike people, who prevent carrying out what the king has decided or do the opposite without the king's knowledge. Therefore Abraham, as a diplomat, wants the reconciliation which has been established with the king confirmed by an oath from the king, in order that in this way the crowd of courtiers may be deterred from having the audacity later on to do anything of this sort without the king's knowledge.

It is pleasing to observe how politely Abraham conducts himself on this occasion. He does not have the courage to demand in plain words that the king swear; for he is a foreigner, but Abimelech is a king. Therefore because it was impolite to demand an oath from one who is not his peer, Abraham proceeds with extraordinary prudence and politeness. He sets seven ewe lambs apart. The king asks why he is doing this, since the covenant has already been made. Abraham answers and begs him to accept them. "Not on your account," he says, "but on account of your courtiers, Phicol and the rest, who perhaps will again attempt dishonesty and will stir up new disputes. Therefore in order that you may guard against this in the future, I want you to swear to me publicly. Although I do not dare demand this, I nevertheless request it with those seven ewe lambs as with crude letters."

It should be noted in this passage that the Hebrew word שָׁבַע is ambiguous. It has the two meanings — "seven" and "oath" — just as in German the word *hutt* means both a "hat" and a "guard," and the word *rad* denotes "advice" and "wheel." Accordingly, in this passage the word שָׁבַע has both meanings: both swore and, if I may express myself in this manner, both "sevened." Abraham set apart seven ewe lambs. Therefore he indicates clearly that even though he does not demand the oath, he nevertheless wants the king to swear.

Accordingly, Abraham wants to exact the oath from the king by means of extraordinary wisdom and a very fine hint, since to demand it openly would be rather impolite. He puts seven sheep before the king, and because the word שֶׁבַע has the two meanings "seven" and "oath," Abimelech understands what Abraham wants. It is just as if some mute came to me and pointed to a wheel. In this instance, because of the homonym, it is easy for me to guess that he is seeking advice. For the German word *rad* has the meanings "wheel" and "advice." Thus by means of the word for the number seven Abraham puts the king in mind of an oath. For it would have been impudent openly to demand an oath from a person of higher rank. I believe that among the Germans this is the origin of the custom of using seven witnesses when drawing up wills and of employing the word "seven" for trustworthy evidence; for we say: *Man musz ims besibnen;* that is, he is so skeptical that he does not believe unless he hears seven witnesses.[76]

Accordingly, when Abraham deals with the king in such a diplomatic manner, this is an outstanding example of respect for the government. The king's forbearance in yielding to the prophet is also outstanding. Reminded by this figurative act, he does not refuse to take the oath.

The Egyptians, more than other nations, had the custom of speaking by means of images or pictures like the hieroglyphics that are found in Philostratus.[77] When they intended to say something about Jupiter, they drew a scepter with an eye above it, just as astronomers still write the name "Jupiter." Because of its straightness the scepter signified justice to them. But the eye signified prudence. For if justice is devoid of the latter, it becomes injustice, as the proverb bears witness: "The height of right is the height of wrong."[78] In ancient times people used such written symbols.

Therefore it is the purpose of this careful description to give us instruction, in order that we may learn how the saintly patriarchs conducted themselves in civil affairs, how respectfully they treated the government, and how kindly disposed the government was toward its subjects. And what can this life have that is finer than a just government and subjects who love their ruler? Where this is the case, there is a paradise in the true sense of the word, and there God has

[76] The number seven is, of course, a sacred and mystical one not only in Hebrew and German usage but almost universally.

[77] Cf. the references in *Luther's Works*, 1, p. 26, note 42, on cosmological tables.

[78] Cicero, *De officiis*, I, 10, 33; cf. *Luther's Works*, 13, p. 150, note 12.

given His blessing. But if the government is blind and unjust, and the people are wicked and unruly, what kind of wickedness would you not find there?

Moses states that from this pact the place was named בְּאֵר שֶׁבַע, that is, "the well of seven," or "the well of the oath" — the oath which was brought about by means of the seven ewe lambs. For שֶׁבַע has both meanings: "seven" and "oath." You may call these matters civil or moral; but they should be carefully noted, and they are full of comfort, in order that we may not think — as the Anabaptists do — that Christians must cast aside the common works of civil life. For God did not found the church in order to do away with either the household or the state. No, He founded the church in order to strengthen the household and the state through the church. Therefore Abraham, the father of the promise and the king of kings in this land, does not refuse to swear and to make a pact with the king and his court.

Therefore one should not refuse or shun civic duties under the pretext of religion, as the monks do. For this reason they hide in monasteries, in order not to serve anyone. They are a blind kind of men, and they devote themselves to a reprobate frame of mind, and for this reason they care about neither the First nor the Second Table. But they receive a reward befitting their ungodliness. While they avoid the inconveniences connected with the household and the government, they plunge into the worst and most hideous vices, more than any laymen, as they call them.

Let us, then, wisely consider God's ordinances and the examples of the saintly patriarch Abraham, who has given us abundant instruction concerning all matters of the church and has provided the pattern of his godliness not only in the ecclesiastical way of life, as a prophet of God, but also in matters pertaining to the government and the household. There must be rulers in this life, and the church has not been appointed to destroy the household and the government. No, it has been appointed to restore them. Nor should kings forget their duty; they should be just and mild toward their subjects, and the subjects should obey them. At this time, however, one can wish for this, but one cannot have it. I am surprised, however, that the place called Beer-sheba was not made famous by the Jews through some special idolatry, as were other places at which the saintly patriarchs lived. It should be enough for us to be taught to know that the godly also serve God when they undertake civic duties.

33. *And Abraham planted trees at Beer-sheba and called there on the name of the Lord, the everlasting God.*

34. *And Abraham sojourned many days in the land of the Philistines.*

Whenever this little statement is made — that the patriarchs called or cried out in the name of the Lord, or that they built an altar — it denotes that a certain place was appointed for teaching and hearing the Word of God. For if the church is to be preserved, there must be some pious prince to provide quarters for it and grant it room and peace, so that the doctrine and the Word of God can be spread. At that time Abimelech was such a person. Under him the house of Abraham, in which the church was, had peace and quiet; and the Word was spread among the heathen by Pope or Bishop Abraham, who, wherever he went, took with him the Word, the worship, the religion, and everything.

Here, too, Moses mentions a civic or domestic work, namely, that Abraham planted a grove. For the word אֵשֶׁל, like the noun "tree" among us, is general, in order that you may understand that not only a garden with fruit-bearing trees was planted but also forest trees for the benefit of cattle.

"Why," says a monk, "does Moses write this? Why does he not rather write about fasts and prayers and coarse garments?" But, as I have often said, Moses is doing this against the monastic clods, who disregard God's commands and walk in self-chosen forms of religious worship. Such people do not see the command of God: "Bring the earth under your dominion, and cultivate it" (cf. Gen. 1:28). For it is God's will that the earth be planted and cultivated, not only for the sake of men but also for the sake of food for the beasts.

Accordingly, this, too, is a civic but good and saintly work, which is not only permitted but is even commanded by God, in order that we may provide for ourselves and our descendants — and, in addition, for the beasts — by cultivating the earth, lest we be like the monks, who, like lazy drones and caterpillars, do not work at all but merely devour what others produce and even revile with insults those who work, while they call this work, which was commanded by God, a work of laymen and rustics.

Abraham is saintlier than all the saints in the New Testament. Yet he is engaged in this work of laymen, not only on account of the foreigners who arrive, in order that they may have shade in which to sit, as Lyra explains,[79] but on account of the requirements of his household, and especially on account of God's command: "Bring the earth under your dominion, and cultivate it." Besides, there is also a third reason, namely, in order that a more abundant crop may enable him to give alms.

Meanwhile Abraham is busy with his main duty. He builds a sanctuary, not of stone, as we do, but he designates a place where he preaches in the name or through the name of the Lord. When the letter ‍ב‍ is prefixed, this expression means to teach and preach. When, however, the letter ‍ב‍ is not prefixed to the noun שֵׁם, but the expression is simply "to invoke the name of the Lord," then it means to pray or invoke.

Moreover, note should be taken of the name of God in this passage. Moses says: "He called or cried out in the name of the Lord, אֵל עוֹלָם, the God of the ages or of the world." For the word עוֹלָם is ambiguous, since its meaning is age or eternity and world. Furthermore, אֵל is also applied to creatures, and in Moses it is used to refer to the most excellent and finest fruits and is generally explained as meaning "strength."

Therefore it pleases me that in this passage God is designated as אֵל עוֹלָם, as though one meant to call Him the force and power of the world, which fills all things in the world, as the poet puts it: "From Jupiter the Muses have their beginning; of Jupiter all things are full," [80] a saying which he no doubt derived from the ancient tradition of the patriarchs. For whatever the world has, exists and is preserved by the Word of God. God created the world, and He preserves the world; thus this אֵל עוֹלָם, God, is the power of the world through whom the world is and has whatever capacity it has.

Abraham gives this name to God, since he had been taught by his experience. For he saw that God stands by His own with ready help, in such a way that He inclines the heart even of the king and the nobles to whatever He wants, yes, that He fashions the hearts individually, that is, gives counsel and impulse to do what is right and proper. Nevertheless, here sin, of which God is not the author, is excepted. We maintain that God is the Author of all acts that are just. But sin is not an act; it is a privation.[81]

---

[79] Lyra *ad* Gen. 21:27.

[80] Vergil, *Eclogues,* III, 60.

[81] This is the Augustinian definition of sin as *privatio boni.*

CHAPTER TWENTY-TWO [1]

1. *After these things God tested Abraham and said to him: Abraham! And he said: Here am I.*

2. *He said: Take your son, your only son Isaac, whom you love, and go to the land of Moriah, and offer him there as a burnt offering upon one of the mountains of which I shall tell you.*

WE have heard that outstanding trial with which Abraham was tested when he cast out his son Ishmael. After Ishmael had been cast out, peace was granted to Abraham under King Abimelech. But then another trial came, by far the greatest, in comparison with which the earlier ones are almost nothing. Thus Holy Scripture is everywhere in agreement with itself. It describes the true children of God as being continually exercised in both kinds of life — the active and the passive — yet without any display of ceremonies; and it points out the good fruits on a good tree. For they are walking in the obedience which they owe God and in true love toward men, and yet they are overtaken by various trials and perils.

But because Abraham is the foremost and greatest among the holy patriarchs, he endures truly patriarchal trials which his descendants would not have been able to bear. Abraham, now happy and confident, is altogether carefree; for Isaac, the son of the promise, has now grown up and was approximately 20 years old. His body was so

[1] In the margin of the original edition the following comment appears: "Luther began this chapter on October 27, 1539, the day after that famous and outstanding man, Doctor Sebald Münsterer of Nürnberg, had been buried; shortly before that, two very promising young men named Geuder, from the nobility in Nürnberg, were buried also. Therefore he began his lecture in this manner: 'I am not lecturing because I want to keep you here at a time when there is fear about the danger of a pestilential plague. For if a plague is imminent, everyone who wishes should take flight, especially those who are fearful. Holy Scripture (Deut. 20:8) commands such people to go back from the camp, lest they make the heart of their fellows fearful. As for me, I do not fear a raging pestilence at the present time but believe that fear itself is the chief cause of this calamity.'" Sebald Münsterer had been a professor of law at Wittenberg; upon his death Luther took Münsterer's orphaned children into his own home.

[91]

strong that he could bear the burden of the wood needed for the burnt offering.

Accordingly, when both parents loved him exceedingly, because he had been born to them in their old age and had the promise of God concerning the future blessing of the entire world, and both were very happy because of this, and peace had been established in the house by the expulsion of Ishmael and outside the house by the reconciliation with the king, and the solicitous parents were now considering the choice of a wife, evidently in order that the Promised Seed might soon be raised up — behold, these very fine plans and very pleasing thoughts of the parents about the marriage of their son are upset and confounded by a single word, namely, by the Lord's command to Abraham to take his son and sacrifice him.

Therefore Abraham's heart was wounded far more deeply now than previously, when he cast out Ishmael. But it is impossible for us to comprehend the greatness of this trial. The reason is that Isaac had the promise of the future blessing. Therefore the command to kill him was all the more painful.

The verb "to tempt" must be particularly noted, for it is not put here needlessly. Nor should it be treated as coldly as James does (1:13), when he declares that nobody is tempted by God.[2] For here Scripture states plainly that Abraham was actually tempted by God Himself, not concerning a woman, gold, silver, death, or life but concerning a contradiction of Holy Scripture. Here God is clearly contradicting Himself; for how do these statements agree: "Through Isaac shall your descendants be named" (Gen. 21:12) and "Take your son, and sacrifice him"? He does not say that some bandit would come and secretly carry off his son; for in that case Abraham could have continued to have hope concerning the life and return of his son. But he himself is commanded to do the slaying, evidently in order that he may have no doubt that Isaac has actually been killed.

In this situation, then, would he not murmur against God and think: "This is not a command of God; it is a trick of Satan. For God's promise is sure, clear, and beyond doubt: 'From Isaac you will have descendants.' Why, then, does God command that he should be killed? Undoubtedly God is repenting of His promise. Otherwise He would not contradict Himself. Or I have committed some extra-

---

[2] See also Luther's prefaces to the Epistle of James, *Luther's Works,* 35, pp. 395—397.

ordinary sin, with which I have deeply offended God, so that He is withdrawing the promise"?

By nature we are all in the habit of doing this. When some physical affliction besets us, our conscience is soon at hand, and the devil torments it by assembling all the circumstances. Therefore a troubled heart looks about and considers how it may have offended God most. This leads to murmuring against God and to the greatest trial, hatred of God.

Abraham, too, had thoughts like this: "Behold, the Lord promised and gave me a son. As a result, I became happy and was restored to life, as it were. But perhaps this gift made me too proud, and I was not as thankful to God as I should have been. Therefore He regrets His promise."

This trial cannot be overcome and is far too great to be understood by us. For there is a contradiction with which God contradicts Himself. It is impossible for the flesh to understand this; for it inevitably concludes either that God is lying — and this is blasphemy — or that God hates me — and this leads to despair. Accordingly, this passage cannot be explained in a manner commensurate with the importance of the subject matter.

We are frequently tempted by thoughts of despair; for what human being is there who could be without this thought: "What if God did not want you to be saved?" But we are taught that in this conflict we must hold fast to the promise given us in Baptism, which is sure and clear. But when this happens, Satan does not cease immediately but keeps crying out in your heart that you are not worthy of this promise.

But in this situation there is need of the fervent prayer that God may give us His Spirit, in order that the promise may not be wrested from us. I am unable to resolve this contradiction. Our only consolation is that in affliction we take refuge in the promise; for it alone is our staff and rod, and if Satan strikes it out of our hands, we have no place left to stand. But we must hold fast to the promise and maintain that, just as the text states about Abraham, we are tempted by God, not because He really wants this, but because He wants to find out whether we love Him above all things and are able to bear Him when He is angry as we gladly bear Him when He is beneficent and makes promises.

Thus Abraham was unable to believe that he was merely being

tested. Otherwise he would have remained sure of the promise and would have thought that God is acting as parents are sometimes in the habit of doing when they tempt their children and take away a treat or something of that sort which they soon return to them. But when God commands that Abraham's son should be taken away, He leaves no hope but simply confronts Abraham with a contradiction. And God, who formerly seemed to be his best friend, now appears to have become an enemy and a tyrant.

Accordingly, Abraham is being more severely tried than Mary when she lost her Son at Jerusalem; for even though she, too, thought that she was being punished for not watching over her Son more carefully, she nevertheless still had the sure hope that He was alive. But here God, who had given the son, commands that the son be killed by the father himself. What hope, then, could the father have? He surely could not have been aware of this, that he was only being tried and that God was not speaking in earnest, just as we buoy ourselves up with the thought that God, even though He seems to be angry, nevertheless does not hate us or is casting us aside but sometimes, as Isaiah (28:21) says, does a strange work and simulates anger, in order to kill the mind of the flesh, which is opposed to God, as Job says: "Even though He slays me, yet will I hope"; for he is sure that God has something else in mind and is not really [3] angry.

These events are recorded for our comfort, in order that we may learn to rely on the promises we have. I was baptized. Therefore I must maintain that I was translated from the kingdom of Satan into the kingdom of God. Someone else has entered into marriage, and there, as usually happens, various inconveniences present themselves. Therefore he should turn his attention to the Fourth Commandment and consider that this kind of life is pleasing to God, for He commands that parents should be honored and thus indicates that this kind of life is pleasing to Him.

One must act similarly in all other trials. Wherever we experience the opposite of a promise, we should maintain with assurance that when God shows Himself differently from the way the promise speaks, this is merely a temptation. Therefore we should not allow this staff of the promise to be wrested from our hands.

Nearly all people are tempted by despair, and the godlier they are,

---

[3] All editions have *fere* here; but we have read *vere*, which seems to make better sense.

the more frequently they are attacked with this weapon of Satan. What else should you do in this situation than say: "I know that I am baptized and that God, for the sake of His Son, has promised me grace. This promise will not lie, even if I should be cast into utter darkness. Therefore what Satan suggests to me is not God's will; but God is tempting me in this manner, that it may become manifest what is hidden in my heart. It is not that God does not know this, but that I do not know it. He Himself wants to make use of this occasion to crush the head of the serpent in me (Gen. 3:15). For the heart of man is unsearchable; and φρόνημα, or the mind of the flesh, is enmity against God" (Rom. 8:7). Nor does man perceive this except through the word of the Law, through which the head of the serpent is killed, in order that we may be made alive, as Scripture says (1 Sam. 2:6): "God brings down to Sheol and raises up."

I have stated what Abraham's trial was, namely, the contradiction of the promise. Therefore his faith shines forth with special clarity in this passage, inasmuch as he obeys God with such a ready heart when He gives him the command. And although Isaac has to be sacrificed, he nevertheless has no doubt whatever that the promise will be fulfilled, even if he does not know the manner of its fulfillment. Yet he is also alarmed and terrified. For what else could the father do? Nevertheless, he clings to the promise that at some time Isaac will have descendants.

Human reason would simply conclude either that the promise is lying or that the command is not God's but the devil's. For there is a plain contradiction. If Isaac must be killed, the promise is void; but if the promise is sure, it is impossible that this is a command of God. Reason cannot do anything else, as experience shows in less important matters.

The Sacramentarians regard it as a contradiction that Christ says (Matt. 26:26; Mark 14:22; Luke 22:19; 1 Cor. 11:24): "Take; this is My body," and yet that Christ is sitting at the right hand of the Father.[4] From this they conclude that therefore only bread and wine are distributed in the Lord's Supper, not the body and blood of Christ. Likewise (John 6:63): "The flesh is of no avail." In the Supper Christ gives His flesh; therefore Christ's flesh is not in the Supper. This is truly rushing into Holy Scripture with unwashed feet and following the blind judgment of reason.

---

[4] On this argument cf. *Luther the Expositor*, p. 140.

Even though there is a clear contradiction here — for there is nothing between death and life — Abraham nevertheless does not turn away from the promise but believes that his son will have descendants even if he dies. Let us, too, learn to do the same thing. Yesterday we buried our very dear friend Dr. Sebald.[5] Therefore he is now lamented as though he were dead. But we know that he is living; for inasmuch as he died in the true confession of the Son of God, and God is not the God of the dead but of the living (Matt. 22:32), he, too, lives.

Thus Abraham relies on the promise and attributes to the Divine Majesty this power, that He will restore his dead son to life; for just as he saw that Isaac was born of a worn-out womb and of a sterile mother, so he also believed that he was to be raised after being buried and reduced to ashes, in order that he might have descendants, as the Epistle to the Hebrews (11:19) states: "God is able to give life even to the dead."

Accordingly, Abraham understood the doctrine of the resurrection of the dead, and through it alone he resolved this contradiction, which otherwise cannot be resolved; and his faith deserves the praise it receives from the prophets and apostles. These were his thoughts: "Today I have a son; tomorrow I shall have nothing but ashes. I do not know how long they will lie scattered; but they will be brought to life again, whether this happens while I am still alive or a thousand years after my death. For the Word declares that I shall have descendants through this Isaac, even though he has been reduced to ashes."

I have said, however, that we cannot comprehend this trial; but we can observe and imagine it from afar, so to speak. Moreover, you see that the passage does not deal with a work, as James says in his letter (2:21), since as yet no work has occurred. It is the faith that we admire and praise.

Therefore one should hold fast to this comfort, that what God has once declared, this He does not change. You were baptized, and in Baptism the kingdom of God was promised you. You should know that this is His unchangeable Word, and you should not permit yourself to be drawn away from it. For although it can happen — as with those who were on the way to Emmaus (Luke 24:28) — that He pretends to want to go farther and seems to be dealing with us as though

[5] See p. 91, note 1, on the burial of Sebald Münsterer.

He had forgotten His promises, faith in the Word must nevertheless be retained, and the promise must be stressed — namely, that it is true and dependable — even if the manner, time, occasion, place, and other particulars are unknown. For the fact that God cannot lie is sure and dependable.

When I am being killed, I see the ways and particulars by which my life is destroyed; but I do not see the particulars through which life will return, neither the time nor the place. Why, then, do I believe what I do not see anywhere? Because I have the promise and the Word of God; this does not permit me to discard the hope of life or to have any doubt about the inheritance which is Christ's, through whom we have been adopted as children.

Up to this time Abraham had thought that his son Isaac would marry and beget children at the place where he was at that time. All this falls through, for here is God's command that he should kill his son. Therefore even though those particulars of place and time are lost, Abraham does not for this reason have any doubt about the matter itself; for he knows that his son will have descendants, even after a thousand years.

These trials of the saintly patriarch have been set before us in order that we may be encouraged in our own trials and say with Abraham: "Though my son Isaac dies, nevertheless, because he believes in God, the very grave in which his ashes will lie will not be a grave but will be a bedchamber and a sleeping room." "On the contrary," says reason, "the opposite is manifest. The flesh turns to dust, and worms consume it." But this neither hinders nor annuls the Word of God; for these two statements which God makes to Adam — "You are dust, and to dust you shall return" (Gen. 3:19) and "The Seed shall crush the head of the serpent" (Gen. 3:15) — belong together.

Here the Jews speak of four revelations which did not occur at the same time, as Lyra relates for the purpose of showing the greatness of the obedience and the boundless power of faith.[6] But there is no need here for such subtlety, for in my opinion these things happened at one and the same time. "Take not a male servant or a female servant, not Ishmael, but your only son, Isaac, whom you love."

Thus God strengthens His command and makes it harsher and more painful, as though He were saying: "After this you will not be

[6] The Jewish exegetical tradition is collected in Lyra *ad* Gen. 22:1-2.

the father of such a son, and you will not have him whom you love so much; for I want you to offer him to Me, not like the other first-born, who were kept,[7] but to kill him. Accordingly, Abraham has now nothing more, so far as the promise is concerned, than he had before Isaac was born; and yet, because of God, he is ready to give up not only his son, Sarah, his inheritance, his house, and his church but even his own life. Isaac's death included all this, inasmuch as the promise was attached to Isaac.

The text says nothing about Sarah, whether she was aware of this command or not. Perhaps — because she was too weak to be able to stand that great shock — Abraham concealed this matter from her. For it is harsh when the text says: "You shall offer your son," not as a gift or as a thanksgiving, as the first-born in Israel used to be offered, but as a burnt offering, so that he is simply reduced to ashes, and the hands of the father had to be defiled with the blood of his son.

What do you suppose the sentiments of Abraham's heart were in this situation? He was a human being, and, as I have stated repeatedly, he was not without natural affection. Besides, the fact that he did not dare divulge to anyone what was happening made his grief greater. Otherwise all would have advised against it, and the large number of those who advised against it would perhaps have influenced him. Therefore he sets out on the journey alone with young slaves and his son. It is a momentous command and far harsher than we are able to imagine. Yet the fact that the text clearly states that God was doing this to test him is full of comfort. If Abraham had known this, he would have had fewer worries. But now he is absorbed in the thought that his son has to be sacrificed and that at some time and in some manner or other the promise has to be fulfilled.

The Lord even designates a definite place away from his home, in the land of Moriah. Furthermore, Moriah is approximately 10 German miles distant from Beer-sheba, unless the cosmographers are mistaken.[8] This is a journey of about three days, for he had a donkey along to carry wood and food. Consequently, their progress was rather slow.

[7] Apparently a reference to Lev. 12:2-8, as interpreted in Luke 2:22-24.

[8] Beginning with the edition of 1541 (thus shortly after these lectures on Gen. 22), Luther's translation of the Bible carried the following gloss on this passage: "Moriah means fear of God, reverence toward God, worship of God; for the patriarchs Adam, Noah, and Shem honored, feared, and served God on the same mountain. We unsophisticated Germans would probably call it Holy Hill, or the place where God is served with praise, petition, and thanksgiving."

Furthermore, as 2 Chron. 3:1 records, Moriah is that hill near Mt. Zion on which Solomon built the temple in Jerusalem where the city slopes down toward the north. But the hill gave its name to the entire land, so that it was called the land of Moriah. To this day the Turks call the hill by that name and regard it with pious reverence. Thus it often happens that an entire land gets its name from one place. Just as all Saxony gets its name from the castle Saxenburg, so at that time that entire region got the name Moriah from Mt. Moriah. Here Jerusalem was located. At that time it was called Salem and also Jebus, and it was governed by the patriarch Shem.

Moriah is written with a double י, and the Hebrews debate very solicitously about its etymology. In this passage Jerome translates it as a common noun: "Go to the land of the vision." [9] But this etymology is rejected by all as being too foreign to grammar. Others think that it got its name from myrrh, so that Moriah means "The Lord is my myrrh," because there the Lord should have myrrh, that is, His worship. For myrrh and frankincense, with which offerings of incense were made, used to grow there. And the etymology fits; for מֹר is "myrrh," י is the enclitic pronoun "my," and יָה is the name of God.

Although I do not object to this etymology, I nevertheless am not adopting it, chiefly for the reason that the Jews, as is their habit, understood only the outward form of worship with incense; they neither understand nor perform the true inner forms of worship.

Accordingly, the opinion of those who derive the word from the verb יָרָה, meaning "to teach," from which is derived תּוֹרָה, "law" or "instruction," so that the meaning of מֹרִיָה, that is, "the Lord who teaches," is that on this mount God teaches and is heard, as the prophets state (Is. 2:3): "Out of Zion shall go forth the Law, and the Word of the Lord from Jerusalem" — this opinion, it seems to me, is preferable and better.

This etymology seems to me to have greater merit and to be more suitable so far as both meaning and grammar are concerned. But I do not claim for myself discernment enough in this language to make a decision. Burgensis, too, agrees with this; for his translation is "The Lord is my Instructor, or He who teaches me." [10]

The third etymology pleases me most of all. Yet I do not reject the others; for they derive מֹרִיָה from the verb יָרָא, which means "to

[9] The Vulgate translation reads: *Vade in terram visionis.* See also p. 101.

[10] Paulus Burgensis (cf. *Luther's Works,* 1, xi) *ad* Gen. 22:2.

fear." Everywhere there are testimonies of Holy Scripture that fear of God is worship of God. For just as the terms "man" and "risible" are interchangeable,[11] as the dialecticians say, so are fear and worship of God. God does not care for myrrh or incense if there is not present the fear on which Holy Scripture everywhere insists most of all, namely, that we should obey the Word of God, as, for instance, in the Book of Jeremiah (7:22-23): "I did not speak to your fathers concerning burnt offerings and sacrifices. But this command I gave them: 'Obey My voice, and I will be your God, and you shall be My people; and walk in all the way that I have commanded you, that it may be well with you.'"

Accordingly, reverence and fear constitute the true and God-pleasing worship. If Abraham had killed his son because of foolish zeal and with contempt for the Word of God as Ahaz did (2 Kings 16:3), it would indeed have been myrrh, that is, a difficult and painful sacrifice that distresses the heart. But God does not look at the outward work; He looks at the heart itself. If it is right and fears God, God is pleased with whatever one does.

Therefore it is my opinion that this word מֹרִיָּה properly denotes θεοσέβεια, or reverence and fear of God. For this reason in Is. 29:13, where the Hebrew has "their fear is a commandment of men," the Septuagint has "In vain do they worship Me, teaching as doctrines the precepts of men." Christ, too, quotes the passage this way (Matt. 15:9).

In the same Book of Isaiah (11:2) it is called the spirit of fear, that is, of the worship of God. Thus that land, as well as the hill, got its name from the true worship of God. But this worship is found only where God Himself teaches.

And what the Jews maintain seems to be true, namely, that in that very place Adam, Abel, and Noah brought sacrifices. Certainly Shem had his abode there. By him the true worship of God was spread abroad in the world. Here, too, applies what we stated above, that before the Flood Paradise was near that land, and that Adam dwelt in the neighborhood of Mt. Moriah after he had been driven from Paradise.[12] Consequently, even before the Flood it was a famous place

[11] Zachary Coke's *Logick* of 1654 (which rested on the manuals of logic to which Luther seems to be referring here) stated: "Man is risible, and every risible thing is a man." Cf. *Oxford English Dictionary*, VIII, 712.

[12] See *Luther's Works*, 1, pp. 87—91, for Luther's discussion of the location of Paradise.

because of the worship of God, and it remained famous up to the time of Christ. But after the Holy Spirit was bestowed, the Gospel was spread from there into the entire world; and no longer was either the worship of God or the church confined to that small corner of the Jewish land.

Thus I gladly agree with those who believe that Moriah received its name from the Hebrew word which denotes "to fear, worship, and revere God," as though one called it in German *heyligstat*, a holy place, a house of God, because this place was the temple and house of God from the beginning of the world, was venerated by Adam and Noah, and was inhabited by the eminent patriarch Shem, just as today there is a Moriah which extends as far as the world, just as Jerusalem does; that is, God is adored and worshiped not only in one definite place but everywhere in the world, wherever there is a congregation of the godly.

Opinions vary as to how God revealed this command that Abraham should kill his son. The majority say that it was done at night through a vision; others suppose that, as was usual,[13] this revelation was made to the patriarch Shem and that he gave this command to Abraham by divine authority. But whatever may be the case, it is certain from what Moses says that it was God's will that Abraham should be put to the test by this command.

As to the translation of Jerome, who made an appellative of the proper noun, he deserves indulgence. For it is characteristic of the Hebrew language that it is entirely etymological even in the case of proper nouns. Therefore just as he allowed the proper name of the place to remain in Chronicles, so he should also have allowed it to remain in this passage. But the verse which comes later, where it is recorded that Abraham called the name of this place The Lord Will See, misled him. Consequently, here, too, he translates: "Go to the land of the vision."

If there are some who want to look for an allegory, Moriah was the Word of God and faith in the Word. For these two are correlative; there can be neither faith nor worship of God where there is no Word, and wherever the Word is, there must be some who believe. Where, then, these two are, there follows the third, namely, the cross and mortification. These three make up the Christian life. But more about this elsewhere.

[13] On Luther's interpretation of the appointment of Shem as a messenger of God cf. *Luther the Expositor*, p. 104.

In this passage, however, special note should be taken of the adverb of place. "Offer your son to Me *there* as a burnt offering." It was not permitted to sacrifice or to set up the worship of God everywhere. No, this could be done only in that place which God chose. Therefore the prophets severely rebuke the Jews who sacrificed elsewhere than in the place commanded by God; and in this passage not only the place but also the person and the sacrificer are specifically named. "You, Abraham, must offer your son, not cattle; you must offer Isaac, not Ishmael." All the details are exclusive.[14]

For God does not want us to serve Him with our self-chosen works. Therefore He prescribes everything in His command, and so positive and stern a command at that. Consequently, if the person, the place, or the time is different, you are mistaken and not only do not worship at all, but you even irritate Him and provoke Him to hate you and be angry with you.

The Jews were not Abraham; that is, they did not have a command, as Abraham did, about immolating their children. Indeed, the Fifth Commandment forbade in general all kinds of homicide. Yet Ahaz thought that he was rendering God a splendid service if he made his children pass through fire (2 Kings 16:3). The antecedent was as follows: Even a son must be killed on God's account, as the example of Abraham teaches. "Therefore," he said "I, too, shall kill my son." But this is a false conclusion because of the dissimilarity.[15] It was by a special and new command that Abraham was ordered to immolate his son; this command Ahaz did not have. Therefore he should have undertaken nothing contrary to the clear commandment of the Decalog.

3. *So Abraham rose early in the morning, saddled his ass, and took two of his young men with him, and his son Isaac.*

This account deserves to have each word carefully examined. Abraham rose early in the morning. He did not delay; he did not argue. Nor did he ask, as Adam did in Paradise: "Why does God give this command?" He listened neither to his flesh nor to the serpent. Indeed, he did not make the matter known even to Sarah; but when he heard God's command, he hastened without any hesitation to carry it out.

14 Cf. p. 64, note 55.

15 Cf. Aristotle, *Prior Analytics*, Book I, chs. 27—28.

This is an extraordinary example and a description of perfect obedience, when so suddenly and at one and the same time Abraham thrusts out of sight and does away with everything he used to hold dearest in his life: his home, his wife, and his son who had been so long expected and upon whom such grand promises had been heaped. Consequently, we admire in vain the saints of the New Testament [16] and read about their fastings and chastisings without discernment; for no matter what kind of men they were, if they are compared with Abraham, their saintliness and virtues become altogether vile and filthy. They do not know what it means to kill the son of promise — the son on whom rested all the hope and strength of the aged father, all of which perishes so unexpectedly in a single moment with the life of his son. This is truly denying oneself and forsaking everything. Elsewhere we read that some cast aside their gold, silver, and wealth, and that others cast aside wife and children and risked their lives because of their confession; but there never was an apostle, a patriarch, or a martyr who could have shown this obedience so unwaveringly.

Let us remember, however, that in this entire account one should pay special attention to the Word and command of God, which glorifies all the works of believers and makes them grand, no matter how small they are. Similarly, the works done without a command, even though they are most saintly in outward appearance, are nothing but filth, like those of the pope or other fanatics.

Next there is a description of Abraham's ready and eager heart. Moses states that he rose, did not delay, and did not hesitate. When we are sure about God's will and believe that He has commanded what we have under consideration, the matter must be undertaken, not with trepidation or hesitation but with the utmost eagerness, even if one had to expose oneself to a thousand dangers or to death itself. For the Word of God cannot be without effect. But when we obey God's command, the outcome determined in advance surely follows, even though the very gates of hell fight against it. Thus David says in Ps. 119:50: "Thy Word is my comfort in my affliction"; that is, because I had Thy Word, my heart was ready and eager to endure all dangers, and Thy Word gave me life.

For it is most certainly true that when anyone in his vocation is convinced in his heart that God desires and has commanded in His

[16] By "the New Testament" here Luther means the entire Christian era, not merely the first century.

Word what he is doing, he will experience such force and effectiveness of that divine command as he will not find in the oration of any orator, either of Demosthenes or of Cicero. That command states all the details. It tells what is profitable and what is good in the matter; it points out and suggests to the heart that God has in view unlimited designs far above our understanding. And when the heart has been provided with this confidence, it proceeds boldly and is not anxious about the possible or the impossible, the easy or the difficult, as St. Paul has magnificently described this confidence and security of the godly in Rom. 8:35 ff.

If Gideon and Samson had not had the Word of God, they would never have performed such great deeds but would have succumbed to the hardship and the great number of their enterprises. But because they believed the Word, these were their thoughts: "I have been called for this, and I have the command to attack the Philistines, the Midianites, etc.; therefore I shall proceed boldly." It is faith that produces these marvelous works, just as Christ says in John 14:12: "He who believes in Me will also do the works that I do; and greater works than these will he do."

But we do not find these facts in the heathen accounts; nor do we Christians have sufficient understanding of them, because we are sound asleep and do not believe God when He commands, threatens, punishes, or promises. We lack understanding. Those saintly heroes and fathers — Abraham, David, etc. — believed, and therefore they performed such difficult things. It is related above how Abraham routed four kings with a small force. He achieved that victory by no other means than faith, which relied on the command and call of God.

Thus in this account Abraham overcomes his trials by faith. And without a doubt he had very great trials. He knows that God has given him a command. Therefore he hastens to carry it out without regard for a contrary opinion of Sarah or of the domestics or of any other creature. What is stated in the psalm (119:50) is firmly impressed on his heart: "Thy Law is my very great comfort, because it gives me life." In the same way let him who has a sure Word of God, in whatever vocation he may be, only believe and have courage, and God will undoubtedly grant a favorable outcome.

We do not have commands about extraordinary and unique things of this kind, and perhaps we would be incredulous even if we had them, as a similar example concerning incredulous King Ahaz is described in Is. 7. The two very powerful kings of Syria and Israel were waging war against him. Moreover, Scripture says (Is. 7:2) that "his heart and the heart of his people shook as the trees of the forests shake before the wind." Then the Lord sends His prophet to Ahaz with a new command (Is. 7:4): "Take heed, be quiet, do not fear, and be not faint. For these two kings are not kings before Me; they are burning firebrands, nay, even stumps of smoking firebrands. Just have confidence, and do not be afraid." What is more, the Lord bids him ask for a sign, so that his heart and faith may become stronger. But what does Ahaz do? "I will not ask," says he (Is. 7:12), "and I will not put the Lord to the test." We, too, would be people of that kind and would not accept it, even if God gave us some new command.

At this time, in the present danger of the plague,[17] we are in a state of trepidation. It is as though we did not have the command to live and to call upon God. We have a most dependable Word uttered by the mouth of the Son of God (John 11:25-26): "I am the resurrection and the life; he who believes in Me, though he die, yet shall he live, and whoever lives and believes in Me shall never die." But who is interested in this Word or pays any attention to it? Similarly, anyone can be certain about his calling from the Word of God, whether it is a calling in civil life or in the church. But there is nothing we neglect more than our duty. The negligence and idleness of the government is familiar to all. The bishops and the pastors remain silent like dumb dogs (cf. Is. 56:10) and do not believe that they are what they are; they strive for riches and honors, but they do not perform their tasks. Meanwhile we complain that we lack the opportunity to do good works.

We have the command that applies to us all, namely, that we should love God and fear no one — not the devil, not the Turk, not the plague — when we walk in our ways, even if our life is in danger, in accordance with the passage (Ps. 27:14): "Wait for the Lord; be strong, and let your heart take courage." But who heeds this? Nobody. For nobody believes that God has commanded confidence and has condemned despair. Therefore this passage deserves careful consideration, in order that we may learn true obedience toward God and how important it is to have the assurance of a command from

---

[17] See p. 91, note 1.

God and with what great confidence this fills the hearts of the godly. We assuredly should have sought for this in the remotest limits of the world, but there is no need of a long journey or of a painstaking search. Our home, body, and heart are full of commands of God; yet we do not believe. Therefore we feel no joy; nor do we have any light or understanding with regard to that spiritual pride and confidence that is based on the Word of God and His commands.

It is for this reason that the examples of the fathers, in which the efficacy and power of the Word of God and of faith are prominent, should be exalted and carefully emphasized, as David boasts (Ps. 119:50): "These are my comfort, namely, Thy utterances." Relying on these utterances, he killed a bear, a lion, and the Philistine Goliath, and performed other difficult and remarkable feats. When he was driven out of the kingdom by his son, he held fast to the same comfort, and his thoughts were as follows: "I was chosen king by the authority and command of God, not because of my own desire but to the glory of God. Since I am sure of this, I shall not become perturbed; nor shall I be afraid." And with this confidence he appeals to God (Ps. 7:6): "Arise, O Lord God, in the command which Thou hast given me," as though he were saying: "If it is Thy desire to cast me aside, it is good; but if Thou desirest that I be and remain a king, I shall rule even against the will and opposition of the gates of hell." With this word he overcomes and kills both his son Absalom and his wicked counselor.

Thus in this unbelievable trial it was Abraham's sole consolation that he knew he had a command from God. He surely would not have fled from the plague or from many thousands of Turks, because his heart held fast to this confidence: "I believe in God Almighty." But what are 10,000 Turks in comparison with Almighty God? Therefore he does not delay at this point, but he immediately takes hold of the command and is ready to carry out the sacrifice.

We should learn to understand this power of the Word of God — this power which the Holy Spirit is wont to exalt so much that He makes it greater than every creature, hell, death, and the good and bad angels. Yes, He even makes it equal to God, as it actually is, inasmuch as in Rom. 1:16 Paul calls it "the might and power of God"; and indeed one should feel the same way about the spoken word. Abraham understood this very clearly; therefore he had no doubt that Isaac, even if he were to die, nevertheless would be revived and that his progeny would live on, because God does not permit His command and promise to be of no effect.

In Ps. 91:7, 11 it is stated: "A thousand will fall at your side, and ten thousand at your right hand; but it will not come near you. For He will give His angels charge of you to guard you in all your ways." He who holds firmly to this promise and meanwhile diligently does his duty in his place, which he knows has been assigned to him by God, even if some dangers or obstacles are put in his way, nevertheless has no doubt about a happy issue and favorable outcome but is convinced in his heart that all the angels will come flying from heaven to help and defend him rather than that any godly undertaking in accord with the Word of God should be in vain and useless. What you undertake on the strength of His Word must succeed, even though there were to be no angel remaining in heaven.[18] In this the sacred accounts are therefore superior to the histories of the heathen; for in the former everything happens by God's command, but in the latter it happens by chance and by the plans of men.

And this is the meaning of the words "Abraham rose early in the morning." He did not argue about the outcome, but these were his thoughts: "I am sure that something better will happen than I am now seeing — not through my strength or that of my people but through the power of the command of God. Therefore I shall obey the Lord, who is giving me the command and is calling me." Thus Joab says to his brother (2 Sam. 10:12): "Be of good courage, and let us play the man for our people, and for the cities of our God; and may the Lord do what seems good to Him." Such people are ready for every good work; all the rest are reprobate, because even a slow obedience is no obedience at all.

He saddled his ass.

All these details are so carefully described in order to show that even the delay exercised his faith to no small extent. The father himself had to look for the wood, cut it, and place it upon the ass for the purpose of burning his son. Meanwhile he undoubtedly felt very great trepidation of the flesh. He did not have a heart of iron, but he was of a very tender nature; and in his mind he continually con-

---

[18] In the original this sentence appears in German, presumably because Luther shifted from Latin to German here, as he probably did more often than the present text of the lectures indicates.

templated the thought of the burnt offering at which his only son, who had been promised him as the hope of the future Seed and of progeny, had to be sacrificed, and with the very wood which the father is gathering. Should he not have deliberated further in a matter so sad and astonishing? Should he not have taken counsel with Sarah, the child's mother? These things are indicated by those seemingly useless words; otherwise this could have been described very briefly. But Moses wants to indicate what emotions Abraham felt at every moment — emotions which undoubtedly were accompanied by inexpressible groans, sighs, sobs, and fatherly tears. But he himself saddles the ass and does not assign this task to the slaves. He is so wrapped up and so absorbed, as it were, in reverence and fear of God that he scarcely realizes what he is doing.

And he took two of his young men with him.

The Jews argue about who those two slaves were.[19] Ishmael has been cast out; yet they maintain that one of the young men was Ishmael and that the other was Eliezer, the overseer of Abraham's house who has been mentioned above (15:2). Whoever they were, they surely were most faithful. For they follow and respect their master without resorting to any subterfuges. But the Saracens have invented horrible lies on the basis of this text. They tell the fictitious story that Ishmael was immolated in the place of Isaac, who, they say, ran away and did not obey his father. Hence they boast that they are the sons of Sarah; for, as they say, Isaac was not sacrificed, but Ishmael was sacrificed in his brother's place.[20]

It is the perpetual custom of all heretics to transfer to themselves the glory of the church and the people of God, for everybody wants to be nearest to God. And this temptation has existed among men from the beginning of the world. Thus today the heretics and the pope want to be the church. The Turk wants to be the people of God. Christians, however, are deprived of their rightful title and honor. This is the course of the world from the beginning to the end. Cain is its originator, and it will persist through all ages. The

---

[19] These rabbinic materials are cited in Lyra *ad* Gen. 22:3.

[20] "Muslim theology also knows the story given in Genesis xxii. But there are several theologians who say it was not Ishāk but Ismā'īl that was the dhabīh. For this view, the sayings of 'Abd Allāh ben 'Omar, Ibn 'Abbās, al-Sha'bi, Mudjāhid are quoted." A. J. Wensinck, "Ismā'īl," *The Encyclopaedia of Islam*, II (Leyden, 1927), p. 544; see also p. 70, note 59.

false church arrogates to itself the title of church of God. Idols seize the name and the honor of God. Therefore almost more sins are committed against the First Table than against the Second. For this reason Isaac, too, is declared to be disobedient and a runaway.

AND HIS SON ISAAC.[21]

After Abraham has received the command, he sees nothing else. Everything fades out in him: Sarah, the domestics, his home, and Isaac. This is true mortification; this is sitting in ashes and sackcloth. Away with Antony, Hilarion, and others! Yes, they performed great and difficult works; but not one of these works was the mortification of that head of the serpent — namely, of reason and man's will — which the monks and hypocrites of their kind rather bring to life and strengthen when they are puffed up with their righteousness, merits, and works of supererogation.

It is a great and truly bitter sorrow to lose the son obtained by so many prayers and tears, and to lose the hope and glory through which he had hoped that he would be the father of the Blessed Seed. In this sorrow he nevertheless comforts himself and maintains that he will have descendants, if not within his lifetime yet after his death, just as Sarah comforted herself (ch. 16) when she thought: "I shall not be the mother of this Seed, for I have not been worthy. Therefore let another be the mother, namely, my slave woman Hagar. Only may the Lord give some offspring!" These are true mortifications. They do not happen in deserts, away from the society of human beings. No, they happen in the household itself and in the government, and from this one can surely form an opinion about Abraham's extraordinary obedience, which extended to his innermost being.

And he cut the wood for the burnt offering, and arose and went to the place of which God had told him.

Everything appears to indicate a delay. Abraham has 318 servants (14:14), yet he himself is a servant of servants. These facts are related in order to bestow praise on his remarkable obedience. He gives no order to anyone but does everything himself, and quickly at that, because he is impelled by the command which rules and lives in him.

[21] In the original this also appears in capitals.

4. *On the third day Abraham lifted up his eyes and saw the place
afar off.*

It is my opinion that the place of the sacrifice was not more than
a quarter of a mile distant from the place Abraham ordered his
servants to halt. Jerusalem, or Mt. Moriah, even though it was a rather
high place, nevertheless could not be seen from a distance, because
the region round about it was mountainous. I am truly surprised
that the father did not die from that bitter and persistent grief, for
he had to make a journey of three days. If that struggle had lasted
one or two hours, he would have prevailed rather easily. Therefore
this delay makes his obedience greater. Meanwhile he thought: "Behold, I am walking along with my son, who is my greatest hope
and a young man; he has to die." During these three days he endured this kind of torture of his flesh and at the same time the darts
of Satan. Nevertheless, he had to endure it in silence because of the
command, and since he relied on this, he was strengthened and
preserved.

5. *Then Abraham said to his young men: Stay here with the ass;
I and the lad will go yonder and worship, and come again to you.*

If the slaves had been present, they would not have allowed the
father to do what he intended; or they would have suspected that
he was out of his mind. But if they had been unable to prevent him,
they would nevertheless have shouted aloud, and by closing their
eyes they would have avoided seeing so great a crime.

6. *And Abraham took the wood of the burnt offering and laid it on
Isaac his son.*

There is another delay, and Abraham's grief breaks out anew when
he places the wood on his son. "O my son, if you or your mother
knew what kind of wood you are carrying! You think that you are
carrying it to a sacrifice, but you do not know that you yourself will
be the burnt offering."

And he took in his hand the fire and the knife.

It was not a sword, and the picture commonly painted of Abraham about to kill his son is incorrect.[22] It was a knife, such as butchers

---

[22] The sacrifice of Isaac was a favorite theme in medieval art; perhaps the
best-known representation is the sculpture in the north porch of the cathedral
at Chartres.

and priests were accustomed to use. Isaac lay on his back on the heap of wood. His face was turned toward heaven, and Abraham wanted to strike his throat, as butchers commonly kill calves. First the ass carried the wood, and the slaves carried the fire. But Abraham took these from them and placed the wood, a burden for asses, on his son, because he was not a boy but a young man about 25 years old. He himself carried the fire. Then indeed various ideas must have arisen in the minds of the slaves.

So they went both of them together.

These two were alone as they walked in the desert. The whole world is ignorant of what is going on here, and there was no one at hand to encourage the sorrowful father. The son, however, does not know that he is to be killed. Nowhere else in Holy Scripture is a walk like this described. There were two. Who were they? The very dear father and the dearly beloved son. In what frame of mind were they? This was their frame of mind: Isaac was unaware of the situation. Nevertheless, he was ready to obey. Abraham was fully determined to immolate his son and reduce him to ashes.

7. *And Isaac said to his father Abraham: My father! And he said: Here am I, my son. He said: Behold, the fire and the wood; but where is the lamb for a burnt offering?*

8. *Abraham said: God will provide Himself the lamb for a burnt offering, my son. So they went both of them together.*

At this point there is surely profound emotion, and there is powerful pathos. Moses did not want to pass this over. Isaac, the victim, addresses his father and stirs up his natural love, as though he were saying: "You are my father." And the father says in turn: "You are my son." These words penetrated into and upset the heart of the father. For the son says: "Behold, the wood; but where is the lamb?" It is evident that he is solicitous about the glory of God, for he knows that his father is about to offer a burnt offering at which he himself wants to be the onlooker. Therefore he gives him a reminder lest perchance he forget the sacrifice because of the very great intentness and devotion of his heart. "Where is the lamb," he says, "for the burnt offering?" Then his father should have answered him: "You will be the lamb." But he does not say this. Then he adds: "God will provide it"; and in this statement he at the same time included God's command.

Abraham does not want to torment his son with a long torture and trial. Therefore he does not yet disclose that Isaac himself must die. Nor does Moses point out that while they were walking along during these three days Abraham urged his son to become accustomed to thoughts of death. Abraham seems to have said nothing about this and to have waited until the very moment he would put the knife to Isaac's throat.

It is certainly amazing how Isaac was able to cast aside so suddenly all fondness for this life and to forget father, mother, home, the promise, and finally life itself, which he had barely begun. All this could not be overcome without great sorrow and grief. For the saints are not blocks of wood and devoid of feeling; but they are human beings, and the emotions and affections implanted in human nature are present in them to a higher degree than they are in others. It was surely extraordinary faith through which Isaac was able to turn away so suddenly from life and to hand himself over to death. For he thought of nothing else, and with his physical eyes he saw nothing else than the destruction that confronted him.

9. *When they came to the place of which God had told him, Abraham built an altar there and laid the wood in order.*

Up to this point Moses has described the example of obedience of both, the father as well as the son, in a long narrative and has kept the reader in suspense to the point of weariness with extraordinary expectation. Now that the altar has been built and the epitasis has come, Moses has nothing to say. He either does not venture to state what took place, because the subject matter is greater than can be expressed by any eloquence, or his tears made it impossible for him to write. He lets the amazement and surprise remain in the hearts of his readers and wants them to form their own idea of a situation which he is unable to describe adequately with words.

Now that the altar was built, the knife ready, and the fire kindled, some conversation between the father and the son must have occurred — a conversation through which Isaac was apprised of the will and command of God. The father said: "You, my dearly beloved son, whom God has given me, have been destined for the burnt offering." Then the son was undoubtedly struck with amazement and in turn reminded his father of the promise: "Consider, father, that I am the offspring to whom descendants, kings, peoples, etc., have been promised. God gave me to my mother Sarah through a great miracle. How, then, will it be possible for the promise to be fulfilled if I have been killed? Nevertheless, let us first confer about this matter and talk it over."

All this should have been recorded here. I do not know why Moses omitted it. But I have no doubt that the father's address to his son was extraordinary, and I think that its main topic was the command of God and the resurrection of the dead. He probably said: "God has given a command; therefore we must obey Him, and, since He is almighty, He can keep His promise even when you are dead and have been reduced to ashes." No doubt Isaac was previously instructed in this doctrine, understood it very clearly, and believed it just as much as Abraham did, because they are examples of faith. But faith includes the promise which has been related above (ch. 15).

Thus it was the father's address to his son which reconciled these two contradictory propositions: Isaac will be the seed and father of kings and of peoples; Isaac will die and will not be the father of peoples. Those contradictory statements cannot be reconciled by any human reason or philosophy. But the Word reconciles these two, namely, that he who is dead lives, and he who lives dies. Thus we live, and yet we die; for even though we are now living, we are reckoned as dead because of sin, and though we have died, we are reckoned as living. On this occasion these statements were treated and discussed between the father and the son, and they were believed not only by Abraham but also by Isaac. For Isaac dies in faith in the promise that he will be a father. Therefore Isaac dies and lives; he becomes ashes and the father of peoples.

The sophists and the rabbis understand nothing in this passage, because they do not see the heart of Holy Scripture, which deals with the resurrection of the dead, life, victory over death, and the destruction of sin, but not with transitory and worthless things. At the same time one can also see here whether there is any faith without works and whether works are condemned when the righteousness of faith is taught. How many very excellent works and how many instances of the saintliest obedience occur at the same time in this one example!

And bound Isaac his son and laid him on the altar, upon the wood.

10. *Then Abraham put forth his hand and took the knife to slay his son.*

Moses sums up that remarkable and amazing account in one short sentence. At this very moment the father is about to cut the throat of his son. The son, with his eyes lifted up to heaven, presents his throat and waits to be reduced to ashes. Thus God brings both into extreme danger of their lives. If on that occasion there had been no faith, or if God had slept for a single moment, the life of the son would have been done for, because the knife is ready, the son is bound and placed upon the heap of wood, and the thrust is aimed at his throat. These are works of God by which He shows that He takes care of us in the greatest dangers and in the midst of death.

The Jews discuss what kind of binding this was.[23] I think that Isaac was bound just as a butcher binds a sheep or a goat with a rope and grasps the animal with one hand and holds the knife in the other. At that moment Abraham also wanted to kill his son in this manner.

But why does Abraham bind Isaac? Not because Isaac was thinking of running away and did not want to obey his father, but in order to conform to the rite of the burnt offering. For Abraham had to assume the mood and procedure of a priest who is killing a calf. Therefore he employs a similar procedure and rite. He places Isaac on top of the wood, like a calf that is now to be killed, and at the same time he moves the knife close to the throat. Why is no compulsion or restraint indicated in this passage, but only the rite and procedure of the priest or slayer?

I could not have been an onlooker, much less the performer and slayer. It is an astounding situation that the dearly beloved father moves his knife close to the throat of the dearly beloved son, and I surely admit that I cannot attain to these thoughts and sentiments either by means of words or by reflecting on them. No one else should have expounded this passage than St. Paul. We are not moved by those sentiments, because we do not desire to feel and experience them. The son is obedient, like a sheep for the slaughter, and he does not open his mouth. He thought: "Let the will of the Lord be done," because he was brought up to conduct himself properly and to be obedient to his father. With the exception of Christ we have no similar example of obedience.

---

23 Both the rabbinic materials and the Christian adaptations of them are cited at length in David Lerch, *Isaaks Opferung christlich gedeutet* (Tübingen, 1950).

11. *But the angel of the Lord called to him from heaven and said: Abraham, Abraham!*

Here you see with what unconcern the Divine Majesty toys with death and all the power of death. Here God is playing with His patriarch and his son, who together experienced the utmost distress and won a very great victory over death. For not only was Isaac ready to die, but his father Abraham actually dies seven times because he is wholly preoccupied with thoughts about the sacrifice and death of his son.

Natural death, which is the separation of the soul from the body, is simple death. But to feel death, that is, the terror and fear of death — this indeed is real death. Without fear death is not death; it is a sleep, as Christ says (John 11:26): "He who believes in Me will not see death." For when fear has been removed, the death of the soul has been removed.

Therefore let us agree on this description of death: Death has a soul and a body. The body is the destruction of death for the soul, and the death of the soul is the fear and horror of death. But if the soul of death has died, the death of the body is a sleep. Here in Abraham was the death of the soul, because he had no doubt whatever but was convinced beyond all doubt that Isaac had to be sacrificed and had to be killed at that moment. But whenever a human being stands in fear of death, that is, has the conviction that he must die, then he feels the violence of real death to such an extent that he cannot hold up. Then he dies in the truest sense of the word, not when the separation of the soul from the body takes place.

Two amazing instances of deaths of this kind are combined here in the utmost patience and obedience. It would have been more bearable for Abraham to die a natural death even seven times rather than be an onlooker, yes, the slayer of his son. Thus both are killed, since they see and feel nothing else than death. Nevertheless, they did not die in the sight of God, as we shall hear later on; for they regard death as a sport and a jest, no differently from the manner in which we are in the habit of playing with a ball or an apple.

But the victory of Abraham, Isaac, and all the saints is faith. He who has faith overcomes the fear of death and conquers and triumphs eternally. About this 2 Cor. 1:9 says: "We have set our hope on the living God who raises the dead." Indeed, we have scarcely a single trace of this faith. For we believe so long as we do not feel death; but when death makes its appearance, fear and horror follow at once.

Therefore it is something wonderful and impossible for reason to believe that God can, and wants to, do away with death and change it into life. But it is far more astonishing that Abraham and Isaac were convinced that this entire action was sport and not death. Anyone readily believes that for God indeed death is sport; but if I am to maintain the same conviction for myself and in the case of my body — that death is not death — no physician, no philosopher, and no lawyer will ever convince me of this.

For who will associate and reconcile these statements: Death is not death; it is life? Moses himself asserts the opposite. For if you listen to the Law, it will tell you: In the midst of life we are in death, according to that ancient and pious hymn in the church.[24] But this has reference to the Law alone. The Gospel, however, and faith invert this hymn and sing thus: "In the midst of death we are in life. Thee we praise as our Redeemer. Thou hast raised us from death and hast saved us." For the Gospel teaches that in death itself there is life, something which is unknown to and impossible for the Law and reason. Hence Paul exults in Col.[25] 2:15: "He disarmed the principalities and powers and made a public example of them." Likewise in 2 Cor. 6:9: "As dying, and behold we live." This is the power of faith, which mediates in this way between death and life, and changes death into life and immortality, which, as faith knows, has been bestowed through Christ.

By this deed, as though by some show, God wanted to point out that in His sight death is nothing but a sport and empty little bugaboo of the human race, yes, an annoyance and a trial, as, for example, if a father sports with his son, takes an apple away from him, and meanwhile is thinking of leaving him the entire inheritance. But this is difficult to believe; and for this reason the heathen, who have no knowledge of this will of God, which He reveals in His Word, are altogether without hope (1 Thess. 4:13).

But Christians, who have the Word, should hear it with all eagerness and should meditate on it, in order that their hearts may be stirred up, so that, however much they may be weighed down by the burden of sin and the hindrances of Satan, they nevertheless may

---

24 Cf. *Luther's Works*, 13, p. 83, note 16.

25 Here the original has "Cor." instead of "Col."

attain to that glory and knowledge of God's mind and of immortality and be able to believe that this statement is true and unshakable: "Death is a sport." This is what Abraham believed and felt, and with this confidence he conquered death. The thoughts of his heart were these: "My son Isaac, whom I am killing, is the father of the promise, and this proposition is absolutely true. Consequently, my son will live forever and will be the heir. Therefore even if he has to die now, he will nevertheless not die in reality but will rise again."

Accordingly, faith reconciles opposites and is not an idle quality, as the sophists say;[26] but it has the power to kill death, to condemn hell, to be sin for sin, and a devil for the devil to such an extent that death is not death, even if everybody's reason should bear witness that death is present. Of this Abraham is very sure. He thinks: "I am reducing my son to ashes. Nevertheless, he is not dying. Indeed, those ashes will be the heir." Is this not playing in such an important and difficult matter — a matter in which all men are twice as childish as usual?

But these things have not been recorded for the sake of Abraham, who is long since dead, but to encourage and stimulate us, in order that we may learn that in the sight of God death is nothing and may sing: "In the midst of death we are in life. Whom shall we praise except Thee, our God?" This is the evangelical hymn; the other one has to do with the Law. The patriarchs and spiritual men understood these truths clearly. We deal with them daily and with great clarity. But how few there are who believe and heed them! To be sure, such people differ in no wise from those who do not hear. Indeed, even though they hear, they do not hear, because they are dead in sins and avarice. In the Old Testament the scribes, the priests, and the ungodly, who did not understand these things, are like them; but David, Isaiah, Samuel, and Jeremiah had the understanding of the Holy Spirit and were able to see that Isaac and his father Abraham, even though they die, nevertheless are living. Here Abraham is killed seven times. Nevertheless, he remains alive, and physically at that. In one moment Abraham the father and Isaac the son are killed and live.

We do not understand these things. Yet they must be thought about, in order that we may understand as much as we can. I certainly

[26] This view of faith had been a matter of controversy between Bonaventure and Thomas Aquinas; cf. the latter's *Summa Theologica*, II-II, Q. 4, Art. 4.

admit my dullness; my donkey remains standing below and cannot ascend the mountain. Thus all who are not well informed in the doctrine of faith remain asses and cannot grasp these thoughts, namely, that death is life. Thus Peter, who denied Christ when he was in danger of death, was a lazy beast. Indeed, he was not even like an ass; for he not only does not come to a halt at the foot of the mountain, but he leaps back at once and runs away.

Therefore let us remember this sight which Moses has set before us, and let us remember that jesting of the Divine Majesty in the matter of death, in order that we may learn to believe that death is life. For how many, I ask, are there who know this? Consider what we do when we look at or are present with those who are at the point of death, or when our own life is in danger. If we were minded like Abraham and his son, we would say (Ps. 118:17-18): "I shall not die, but I shall live. The Lord has chastened me sorely, but He has not given me over to death." [27] Even though I shall be buried and be consumed by worms, nevertheless I shall live. "But you will die," objects the flesh. No, but it is a chastisement.

Abraham and Isaac saw and knew nothing else, and the matter itself and the entire action were in no wise different from their thoughts. Nevertheless, they maintain that it is some sport, not death. In like manner Paul scoffs at death and exults (1 Cor. 15:55): "Death, where is your sting?"

Let us, too, learn this, in order that we may be able to say in the midst of death: "Farewell, leaves and grass! I shall not die; but I shall live, just as Isaac thought when the knife was being aimed at his throat." But if we still fear and tremble at the thought and sight of death, let us acknowledge our ignorance, and let us not boast that we are theologians.

All people can see death, and the heathen and the ungodly realize that death is death. But this is the wisdom of Christians and the unique teaching of the church — the teaching to which Abraham holds fast: "Though I am killing my son, I have him alive." And Isaac: "Though I die, I shall not die when you cut my throat and reduce me to ashes. To be sure, I shall be turned to ashes. Nevertheless, I shall live, and I shall beget heirs of the entire world."

But previously the text has stated correctly: "So they went both of them together." Except in those two, this reflection about death did

27 Cf. *Luther's Works,* 14, p. 45, note 4.

not exist in the entire world. When Isaac's throat was about to be cut, he thought: "Into Thy hands I commit my spirit (Ps. 31:5). I shall not die, but I shall live; and I shall return, because God will not lie. I am the son of the promise. Therefore I must beget children, even if heaven collapses." Consider whether this is not dying a sure death and nevertheless living a surer life. Hence the prophets in Holy Scripture everywhere proclaim the resurrection of the dead, and this passage clearly points out a resurrection even into this physical life. How much more into the future life!

But all this has its source in the First Commandment; for in it is contained the doctrine of faith and of the resurrection of the dead. "I, the almighty Creator of heaven and earth, am your God; that is, you must live the life I am living." If He were speaking these words to oxen, they would live forever. But they are said to us — to us, I say. He does not say to them: "You must eat chaff, wheat, and grass." No, He says: "I am your God."

Furthermore, to be God means to deliver from all evils that burden us, such as sin, hell, death, etc.; for in this manner the prophets regarded and interpreted these words. The heathen know God solely as the Creator; but in the First Commandment you will find Christ, life, victory over death, and the resurrection of the dead into eternal life, and finally the entire Old and New Testament. But only those who have the Holy Spirit and pay attention to what God says and does see this. Even though the others constantly hear these things, yet they do not concern themselves with them.

Therefore let these two, Abraham and Isaac, be examples of this article concerning the resurrection of the dead, because both believe that God is not only able to raise the dead but most assuredly wants to do so, and that He deals with men about the necessity to slay death, which nevertheless is not death for Him but is a sleep, which is a brother [28] and blood relative, so to speak, of death; for when a human being is buried, he is not dead for God, but he sleeps.

Thus it can be said about Isaac when he is reduced to the dust from which he was taken: "He is not dead ashes; he is the son of the promise — the son who begets kings." Let us have the same thoughts about our dead and about our bodies. This food of worms will not remain dust; but it will live again, because we hear Scripture saying that in the eyes of God death is some childish sport and is

[28] The idea of sleep as the brother of death appears in the *Iliad*, XIV, 213, though it may be even older; by Luther's day it had become proverbial.

also such for all Christians, who believe in the God who gives life to the dead (Rom. 4:17) and regards the deceased as living.

This is the Christian doctrine and the wisdom of God, the science of the saints, the sublime knowledge beyond the comprehension of the world: "Death, where is your sting? Where is your victory?" (1 Cor. 15:55.) In the midst of death we are in life. "I shall not die" (Ps. 118:17). Let him who has this skill give thanks to God. But we must take pains that we not only speak of it theoretically but cling to it in fact and with our whole heart.

If it is asked from what source the fathers drew this wisdom, Paul answers (1 Cor. 10:4): "From the spiritual Rock which followed the people in the desert," that is, from the knowledge of Christ, the promised Deliverer.

The Law and carnal wisdom do not understand these things, just as at that time that sight of the two was hidden to the entire world but was known and highly pleasing to God and the angels, while for men and devils it was horrible and frightening. For whenever the devil sees a human being acting in faith, he is frightened, in accordance with the statement in 1 Cor. 4:9: "We have become a spectacle to the world, to angels and to men." If this is understood of the wicked angels, it is a horrible spectacle; if it is understood of the good angels, it is a pleasing spectacle, as is stated in 1 Peter 1:12: "Into which angels long to look." For God and the angels are glad to look at those wonderful works: the victory over death, the destruction of sin, Isaac returning and restored to life from the ashes, and made the father of nations from nothing.

There was a great light of faith in that young man. He believed in God the Creator, who calls into existence the things that do not exist (Rom. 4:17), and commands the ashes that are not Isaac to be Isaac. For he who believes that God is the Creator, who makes all things out of nothing, must of necessity conclude that therefore God can raise the dead. "Why is it thought incredible by any of you that God raises the dead?" asks Paul (Acts 26:8).

Hence these examples show that we should learn to believe that life and death are alike for the godly. If they live, they die; if they die, they live, just as is taught and pointed out throughout the entire New Testament that all the works of Christians are wonders. Ps. 4:3: "The Lord makes His saint wonderful." Christ says (John 14:12): "Greater works than these will he do who believes in Me, and I go to the Father," that I may be almighty in you. These marvelous works terrify the demons, delight the angels, and comfort the godly.

But away with the ungodly, lest he see the glory of God! For the world does not see the Spirit of truth; nor does it know Him. "You know Him, for He dwells with you and will be in you" (John 14:17). The Jews indeed saw Christ raising Lazarus (John 11:45), and Peter healing with his shadow (Acts 5:15). Thus our opponents see that we want to take care of all men with the Gospel. They also see our works of love, humility, and patience. But even though they see, they do not see. Even if the Holy Spirit displays such works as unmistakably strike their very eyes and ears, so that they can be grasped with the hands, they nevertheless do not see. Therefore they speak irreverently against us and against the Spirit, who speaks and works in us, and they cry out that all this is the work of the devil.

But the Holy Spirit has been clearly exhibited to their eyes, and His works and wonders are seen in the Word and in the sacraments. Consequently, even the stones, if they were not devoid of reason, could see and bear witness. Yet they do not see. Why? Because Christ says (John 14:17): "The world cannot receive Him."

But he who [29] can believe in accordance with the First Commandment that God is the Creator of heaven and earth will not argue or have any doubts about the resurrection of the dead. On the other hand, he who does not believe that God can, and wants to, raise the dead believes nothing at all, just as the pope, the cardinals, and the bishops do not believe in a resurrection of the dead. Therefore one concludes on the basis of an infallible inference that they do not believe that there is a God. Because they deny His works, they believe nothing about His majesty and power, of which one is aware in the resurrection of the dead.

Therefore let him who is able to do so expand upon this account and meditate on it with all his heart, in order that he may have it as an excellent example for the strengthening of faith and then for refuting the foolish ideas concerning the obedience of the papists and concerning the monastic vows on which they bestow high praise. But they regard this account with supreme contempt, because Abraham was the head of a household, a layman, and a husband. They say: "These are civil and mundane works. We do spiritual works. We forsake the world."

---

[29] Here the Weimar edition has *quia*, but with the Erlangen editors we have read *qui*.

But if someone wanted to persuade the monks that Abraham was a priest and bishop, they would proclaim him a heretic. For they define a priest as one who has a long robe and a shaved head, who reads the canonical hours. Apart from this notion they know of no priest, just as though God approved of those priests who howl in the church. They are priests of the devil; but Abraham is truly a priest, because he sacrifices not only cattle but his son. And here indeed the rite of immolation is described. Abraham bound Isaac and wanted to kill him like an animal.

To this they give no consideration, nor do they place much emphasis on it. For Abraham does not have a shaved head. He has no chasuble or anointed fingers. He grows a beard and is a husband. Had he had a harlot and illegitimate children, they would have greater praise for him.

But we, in turn, detest them and condemn them as idolatrous and devilish, and we declare that those are true priests who believe the Word of God, offer the sacrifice of praise and of the cross, and do not walk about in long garments but walk about in the gifts and jewels of the Holy Spirit: faith, patience in death, and the expectation of another and better life.

Let these statements be enough about this truly spiritual account which I indeed, being carnal and one of the feet of the ass that does not ascend the mountain, cannot fully comprehend or expound. Nevertheless, I, insignificant as I am, wanted to present as much as I could consider and understand.

11. *But the angel of the Lord called to him from heaven and said: Abraham, Abraham! And he said: Here am I.*

Here one can see how the saints are admirable to the angels and God's showpieces. For they themselves are works of God. An angel from heaven was present here and observed Abraham during the entire action. Indeed, God Himself in heaven and all the angels were onlookers. Nor did the angel come flying from afar from the ends of the world, but he stood over Abraham, fixed his eyes on Isaac, and saw how Abraham bound his son and brought the knife close to his throat, and how the son proved his obedience and willingly awaited the thrust.[30] Perhaps Abraham shed tears. His son lay on his back

---

[30] We have accepted the suggestion of the Erlangen editors and read *ictum* for *istum*.

with his eyes fixed toward heaven. These things the angel beheld, and when the knife has already been drawn, he cries out and calls Abraham by name. So close do the angels post themselves and direct their eyes toward us when we are godly.

This obedience gave God extraordinary pleasure. For of all the sacrifices the one most acceptable to God is this: to kill sin, to live in righteousness, holiness, obedience, and mortification of the flesh. This is indeed painful and difficult for us; but one must learn to accustom oneself, as Paul says (Rom. 12:2), to "what is the good will of God."

We merely talk about these things, but Abraham and Isaac actually did them. And this is the perfect will for God. It has not even begun in us. To God it is well-pleasing and good; to us it is unpleasant and disagreeable. Nothing is more agonizing than the mortification of the flesh and sin. For this reason it seems horrible and impossible, and we shun and hate it. Nevertheless, one must accustom oneself to it and make a beginning, in accordance with the example of Abraham, who does not shun it but waits for it with the utmost readiness. The purpose of his being here is that his son may be killed and that life may follow death.

This is a work done in faith — a work in which the angels are wont to rejoice, even in us, when we are engaged in a Christian office and work. Compared with this, the righteousness and obedience of the papists is not only obscured but seems altogether filthy and loathsome, because these are all self-chosen works. Similarly, many kings and people have imitated the example of Abraham; but they sinned grievously and had no understanding of true mortification.

In *The Lives of the Fathers* there is a story about a certain hermit who had withdrawn into the desert with his only son. It was his intention to forsake the world. When the boy wept there, he wanted to throw him into a nearby river and drown him.[31] The monks greatly exalt and praise this work and liken it to Abraham's work. But it is like the work of the devil in Paradise. And if the hermit had killed his son, he would have been a murderer. So would any others who would have followed his example or approved of it. The reason is this, that without the Word no obedience pleases God.

But the papists, those priests of Baal, do not accept this reason

[31] This is apparently a reference to the anecdote told in *Vitae Patrum*, IV, 45, *Patrologia, Series Latina*, LXXIII, 842.

but cry out stubbornly against it and declare that we condemn good works. We, however, assert that a good work is what is done in faith and in obedience to God by a man who believes that God is the Creator, the Preserver, and the One who raises from the dead. But a monk, a priest of Baal, a Turk, and a Jew does not walk in the obedience of God, does he? Not at all, because he has no command of God.

Thus Ahaz did a great work (2 Kings 16:3), but it was contrary to God and His Word. Therefore the statement in Micah 6:7 is correct: "Shall I give my first-born for my transgression?" The answer is no, because there is no command to do so. Abraham had an extraordinary command of God. But others did not have the same command, for God does not say in general that anyone who offers his son to God pleases God.

We cannot all do one and the same work, just as in the case of the human body there must be different functions of its different members. The feet do not make anything; the hands do not walk. But there is one obedience and one Holy Spirit. But obedience should be certain concerning faith, which does not exist where there is no divine promise. Nor do the works please Him where there is no command of God. The papists and the Turks are full of faith. But it is an invented faith, because they say: "This is how I shall believe; therefore I shall please God in this manner." But this is something self-chosen in accord with one's own imagination. Consequently, it is a devotion that pertains to the devil, not to God.

Accordingly, this extraordinary example of Abraham should not be dragged along as a precedent to be followed; but we should imitate his obedience and his faith in the resurrection, in the killing of sin and death which takes place in Abraham and in his son. Then let everyone, in his own place and station, remain in the same faith, and let everyone obey God. In this manner we shall be partners of the angels, guests and table companions in the kingdom of God.

Besides, at this point the question can be raised why the angels have appeared less frequently among us and generally in the New Testament than in the Old Testament. My answer is that this happens because the Son, the Heir of all things, has appeared and has been sent. Indeed, previously ministers and messengers were sent out in advance, as is customarily done by princes and kings in the world, to remind the people of the coming of the Lord; but when He Himself is present, there is no need of ministers and forerunners.

After God had sent His Son, He revealed all things and filled the earth with heavenly wisdom, to which the signs and wonders performed by Christ bear witness, as St. Paul says 1 Tim. 3:16: "God was manifested in the flesh, justified in the Spirit, etc." For this reason appearances of angels should not be wished for.

After Christ's manifestation the devil horribly deluded the world by sending into it apparitions and wicked angels, as the examples of bygone times show. But this was a punishment for the ingratitude of people who despised the Lord when He Himself was present and who sought new revelations out of empty curiosity.

Thus at the beginning of the restoration of the Gospel,[32] Münzer, Carlstadt, and the Sacramentarians arose. They abandoned the Gospel, which had been given through the Holy Spirit from heaven, and were on the lookout for extraordinary illuminations. Some arrived at such a degree of folly that they boasted of hearing the voice of God speaking in heaven.

At this point it was imperative that the truth and light of the Gospel be adduced in contradiction, and one had to contend against fanatics of this kind who believed that the will of God is to be investigated apart from the Word. Such people were formerly the enthusiasts, likewise the Manichaeans and all the heretics. They all wanted to be like the patriarchs, to whom the oracles of God were revealed more and more clearly until Christ, the Light Itself, came into this world.

Thus the popes have invented new ravings on the basis of a false understanding of the promise of Christ when He says in John 16: 12-13: "I have yet many things to say to you, but you cannot bear them now. When the Spirit of truth comes, He will guide you into all the truth." They have made up the falsehood that not everything necessary for our salvation was transmitted by Christ and the apostles, but that many pronouncements were held back for the bishops and for themselves — pronouncements to be set forth more and more clearly to the church.[33]

[32] By "the restoration of the Gospel" Luther means the Reformation; cf. *Luther's Works*, 24, p. 47, note 28.

[33] See, for example, Nicolaus Herborn, *Locorum communium adversus huius temporis haereses Enchiridion* (1529), X, ed. Patricius Schlager, *Corpus Catholicorum*, 12 (Münster in Westfalen, 1927), p. 49.

To all these ravings one should adduce in contradiction the words of Christ (Luke 16:29): "They have Moses and the prophets." Likewise: "The Lord Himself is coming. Here let the gates be lifted up that He may come in" (cf. Ps. 24:7-8). For He is not a servant, as Moses or the ministering spirits are; He is the Lord Himself.

These things should be taught, and they should also be transmitted to our descendants, in order that they may shun and abhor the revelation of new doctrines and may observe the heavenly command (Matt. 17:5), "Listen to Him," that is, to the evangelists and the apostles. Let them read and listen to these, likewise to the Old Testament, which bears faithful testimony concerning all these things.

But if anything beyond this is revealed, it must have the analogy of faith and must be a revelation of the understanding of Scripture; otherwise it is of the devil. Satan has indeed often tempted me to demand a sign from God, just as he also tempted Augustine, who prays that no angel appear to him.[34] But far be it from me to yield to this temptation. Without an appearance of angels, and strengthened by the Word alone, the martyrs met death for the sake of the name of Christ. Why should we, too, not be satisfied with the same thing? Baptism is a sufficiently manifest and clear appearance. So are the Eucharist, the Keys, the ministry of the Word. They are equal to — yes, they even surpass — all the appearances of all angels, in comparison with which Abraham had only droplets and crumbs.

Hence I am not concerned about angels, and I have the habit of praying God daily not to send any angel to me for any reason whatever.[35] But if one were to present himself, I would not listen to him; but I would turn away, unless he were to point out something concerning an exigency of the state, just as all pleasant and happy dreams in civil matters are sometimes wont to make us glad.[36] Yet I do not know whether even in such an event I would want to listen to him and believe him.

[34] Luther may be thinking of Augustine, *De vera religione*, 55, 110, *Patrologia, Series Latina*, XXXIV, 170. For Augustine's exegesis of the passage at hand cf. *De Trinitate*, Book III, ch. 11, 25.

[35] Luther is referring here to angels as bearers of private revelations, for his own morning and evening prayers contained the petition: "Let Thy holy angel [or angels] have charge of me," *Small Catechism, The Book of Concord*, pp. 324 to 325.

[36] See the earlier discussion of dreams in these lectures, *Luther's Works*, 3, pp. 11—12.

But in spiritual matters we should not regard the angels as necessary, because God's promise has been amply displayed and made manifest in Christ. He has left me His Word, with which I instruct and strengthen myself. Nor is it the case that I fear that He is so fickle and changeable that sometimes He proclaims one doctrine and sometimes another. Thus Num. 23:19 states: "God is not man, that He should lie, or a son of man, that He should repent." We have the Word of God, the Eucharist, Baptism, the Ten Commandments, matrimony, ordinances of the state, and the administration of the household. Let us be satisfied with these and occupy ourselves with them until the end of the world.

Gregory, as can be observed in his dialogs, put faith in absolutely all apparitions.[37] Thus, among other things, many things were invented concerning the Festival of St. Michael: that Michael consecrated a church on Mt. Gargarus, that he stabbed an ox which had plowed on that festival day.[38] I would have said: "What do you have to do with Mt. Gargarus, whose lord is the King of Apulia? You are not Michael; you are the devil."

The books of the papists are full of such lies, and this is our own fault. Because we were unwilling to listen to the Lord and demanded angels, revelations, and apparitions, we, to our own great harm, find in abundance what we sought.

This is Paul's opinion in 2 Thess. 2:10-11: "Because they refused to love the truth and so be saved, therefore God sends upon them a strong delusion, to make them believe what is false." We have despised that teacher of whom it was said (Matt. 17:5) "Listen to Him," and also (Luke 4:18), "The Spirit of the Lord is upon Me, etc." We had itching ears, and when we turned them away from the truth, we wandered into myths (2 Tim. 4:3-4). For this reason we have found people who scratched our ears.

If I were a king and had sent my only son to someone, at the same time offering him the kingdom and all its riches, and he spurned so great a favor, I would send him trouble and all kinds of evil. Similarly, when we did not accept the Gospel which was confirmed by signs from heaven, did we not deserve to get an entire legion of devils in place of the one good angel Abraham saw?

[37] Luther frequently makes this complaint about Gregory I; see, for example, *Luther's Works*, 22, p. 273; 24, p. 370.

[38] Cf. also *Luther's Works*, 3, p. 232.

12. *He said: Do not lay your hand on the lad or do anything to him.*

At this point another question arises. How was Abraham able to obey the voice of the angel and to refrain from killing his son? What if he had been in doubt and had thought that it was not an angel but a devil? For he had God's explicit command: "Kill your son and offer him as a burnt offering." In spite of this command he is ordered to spare the lad.

The earlier trial was in conflict with the promise of the Seed. But this has been overcome, since Abraham had now made up his mind about being obedient, and Isaac had accepted the comfort that even though he would be reduced to ashes, the promise would nevertheless remain, and God would raise him from the dead. In spite of all this the angel now cries out and says: "Do not do anything to the lad." Here Abraham's trial conflicts with the command, just as his previous trial had conflicted with the promise.

My answer to the question is this: Holy Scripture declares that it was a real angel, not a counterfeit one, who was bringing the real Word of God. Abraham believed that he would not be speaking in vain, and, when he was now determined about killing his son, the Holy Spirit cautioned him within through the word of the angel as though through an external instrument and restrained the spirit and faith in him. But without the external word Abraham would not have believed the opposite; nor would he have changed his mind.

Then it is also credible that by some extraordinary and secret impulse Abraham restrained his hands contrary to the command, just as in the Old Testament the prophets did many things contrary to the Word, as when Elijah builds an altar on Mt. Carmel and kills the prophets of Baal contrary to what Moses had commanded (Deut. 12:5): "In the place which God will choose, there you shall bring your sacrifices." Elijah did not observe this; neither did Elisha. Likewise there were many prophets in Israel who did not come to Jerusalem to teach there.

All these men had an extraordinary impulse with some prerogative. Thus Samson had a special spirit when he tore the lion to pieces (Judg. 14:6) and without weapons slew a thousand Philistines with the jawbone of an ass (Judg. 15:15). Those extraordinary impulses and heroic spirits are beyond the ordinary rule and conduct, just as we observe some differences among rulers and princes in their direction of state affairs. Some observe the statutes and the common law,

but others do not. Alexander, for example, does not allow himself
to be bound by any laws but forces his way through by some impulse of his. This could not be done at all by others.[39]

We see this in the examples of the heathen. How much more
God has reserved heroes for himself among His own people! With
300 soldiers Gideon destroyed the army of the Midianites. Abraham,
as related above, overcame the four kings with a small band. These
are not ordinary examples; they are miracles which God reserves for
Himself. Thus it is possible that God gave to Abraham a hidden and
special impulse not to kill his son. It seems that in this manner
a simple answer can be given.

But the text adds an outward distinguishing mark, because it
states explicitly that the angel came from heaven. He did not come
after the fashion of Satan. God has established a wonderful distinction. The good angels come with terror, that is, with some majesty.
Thus Ps. 104:4 calls the angels, or ministers, a burning fire. Consequently, the people to whom they came are frightened. Mary, for
example, is very much afraid when she sees the angel (Luke 1:29).
The same thing happens in Dan. 8:17. Accordingly, the angels bring
with them a certain majesty.

Thus on this occasion the angel came down from heaven; and
heaven undoubtedly was opened, a strange light appeared, lightning
and fire were seen, and at the same time there was a multitude of
angels. Thoroughly frightened by this majesty, Abraham dropped the
knife and at the same time the thought of killing. Similarly, the
angels appeared on Mt. Sinai with fire and thunder, so that the
people were thrown to the ground. Eventually, however, the good
angels depart with joyfulness and leave the hearts serene and cheerful. This is God's procedure when he sends good angels; and by this
sign Abraham, too, was reminded that a real angel was there.

But a wicked angel, like a serpent, creeps along softly and gently
until he decoys people into smugness and sin. Then he goes away,
leaving horrible fear behind.

In the second place, Abraham has the analogy of faith, because
the angel does not bring him a word that is contrary to the promise.
No, what he says is in agreement with the statement (21:12), "Through
Isaac shall your descendants be named." For the spirits must be

[39] On these *Wundermänner* like Alexander, who "have a special star," see
Luther's discussion, *Luther's Works*, 13, pp. 154 ff.

judged by the analogy of faith. When Satan, for example, commands me through the pope to worship Benno, that notorious idol of Meissen, I examine this command in relation to the rule and norm of faith and see whether it is in agreement with it.[40]

But the analogy of faith is this: "There is no other name under heaven given among men by which we must be saved" (Acts 4:12). Thus there is no analogy between Christ and James of Compostela.[41] Therefore I reject James as an idol, even if an angel were to preach a different gospel (Gal. 1:8) or the idol were to raise the dead.

The promises are simply not subject to modification and change. For this reason Abraham also observed what had been commanded previously, but in such a manner that he examined it in relation to the analogy of the promise concerning the Seed that would come. Lastly, the final cause should also be considered. Therefore there follows:

For now I know that you fear God, seeing you have not withheld your son, your only son, from Me.

The angel wants God to be feared. That final cause the devil does not prescribe. Yet that result, namely, the fear of God, does not exist unless one first has the Word of God. Thus those who have both the discernment of the Spirit and faith can at any time establish the outward difference between the apparitions. For the evil spirit cannot avoid seeking his own glory, just as ungodly and false teachers propose new and unheard-of things, in order that the world may admire their wisdom, not in order that God may be feared.

The second and most certain proof of a good angel is that he comes from heaven. In the third place, there is also agreement with the analogy of faith. Influenced by these considerations, Abraham obeyed the voice of the angel who annulled the command about sacrificing his son. In addition, the Holy Spirit, who is always connected with the Word, undoubtedly had a hand in what took place here.

Passages like this, which seem to be contradictory, give rise to extraordinary debates among clever persons who are vainglorious.

---

[40] Benno was Bishop of Meissen at the end of the eleventh century; Pope Hadrian VI canonized him on May 31, 1523, calling forth Luther's treatise *Against the New Idol and the Old Devil*, W, XV, 170 ff.

[41] The Spanish shrine of St. James, Santiago de Compostela, was a favorite goal of medieval pilgrimages and a favorite object of Luther's polemics; cf., for example, *Luther's Works*, 22, p. 250.

For the devil looks for contradictions; and when he gains nothing by them, he invents fallacies: "God would not be contradicting Himself and have lied, would He? First He commanded Abraham to sacrifice his son; now He forbids it." But we Christians must think and speak about these matters both with respect and with the fear of God, and we must recognize that it is God's nature to do contradictory things when things are contradictory. Nevertheless, this wonderful guidance of the saints reminds us pleasantly of many things and abounds in comfort. And indeed the godly — if this were possible without violating the majesty and truthfulness of God — could employ these expressions: "God is pretending, lying, simulating, and deceiving us," as we have the habit of saying in our proverb: "If it is true, it is a big lie." [42] For when they have to meet death, they can say to God: "It is not death; it is life. Thou art playing with me as a father plays with his son. Thou sayest one thing but hast something else in mind." This is a salutary lie for us.

And how fortunate we would be if we could learn this art from God! He tempts us and proposes a strange work, that He may be able to do His own. Through our affliction He seeks to get His sport and our salvation. God said to Abraham: "Kill your son." How? With playing, simulating, and laughing. Surely a happy and delightful sport!

Thus God sometimes pretends to be withdrawing rather far from us and killing us, but who believes that He is pretending? Yet with God it is a sport and — if we were permitted to express it in this way — a lie. It is indeed a real death that all of us will have to meet, but God does not carry out in earnest what He is showing. He is pretending and is testing us whether we are willing to give up the present things and life itself for God's sake.

Thus Moses says in Deut. 13:1 ff.: "If a prophet arises among you, or a dreamer of dreams, etc., you shall not listen; for the Lord your God is testing you, to know whether you love Him with all your heart and with all your soul."

These are not the words of an angry judge, but they are fatherly words which say: "I have given you My Word, that you may accept it with a tranquil heart, etc.; but I shall send false apostles and test you, whether you are willing to love Me and My Word in earnest."

Thus a father takes an apple away from his boy under some pre-

---

[42] Here Luther once more breaks into German.

tense, not because he wants to deprive him of it but merely to make a test whether his son loves him and believes that his father will give it back. If the son gladly gives up the apple, the father is pleased with his son's obedience and love.

Thus God's testing is a fatherly one, for James says in his letter (1:13): "God is not a tempter for evil"; that is, He does not test in order that we may fear and hate Him like a tyrant but to the end that He may exercise and stir up faith and love in us.

Satan, however, tempts for evil, in order to draw you away from God and to make you distrust and blaspheme God. God sports with the children He loves and, as it seems to the flesh, shows Himself angry and dreadful. Hence there arise the well-known laments "I am driven far from Thy sight" (Ps. 31:22) and "Hide not Thy face from me" (Ps. 27:9). But these are merely instances of sporting. God will not deceive or cheat you. Just hold fast to His infallible and unchanging promise. Even though you should lose honors, riches, and life itself, you should nevertheless not maintain that God is angry with you and therefore has cast you aside; but you should expect other far more excellent gifts, honor, and a better life from Him, as Job 13:15 states: "Even though He kills me, I will hope in Him."

As for the rest, the fathers have interpreted the verb "I know" in this passage as "I have caused you to come to know," [43] that is, to realize that you are one who fears God, just as Peter admonishes us to make our call and election sure and firm by doing good works (2 Peter 1:10). If someone has overcome a trial in this manner, he is made more certain of God's help and can say: "This is sure proof that I have been helped by God, because by my own powers I would not have been able to achieve this." Thus the fruits of the Spirit are called evidences of faith which assure us of our election and call.

Furthermore, in this passage the rule concerning God's twofold cognition or vision should be observed. When Holy Scripture says: "God saw," there a twofold cognition is posited: the one, eternal and invisible, by which God sees things before they are in existence; the other, by which he observes things that exist. By means of that second vision, with which He looks at existing things, God did not see Mary before she existed, and yet He saw her from eternity. Thus God saw all the creatures before they were made, and now that they have been made, it is also said that He sees or knows them.

---

[43] Cf. pp. 152—154 on the causative significance of the Piel and Hiphil in Hebrew.

God is speaking in the same manner in this passage: "Now I know"; that is, now I judge and see in fact that you fear God. Augustine's distinction between morning and evening knowledge has reference to this.[44]

God has some characteristics that are similar to the human power of comprehension. Therefore I think that this expression, "Now I know," must be understood in a simple manner, although I do not reject the explanation of the fathers that God is speaking in human fashion, as though then at last, as a result of that obedience, He had perceived Abraham's godliness and true fear.

Most delightful are the descriptions of this sort, when Scripture speaks about God as if He were a human being and attributes to Him all human qualities, namely, that He converses with us in a friendly manner and about matters similar to those which human beings discuss; that He is glad, is sad, and suffers like a human being because of the mystery of the future incarnation.

Our reason for reading and searching the Old Testament is to see foretold, not only in words but also by means of various figures and deeds, that Christ would become man.

Thus we love those expressions of Scripture when God is described in terms of human form and actions: "Why do You sleep?" (Ps. 44:23); "The eyes of the Lord are toward the righteous" (Ps. 34:1); "Thou openest Thy hand" (Ps. 145:16); and any others like them. They are transferred from human beings to God because of the feebleness of our understanding.

And let us be satisfied with this picture, as it were; and let us shun that inquisitiveness of the human intellect, which wants to investigate His majesty. For God's incarnation was foretold in order that we might have a definite pattern for recognizing and taking hold of God.

Next the question is usually considered at this point whether Abraham was justified on the basis of his works, as James argues in his letter (2:21). Because the text says: "Now I see that you are righteous," he wants to conclude from this that previously Abraham was not righteous. But the answer, which the words themselves point out, is easy. For it is one thing, even grammatically speaking, to be righteous and another thing to know that one is righteous.

Abraham was righteous by faith before God acknowledged him

---

[44] Cf. also *Luther's Works*, 1, p. 4, on "morning and evening knowledge."

as such. Therefore James concludes falsely that now at last he was justified after that obedience; for faith and righteousness are known by works as by the fruits. But it does not follow, as James raves: "Hence the fruits justify," just as it does not follow: "I know a tree by its fruit; therefore the tree becomes good as a result of its fruit."

Therefore let our opponents be done with their James, whom they throw up to us so often.[45] They babble much but understand nothing about the righteousness of works.

Indeed, even the sophists make a distinction between perceived being and substantive being.[46] The righteous man does not become righteous by being perceived as such. But he who has been justified by faith, as was stated above about Abraham (ch. 15), is perceived as righteous by the fruits and works.

But one should also note in this passage that when Abraham is praised as one who fears and reveres God, the statement refers not only to his faith but also to his entire worship, to the tree with its fruits, inasmuch as for the Hebrews to fear God is the same as to worship God or to serve God, to love and honor God.

Thus Ps. 14:5 — "They feared where there was no fear" — is not speaking of dread because the ungodly have no dread. No, it is speaking of the worship of the ungodly. They worship God where He is not to be worshiped. Their conscience is seared, as Paul calls it (1 Tim. 4:2), that is, artificial or false, unreasonable, not natural, not true, as when the pope forbids marriage and the eating of meat. Accordingly, the ungodly want to fear God, that is, to worship Him, where there is no true worship of God.

Thus when it is stated (Matt. 15:9): "In vain do they worship Me with the precepts of men," this means the same as saying that they fear Me in vain. For in Holy Scripture the fear of God is the highest form of worship. Hence Jacob (Gen. 31:42) calls the Lord God "Fear" and "Awe." By this he understands nothing else than the Deity Itself.

Accordingly, the ungodly want to be reverent and humble; they walk with their necks bent and their heads shaking like a reed. They desire to appear to be fearing God above all men. Yet they fear and worship in vain.

[45] See, for example, Herborn, *Enchiridion* (cf. p. 125, note 33), III, p. 26.

[46] Luther is referring to a scholastic distinction between *esse cognitum* and *esse substantivum*.

This is truly a common evil throughout the entire world. Our fear, worship, and esteem equal the worship of the angels (Col. 2:18); but our conscience is false and seared. Thus the priests of Baal endured some extreme tortures; they pricked themselves with knives and awls until they bled (1 Kings 18:28). But those were self-chosen marks and not those of which Paul says (Gal. 6:17): "I bear the marks of my Lord."

On the other hand, where fear should be greatest, the ungodly do not fear at all. Indeed, they are exceedingly bold in despising the true worship and treading the Word of God underfoot.

God should be feared nowhere except in His Word, in accordance with the command which says: "You shall not worship strange gods, and you shall not make for yourself a graven image, whatever it may be" (cf. Ex. 20:3-4). Where God is revealed in his Word, there worship Him, there exercise your reverence; then you are fearing where you should fear and tremble.

It is for this reason that we tread underfoot the pope and the sects, who establish forms of worship outside, and contrary to, the Word of God. We do not fear or respect them. They, in turn, condemn the true religion and doctrine and call it heretical. Accordingly, they fear where there is no fear; and where they should fear, they do not fear.

Up to this point Abraham has made ready the sacrifice with his son, although it was not carried out but was merely a preparation for the sacrifice.

13. *And Abraham lifted up his eyes and looked, and behold, behind him was a ram, caught in a thicket by his horns; and Abraham went and took the ram, and offered it up as a burnt offering instead of his son.*

It has been stated above that we can believe piously and reverently that the angel came with extraordinary majesty, with wind and flame, and that Abraham, thoroughly frightened, fell on his face, or at least listened on bended knees when the angel said: "You fear God." But after forbidding the killing the angel disappeared. There Abraham remains alone with his son; and when they lift up their eyes and look about, they see a ram behind them. (The emphasis is on the phrase "behind them.") The ram is held fast. He has been caught in the tangled and intertwined briars.

The Hebrew word סְבַךְ properly denotes wild branches that are spread out and grow without any definite order. Those branches held the horns of the ram.

In Ps. 74:5 we read: "At the upper entrance they [Thy foes] hacked the wooden trellis with axes." This means that God's foes stormed against the sanctuary exactly as if a forest or a vineyard planted with trees were being cut down, or as if the temple or sanctuary were a jumbled and tangled forest. Others have imagined that סְבַךְ is the name of the place.[47] But it is a common noun. The ram was at the foot of the mountain. He was held back among the briars and bushes.

At this point it is customary to ask where this ram came from. The Jews say that he was created on the sixth day together with the rest of the animals and that by a divine decree he was preserved up to that time.[48] We Christians know that with God creating and preserving are identical. No one who knows the Creator's power will discuss rather inquisitively where the ram came from. Scotus discusses where God will get the fire with which to burn the world on Judgment Day.[49] What more stupid question or thought can there be? Evidently the only mistakes wise men make are enormous mistakes. But in order to say something concerning the question that has been put, let us remember this, that Holy Scripture points out that God is wont to bring forth through the voice of an angel or some servant things that did not exist or to multiply things that do exist.

At the word of the man Moses water flows from the rock and quails are scattered throughout the camp. If God has one quail, He has 100,000 or an unlimited number. Thus He takes five loaves and feeds 5,000 persons.

If we believe that everything was created by God's power out of nothing, why should we not also believe this, that He can multiply and increase what is already in existence? Where do snow and rain often come from so suddenly? Now the sky is clear; one moment later, when He pleases, He sends snow or rain.

---

[47] The word was interpreted as a proper noun in the translation of the Septuagint: Σαβὲκ τῶν κεράτων.

[48] Cf. the materials collected in Louis Ginzberg, *The Legends of the Jews,* I (Philadelphia, 1954), p. 282.

[49] Cf. Claudius Frassen (ed.), *Scotus Academicus,* IV (Rome, 1900), pp. 422 to 431.

In 1 Kings 17:14 Elijah tells the widow of Zarephath: "The jar of meal shall not be spent, and the cruse of oil shall not fail." Through this word the widow and her family are supported during that entire time of famine. Indeed, even her son, who had died, is brought back to life. Thus in 2 Kings 4:42 Elisha commands his servant: "Give the people bread. They shall be satisfied"; and 100 men were satisfied with 20 loaves of barley bread. How much more, therefore, are the angels able to do this! For God it is not impossible to produce — through a power that is, so to speak, ordered and mediated [50] — a ram from the briars themselves when the angel speaks. How much more could He do so if He wanted to make use of His unmediated power, as when He changes the fire in the furnace into something that cools! [51]

Therefore I find no fault with saying either that the ram was brought there by the angel or that he was brought into existence at the angel's command. I prefer to believe the latter.

Nevertheless, it does not seem to have been a rash statement on the part of the fathers when they said that the ram was provided from the beginning of the world; for they knew about Christ, the woman's Seed, and understood this ram to be a figure of Him.

For Christ existed before the creation, as Paul says (Titus 1:2): "God, who never lies, promised ages ago." Hence before the ages, from eternity, Christ was destined by divine providence to crush the head of the serpent, to become the sacrifice for the human race, to kill sins, and to give us life. But He waited until the predetermined time of His appearance arrived. This is a sufficiently good allegory. I do not disapprove of it.

But after they had seen the ram — no matter how he had been brought there by God — Abraham took him and offered him as a burnt offering in his son's place. There Isaac was the acolyte and assisted his father in bringing the sacrifice. Moreover, that ram was a sign by which Abraham was convinced that the ram was to be offered, not Isaac. Thus some sign is always attached to the Word, for Abraham realized at once that the ram had been provided by

[50] Luther is employing the scholastic distinction between *potestas ordinata* and *potestas absoluta;* cf. Thomas Aquinas, *Summa Theologica,* I—I, Q. 25, Art. 5.

[51] This is probably an allusion to the story of the three men in the fiery furnace, Dan. 3:8-30; it may be a paraphrase of the apocryphal addition to the story: "But the angel of the Lord came down into the furnace . . . and drove the fiery flame out of the furnace, and made the midst of the furnace like a moist whistling wind."

God for the sacrifice. Otherwise it would have been useless for him to prepare the altar and the other things necessary for the sacrifice.

14. *So Abraham called the name of that place The Lord Will See; as it is said to this day: On the mount the Lord will see.*

It is the universal opinion of all translators that one should keep the passive voice in this passage and read: "On the mount the Lord will be seen." And I have no doubt that Jerome originally translated it this way. But it was changed because of the error of some wiseacre or scribe who thought that the latter clause should be in harmony with the one that precedes it.[52]

About the mountain, or rather about the land of Moriah, we have spoken above. It was a place for revering and worshiping God, and on it the fathers brought sacrifices.

But I prefer to follow the opinion of Burgensis, who is both versed in the Hebrew language and scholarly in interpreting the meaning of Scripture.[53] He thinks that one should read: "On the mount the Lord will see," and as his reason for this opinion he states that above Abraham had answered his son's question about the sheep: "The Lord will see"; that is, "He will provide." It is as though he meant to say: "Even if we do not know, He knows where we shall get the sheep for the burnt offering. Let Him see to it."

I cannot condemn this explanation. For the Lord did see; that is, He took care that those words of Abraham to his son — "The Lord will provide" — were fulfilled. Because of this the name The Lord Will See was given to the mountain, as though Abraham were saying: "The Lord is looking at and caring for this place."

And this meaning has reference, as it were, to Mt. Moriah, on which God was worshiped. Accordingly, this name, The Lord Will See, has a correlative relation, so to speak, to those who are on the mountain and worship God; for God, in turn, has regard for them and hears them. Therefore this mountain, which long ago was sacred because of the religious practice of the fathers — as was stated above — is now also consecrated by God Himself, since He sanctifies and cares for both the place and those who come there as worshipers.

Consequently, the name of the mountain abounds in comfort; for

[52] Jerome, *Liber hebraicarum quaestionum in Genesin, Patrologia, Series Latina,* XXIII, 1021.

[53] Paulus Burgensis (cf. p. 99, note 10) *ad* Gen. 22:14.

it implies a relation between him who fears — that is, calls upon God and gives thanks — and God, who accepts or hears vows and prayers — between him who adores and Him who is adored.

Inasmuch as the place had been appointed previously for the worship of God, Abraham is now fully assured that God is present there and inclines His eyes and ears toward all who worship and adore at this place.

Therefore even though it is more correct to retain the passive, as the Hebrews want to do, nevertheless the word has commonly been turned from a passive into an active, so as to signify that God is at that place and directs watchful eyes toward those who worship Him.

Thus when Jacob was on his way to Mesopotamia and at night in a dream saw a ladder and the angels of God ascending and descending on it, he said: "How awesome is this place! This is none other than the house of God and the gate of heaven" (Gen. 28:17); that is, at this place God has to be feared, here thanks must be given to Him and sacrifices brought. Thus this mountain, The Lord Will See, was regarded as sacred throughout all posterity, and the fathers, because of some feeling of piety and reverence, included it in their worship, so that he who wanted to see God came there because God would not only appear and be seen there but would also see.

It is as though they meant to say: "Now it should be called Epiphany, because God looks, appears, is heard, is seen, and reveals Himself through the Word, through hearing prayers, and through all His other benefits." This is an improper use of the word and a change in the meaning, not, however, with evil intent but rather for giving comfort.

But because God not only sees, and looks at, this place — which would not be enough for us — but is also seen by us and appears to us, it follows that "The Lord will be seen" was read where formerly "He will see" used to be read. Moreover, I think that mountain was the place for oracles. Rebecca later on consulted that "He will be seen" (Gen. 25:22); that is, she sought advice from the patriarch Shem, who was a priest of the Lord and undoubtedly taught and preached at that place.

15. *And the angel of the Lord called to Abraham a second time from heaven and said:*

This is the last conversation the Lord had with Abraham, and now the account of Abraham will be brought to a conclusion. But at this point I urge again what I have stated repeatedly, namely, that in the Holy Scriptures and the accounts they record one should take note above all of the Word and addresses of God, which one does not hear in legends that do not say anything. Holy Scripture alone has the appearances of the Lord.

Moreover, how impressive Abraham's glory is, since he enters so often into conversation with God! We find that God conversed with him eight times. Our legends in the churches of the Gentiles have nothing like this, and it is an absurd procedure on the part of all men to regard works with greater admiration than that with which they regard the Word of God, who is the Author and Producer of all marvelous and most difficult works. Nevertheless, we turn our eyes toward the works alone; but we suppose that the voice of God is the voice of human beings. For no difference is perceptible between the word of man and the Word of God when uttered by a human being; for the voice is the same, the sound and the pronunciation are the same, whether you utter divine or human words. For this reason we withdraw from the majesty of the Word and are not concerned about that "The Lord will be seen" or the appearance of God. We pay no attention to God when He speaks with us. Meanwhile we admire those revolting works of the Carthusians.

Therefore the Word of God must be given consideration first of all; and if someone were to perform all sorts of miracles, yes, even to raise the dead, and comes without the Word, he must be repudiated. All the apostles and prophets have diligently given this warning, and in Deut. 13:9 ff. Moses says that a false prophet and inventor of dreams must be killed, "because," as he states, "he has spoken to draw you away from the Lord your God."

We should be disturbed by our danger and be prudent, because the pope has established his tyranny without the Word by miracles of that sort. Thus they make the silly assertion about Pope Sixtus that when once upon a time he was in peril at sea, he gave an order to the sea and said: "If I am the vicar of Christ, let the boisterous sea be still," and that this suddenly happened.[54]

By this miracle they have proved that the pope is the vicar of Christ, just as they have deceived the wretched people with many other miracles, either true or invented, and likewise with the piety, abstinence, vigils, and hardships of the monks.

[54] Apparently a reference to the legends about Pope Sixtus II (d. 258), whose name is mentioned in the Canon of the Mass.

We ourselves should bear this in mind and also impress it on our youth, that they may learn to beware of and hate these hideous works and, on the other hand, to love the Word of God and to esteem it highly. For it is above all things and creates all things: that most beautiful sun, the soul, the body, and whatever this world contains.

Why, then, do we bestow such great praise on the works themselves, no matter how splendid they are? Let us rather marvel at the Performer and Author of the works and first of all be sure whether the things that are praised as miracles were done through the Word of God or not.

But the papists say: "How could those things be done if they were not the will of God?" This is indeed correct. God wants and permits these things to happen as a punishment for the loathing and contempt of the Word. Paul says that God has sent them, not a simple error but a power and ἐνέργεια of error to permeate and overcome them (cf. 2 Thess. 2:10-11).

Therefore let the pope above all prove by the Word of God that Pope Sixtus is the vicar of Christ. "It is written," they say, "in Matt. 16:18: 'You are Peter, and on this rock I will build My church.'" Very well! But by this very statement Christ wants Peter to be a confessor and minister of the Word, not a tyrant who would burden consciences with human traditions. Nor should he destroy the knowledge of Christ; for this is being the Antichrist, not the vicar of Christ.

Therefore even if either Sixtus or anyone else were to raise the dead, I would spit in his face and say that he is impelled, not by the Holy Spirit but by an unclean spirit, because he does not bring a Word of God.

Accordingly, we set the Word in opposition to works, just as they, in turn, set works in opposition to the Word. To be sure, they have this advantage, that men are more impressed by the outward appearance and splendor of works than by the Word; but we discuss these accounts so painstakingly in order that consideration may be given to the main point in them. They themselves do not see this; but they say that Abraham was a layman, that he had domestics, and that he wandered about in countries as a poor man and an exile. They do not see that he was full of patience, humility, and love. They pay far less attention to the words God speaks with him. If praise were bestowed on strange and quaint dress, fastings, and pious gestures, they would applaud and commend him. But because he had a wife, domestics, and cattle, they say that he is a carnal-minded man. But away with them and their hideous works!

Let us stoutly maintain and believe that the Word of God is all in all. If you believe this, great and wonderful works will not be lacking; but they will be of such a kind that they do not catch the eyes of the wicked and are not acknowledged by the world.

Through the Word and prayers we have done many difficult things. By means of prayers we are still preserving peace and are thwarting the efforts and plots of our adversaries. But the godly alone see these things. They have the Holy Spirit and esteem highly those truly spiritual and wonderful works: Baptism, the Eucharist, absolution, constant attendance in one's calling, and obedience to parents and superiors. Because all these things are common and done every day, the papists disdain them.

16. *By Myself I have sworn, says the Lord.*

The majestic God not only promises but also swears, and indeed by Himself, as the words indicate. If He had a greater one than Himself, He would gladly swear by him; but because He does not, He swears by Himself. Our people have the custom to swear "by their troth" and "upon their soul." This is not a trivial oath, although, if one takes people into consideration, it is a very trivial one, because they are deceitful and untruthful. Actually, however, it is no different from swearing by God Himself.

Just as Christ explains in Matt. 5:34 ff.: "But I say to you: Do not swear at all, either by heaven, for it is the throne of God, or by the earth. And do not swear by your head, for you cannot make one hair white or black." Hence it will be far [55] less permissible to swear by the soul; and the reason is this, that an oath by the hairs, heaven, the earth, etc., is taken by a creature of God, that is, by what is not ours or in our power. Therefore oaths of that kind include God Himself, even though the name of God is not expressed. Thus whenever the Holy Scriptures say: "As my soul lives," this is an oath by God, whose creature the soul is.

Moreover, the fact that God swears by Himself is something great and wonderful. The author of the Epistle to the Hebrews saw this here and weighed it carefully (6:13). For it is an indication of

[55] We have followed the Erlangen edition and read *multo* here rather than *multa,* as the Weimar edition has it.

a heart burning with inexpressible love and with a desire for our salvation, as though God were saying: "I desire so greatly to be believed and long so intensely to have My words trusted that I am not only making a promise but am offering Myself as a pledge. I have nothing greater to give as a pledge, because as surely as I am God, there is nothing greater than I. If I do not keep My promises, I shall no longer be He who I am."

This is surely something astounding and worthy of the highest degree of attention. For this is what the divine truth wants to point out: "You, man, are fickle, inconstant, and changeable; therefore I am adding My unalterable oath. With this I want to bear witness that rather than deceive you I shall not be God."

If God had sworn merely with the words "I shall sooner let heaven, the earth, the sun, the moon, and the very beautiful structure of the entire world perish than permit My promise to become of no effect," it would surely be something of great importance and no less marvelous.

But God adds something else — something of far greater moment, far more sacred: "I, who am God and have the power to destroy or to create heaven and earth, swear and give as a pledge, not a creature, not heaven and earth, but Myself, the Creator of all things."

This sacred oath will condemn all those who do not believe, just as it stirred up and increased the faith of the holy fathers in a marvelous manner. For they thought: "God has promised life and deliverance from death and the devil, and He has sworn by Himself. This is our אוּרִים and תֻּמִּים (Ex. 28:30). Therefore if we do not believe, we shall be condemned."

Accordingly, let us also bear in mind that God enlarges His promise to such an outstanding extent that it surpasses all thinking and faith; for He strengthens and confirms it by His majesty, in order that we may have no reason whatever to mistrust and doubt.

Surely, this is condescension. God accommodates Himself completely to our weakness. It should be enough if He moved one finger to bear witness of His fatherly goodwill toward us. But now He offers us His Word, and He not only promises but even takes an oath and invokes evil upon and curses Himself — if one were permitted to speak this way — in order to bless us.

Moreover, we should refrain from debates about predestination and from similar discussions. They are fraught with danger and mischief, because they inquire into the will and hidden counsels of God apart from the Word. They want to investigate and explore too inquisitively why God has revealed Himself in one way or another, and why He so earnestly endeavors to persuade our will to believe. The inquisitiveness of Adam is well known. In Paradise he sought God apart from the Word, just as Satan did in heaven. Both found Him, but not without great harm.

Therefore let us learn that God must be apprehended, not with our reason but as He has revealed Himself and has condescended to speak and deal with us in human fashion. Indeed, we should joyfully welcome the Divine Majesty, who comes down to us with such humility that He not only invites us to Himself with promises but by inserting an oath even compels us to accept what the Word offers.

This same doctrine is set forth in an excellent manner in the Epistle to the Hebrews (6:16-18): "Men indeed swear by a greater than themselves, and in all their disputes an oath is final for confirmation. So when God desired to show more convincingly to the heirs of the promise the unchangeable character of His purpose, He interposed with an oath, so that through two unchangeable things, in which it is impossible that God should prove false, we who have fled for refuge might have strong encouragement to seize the hope set before us."

What could be said or thought that is surer and more powerful for increasing and strengthening our faith? And what else are we doing with our incredulity or doubt than accusing God of lying when He promises and swears, and saying, while we defy Him to His face, as it were: "Lord God, Thou art lying!"?

But how many are there who would pay any attention to such an awful and exceedingly common blasphemy — a blasphemy which by nature is firmly established in the hearts of all human beings? For they either smugly despise and hate the words and promises, or if they sometimes hear them, they say that they have doubts and do not know whether God is compassionate to such an extent and whether He is concerned about and hears those who call upon Him, and especially the unworthy and sinners.

But when the heart has doubts, as that person says,[56] it is also driven in a short moment to blasphemy and despair. For this reason St. Paul so often urges us to have full assurance (πληροφορία), that

---

[56] A quotation from Terence, *Andria*, I, line 268, with some additions.

is, a firm and unshakeable knowledge of God's will toward us, which gives assurance to our consciences and fortifies them against all uncertainty and mistrust.

The teaching of the pope is all the more detestable because it not only disregards this but even wickedly maintains that one should have doubts; that is, he publicly declares God a liar, even though He promises, swears, pledges His majesty, and curses Himself.

But how much evil there is in a wicked and blasphemous dogma the outward sins prove: greed, lust, and shameful acts of every kind, which, like the evil fruits from a corrupt tree, originate from a blasphemous heart which does not think that God is truthful, whether He promises, commands, or threatens those who transgress His commands.

Therefore the Epistle to the Hebrews earnestly reminds us of the immutability of God's counsel and promise, lest we attribute fickleness and untrustworthiness to God.

Thus Paul says in his Epistle to Titus (1:2): "God, who never lies." "What purpose does it serve," you will say, "to give these admonitions so carefully? For who has had the audacity to say that God lies? Do not the pope, the Turks, and the Jews also maintain that God is truthful, just, wise, and good?"

But when they say this most, they imagine most of all that God is untruthful, unjust, and unwise; for they have no other knowledge of God than a philosophical or metaphysical one, namely, that God is a being separate from the creatures, as Aristotle says — a being that is truthful and contemplates the creature within itself.[57] But of what concern is this to us? The devil, too, has such a knowledge of God and knows that He is truthful. But when knowledge is imparted about God in theology, God must be known and apprehended, not as remaining within Himself but as coming to us from outside; that is, we must maintain that He is our God.

That first Aristotelian or philosophical god is the god of the Jews, the Turks, and the papists; but he is of no concern to us. But our God is He whom the Holy Scriptures show, because He gives us His epiphany, His appearance, אוּרִים and תֻּמִּים, and speaks with us.

Therefore it is to be deplored that we do not side with and believe this God, who has revealed Himself to us by the Word and by signs. We all have this blasphemy spread through our flesh and

---

[57] See, for example, Aristotle, *Nicomachean Ethics,* Book X, ch. 8.

blood: "I do not know whether God has such great concern for me as He has promised in His Word. I doubt it." What else is this than to think or say that God is a liar?

If lusts, greed, and other sins alone were ruling in us, God would not be so angry. But this root and source of all evils He detests and punishes in an awful manner. In the sacred accounts many kings are praised because of all sorts of good qualities: moderation, generosity, justice, and the like, which human discipline can bring about. What Scripture complains about in regard to them is that they did evil before the Lord, that is, that they disregarded God, who spoke and promised, and worshiped calves and idols, as Jeroboam and others did. For so great is the perversity of the human heart that it accepts strange gods far more readily and eagerly than it maintains that this God, who has revealed Himself through His promises and signs, is truthful. How great a kindness it is that He has redeemed us through His Son! But how difficult it is for us to believe this can be seen in the perils of the plague, famine, exile, and punishments in which we, utterly without any confidence, are troubled and alarmed to the point of being virtually without any hope and promise!

What is the reason? Because on account of original sin there is inherent in us this evil which causes our heart to cry out continually against the promises of God and to grumble that familiar charge: "God is lying; His oath is not true."

If we were able to believe firmly that God will keep His promises and that the oath with which He has pledged his Deity and has given His Son as a sign will be sure, then we would regard death, want, shame, and hell as if they were life, riches, glory, and heaven, just as they differ in no wise before God. But because this does not happen, it is a sure proof of our unbelief and mistrust.

Therefore the papists, the Turks, and the Jews believe absolutely nothing at all. Nor do they understand what sin, mercy, righteousness, truth, and grace are; all these are mere puzzles for them. Yet they want to appear wise, and they are indeed, but in their way, namely, in philosophy, not in the kingdom of heaven, because they have absolutely no understanding of spiritual matters but despise them.

And how would they care about them and be greatly affected by them when we, who want to be godly, find that awful evil in us that we do not rejoice every moment in spirit over that inexpressible mercy of God toward us and do not laugh at and despise death, the world, and the devil?

But this serves to glorify the marvelous patience and mercy of God, who forgives not only past but also present sins and with great tenderness of heart puts up with this common indifference toward His grace.

We have Christ's command. To it a promise is attached. At the same time there is a threat. "Everyone who acknowledges Me before men," He says, "I also will acknowledge before My Father who is in heaven" (Matt. 10:32). "He who does not take his cross and follow Me is not worthy of Me" (Matt. 10:38). In John 12:25-26 He says: "He who hates his life in this world will keep it for eternal life. If anyone serves Me, he must follow Me; and where I am, there shall My servant be also."

Those who are not moved by these and similar statements but put the welfare of the body and the goods of this life ahead of acknowledging Christ assuredly do not hold any other opinion than that God is untruthful when He promises or threatens.

How often it is repeated in the Psalms: "Wait for the Lord; be strong, and let your heart take courage; wait for the Lord!" (Ps. 27:14.) "Love the Lord, all you His saints! The Lord preserves the faithful but abundantly requites him who acts haughtily. Be strong, and let your heart take courage, all you who wait for the Lord!" (Ps. 31:23-24.) We know all this, and it is pointed out to us daily; yet we neither believe nor follow God, who calls us to confess the Word and promises help and deliverance. There certainly is no reason for us to think that God is pleased with that doubt and mistrust in us. Indeed, this one sin is by far the gravest of all the sins which will condemn the world and the unbelievers. For the magnitude of the sin can be gauged from the magnitude of God's promise, oath, pledge, and imprecation.

Therefore whoever has either a droplet or a spark of that spiritual trust should know that it is a blessing of God and an extraordinary gift. If we firmly and unquestioningly held promises of this kind as true, there would be given to our hearts strength far greater than our fear of the world or the devil or all the gates of hell.

Accordingly, these things are dealt with rather frequently, in order that we may stir up our hearts and finally begin to learn at least with the abecedarians; for we shall never be doctors and rabbis in this wisdom. Would that we were pupils of Christ!

Secondly, in order that we may remember that Holy Scripture

gives instruction concerning other and far loftier matters than the arts and the books of the philosophers, which know nothing about God's boundless mercy and truth and have no understanding of how enormous a sin it is when all men attribute the crime of lying to God. For they are unacquainted with the promises we have because of God's kindness.

Hence these words of God's oath should be carefully weighed. God admonishes us like a most compassionate father, spurs us on, and urges us in whatever ways He can; He promises, swears, and pledges Himself with an imprecation of Himself — if it is permitted to speak this way — solely in order that we may believe Him.

But here all the saints had their troubles. It is not without reason that Paul says (Titus 1:2): "God, who never lies." Perhaps he himself was tempted, and perhaps he himself wrestled with that doubt concerning God's mercy and truth. It is as though he were saying: "God has promised, but the world does not want to believe. Indeed, it is difficult for me to overcome my mistrust." For he undoubtedly added this little statement with indignation.

We, too, should acknowledge our wretchedness and weakness. For inasmuch as we are satisfied to some extent with those firstfruits which we have received and do not desire to make progress and advance, we are altogether sluggish with regard to prayer, confession, and giving thanks, and do not maintain that God's oath is true but for the most part have doubts and to that extent think that God is lying and deceiving.

Therefore let us not justify ourselves if God should want to enter into judgment with us, but let us humble ourselves in faith and acknowledge our sin. Let us be sorry that we still have those horrible dregs and remnants of sin through which we make God a liar so far as we are concerned. Furthermore, let us cry: "Have mercy on me, O God, according to Thy abundant mercy, etc. Forgive us our debts."

If we boast of our righteousness and despise weak brethren, it is sure that we do not understand anything about this doctrine, just as the Pharisee in Luke 7:36 ff. despises and condemns the woman who was a sinner. But Christ, on the contrary, counters with: "Know yourself. You do not believe Me when I swear and pledge My majesty. That is the greatest sin; you do not regard Me as God, but you make a graven image for yourself out of your own righteousness."

Our trust will be perfect when life and death, glory and shame, adversity and good fortune will be alike to us. But we shall not attain this through speculation; it will have to be learned in trial and prayer. For here there is no argument about the words "God is truth"; but there is an argument about the subject matter, namely, that God does not lie when He swears and when He promises the greatest blessings, life, and deliverance from sin and hell, and when He so firmly assures every one of us: "You, human being, shall surely live, or I Myself shall not live. Hell has been overcome and destroyed for you, or I Myself shall be destroyed and cease to be God. Indeed, in order that you may have no doubt, you have My Son given to you as a gift."

To believe these most glorious promises and to expect these blessings from God with firm confidence is true faith. And God wants our hearts to be aroused to this confidence not only by the examples of Abraham and others — and not only by His promises — but also because He has given His own Son for us, to be a gift and a pledge of heavenly blessings.

When we compare this doctrine with the traditions of the Jews and the papists, we observe a horrible darkness among both. They teach nothing at all about these matters. "Why do we need faith?" say the papists. "Good works have to be done." Those poor foolish people know nothing about the power and nature of faith. They understand as much about these five letters — F-A-I-T-H — as this paper does.[58] The paper presents five letters to the eyes of the readers. Thus those people know nothing more about faith. They suppose that it is a useless reflection or merely a knowledge such as demons have; they do not know that faith means to believe, and give assent to, God when He promises and swears. To be sure, they are aware that there is a God. So are the demons. But this is not sufficient for us. Indeed, it does not concern us at all, because it is outside us.

True faith draws the following conclusion: "God is God for me because He speaks to me. He forgives me my sins. He is not angry with me, just as He promises: 'I am the Lord your God.'" Now search your heart, and ask whether you believe that God is your God, Father, Savior, and Deliverer, who wants to rescue you from sins

[58] This is another indication that the commentary is not a verbatim transcript of Luther's lectures but an adaptation by his editors.

and from death. If you become aware that you are wavering or uncertain, consider how to correct that doubt through constant use of the Word of God.

Accordingly, let us strengthen and fortify ourselves against the doubts of the papists, and let us learn that for God the only completely pleasing worship and obedience is faith, that is, to believe and trust our God when He swears so solemnly.

Besides, this one passage is the only place in which Holy Scripture states that God swore.[59] From it has flowed everything said in Ps. 110:4 and in Ps. 132:11 about the oath sworn to David. For just as the promise of the Seed of Abraham was transferred to the Seed of David, so Holy Scripture transfers the oath sworn to Abraham to the person of David.

David understood this oath in no other manner than as if it had been given to him; and he bestows great praise on it in Ps. 110, where he speaks about his Lord. For he occupied himself diligently with the study of Holy Scripture, and, since he had the promise concerning the seed and fruit of his body, he drew many conclusions from this passage in an ingenious and godly manner and applied them to himself.

For David thought: "God swore to Abraham in the promise of the Seed. Without a doubt this oath pertains to me too." For this reason he repeats it so many times and comforts himself with it so powerfully in Ps. 89:35 and in Ps. 132:11.

Why does David do this? Because he thinks: "Through the promise given to me I am convinced that the Seed of Abraham, which came down through so many fathers, has come into my tribe, into my line, person, and body. Therefore whatever was said or promised to Abraham must by every right accrue to me."

This was indeed an extraordinary glory and a great distinction. No doubt it puffed up his heart to some extent, and for this reason a humiliation followed. He fell into a hideous sin, lest he become inordinately proud.

Next, because the blessing is attached to the Seed of Abraham, David concluded further that this blessing had to be applied to him and his Seed: "That Seed of Abraham is now my Seed. The Messiah will be my Son and my Lord. And I am he to whom the promise is

[59] It is noteworthy, as Luther indicates, that all other references to God's swearing in the Bible put it in the past — perhaps in an allusion to this passage. Cf. Ps. 89:35; Ps. 95:11; Is. 14:24; Is. 62:8; Luke 1:73; Heb. 3:11; Heb. 6:17.

attached, just as it was attached to the person of Abraham." Moreover, Matthew alludes to this when he speaks of "the Son of David, the Son of Abraham" (1:1).

Furthermore, David concludes that blessing is a mark of priests, not of kings, as Melchizedek blesses Abraham (Gen. 14:19). "But my Seed is the Son of a king," says David. "Yet He is the One who blesses; therefore He will be both King and Priest." In this manner David, enlightened by the Holy Spirit, unfolded, and reflected on, this oath. Consequently, he had no doubt at all — indeed, he even proclaimed in eloquent terms — that the Messiah, his Son, like a son born from a king, would be a King, yet a King who would bless and for this reason would also be a Priest.

But because David was not of the priestly or Levitical tribe, he considered why God did not take the blessing from among the tribe of Levi, namely, for the obvious purpose of pointing out that the Levitical priesthood was to be abolished, but that Christ's priesthood would be eternal and unchangeable. For the blessing promised to Abraham is eternal. From this David concluded that Christ was a Priest after the order of Melchizedek — a Priest whose beginning and end are unknown.

Thus not only the author of the Epistle to the Hebrews but also the fathers and prophets saw, and marveled at, the abundance of God's grace, which pervades the entire promise and the oath. Therefore they pondered this text with the utmost zeal, and David's most beautiful psalms originated from it. The saints in the New Testament also extol this oath with great joy. Thus Zechariah sings (Luke 1:73): "The oath which He swore to our father Abraham, to grant us." And Mary says (Luke 1:55): "As He spoke to our fathers, to Abraham and to his posterity forever."

Because you have done this and have not withheld your son, your only son,

17. *I will bless you, and I will multiply your descendants as the stars of the heaven and as the sand which is on the seashore. And your descendants shall possess the gate of their enemies.*

18. *And by your Seed shall all the nations of the earth be blessed, because you have obeyed My voice.*

These words are the subject matter and the gushing fountain, as it were, of many of the prophecies and addresses of Isaiah, David,

and Paul. Moreover, they agree with the preceding promises, which
are found in Gen. 12:3: "In you all the families of the earth will be
blessed" and in Gen. 15:5: "Look toward heaven, and number the
stars, if you are able; so shall your descendants be." But this promise
is clearer and more explicit.

Above God said: "In you, Abraham, all the families of the earth
will be blessed." There his Seed is included, but it is not expressed.
But in this passage it is expressly stated: "In your Seed." In opposition
to the nonsense of the Jews, however, Paul declares and explains
that this Seed is Christ (Gal. 3:16).

Then all nations are mentioned. Hence this promise also pertains
to us Gentiles and to all who will ever hear and accept it, not only
to the Jews.

To be sure, the promise was not spoken to us, and in this the
Jews surpass us; but we are nevertheless the persons of whom God
is speaking. The first Person is God, who speaks; the second person
is Abraham; and we Gentiles are the third. Therefore we should
reverence and sincerely love the passage before us. If the words
sounded like this: "In your Seed your people will be blessed," we
would have been excluded there; but because He is speaking about
the nations and about ourselves, we may certainly rejoice in that
blessing.

These words truly deserve to be written in large letters of gold
and to be continually before our eyes and in our heart. For this is
our glory in the blessing through the Seed of Abraham — the blessing
we boast of and praise no less than the Jews.

Of course, God did not speak or swear *to* us; but He spoke *of* us.
So far there are differences that concern only the person, because
the Jews are the second person, and we are the third. But the first
Person, which is God, who is speaking, addresses both. It is His
desire that first the Jews and then the Greeks, as Paul is wont to say
(Rom. 1:16) — and he leaves the Jews their prerogative — come to
faith and enjoy all the good things the Blessed Seed of Abraham
brings, that is, Christ Jesus, the Salvation and Blessing of all nations.

Finally, it is certain that we dwell and live at some place on earth,
just as the Jews dwelt on earth; for the text adds the words "all
nations of the earth." Hence we shall share in the blessings also
for this reason.

The verb "to bless" must be carefully noted, because it differs
from the one that appears above (ch. 12). Moreover, the exact

meaning of the word must be determined on the basis of the Hebrew conjugations, in accordance with which the meanings of verbs vary.[60]

The first conjugation includes the neutral or absolute verb — as "I run," or when I say "I teach," "I bless" — without the addition of a word which it governs, so that the action is not transitive; for I am not saying that God is blessing a man or anything similar.

But the same verbs in the second conjugation are construed with the accusative, as "he teaches rhetoric," "he blessed a man." Here the act of blessing is directed toward someone else.

The third conjugation is transitive — and it occurs very frequently in the Holy Scriptures — as if I were to say in Latin *doctifico*, that is, "I cause to teach," or *amatifico*, that is, "I cause you to love." Thus *benedictifico* means "I make you blessed." And this conjugation is appropriate for God alone. For He causes to be wise; that is, He gives those good things. Yet it can also be used of human beings, as "Moses causes to teach the people"; that is, he causes Aaron to teach the people in order that the people may learn.

The fourth conjugation includes those verbs which express an action that is not directed toward another but is directed back to the agent, as when I say "I bless myself," although no reflexive pronoun is added. But the nature of the verb includes this reflexive meaning, "toward myself." The Germans and the Latins add a pronoun, because they do not have verbs of that kind. The inchoatives — *calesco*, for example — resemble them somewhat but do not correspond to them in every respect.

Here belong, then, the transitive reciprocal verbs, or those that are reflexive in their action, as the grammarians call them. For example: "My soul will praise itself in the Lord"; that is, I rejoice, and I exalt myself; or my soul glories, that is, greatly exalts itself and regards itself as worthier than heaven and earth, but in the Lord. The strict meaning is that through the power of another one does something that he is unable to do by his own power.

We express this by means of the passive: "In the Lord my soul will be praised." Likewise: "The nations will be blessed." But it is God who blesses, and Christ is the Seed through whom He blesses, or, in the reflexive conjugation: "They bless themselves"; that is, that blessing of God through Christ, who blesses, comes to the

[60] On the sources of Luther's knowledge of Hebrew cf. *Luther's Works,* 2, pp. 33—34.

nations when they apply the blessing to themselves, so that they say: "I am blessed, not in myself but in the Seed." Thus, for example, when I say: "I praise and glorify myself, but in the Seed," I am glorying in the glory and power of another, as Paul says in Gal. 2:20: "I live, but Christ lives in me." I am proud of my salvation and of the forgiveness of my sins. But through what? Through another's glory and pride, namely, Christ's.

Moses employed the same word in Deut. 29:19, where, after recounting the benefits and confirming the divine covenant, he opposes the smugness and hypocrisy of the ungodly with a tacit reproach. He speaks of "one who, when he hears the words of this sworn covenant, blesses himself in his heart, saying: 'I shall be safe, etc.'"; that is, the ungodly will be moved neither by the promise nor by the threats but will say: "Let either God or Moses curse. What do I care? I bless and comfort myself."

Thus in Jer. 9:23-24 we read: "Let not the wise man, the mighty man, the rich man glory, etc.; but let him who glories glory in this, that he knows Me." In this passage there is a reflexive meaning in each part. The wise man, the strong man, the rich man who praises himself should not praise himself in wisdom, etc.; but he who praises should praise himself in the Lord. In German we add the pronoun: *Erneeret sich, beisset, frisset sich,* which the Hebrew verb includes by virtue of its nature. Therefore in accord with the idiom of the Hebrew language you will translate more properly as follows: "In your Seed all nations will bless themselves." [61]

My purpose in presenting these facts rather carefully and in bringing them to your attention has been to encourage those who want to study the Holy Scriptures to apply themselves to the Hebrew language, in order that they may be able to refute the nonsense of the rabbis even on the basis of grammar. For there is great danger that with their glosses the rabbis will again obscure and falsify the Holy Bible. It has been stated elsewhere, however, that there is a twofold blessing: a blessing in words and a blessing in actuality. The blessing in words consists of praises and commendation. It is with the verbal blessing that the Jews understand this passage to be dealing, since they insist on it alone.

The blessing in actuality is truly divine; for when God blesses,

[61] Here in Gen. 22:18, as in Gen. 12:3, Gen. 18:18, etc., the Revised Standard Version translates accordingly: "shall bless themselves."

the result is the thing itself or that which is said, in accordance with those well-known statements: "For He commanded, and they were created" (Ps. 148:5) and "God said: 'Let there be light'; and there was light" (Gen. 1:3). He is One who blesses with effect and does all things through what He says, because His Word is the thing itself, and His blessing is an abundant blessing, physically as well as spiritually.

Properly, however, a blessing denotes an increase, as the angel says to Hagar (Gen. 16:10): "I will greatly multiply your descendants," and about Ishmael (Gen. 17:20): "I will bless him and make him fruitful and multiply him exceedingly." And it is not a verbal blessing but a blessing in actuality — although physical — that Ishmael will beget twelve princes. Hence we repeatedly read in the Holy Scriptures (Gen. 48:9): "They are my sons, with whom God has blessed me."

The Jews take this passage to mean solely a verbal blessing, namely, that all nations will praise themselves in the people of the Jews and will admire and praise the blessing of this people.[62] My reason for calling attention to this is that no one should be bothered by the glosses of the Jews. They explain these words as follows: The seed of Abraham will be blessed; that is, everything will be bestowed on them in abundance, so that all nations will marvel, bless themselves and be glad that they can share and have part in these blessings.

Thus the Jews exalt themselves above the Gentiles and want the Gentiles to be subject to them solely because of the physical blessing. But if you consider the historical accounts, you will find that because the Gentiles — the Syrians and the Persians — had a world empire, they surpassed the Jews by far and were much more powerful.

Hence this blessing does not subject the Gentiles to the Jews like slaves. For it would be more correct to call it a curse than a blessing if the Gentiles had no other glory than that which would stem from the arrogant rule of the Jews.

But the Gentiles have been the masters of the Jews and have kept them in subjection by severe bondage. Therefore other good things must be tendered by the blessing, namely, heavenly and eternal ones, which the Gentiles enjoy the same as the Jews do. Thus the true and divine blessing is promised to the Gentiles, not subjection and bondage, as the Jews dream.

[62] See the related discussion earlier in these lectures, *Luther's Works*, 2, pp. 261—262.

Burgensis correctly and piously puts us in mind of the same thing, namely, that the text is not dealing with a human blessing — or, in accordance with the distinction we made above, a verbal one — but with a divine one, that is, with divine favors and with an abundance of heavenly good things, as a result of which the Gentiles will praise themselves in that Seed.[63]

This is the true and genuine meaning, since St. Paul, too, has the same explanation, namely, that the Gentiles will be highly elated and will call themselves blessed, lords of heaven and earth, as he says in Eph. 1:3: "Who has blessed us in Christ with every spiritual blessing in the heavenly places."

Without a doubt the more intelligent Jews, who believe at least in the resurrection of the dead, will go over to the same way of thinking. For since their fathers did not obtain the promise concerning the physical blessings, they will have to concede to us that this promise must be understood of a blessing different from that which pertains to this wretched and miserable life, in which the ungodly are richer in other respects than the godly.

But after we have made clear the force and exact meaning of the verb, it is now necessary to consider the fact that "in your Seed" is added. All nations will bless themselves, will be proud, and will boast that they are saved, blessed, and richly supplied with all spiritual gifts. But how will they do so? They will not do so in themselves, will they? No. But they will glory in the victory over death, in the abolition of sin, and in the gift of eternal life, not because of their own merits and righteousnesses, but "in your Seed."

All glory and confidence of most wretched sinners will not consist in this, that they are praiseworthy and righteous in themselves. No, they will declare that they are holy, redeemed, and washed with the blood of Christ, and that they have been translated from the kingdom of darkness into the kingdom of light (cf. Col. 1:12-13).

The Jews, on the other hand, want to be conspicuous and to be proud because of their wisdom, fortitude, power, and wealth. But that is not what this blessing promises; it teaches that one should glory in the Lord, just as Jeremiah (9:24) most gravely urges the same thing over against the persistent pride innate in the Jews.

In the same way we repudiate the vain confidence of the work-righteous — the confidence they have in vows, in the cowls of the

[63] Paulus Burgensis *ad* Gen. 22:18.

Carthusians and the Minorites. Not even the saintliest persons, whether Peter or Paul, may flaunt their works, even though they may have raised the dead. Thus Paul is so far from being puffed up on account of his pharisaical righteousness and the other gifts he mentions in his Epistle to the Philippians (3:4 ff.) that he counts "everything as loss because of the surpassing worth of knowing Christ Jesus, our Lord."

Hence all glorying is excluded by the phrase "in your Seed," which is added to the promise. That Seed sets aside all other blessings and the glory of one's own righteousness and bestows His on us, namely, "that which is through faith in Christ, the righteousness from God that depends on faith" (Phil. 3:9). Therefore all nations will bless themselves in no other than "in your Seed." In Him are all the treasures of wisdom, righteousness, and holiness; and whatever there will be anywhere among them that is praiseworthy they will have in its entirety through this Seed.

Similarly, St. Paul says (1 Cor. 1:30-31): "Whom God made our wisdom, our righteousness and sanctification and redemption; therefore, as it is written: 'Let him who boasts, boast of the Lord.'" He is our life, salvation, and peace. "I am the resurrection and the life; he who believes in Me, though he die, yet shall he live" (John 11:25).

Abraham was endowed with many extraordinary virtues and gifts which he surely should have acknowledged and praised; but he has no glory before God, because all glorying is excluded. How much more shall we reach the same conclusion about the other saints, no matter how much merit they have, whether of congruity or of condignity!

Because God blesses solely in this Seed of Abraham, He also wants us to be blessed and to bless ourselves in this Seed; that is, we should glory and maintain with assurance that this Seed is ours and belongs to us with all its good things and heavenly treasures.

Burgensis, who, fortunately enough, was converted from Judaism, was aware of the same thing when he said that the verb "to bless" implies, as the author and bestower of the blessing, not the nations but the Seed of Abraham, namely, that He is the principal, effective cause of that blessing.

And He is not only the effective cause; but He is also the formal cause, that is, the blessing itself. For from Him and in Him we are the blessed of Christ and the anointed, and every one of us can make this boast: "Christ is my formal blessing, anointing, life, and salvation, because I cling to Him; and by this One who blesses I am designated as blessed, and I call myself blessed."

Therefore the Hebrew way of expressing itself in the case of the verb "to bless" should be carefully noted and pondered: "All nations will bless themselves." For it denotes that full assurance (πληροφορία) and nature of faith that I must maintain with certainty and without any doubt that I am blessed and declare myself truly alive, saved, righteous, and blessed. Otherwise I do wrong to the Seed of Abraham, namely, to Christ, the Author of life and salvation.

For the promise does not depend on my merits or works; it depends on the Seed of Abraham. By Him I am blessed when I apprehend Him in faith; and the blessing clings to me in turn and permeates my entire body and soul, so that even the body itself is made alive and saved through the same Seed.

And that begins in this life through faith when the soul, weighed down by death and sin, is buoyed up and receives the comfort of life and salvation. At some later time, in the resurrection of the dead, the body will follow the soul without any hindrance — not instrumentally but effectively and, as it were, formally [64] — to the point that our lowly body will be changed "to be like the glorious body of Christ" (Phil. 3:21).

But this confidence and saintly glorying is obstructed in us in many ways. For the evil conceived because of the fault of original sin is born with us. I am speaking of the pride and presumption which cause men to be arrogant in regard to their strength, wisdom, might, and wealth.

Nothing is easier for flesh and blood than to bless itself and to exalt itself before God — but on account of its own righteousness and holiness. But this blessing of the flesh must be mortified and killed like a most deadly poison. And before we apprehend that other blessing, we must consider and recognize the curse through which we have been plunged into sins and horrible corruption, namely, unbelief, blasphemy, smugness, and other maladies and lusts without number.

When God declares that the nations are to be blessed, He points

[64] Luther is employing the distinction among causes from Aristotle, *Physics,* Book II, ch. 3.

out that they are cursed. For God does not say this in vain, but He indicates that they are without a blessing and that they fall short of the glory of God. This conclusion is unavoidable and cannot be escaped, just as the apostle Paul places himself under this very same judgment in 1 Cor. 4:4: "I am not aware of anything against myself, but I am not thereby acquitted."

The self-righteous and the hypocrites pay no heed to this; nor do they think that they are cursed, just as the Pharisee proudly boasts (Luke 18:11): "I am not like other men." Therefore the blessing does not apply to them, even though they always have it on their lips and bless themselves — but in themselves, not in the Seed.

But this is a satanic and cursed blessing, and everywhere the prophets contend most sharply against this kind and call the blessings of these people a lie, vanity, an idol, incantations, divinations, etc.[65]

Paul speaks to this effect in Gal. 3:10. "All who rely on works of the Law," he says, "are under a curse." Hence all nations, because they are without the blessing, are under the curse and sin, that the entire world may be subject to God. "But the Scripture consigned all things to sin, that what was promised to faith in Jesus Christ might be given to those who believe" (Gal. 3:22). These truths, and many like them, had their source in this promise as in a most abundant spring.

But these words of the divine judgment are not so pleasant for flesh and reason, for all men, even those who are openly ungodly and villainous, avoid the confession of sin. Hypocrites in particular resent it very much when they hear that the doctrine of the Gospel censures their sins and wickedness. They all readily acknowledge the blessing and boast of it, but they never permit it to be said that they are cursed and damned because of sin. Indeed, they even hate those who teach and censure them, and they persecute them in a hostile manner.

Therefore we should know that this passage does not pertain to satisfied and stiff-necked people and those who are inflated by their own righteousness. No, it pertains to those who have been humbled and afflicted; whom sin troubles and torments; who feel the curse and wrath of God which threatens the cursed and the sinners; who, even if they have righteousness, wisdom, and other gifts, nevertheless declare loudly that these are nothing but masks and a shadow, and com-

[65] Luther is apparently thinking of passages like Mal. 2:2.

plain that of all people living they are the most wretched and for this reason implore the mercy and grace of God.

Thus David was very powerful, and he was rich. Yet because he knew that he was under the wrath of God, sin, death, and the power of the devil, he thinks: "Of what advantage are all the riches of the entire world to me, since they do not bless me or bring life and eternal salvation?"

Similarly, all nations which recognize with a troubled spirit that they are condemned and that trust in their own gifts and powers has been killed — even though they walk along in splendor and in the glory of the most excellent gifts of the Spirit, as David and others do — nevertheless regard themselves as most wretched and most cursed, because they feel the power of sin and the terrors of hell and of the wrath of God. To them, therefore, this promise should be pointed out. The prophets drew all their comforting discourses from it.

In the New Testament we have this promise elucidated and explained in an excellent manner. In Gal. 3:16 St. Paul states with beautiful clarity that this Seed is Christ. Undoubtedly the Holy Spirit enlightened and taught him. For the Jews and the entire wisdom of the flesh in no wise understand or concede that this one Seed is Christ.

In the second place, it is also explained that this Seed of Abraham is true man and true God. He is a man because He became flesh and the son of the Virgin. This the Jews do not deny, since He is the son of Abraham. The blessing, however, proves that He is God; for the nations are under the curse, as are all creatures. Therefore He is not a creature and not from the Gentiles. Otherwise He would also be cursed. But He not only blesses others, but He Himself is also formally blessed, so that in this way the entire world is blessed. This can be said of no heathen. No one has ever had the right to claim for himself that he blessed himself and others and delivered from death.

Therefore Burgensis excellently stresses the fact that the blessing fits the Creator alone and not any creature. Hence He who blesses must be true God, because to deliver all nations from the curse is a work of God, not of man or of angels. And so that Seed is true God and man in one Person. He is man because He is of the Seed of Abraham; He is God because He bestows the blessing.

In the third place, He must be the kind of man who was born without sin. In this particular, then, our faith is wonderful. We believe that He is man and yet not born from blood, because He was not conceived in original sin. For the blessing and the curse cannot stand side by side, which would happen if He had been conceived in sin.

Accordingly, Mary did not conceive this Seed in the natural manner. She is not a mother like the mothers of all nations. She had to be a mother and give birth to a new man. But she was a pure mother and a virgin who conceived, not from a man or from an angel, whether good or bad, but from the Holy Spirit (Luke 1:35).

Thus Paul, Isaiah, and the other prophets pondered this passage carefully and did not read the promises carelessly and superficially, as we do. For when God speaks, He utters words that are of such importance and so sublime that heaven and earth cannot comprehend them.

These words speak of most weighty matters — matters that surpass all the understanding of the whole world, namely, that all nations are under sin, death, and eternal damnation. To be sure, one may conclude this a posteriori and from the effect — for we all feel the perils and countless misfortunes that are more painful than death itself — but we do not know the cause. Far less do we see deliverance.

Consequently, the cause is pointed out in this promise, which bears witness that all nations are under the curse and power of the devil and nevertheless offers deliverance if they recognize their wretched state and do not despair but believe in the Seed and bless themselves because of this Seed, boast of life, and individually apply this deliverance to themselves by faith and say: "I am no longer a sinner; I am righteous. I am not cursed; I am blessed through the Seed of Abraham — the Seed who is true man, born of the descendants of Abraham, and true God."

This blessing is so powerful and efficacious that it is able to destroy and abolish both death and the entire curse which was brought on as a result of original sin.

Moreover, the fact that God, as is stated in the Epistle to the Hebrews (2:16), is concerned with the descendants of Abraham, not with angels, is an incalculably great honor to that wretched mass of the human race. For it was not difficult or impossible for Him to bring His Son into the world without a mother. But He wanted to make use of the female sex.

He could likewise have formed a body suddenly from a virgin, just as He formed Adam from clay and Eve from a rib of Adam. He did not choose to do this, but He adhered to the order which He Himself had established. For a maiden has been created in such a way that she should conceive, be with child for nine months, and give birth. Therefore He wanted His Son to be conceived, carried and born in the womb of a maiden, not formed from clay and not conceived by a male.

It is surely a great comfort that it did not please God that His Son should become man from any other material than the human race. He wanted His Son to become our brother and to adorn us with the exceedingly great honor of having a God born and made man in our flesh and blood.

These facts are so grand and sublime that they cannot be apprehended and understood in any other manner than by faith, which produces in us that spiritual confidence through which we firmly believe that we have eternal peace in heaven and on earth — not in ourselves, of course, but in the Seed of Abraham.

But here every thought and presumption of one's own righteousness must be put aside. Moreover, that Seed must be carefully separated from all works. For the Seed of Abraham conceived by the Holy Spirit is not my work. But our righteousness and the Seed are distinct things. Works, of course, are called, and actually are, blessings. Of these John 14:12 says: "Greater works than these will he do." But they are truly good only if the blessing is there first.

The blessing of the Seed, however, is the work of another; it is not our own. Therefore justification must be ascribed neither to the righteousness of the Law nor to the papistic traditions; but I shall bless myself in Christ Jesus, our Deliverer, so that he who boasts, boasts of the Lord (1 Cor. 1:31). In Ps. 105:3 we read: "Glory in His holy name." Then we shall boast with confidence and everlasting joy.

Up to this point we have concerned ourselves with the affirmative meaning of this passage, that is, with faith in Christ, the Seed of Abraham, and apart from the worthiness and merits of works. For the text states clearly that although in themselves all nations are accursed and without any worthiness and righteousness, yet they will bless themselves with a blessing that belongs to another.

Accordingly, every blessing apart from this one is condemned. So are all wisdom, righteousness, power, and whatever man possesses in accordance with his origin and his birth from Adam. However much we may prosper in the wealth and goods of the entire world, that physical blessing is condemned as long as the curse remains; nor are anyone's prestige and glory great enough to make him an exception here. For "all nations" means all mankind.

These statements agree properly and in a godly manner with our doctrine of justification and faith, which the papists condemn and persecute as false and heretical. They call us "solafideists," [66] because we attribute righteousness to faith alone.

But we are not the originators of this doctrine. Enlightened by the Spirit of Christ, we have drawn it from these and similar promises. Manifestly, every thought of and trust in a righteousness of works is rejected here, and in this one blessing through the Seed of Abraham righteousness, salvation, and life are included.

But because they so brazenly contradict the plain truth, it is also worthwhile to deal with the point of view which denies or opposes our doctrine — the point of view they maintain together with a new explanation they have recently invented to cover up their error.[67]

They do not attribute righteousness simply to works. No, they attribute it to works joined with faith, because they see that they have been caught in a manifest and disgraceful error, namely, that they have taught works alone, without faith, and based on human traditions at that. Therefore they are now making a slight change, and instead of their traditions they are demanding the works and the righteousness of the Law for justification.

Since not even this, however, is enough to turn aside the disgrace they deserve, they resort to patching faith on the works and declaring that justification comes neither from works alone nor from faith alone, but that faith together with works justifies because faith without works is dead.

Let us, then, examine this negative proposition. The affirmative proposition we stated above, namely, that we are reckoned and pronounced righteous through faith alone. This is confirmed on the basis of the passage in which it is stated that the nations will bless themselves, not in their own wisdom and righteousness or in the Law but

[66] We have translated *solarii* with "solafideists," also on p. 167; cf. *Luther's Works*, 26, p. 138.

[67] Cf. *The Disputation Concerning Justification* of 1536, *Luther's Works*, 34, pp. 151—196, which discusses and refutes some of these "recent explanations."

in the blessing of the Seed, that is, in Christ Jesus, "whom God made our wisdom, our righteousness and santification and redemption" (1 Cor. 1:30).

The negative proposition is this: Faith alone does not justify, but faith does so in conjunction with works. Furthermore, they attach a crafty declaration or restriction to this proposition. They say: "Although we demand works as necessary for salvation, yet we do not teach that one should put one's trust in works." The devil is sly enough; but he accomplishes nothing, even though he hoodwinks the ignorant and deceives reason.

Since it has been established that trust in works is rejected and condemned, the righteousness of works is altogether nothing. For there can be no true righteousness in men unless at the same time trust is added, according to God's command, by which I am forbidden to lie or to deny that righteousness is what it actually is; for I must not say that it is sin.

Hence if there is any righteousness of works — as they declare, because faith without works is nothing — I must assert and have that righteousness by divine authority; and if I am to be saved, I have to believe that this righteousness avails for salvation and eternal life.

Therefore their teaching that one must not put one's trust in works is a deception and a lie. And the contrary proposition must be maintained, namely, that trust necessarily follows the righteousness of works, because all righteousness and truth brings with it trust, which is the complete reality [68] or the prime energy, substance, and factotum of righteousness.

Similarly, righteousness in the administration of the state and the household cannot exist without trust. How, then, can it be taken away from that righteousness which they want to be righteousness before God? In the administration of the household I must be sure that this woman is my wife and that this child is mine. In the administration of the state I must be certain about my officer of the state, who he is, whose subject I am, who my fellow citizens are, who are joined to me by the same laws. I am not permitted to doubt or waver. Yes, even such great constancy and certainty are required that I do not doubt and do not refuse to spend my life and all my goods for the welfare and defense of home, wife, government, and fellow citizens. But if I doubt that this is my wife, my father, my son, my

_____

[68] Here Luther refers to Aristotle's idea of ἐντελέχεια; cf. *Metaphysics*, Book IX, ch. 8.

prince, or my fellow citizen,[69] then she is not my wife; nor is he my father, my son, my prince, etc. And thus righteousness in the household as well as in civil life is done away with.

Hence all righteousness and truth, whether in the government or in the household, has trust attached to it as its substantial form.

Therefore when the papists declare that they teach righteousness of works and nevertheless say that one must not trust in works, they contradict themselves, and they themselves admit that the righteousness of works is altogether nothing. It is similar in the household. If you have doubts about your wife, whether she is your wife, then she is not your wife; then she is a harlot. For in any righteousness, not only of Christians but also of the heathen and the Turks, there has to be certainty. The Turk is sure concerning his wife, family, emperor, etc. Thus a Christian should maintain that his works are pleasing to God and are good, whether they are performed in the church, in the household, or in the government; and it is a deception when they teach that works must be done, but that one should not put one's trust in them.

Whence come those sermons of the prophets — "They worship the works of their own hands" (Jer. 1:16), etc. — except from the fact that all who want to be justified by their works are in reality idolaters? For they cannot avoid having trust in their works.

Why did I undergo excessive hardships in the monastery? Why did I torture my body with fasts, vigils, and cold? Certainly because I was trying to be sure that through these works I would get forgiveness of sins, etc.

Therefore give this answer: "You are making conflicting statements; you assert a righteousness of works and deny that there is any trust in them, although all righteousness necessarily includes trust. Lack of trust, however, is conclusive proof that no righteousness is there. But if you put your trust in works, you are an idolater."

Is this not teaching things that conflict and imply a contradiction? Who does not see that they are destroying and consuming themselves with their contradictions? Now they maintain justification; now they deny it. To be sure, they do not deny it in words; but they deny it in fact, because they declare that faith with works justifies, and nevertheless they exclude trust.

Their former prattle about human traditions and works of the

[69] We have followed the Erlangen edition and read *civis* here rather than *cives*.

Law is condemned even by their own judgment and confession. But after they have seized upon the word "faith" in such a manner that they deny that it alone suffices for salvation and tack on it the merits of works, they lose faith the same time that they lose the works.

But they adduce what is stated in Luke 17:10: "When you have done all, say: 'We are unworthy servants.'" [70] With these words they defend their dogma that one must not put one's trust in works. But again they stumble disgracefully. For that which they suppose is supporting them overthrows their entire doctrine. Christ condemns not only trust in works but also all righteousness and merits of works. For if one must say that works are useless, it follows of necessity that they are not righteousness and do not avail for eternal life but are worthless and amount to nothing at all.

Therefore all trust, righteousness, wisdom, and whatever else has to do with works is rejected, and the statement that we are justified by faith with works is false. The Blessed Seed alone delivers from death and bestows righteousness and the eternal life that is obtained through faith.

We do not deny that works must be done; but when our opponents commingle the faith that justifies and the works of those who have been justified through faith, we disapprove. To be sure, faith and works indeed fit together well and are inseparably joined; but it is faith alone that obtains the blessing. Therefore we declare that faith alone justifies, because it alone is blessed. Works do not bless; they do not have this glory. No, they are the fruits of the person who has been blessed.

This righteousness of ours comes through faith. Concerning it we should have no doubt; nor should we say that it is useless or vain, lest we hear the words: "Woe to those who call good evil" (Is. 5:20). Therefore I should not say: "I have the blessing, and for this reason I am useless." No, I must say: "I am honest, saintly, righteous, and blessed, because I am such through the righteousness of another, not through my own righteousness. This I can set against the wrath and judgment of God, and I am sure that God cannot deny Himself and cast aside His Son, that Seed of Abraham. Therefore I maintain with confidence and without any doubt that I am righteous and an heir of eternal life."

---

[70] Cf. the *Confutation of the Augsburg Confession*, VI, 6, in M. Reu (ed.), *The Augsburg Confession* (Chicago, 1930), II, 352—353.

This promise embraces almost the entire Christian doctrine, the incarnation of Christ and justification, but not the sacraments, which were revealed later on, when Christ came. Furthermore, it contains a refutation of the papistic doctrine, not only concerning traditions and works but also concerning faith combined with works, which they stress against us "solafideists." This proposition remains unshakable and sure, that faith alone justifies, because all trust of all men is absolutely condemned, and trust is put in the Seed alone.

Therefore we shall conclude in opposition to our opponents: "Your justification, in which you teach that works must be combined with faith, is a lie, because you contradict yourselves, maintain the righteousness of works, and deny trust. When trust is abolished, righteousness itself must be abolished, because certainty and trust are the very life of righteousness."

On the other hand, it is true justification when I am certain through faith that the Blessed Seed, through whom I bless myself, dwells in me. Nor must I have any doubts or suppose that this blessing amounts to nothing or is idle. For the Seed of Abraham does not let me be useless but causes me to abound in fruits. In John 14:12 we read: "He who believes in Me, etc."

But they object and say that in this passage the text has: "Because you have done this" and "Because you have obeyed." From this it seems to follow that Abraham earned the blessing with his works. Hence our works, too, they say, deserve reward. For it is a causal way of speaking when God says: "I will bless you because you have obeyed My voice," as though He were saying: "I would not bless you and the others if you had not obeyed."

This argument, like an iron wall,[71] they oppose to what we have said up to this point, and they easily deceive the unlearned. They say: "What has now become of your statement that all nations will bless themselves in the Seed of Abraham, and also that righteousness through works is condemned? Here Moses says the opposite: 'Because you have acted, and because you have obeyed.' The inference is clear: The blessing is given to Abraham because he obeys and acts. Obeying and acting are works. Hence we obtain the blessing through works."

My answer is: Two questions are involved in this discussion:

[71] Apparently a favorite expression for a supposedly irrefutable argument; cf. *Luther the Expositor*, p. 122.

(1) whether we are justified through works, and (2) whether God does great and wonderful works for the sake of the elect because they are already holy and just through faith.

We are now dealing with the first question: whether we earn righteousness through works or receive it through the grace and mercy of God as a gift, without merit on our part.

But the question is not raised whether he who has been justified through grace and faith earns or procures it from God that God for his sake does miracles and extraordinary works, just as He deals marvelously with His saints (Ps. 4:4) and adorns them in sundry and wonderful ways.

With satanic wickedness they mix up and jumble these two questions, and there is a fallacy of composition and division, as the dialecticians call it.[72] Teachers of that sort deserve ill will and should be censured, because they lead the people astray with nothing but fallacies and make no distinction among the arguments and matters under discussion.

It is first of all the duty of a teacher and dialectician to define and divide properly, then to bring proofs and reach conclusions. Our opponents are not doing the first two things, but they set down their propositions and their conclusion without any definition and division. Because of this confusion they teach nothing that is sound. Instead, they confuse simple minds and lead them astray.

Our question is this: "Can a sinner earn righteousness through good works — either through them alone or through good works in conjunction with faith — or does faith alone justify without works?"

From this question one must distinguish the second: "Does God for the sake of those who are already justified, holy, and appointed heirs of eternal life do the marvelous works of which Ps. 17:7 says: 'Wondrously show Thy steadfast love,' etc.?" They understand this statement as referring to the wonderful works of God that are done in those who already have righteousness and the Holy Spirit, and are sons and heirs of God; and they confuse the works of those who are to be justified with the works of those who have been justified.

Why do they not rather give their answer to this question: "Was Abraham justified, and did he obtain the inheritance of eternal life, through the sacrifice of his son?" To this we say no, and our reason is that he is already justified (Gen. 15:6). And here the text states:

---

72 Cf. *Luther's Works*, 27, p. 31, note 28.

"God tested Abraham." It does not say that He justified him, for he had previously received forgiveness of his sins and righteousness through faith when Moses states: "Abraham believed God, and it was reckoned to him as righteousness." There we do not read: "Because you did, because you obeyed."

Hence their argument has no weight at all; but the meaning of these words is this: "You have done a wonderful work, because you are righteous. I, in turn, shall do a wonderful work with you; I shall give a blessing of all nations through your Seed." Abraham is not justified by this. For of what concern to him was the blessing of all nations, to whom everything stated here applies: "By Myself I have sworn"?

Therefore this promise was not made to Abraham in order to justify him; but it is like a reward and some adornment added by God, so that God might make known that He will bestow boundless benefits on believers and those who call upon Him. For it is a great distinction that Abraham is the father of faith, of the blessing, and of Christ. These are incredible gifts; but he is not justified by them, because he has already been blessed before the blessing of all nations is promised.

When God gives great miracles to His saints, this is far different from justifying them and receiving them into grace. Christ promised believers (John 16:28) that they would receive whatever they would ask from the Father. Likewise (John 15:5): "He who abides in Me will bear much fruit." But they are not justified by these works which they receive from the Father, just as the branches of a vine are not produced by their fruits.

Accordingly, we grant that God shows favor to those who have been justified, that He rewards and endows them with great and wonderful works. But all this would not obtain for them forgiveness of sins and the grace of God unless they were previously among the saints. And because the saints are in grace and have the Holy Spirit, they are equipped for every good work.

If Abraham had not been righteous and had not been endowed with that foremost gift of the grace and mercy of God, if he had not abounded in righteousness and faith, he would never have offered his son; nor would he have obtained this glory of which the pasage before us is speaking.

Thus I pray daily that God may put an end to the pope and the

Turk; but I am not justified by this prayer. Indeed, if I were not righteous, I would not pray. But I feel and experience that these prayers of mine and of the whole church repulse and curb the Turks, the pope and his accomplices. And it is a great favor that the fury of our adversaries is turned away. Day and night they make use of their power and cunning to shed innocent blood.

But this prayer does not produce the church. On the contrary, the church produces the prayer through which it gains that marvelous victory over the plots of Satan, keeps the ferocity of the evil angels at a distance, and gets the protection of the good angels. These are the works and merits of the saints — the works and merits of which Christ says (John 14:12): "He who believes in Me will do greater works than these."

Thus God is saying to Abraham in this passage: "You have done this outstanding work and have been obedient. Behold, I, in turn, will adorn you with an outstanding miracle, not in order that you may be justified but to have you know that God loves His saints and not only calls and justifies them but also makes them great and glorious."

Accordingly, those who have been justified do wonderful works; but they are not justified by their wonderful works. Thus Paul has the glory that he is the teacher of the Gentiles. We glory in our victory over Satan and his followers, because they can do nothing against us. But we are not justified by this glory; for God so loves His saints that He approves of, adorns, and rewards whatever they do, not because of the works per se but because of their faith in the Seed of Abraham — the faith which exerts its power through virtues of every kind.

But if the works of the righteous and their faith could be detached or separated — which cannot be done — then they would be useless indeed, and one would have to say that we are unprofitable servants — which the papists say about that righteousness of theirs — because the remnants of sin, which adhere to us, pollute our works. But faith must be involved at the same time as inseparably joined to the works. And if any blemish remains, it is completely blotted out through the blessing of the Seed.

Therefore I commend this passage to all godly people as abounding in spiritual instruction, and of many and sundry kinds at that. If, when I explained the passage, I did not treat everything as it deserved, a reasonable reader [73] will attribute this to my inadequate ability. Nevertheless, I think that these are the main points.

In the first place, this passage gives amplest confirmation of the doctrine concerning the righteousness of faith, namely, that we are justified by faith alone. For no blessing is to be hoped for except through the Seed of Abraham. The text is clear. All nations — no matter how righteous and wise they are, and no matter with what outstanding gifts they are adorned — nevertheless are not blessed except through your Seed, O Abraham. Therefore they bless themselves, not in themselves but in your Seed.

At the same time the nature of faith is described in this passage. It is the nature of faith to believe with certainty that we are blessed, not through ourselves but through Christ, who is our blessing. Hence we bless ourselves and maintain that we are the ones to whom that blessing belongs, for it is faith which apprehends the blessing.

In addition to that confirmation there is a refutation of our opponents in regard to the righteousness of works. Because works are not that blessing through the Seed of Abraham, it is clear that whatever righteousness or blessing through works is presumed is idolatry and a curse.

The main points of our doctrine are these: We maintain that righteousness comes through faith alone, and we refute the idolatry of the pope. But it follows as a corollary that whatever the papists prate about faith and works is not understood by the papists themselves. And they should be censured above all because they teach doubt and take away from righteousness its substantial form, which is trust.

We, however, preach so much about faith in order that we may maintain the trust and certainty because of which we must be persuaded and sure that we are blessed through the Seed of Abraham.

But one should also note that in this promise Holy Scripture implies not only the divinity of Christ but also the distinction of Persons. It is the Father who promises; but the Seed is the Son, who is promised; and He is distinguished from Him who promises. Accordingly, there are two distinct Persons: the eternal Father, who promises, and the eternal Son, who is promised. This is what the prophets unfolded beautifully on the basis of those words. For they did not read the Holy Scriptures as frigidly as we are accustomed to do, and especially the Jews, who speak foolishly of only a verbal blessing.

[73] See p. 149, note 58.

Thus Isaiah says (65:16): "Whoever is blessed on earth shall bless himself in God. Amen"; that is, if there will be any blessing on earth, it will be in God. Amen. That is, in the true God. Hence Isaiah is pointing out that the Seed of Abraham is true God and that through this Seed the blessing will come, lest the Jews say that we are worshiping a crucified human being. For Isaiah says clearly: "He will be God and God. Amen"; that is, the true God, who keeps His promises. Many such statements have flowed from this passage as from a living spring and a well of living waters.

But let us return to the words of the promise, and let us compare them with the previous ones; for there is a repetition with an addition — which is common in Holy Scripture — so that the promises or previous statements are repeated whenever something new is to be added. The same thing happens here.

The difference, however, is not only in the words but also in the facts. There is a difference in the words when God says: "Your offspring shall possess the gates of your enemies." Above He said: "I will curse those who curse you," which amounts to the same thing. But there is an actual difference in the addition of the oath and in the word "to bless," namely, that all nations will bless themselves and will do so in the Seed of Abraham. This makes the promise not only clearer but also more magnificent.

The remaining clauses are easily harmonized. For what the passage before us has — "I will bless you, and I will multiply your descendants" — is stated in ch. 12:2-3: "I will make you a great nation, and I will bless those who bless you, etc."

Thus it is stated in ch. 13:16: "I will make your descendants as the dust of the earth." But in this passage it is expressed in words that are changed a little, namely, "as the sand which is on the seashore." We have pointed out above, however, that a twofold seed of Abraham is indicated.[74] The one is compared to the stars of heaven. These are the saints. The other is compared to the sand on the shore of the sea and to the dust of the earth. These are the ungodly.

Whoever is looking for an ampler exposition would do very well if he compared these statements with the addresses of the prophets, especially, however, with the psalms of David, who was very fond of this passage, as appears from Ps. 110, which he wove from this promise as a most beautiful web.

[74] Cf. *Luther's Works*, 2, pp. 359 ff.

In the first place, David calls Abraham's Seed his Lord. Indeed, he sets Him at the right hand of God: that is, he assigns to Him power equal to that of God. Inasmuch as all nations are to be blessed in Him, He must be distinguished from the nations that are all descended from Adam and for this reason are under the curse. For doing away with sin and death, blessing, and bestowing on men spiritual and eternal benefits are divine works and favors.

Accordingly, David concludes that this Seed, born without the semen of a man, is sitting at the right hand of God. This means that He is equal to God, because He does works equal to the works of God.

But because He is the Seed of Abraham, He must take on human nature; for otherwise God, in His own nature and essence, cannot be called the Seed of Abraham.

In the first place, David drew from this the following conclusion: This Seed is the Son of God and the equal of God, and He is the kind of king who sits at the right hand of the Father.

In the second place, the promise states that He will not only rule but will also bless. At the same time, therefore, He will be a Priest. For not only royal authority but also a priesthood is dealt with, and the name and office of priest embrace the foremost benefits of Christ. Therefore David, enlightened by the Holy Spirit, adds an oath, not in regard to royal authority but in regard to the priesthood: "The Lord has sworn and will not change His mind. 'You are a priest forever,' etc."; that is, my Lord will sit at the right hand of God, but in such a manner that He will not only rule but will also bless.

This is the excellent knowledge David had about Christ, the Seed who was to come from his tribe and flesh; and he undoubtedly realized and was exceedingly glad that such outstanding glory and honor were being heaped upon him in preference to other kings when Nathan brought him the promise (Ps. 132:11): "Of the fruit of your body will I set on your throne." Hence he concluded that this promise was being channeled into his body and seed, and that the Son of God would be born from his offspring.

When David heard that the line of Abraham among the people of Israel would be brought down to his person, so that the Seed would come from his body and blood, he received these tidings with joy. Previously he had never even considered this glory, just as Mary could not hope for the great honor of becoming the mother of Christ.

David thought that the descendants of Abraham had been scattered and that it was not known for sure into which person the promise had been channeled. On this occasion the prophet restricts it to a definite tribe and person, and says: "Of the fruit of your body I will set on your throne."

It was certainly important for David to know that the Son of God would stem from him and that the blessing of all nations would be looked for from his flesh. He congratulated not only himself but also the entire world because of the fact that the promise was repeated and was channeled into his body, so that hearts were no longer uncertain or had any doubts about the source from which the redemption of Israel was to be expected.

We should take careful note of this glory of David, in order that we may learn to differentiate the call, justification, and glorification. Many are called who are not justified; many are justified who are not glorified as Abraham or David were.

Nevertheless, this glory does not affect David's justification; for Scripture itself makes a distinction and teaches that God promises, and bestows on, those who have been justified outstanding and glorious works, which are recounted in Ps. 149:8-9: "To bind their kings with chains and their nobles with fetters of iron, to execute on them the judgment written! This is glory for all His faithful ones." Thus we read that saints have raised the dead.

These are works that invested them with glory. But they were not justified by them, though they were made certain that they were in grace and righteous. For if they had not been previously justified, they would not have performed these works.

I wanted to remind you of these things in passing because of that silly reasoning which I touched on above: "To Abraham it is said: 'Because you have obeyed.' Therefore we are justified by works." For the works of justification and glorification [75] must not be jumbled together.

Furthermore, what is stated in the promise — "Your descendants shall possess the gates of their enemies" — David has expressed in the following words (Ps. 110:1): "Till I make Thy enemies Thy footstool."

[75] We have followed the reading of the Erlangen edition rather than that of the Weimar edition, which lacks the words "and glorification."

This leads to the conclusion that the Seed will have enemies and adversaries, and a variety of them at that, powerful and violent. Yet the victory will be with the sand and the stars, but especially with the only Son. For we see that it happened this way. This people had deadly enemies but many outstanding — also physical — victories over them.

Thus it is related in the books of Judges and Kings that even the godless kings of Israel, Ahab and Joash, won glorious victories over the Philistines, the Syrians, and the Ammonites on account of this Seed, for whom God made the enemies a footstool.

These were victories of the godless, who are compared to the sand on the shore of the sea and to the dust of the earth. But the stars of heaven, that is, the godly, have obtained the true blessing in their spiritual victories, because they have taken possession of the spiritual gates, that is, the bodies and the minds that were subject to the power of Satan. These they have turned to faith; and they have destroyed the gates of hell, the dominion of Satan, of death, of sin, and every kind of affliction of the soul as well as of the body, and have obtained peace in heaven and on earth, so that they no longer stand in awe of hell and are not filled with horror when sin and the threats of the Law accuse the conscience.

These are victories and defeats far more glorious than those of the Ammonites, the Philistines, and others like them. Moreover, this is in most excellent agreement with the first promise, which was given in Paradise (Gen. 3:15) — the promise that the Seed of the woman would bruise the head of the serpent, etc. All the other promises are like this one, except that some are clearer than others.

We, too, who believe that this Seed is our blessing, have good reason to glory and act proudly over against all the gates of hell and against Satan himself with all his scales [76] and mobs. To be sure, we are compelled to bear the hate and cruelty of our enemies; but "in all these things we are more than conquerors through Him who loved us" (Rom. 8:37).

If we are Christians and believe in the Seed who blesses us, what do we care if the devil or the world is angry? For all we care, let them take away what we have, and let them kill the body. They will not for this reason keep us in death, will they? Not at all, for

[76] On this metaphor cf. *Luther's Works,* 13, p. 280, note 47.

we are blessed and are sure of life over against death and of the grace and favor of God over against the hatred of the world.

Thus David comforted himself with this promise and had good reason to be glad that that Seed had been assigned to his house. He calls Him אֲדֹנִי and reasons that He will be a King and a Priest. He is a King because He sits at the right hand of God, who has all things in His hand, as is stated in Matt. 11:27: "All things have been delivered to Me by My Father." He is a Priest because He blesses.

From those premises there follows by a very proper and very easy inference all this: "The blessing of the Seed which was promised to Abraham belongs to my house because I heard from the prophet Nathan: 'Of the fruit of your body, etc.'; therefore Christ, who was promised to Abraham, will be born of my seed." And so the line of descent from Abraham is directed into the body of David.

Finally he also perceives that the Levitical priesthood was not established in order to be everlasting, because another One who will bless is promised, and the office of blessing, which previously belonged to the tribe of Levi, is now transferred to the tribe of Judah.

Here the face of Moses was uncovered completely (cf. 2 Cor. 3: 14-16). Consequently, David could see that the Levitical priesthood was only a shadow and figure. This is also apparent from the fact that before the time of Moses the promise that the blessing would come from his Seed was made to Abraham.

Therefore he saw that a far more excellent priesthood would follow that of the Levites — a priesthood which would bless both Abraham and the Levites, who themselves are under the curse and for this reason are in need of the blessing of the Seed just as others are. Into this situation he then fitted Melchizedek and concluded that because of the eternal Seed the priesthood would be eternal.

This reasoning was clear and easy for David, since the premises are sure: "I am of the tribe of Judah. The Levites are not. And to me there is promised a King and Priest who is to be the blessing of all nations. Therefore whatever was ordained by Moses in regard to the tribe of Levi is only a shadow of things to come, because the real One who blesses was promised long before that ordinance."

Likewise, when God says to Moses in Ex. 25:40: "And see that you make them after the pattern which is being shown you on the mountain," he concluded that the warning about that pattern or type was not given so carefully without a purpose; and he decided that

Moses surely had before his eyes and in view the future blessing through Christ. For Moses is the shadow or figure that preceded Christ, who was to come. Therefore the true priesthood was in existence from the very beginning of the world, first covertly but later on promised more clearly to Abraham.

Thus David and the other prophets carefully examined and pondered this statement. Therefore they were able to interpret Moses correctly and profitably, namely, that the righteousness and the works of laws do not deliver from the curse, but that this comes about only when one believes and accepts with complete trust the Priest who was promised to Abraham.

To be sure, the Levites had been appointed by God as priests; but they were mortal, and therefore they gave a blessing that was only temporal. For as the priest, so the blessing. They could not do away with sin and death; nor could they purify hearts.

Hence David says that Another will come, namely, the eternal Blesser, whose kingdom will have no end. Yes, what is more, Moses covertly indicates by all his ordinances that everything must be referred to the house of David.

Therefore the prophets and all the saints before Christ cry out so often and so anxiously: "Come, O Lord!" as people desirous of looking upon His glory and that light of the Seed of Abraham and David which all the godly in the New Testament enjoy by God's great favor.

Moreover, note should be taken of the explanation of the universal principle, "ALL NATIONS SHALL BE BLESSED," which, of course, in Holy Scripture is a common way of saying that not a single one of the nations is blessed except through this Seed. The same thought occurs in John 1:9: "It enlightens every man," and also in 1 Tim. 2:4: "God desires all men to be saved" — not that all are enlightened, but that the universal blessing, scattered abroad among all nations, comes from this Seed. An exclusive rather than a universal principle is meant,[77] as though one said: "Nowhere is there light, life, and salvation except in this Seed."

Thus our doctrine has been clearly proved, and that of our opponents has been refuted. We are blessed in Christ, not in ourselves; that is, we must maintain with assurance that the blessing

---

[77] The Weimar text reads: *Exclusiva per universali ponitur,* which is grammatically unintelligible.

comes through Christ. Those who oppose this — which the papists are doing — give evidence enough that they have no understanding whatever of the doctrine of godliness.

19. *So Abraham returned to his young men, and they arose and went together to Beer-sheba; and Abraham dwelt at Beer-sheba.*

It is truly amazing that the very saintly patriarch returns from so sacred a place. If such a grand revelation about sacrificing a son were to come to us, and if that glorious promise — "In your Seed shall all the nations be blessed" — were added — likewise the conversation and the presence, not of one angel but of the entire heavenly host — human devotion would surely give the advice that this place should not only be held in reverence but should also be inhabited. Why, then, does Abraham not do this?

In the Books of Kings and in the Prophets one perceives how insane the Jewish nation is in the matter of human religion. They chose mountains, hills, woods, and trees where they could have at least some traces of the deeds of the fathers. Therefore they established forms of worship and sacrifices at Gilgal, Bethel, Dan, and Tabor; for at those places outstanding events took place.

Thus Abraham had very valid reasons for remaining at and venerating this place. He brought a supreme sacrifice at that place of divine worship and reverence. Nevertheless, he did not want to make it renowned by any monument, as we shall hear later about his grandson, the patriarch Jacob, who set up a stone at the place where he had seen the ladder (Gen. 28:18).

Abraham's descendants eagerly visited and venerated places of this kind which were distinguished by the worship of the fathers and their sanctity. For this reason they are so often censured by Moses and the prophets; and with the utmost zeal Moses endeavors to refer all accounts, rites, wonderful deeds, and the entire worship to the place which the Lord chose. "Take heed," he says (Deut. 12: 13-14), "that you do not offer at every place, but only at that place at which there shall be a remembrance of My name."

Therefore he designates for them a definite place and calls it the Tabernacle מוֹעֵד, that is, the appointed, definite, and fixed place. This tabernacle God gave to Moses as a sure sign of the place He had chosen, and He added the promise that He would dwell there, be present, and hear the invocations and prayers of those who call upon Him.

But that very people, which most of all had a sure and definite place of worship, wandered and strayed most of all in uncertain and self-chosen places.

Such is the deplorable perversity of our nature that we do not keep what God commands or regard it highly; but whatever the devil prescribes, this we receive and observe with the utmost eagerness and deference. We erect altars, chapels, churches; we run to Rome and to St. James.[78] But meanwhile we slight Baptism, the Eucharist, absolution, and our calling.

And the pope has concerned himself with this one purpose: to do away with the fixed place or tabernacle, that is, the ministry of the Word. He does not bother about the Word and the sacraments, nor does he make use of them; but he takes them away and horribly torments the people. He fills the entire world with his indulgences, and wherever there are places and self-chosen nooks, he dispenses indulgences in order to give support to his errors and his mania for idols.

On the contrary, God calls us back to the place where the memory of His name is, to our tabernacle, which is the ministry of the Word. Where the Word resounds and the sacraments are administered according to Christ's institution, this is the true tabernacle of God.

If the pope had such weighty testimony in his favor that God had spoken with him at Rome as He did with Abraham on Mt. Moriah, who could resist him? Now, however, by his own audacity, without the Word, he gives support to such idolatrous practices in the name of Peter and fills the entire world with his most impudent lies in order to seize for himself the wealth of the world.

Therefore the example of Abraham, who had most valid reasons for instituting something at this place, is something notable. He was called from Beer-sheba to Mt. Moriah by divine authority; he offered a very great and admirable sacrifice because he was ready to immolate his own son; and he heard the Word of God from heaven in fear and faith. Nevertheless, he undertakes nothing; nor does he call the people together to extol or honor this place.

Moses has given us a detailed account of this as an example and as instruction, in order that we may not attempt or venture anything in divine matters. In other matters, whether of the government or

[78] See p. 130, note 41.

of the household, there is abundant opportunity for you to keep busy and to do your duty boldly in accordance with the Word of God. Thus you are commanded to be bold, brave, and undaunted over against the Turks. But in matters of religion all presumption and rashness, all personal endeavors and preferences, are altogether forbidden, just as they are censured again and again by all the prophets.

To his religious practice Abraham adds nothing over and above his calling. Although this place was most holy, and very saintly persons — angels, Abraham, and Isaac — had stopped and tarried there, he nevertheless turned away from all this and departed. He thought: "I have done what I was obliged to do; I have sacrificed my son just as I was commanded to do. But God is not commanding me to set up a form of worship at this place. Hence I shall venture to do nothing." Thus he refrains from every rash and bold action; he abides in the fear of the Lord and waits for His call, ready to obey and to follow wherever God calls him.

Therefore what this passage teaches is that in matters of religion the question above all others must be "Who has given the command?" Seneca says: "Do not consider who is speaking, but consider what is being said." [79] This rule has a place in the household and in the state; but in the church and in matters of religion it must be turned around, and one must ask who, not what. In man there is some wisdom as a result of the light of reason, which was implanted by God. But because it is characteristic of man to err and to be deceived, one must consider what is being said, not who is saying it; and one should not rely on the person.

But in the church one must consider who is giving the command, what kind of person he is, and how important he is. If this is not done, the devil very easily changes "Who is giving the command, what kind of person is he, and how important is he?" into "What is being commanded, what is its nature, and how important is it?"

Ahaz is thinking of providing a special form of worship for God, and he immolates his son in accordance with the example of Abraham (2 Kings 16:3). But he commits a grievous sin; for God did not command this. He demanded that a מִנְחָה, or calf, be offered. But Ahaz disregards this and seizes upon the what instead of the who.

These facts should frequently be brought to remembrance and

[79] A favorite saying of Luther's or of his editors; cf. *Luther's Works*, 3, p. 287, note 58.

carefully considered in the church, in order that we may be satisfied with the doctrine once delivered (Jude 3). If we had followed it prior to these times, we would never have approved of convents, pilgrimages, indulgences, and sacrifices for the dead. Every pastor would have taught the Word of God in his parish; and the church would have felt satisfied with the Word, Baptism, the Lord's Supper, absolution, and solace in death and life. Then everyone would have done his duty in his civil and household activities, whether he was a servant or a master, an officer of the state or a subject. Those monstrous papistic abominations would never have crept into the church.

Abraham conducts himself in this manner after he has come away from the religious performance, the angels, and the appearance of God on Mt. Moriah, than which no place was more sacred in the entire world; for God's voice and promise resounded there. He turned his back on all this, so highly does he esteem his calling and the ministry of the Word. Since God gives him no command, he does not venture to do anything but returns to the works of the household, governs his domestics, his wife, and his servants, where clearly nothing spiritual or ecclesiastical is apparent. He leaves these things behind on Mt. Moriah. Nor does the appearance of the angels detain him, but he returns to the lads and to the ass.

If some devout hermit or monk were to hear this, he would detest Abraham. For, he who leaves so sacred a place, where God dwells with His angels, and goes to his ass and does the common, filthy, and stableboy chores of the household — is he a saintly patriarch? What sort of sanctity is this? It is astonishing how much those fellows despise these chores. The only thing they regard as piety and saintliness is withdrawal into a deserted corner after abandoning the world, that is, father, mother, and civic duties.

In one place Jerome bestows such high praise on this kind of sanctity that he maintains that the father or mother who stands in the way of a monk about to enter a monastery and desires to draw him back should be repulsed and trampled underfoot.[80] These are wicked and despicable words. Really, Jerome, we tread you underfoot, together with your Bethlehem, your cowl, and your desert; for through the ministry of the Word of God I am called, not to Beth-

---

[80] Cf., for example, Jerome's letter to the monk Heliodorus, Epistle XIV, 3, *Patrologia, Series Latina,* XXII, 547—548.

lehem but to the church, into a parish, to hear the Word of God. There God dwells, there the guardian angels are, and there I hear that I must honor my parents and devote myself in a godly and faithful manner to my calling. If God wants to place me elsewhere, He will call me. Without a call let the devil follow you and others.

Because of the Word and God's command, therefore, I shall honor my parents and not tread them underfoot. But if I renounce Baptism, faith, and obedience to God — which all monks have done — what saintliness or what worship of God can there be?

Christ says (cf. Mark 10:29): "For My sake you will leave brothers, sisters, father, mother, wife, children, and lands." But you should not leave them of your own will or choice when they need your service and support most. Godlessness of this kind had also prevailed among the Jews, since they taught that a sacrifice was a mark of far greater saintliness than obedience to one's parents. Christ inveighs against this in Matt. 15:5. The Jews said: "A קָרְבָּן," that is, a gift and sacrifice, "will be of greater benefit to you than honor"; and thus, under the pretense of saintliness and religious belief, they set aside the position and prestige of parents in order to satisfy their greed.

Just as this doctrine has been treated at great length and carefully explained up to this point, so it must be constantly repeated on account of the adolescents and the tender youth, who are the seedbed of the church, that they may learn that they must stand firmly and remain where God speaks, and that they may accustom themselves to those obligations which are commanded by God, unless they are called elsewhere or driven out, as when tyrants banish and force godly men out of their offices.

To be sure, a free and voluntary choice of a religious life pleases the flesh and seems wholly acceptable to reason. But if you follow its lead, you are doing exactly what those did who forsook the tabernacle and rushed to trees and groves. This is devilish and not a mark of godliness; and Paul also condemns self-chosen acts of religious devotion where there is no Word that calls but only a will that chooses and establishes.

Therefore Moses has carefully recorded that Abraham did not want to remain at that sacred place when he had finished his sacrifice. Instead, he returned to the mean works of a layman and to his forms of worship, which were still unrestricted and not bound to any special place. For he was still wandering about and had no fixed form of worship but brought a sacrifice whenever God commanded him to do so.

Accordingly, Abraham returned to the lads, or servants, and to his ass, and there he undoubtedly prepared a banquet and feasted with his servants and his son; for a sumptuous and merry banquet is an essential part, as it were, of a sacrifice.

Thus the Law prescribed (cf. Lev. 7:28-36) burning the fat and giving the shoulder and breast to the priest when animals were offered. If it was not a burnt offering, the rest of the flesh would belong to those who brought the sacrifice. Then they would sit down before the Lord, feast joyfully, and give thanks to God.

It was also customary among the heathen to feast at their sacrifices, and as a result of this heathen rite we live and dress more sumptuously on feast days. Thus Abraham also sat at the foot of the mountain near his ass and feasted with his servants and his son.

It is surely amazing that after so great a trial, which involved the sacrifice of his son, Abraham was immediately able to be collected and cheerful. Evidently this was their custom, even though feasts after sacrifices had not yet been prescribed by law, as was ordained later on by Moses. Accordingly, after the son had been restored and the ram had been slaughtered, both the father and his son rejoiced heartily and undoubtedly related everything to the servants with great joy and praised God with grateful hearts. After leaving the extraordinarily holy place where they had sacrificed, where the angels had appeared, and where God had made His presence known, they went back to Beer-sheba, whence they had gone forth. They returned to Sarah.

20. *Now after these things it was told Abraham: Behold, Milcah also has borne children to your brother Nahor:*

21. *Uz the first-born, Buz his brother, Kemuel the father of Aram,*

22. *Chesed, Hazo, Pildash, Jidlaph, and Bethuel.*

23. *Bethuel became the father of Rebecca. These eight Milcah bore to Nahor, Abraham's brother.*

24. *Moreover, his concubine, whose name was Reumah, bore Tebah, Gaham, Tahash, and Maacah.*

Syria and Canaan are adjoining regions; but up to this time Abraham did not know what was happening at the home of his brother Nahor, who had remained in Haran with his wife. Therefore Moses records that he received a report about the family and children of his brother, namely, that Milcah had borne him eight sons and his concubine four. This makes twelve persons besides Rebecca.

Holy Scripture makes mention of this genealogy because, in the first place, it makes Nahor a father almost like the patriarch Jacob in respect to the correct and exact number of their male and female children — for he begot twelve sons and one daughter, just as Jacob did — and, in the second place, on account of Rebecca and her betrothal to Isaac, which took place a little later.

Furthermore, this passage throws light on an earlier question in the eleventh chapter [81] and shows that Nahor is older than his brother Abraham because he had such a large number of children, who are enumerated here. Moreover, Bethuel has a daughter Rebecca, Nahor's granddaughter, when Abraham is 80 years old. Therefore one assumes from this that Abraham is not the first-born.

To be sure, among the Jews Abraham is regarded as the first-born, Haran as the second, and Nahor as the third; but if this is correct, how could Milcah and Sarah, Haran's daughters, marry the two brothers Nahor and Abraham? For it follows that Haran married when he was eight years old and begot Sarah, which is altogether absurd. Lyra alone opposes this opinion of the Jews and concludes that Abraham was born last and was sixty years younger than his brother, and he proves this with the credible conjectures and arguments we have enumerated above.

But Stephen — in Acts 7:4 — troubles me more. He says that Abraham departed after his father's death. From this it follows that 60 years have to be added to the age at which Abraham departs, if you consider the account and calculate the years of his father Terah. But if you count from Abraham's seventieth year, as is commonly done in all computations, 60 years are lost, as we also mentioned above, just as in the Books of Kings 20 years are also lost. Thus we lose almost 100 years.

It seems, however, that because of the Last Day, the hour or year of which God has wanted to be unknown, Holy Scripture has hidden these years in accordance with a special plan. For it may be that He is anticipating the thoughts or expectation of the godly by 100, 160, or more years.

[81] Cf. Luther's discussion of the views of Lyra and of Rabbi Solomon on these questions, *Luther's Works*, 2, pp. 237 ff.

The other question — concerning Sarah or Iscah and Milcah — has been dealt with above (Gen. 11:29).[82] There were three brothers: Haran, the first-born, who dies at Ur of the Chaldeans and leaves two daughters, Milcah and Iscah, whom Terah takes under his protection and guardianship. Nahor is the middle brother. Abraham is the third.

These two married two sisters who were their nieces or the daughters of their brother Haran, for at that time marriages of that kind were still not subject to any restriction.

Moreover, Moses states that among those 12 fathers Kemuel is the father of the Syrians. But this name has completely disappeared and perished, and no other mention is made of it in the Holy Scriptures.

Uz gets his name from wood, or from a tree. But he, too, is regarded as the father of the Syrians. This name is also given to the land of Uz (Job 1:1), in which Job was born, as St. Jerome declares.[83] Many maintain that Job was of the family and progeny of Esau, an opinion which I, too, once held.[84] But I have changed my mind and prefer to believe that he must have been born in Mesopotamia, in Syria. Hence it is related in the account about Job that the neighboring Chaldeans laid waste his fields, plundered his house, and carried off his cattle. Therefore I am of the opinion that Job was a powerful and rich lord who occupied some part of Mesopotamia close to the Chaldeans and the Babylonians.

Buz, too, was a ruler and had possession of a part [85] of Mesopotamia. Hence Elihu, the son of Barachel, is called a Buzite, who discourses against the afflicted Job in so hateful a manner and heaps much abuse upon him. Thus it is apparent that Nahor had a rather large and famous church, in which there were many outstanding men. Abraham did not have men of this kind in his church.

But Jerome writes [86] that men very well versed in the Scriptures maintain that this Elihu is Balaam (Num. 23), who was an outstand-

---

[82] Cf. *Luther's Works*, 2, pp. 240—241.

[83] Jerome, *Liber hebraicarum quaestionum in Genesin, Patrologia, Series Latina*, XXIII, 1021.

[84] Presumably this idea was based on Augustine, *The City of God*, XVIII, 47.

[85] Instead of *patrem* in the Weimar text, we have followed other editions and read *partem*.

[86] Jerome, *Liber hebraicarum quaestionum in Genesin, Patrologia, Series Latina*, XXIII, 1021, quoting Jewish sources.

ing prophet and teacher in Mesopotamia to whom [87] oracles of God were revealed, as he himself boasts, and many glorious prophecies were entrusted by God. Therefore when he says (Num. 23:7): "The king of Moab has called me, Balaam, from Aram," that is, from Syria, he points out that he had been called from some region where these fathers, who are enumerated in this passage, lived; and it is evident that they certainly were distinguished men and had a kingdom or empire that was flourishing and well established.

Moses records that Balaam was the son of Beor, whom Peter calls Bosor,[88] and that he lived beyond the river of the children of Ammon, that is, beyond the Tigris or the Euphrates.

Balaam was a great man; but he fell horribly, as the account of him proves. He had most important prophecies, similar to the predictions of Daniel, about Alexander the Great and about the Roman Empire, which would lay waste the kingdom of Israel and Judah. Thus this Balaam is said to have descended from Buz, the son of Nahor; and he lived up to the time of Moses. These two men were the greatest prophets of that age. Balaam was summoned from Mesopotamia against Moses, who came from Egypt; and Balaam really had the Word of God and blessed Israel.

[87] We have accepted the reading of the Erlangen edition and translated *cui* rather than *qui*.

[88] The reference is to the Vulgate of 2 Peter 2:15: *secuti viam Balaam ex Bosor, qui mercedem iniquitatis amavit.*

CHAPTER TWENTY-THREE

1. *Sarah lived a hundred and twenty-seven years; these were the years of the life of Sarah.*

2. *And Sarah died at Kiriath-arba (that is, Hebron) in the land of Canaan; and Abraham went in to mourn for Sarah and to weep for her.*

IN the first place, in order not to appear unacquainted with or not to have read the thoughts of the Jews, we shall review them briefly.[1] For they invent hidden meanings in this passage for the years of Sarah's age, because Moses does not simply state that Sarah lived 127 years, as we usually say, but adds the word "years" to each number: 100 years, 20 years, seven years. They maintain that this is done to indicate that Sarah was as beautiful in her hundredth year as she was in her twentieth, and that she was no less chaste and virtuous in her twentieth year than she had been in her seventh year.

Let us by all means grant them these figments, which were invented with a pious sentiment to bestow praise on the extraordinary virtue and the noble figure of an extraordinarily saintly matriarch who very much deserved such praise. We, too, are in the habit of doing this after the death of friends and relatives. We recount their commendable deeds and virtues, cover up their faults, and mention things that deserve praise. We do so in order to alleviate our grief and longing in this manner.

But it would be silly if one wanted to make from this a general rule or canon and apply it to all numbers of years. Thus when the years of the patriarchs are enumerated above, it would be altogether absurd if a similar comparison of the years of their life were undertaken in the case of each one.

I am surprised, however, that they did not rather consider why Moses uses the plural — "the lives of Sarah" — as though he intended

[1] The source of this information about the Jewish exegetical tradition is Lyra *ad* Gen. 23:1.

to say: "Sarah had lives." A consideration of the years of the lives
of Sarah would be more profitable.

For Moses is referring to the great and infinite variety of changes,
misfortunes, and perils, as well as to the very widely different kinds
of life that Sarah saw and bore. She was born in Babylon, and there
she married. Soon after this she left with her husband and lived in
Haran. Later on she dwelt in the land of Canaan. There Abraham
was a sojourner. Finally he came to Egypt and Gerar. These most
annoying changes and migrations the very saintly mother endured
with great courage, and in regard to every outcome of all her misfortunes she was most patient.

And human life as a whole is actually such that because of the
extraordinary change of all things one can call it "lives"; for we die
as often as a new trial arises, and we become alive in turn when we
are buoyed up and receive comfort.

Observe, I beg you, how great a variety and difference there is in
the life of each person.[2] The first age is that of a seven-year-old boy.
When this has come to an end, another period of seven years follows,
just as philosophers and physicians, too, point out when they discuss
the climacteric years during which striking changes take place. And
Paul says about himself in 1 Cor. 13:11:[3] "When I was a child, I spoke
like a child, I thought like a child, I reasoned like a child; when
I became a man, I gave up childish ways." Such changes are part
of the lives of the human race. For this reason that entire sequence
of ages in each human being is justly called lives, because during
any period of seven years we are changed into a different appearance,
disposition, and understanding. In short, we die and become alive.

During the third period of seven years thoughts about marriage
arise. When you have become a husband, the cares of the household
or of the state follow. When you are elected to the senate, you are
admitted to the deliberations and counsels of the rulers. There you
must put on new manners and a new skin; for many inconveniences,
burdens, and difficulties, as well as the hatred of neighbors and
associates, will have to be borne. Often there will even be a lessening
of prestige and esteem. This variety of new ways and of changes
makes for a variety of lives.

[2] Luther may have derived this information about "the ages of man" from
Aristotle, *History of Animals,* Book VII, ch. 1, and from Horace, *Ars poetica,*
lines 158 ff.

[3] Here the original has "2 Cor."

This is what Moses wanted to indicate when he speaks of "the lives of Sarah." It is as though he were saying: "Sarah, in conformity with differences in places and people, often adopted a different attitude and different ways. When she came to a place where she thought she would live pleasantly and quietly, she was compelled to move and to change her plans and feelings as she did so." For this reason that saintly woman had many lives. More attention should have been given to these things, although it is easy for me to believe that in her hundredth year she was just as beautiful as she was in her twentieth.

Then one should much rather consider how Abraham delivered a beautiful funeral address about Sarah. For in the Holy Scriptures no other matron is so distinguished. Her years, lives, conduct, and burial place are described. In the eyes of God, therefore, Sarah was an extraordinary jewel on whom extraordinary love was bestowed, and she is mentioned deservedly by Peter as an exemplar for all saintly wives. He says (1 Peter 3:6) that she called Abraham lord and that "you are her daughters." To all Christian matrons Peter holds her up as a mother.

Scripture has no comments even on the death of other matriarchs, just as it makes no mention of how many years Eve lived and of where she died. Of Rachel it is recorded that she died in childbirth (Gen. 35:16-19). All the other women it passes over and covers with silence, with the result that we have no knowledge of the death of Mary, the mother of Christ. Sarah alone has this glory, that the definite number of her years, the time of her death, and the place of her burial are described. Therefore this is great praise and very sure proof that she was precious in the eyes of God.

But these facts do not concern Sarah, who is already dead, as much as they concern us, who are still alive. For it is a very great comfort to hear that the departure and death of that most saintly matriarch and of all the fathers, in comparison with whom we are nothing, differs in no wise from our own death but was just as odious and ignominious as our own is. Their bodies were buried, consumed by worms, and hidden in the earth on account of their stench, not otherwise than if they had not been the corpses of saints; yet they were most saintly people, and, although departed, they are actually alive in Christ.

Accordingly, these things are written for our sakes, in order that we may know that the most saintly fathers and mothers underwent the same experiences we are wont to undergo. Nevertheless, it is certain about them that in the eyes of God they live; and I believe that they — namely, Abraham, Isaac, Jacob, Adam, etc. — rose with Christ.

And this seems to have been the reason why Abraham went to so much trouble about the burial, lest his dead Sarah be buried in a foreign land. Later we shall hear the same thing about Isaac. Thus Jacob and Joseph wanted to be buried in the land of Canaan, not in Egypt.

This wish is proof that God implanted this sentiment in them, so that they desired and wanted to be buried in this land, which had been promised to them, with the sure hope that they would be raised with Christ. They wanted their burial place to be there, in order that they might repose not far from the Seed that would come; for Hebron is two or three miles distant from Jerusalem. Hence they undoubtedly rose with Christ for our comfort, lest we fear death when we see the horrible shape of our bodies after death.

Those who have no hope of the future resurrection (1 Thess. 4:13) are not at all concerned about the future life. Nor do they think about it. But these things were written for us in order that we may remember how from the beginning of the world all the saints died and were reduced to the same stench and ashes, as Paul says in 1 Cor. 15:43:[4] "It is sown in dishonor." They underwent the same corruption and dishonor notwithstanding the fact that they were saintly in the flesh and in the spirit.

For thus it has pleased God to raise up from worms, from corruption, from the earth, which is totally putrid and full of stench, a body more beautiful than any flower, than balsam, than the sun itself and the stars.

I am mentioning these things in order that the examples of these saints may influence us; for those who are weak in faith are affected more and are drawn more pleasantly, as it were, to comfort by these less important examples than by the example of Christ. Because Abraham, Isaac, Jacob, and Sarah die in this way, the godly heart, though still weak, thinks: "Why should I object to or shudder at the lot common to all the saints?"

For it is not so much their own weakness that catches the eyes of the weak as that horrible appearance of dead bodies. Therefore

---

[4] Here the original has "1 Cor. 5."

they think: "If I had such a body as Christ had, which death could not corrupt or worms consume, I would await the Last Day with greater courage." When the death of Christ is set before them as an example, it somehow does not seem to be a death, because He rose again on the third day. Hence the weak are affected and strengthened more when they see that the corruption of the bodies of the patriarchs is like our own corruption.

But those who are stronger in their faith simply despise death and proudly scoff at and make sport of it. They say: "What is death? What is hell? Christ, God's Son, died and was put under the Law. He overcame death by dying, and He restored life to us."

If we were so strong and could believe without any doubt that Christ died for our sins and rose again for our justification and life (Rom. 4:25), no terror or fear would cling to us; for the death of Christ is a sort of sacrament which assures us that our death is nothing. But the weak are affected more by examples than by a sacrament, for because of the greatness of the Person of Christ it does not penetrate hearts so easily and persuade them to despise death.

Therefore we cling to examples that are analogous, just as I myself sometimes take more pleasure in the example of Sarah than in that of Christ. The reason is the weakness of my faith. Sarah's death has greater appeal and more comfort for me, since I know that she was a most saintly woman. Nevertheless, I hear that she dies, is buried, and is forgotten in such a shameful manner, as though she had been snatched from the sight not only of men but also of God and the angels. If this happened to her, I shall not be disturbed, even though the same thing happens to me.

But those who have greater strength of heart and faith cherish this sacrament; and because they believe that the Son of God died for them, they scoff at death and regard Satan and hell as a jest, in accordance with 1 Cor. 15:55: "O death, where is thy sting?" and Col. 2:15: "He disarmed the principalities and powers and made a public example of them, triumphing over them in Himself." Here Paul is speaking very mockingly and disdainfully about death.

The reason is that for Paul Christ is not only an example but also a sacrament, which is richer and far more sublime than an example. For the sacrament supplies in manifold ways and without limit whatever is lacking in the example. Sarah did not die for me; nor can she bestow life on me. But it is the majesty and importance of the sacrament that it has life-giving power which will restore life to me in the resurrection of the dead.

The example of Sarah is the rhetoric, as it were, which draws, arouses, and persuades us to despise death; but the sacrament brings about and works in my body what was brought about in Abraham and many saints who were raised from the dead.

Therefore examples should not be scorned, since the rhetoric they employ is pleasant; but because the example of Christ is at the same time a sacrament, it is efficacious in us and not only teaches us, as do the examples of the fathers, but accomplishes what it teaches. It gives life, the resurrection, and deliverance from death.

The examples of the saints teach that one has to die, and they persuade us to bear death with composure. Over and above this, however, Christ's example says: "Arise. Be alive in death. Your putridity will become more radiant and more brilliant than the sun." For Christ's example is a sacrament which bears witness and makes us certain; it not only teaches or persuades but proves and demonstrates necessarily that Christ's death imparts life to us.

Therefore those who are weak and have fearful consciences are doing what is right when they set before themselves the examples of the saints, with which to sustain and gradually stir up their faith more and more. But then they should also remember this, that what is lacking in the example of Christ so far as physical disgrace is concerned (for He was not disgracefully putrefied and consumed) was amply made up for and fulfilled on the cross and in the garden. If anyone had seen that horrible distress and torment of spirit and soul which He experienced in the garden, he would have said: "O how glorious the death of Abraham and Sarah was in comparison with that cross of Christ!" Accordingly, that which was lacking in the body was fulfilled in the spirit.

The arguments about the name of the place vary; for at Abraham's time it was called Kiriath-arba, not Hebron. Above (18:1) it is called the Valley of Mamre. The grammarians are at odds as to why this is done, and the question is still undecided.[5] Our translator has *in civitate Arbeae.* Therefore Arbea is a proper noun. Thus in German we call some cities Halberstadt, Carlstadt, etc.

If one considers the etymology, Kiriath-arba is the same as City of Four or Tetrapolis. Jerome adopts this etymology and says that

---

5 A quotation from Horace, *Ars poetica*, line 78.

this name was given to the place because four patriarchs — Adam, Abraham, Isaac, and Jacob — and their wives were buried there.[6] Concerning Abraham, Isaac, and Jacob there is certainly no doubt; but no one will find it easy to prove that Adam and Eve were buried in Kiriath-arba.

From Joshua (14:15; 20:7) one can gather that Hebron was formerly called Kiriath-arba and that the name was given to the city by a certain prince named Arba, who was powerful among the Anakim, that is, among those giants. He was a prominent man either because of his virtue and wisdom or because of his notorious vices, or he was powerful and famous for some other reason.

Thus among us Carlstadt gets its name from Carl, who was a great man among the kings. Halberstadt is named for a certain Albert, who was very prominent among the nobles.[7] But Arba got his name from a numeral, just as the Latins say Quintius, Octavius, Nonius.

Hence I do not approve of Jerome's opinion when he says that Adam was buried in that place, because such a destruction and confusion of the entire world came about as the result of the Flood that no traces of earlier tombs have remained. Thus the entire world became incomparably worse than that earlier one, both with respect to fruits and with respect to people. Paradise was laid waste and destroyed, and no one knows where Adam or Eve or other fathers were buried. For this reason neither their tombs nor any traces of them have come to light.

People also invent another tale; they say that Adam was buried on Mt. Calvary, where Christ was crucified later on.[8] By this they want to point out that Christ died at the tomb of Adam or where the tree of knowledge stood. These are pious fictions, but to me it seems likely that Paradise was located in the neighborhood of Jerusalem.

But it is astonishing and noteworthy on account of the various migrations, of which we have made mention so many times, that Moses states that Sarah died in Hebron, although shortly before this he related that Abraham, Sarah, and Isaac dwelt at Gerar and were safe because of the favor and protection of King Abimelech.

[6] Jerome, *Hebraicae quaestiones in Libro Geneseos, Corpus Christianorum, Series Latina,* LXXII, 28.

[7] The name Carlstadt is connected with Charlemagne; Halberstadt was founded in 814 and became an episcopal see in 820.

[8] This idea goes back to the early church; cf. *Luther's Works,* 1, p. 310, note 73.

Sarah was 90 years old when Isaac was born. But at this time Isaac is 37 years old. As these years went by, he must have increased in strength of mind and body. He was 20 when he was to be sacrificed. From that time up to the death of his mother Sarah 17 years passed. Meanwhile Abimelech died, and another king, who, as happens, was different from his predecessor, succeeded him. But with the change of kings the attitude of the people also changed, and at court as well as among the people the hatred and envy of Abraham, whom they had seen constantly increasing and acquiring great wealth, broke out afresh. Therefore since he was plagued by unjust hatred and insults and was expelled, he moved away and returned to his old encampment at Hebron. Otherwise he would have had no reason for going away.

But perhaps Abraham is not at home when death comes to Sarah. Perhaps he is busy with the affairs of his household, with selling the lands and possessions he had held at Gerar, or with similar things. God does not reveal this to him; nor does He keep him at home. But He lets him go away. When Sarah was confined to her bed, however, she no doubt sent a messenger to call her husband back. But death overtakes her before he returns. Therefore when he returns to Hebron, he finds his wife dead at home.

These events are recorded for our sakes, lest if at some time the same things should happen to us too, we imagine that we are experiencing something unusual or new in comparison with what happened to those who were very saintly and very dear to God. For the loss of one's very dear wife — and in one's absence at that — is a happening full of distress and grief.[9]

But, as Moses says, Abraham came to mourn for Sarah. He cannot call her back to life, and in the account that follows he no longer calls her his wife; he calls her his "dead one." This is altogether pathetic. He undoubtedly kept before his eyes and in his heart her virtue, her piety, the habit of her entire life, her calm and pleasing ways, her gentle nature, and her respect and love for her husband. As has so often been stated, all these qualities were outstanding in her.

But what about the statement of Moses that Abraham came to mourn and weep? Did a man so great weep, sorrow, put on mourning clothes, and walk about with a sad and downcast expression? Where is that triumphant victor over so many exiles and wanderings

___

9 It will be remembered that these lectures were delivered at a time when the plague was raging in Wittenberg; see p. 91, note 1.

through Syria, Egypt, and the entire land of Canaan? Where is the man who overcame four kings and set Lot free, offered his dearly beloved son (nothing like this is found in any other historical account), was willing to slay his son — who was the hope of future generations and of the promise — and in this manner conquered and killed his loftiest natural affection?

Why, then, does Abraham weep? Why does he not show himself a man in this instance? He conducts himself exactly as if he lacked such a lofty spirit and such heroic impulses and had never been disciplined by any perils or adversities.

My answer is: By this example Holy Scripture shows that mourning or weeping over dead parents, a wife, or friends does not displease God. Indeed, it is wrong not to weep. The world, which is totally leprous, calls the lack of natural affection — which means not being influenced by affection or love for one's wife, children, or relatives — courage;[10] but this is utter madness and is not a virtue.

But the saintly fathers were very softhearted people, and by nature they were purer. For this reason their natural affections surpassed those of others, who were without sensibility. For the saintlier one is and the more intimately one knows God, the more one understands the creatures and is attached to them.

Moreover, it belongs to mourning that you grieve and are sad from the heart, to the extent that a sad face, tears, sighs, and lamenting reveal your grief. It is for this reason that Moses writes clearly and commends Abraham's mourning and lamenting. Observe also how Jacob weeps on account of Joseph (Gen. 37:34-35). Accordingly, the saintly fathers were affected by the misfortunes and disasters of human nature. They wept with those who wept (Rom. 12:15). They were not logs and blocks of wood. No, they had most tender emotions and affections. For they had a knowledge of God. He who knows God also knows, understands, and loves the creature, because there are traces of divinity in the creature.[11]

When in the beginning God created heaven and earth, the first trace of the Father was the substance of things. Later the form was added. In the third place, there was the goodness. But the godly

10 Cf. Luther's discussion of pagan attitudes toward death in his *Commentary on Psalm 90, Luther's Works,* 13, 76-83.

11 This discussion of *vestigia* has its origin in the speculation about *vestigia Trinitatis* in Augustine, *On the Trinity,* for example, Book X, ch. 10:13, on "use" in relation to the Holy Spirit.

alone observe this difference in the creatures. The ungodly have no knowledge of it; for they know neither God nor the creatures, far less their use.

Moreover, the use of a thing concerns the Holy Spirit. He who sees the use of a thing sees the Holy Spirit, he who discerns the form or beauty of a thing sees the Son, and he who considers the substance and continuing existence of things sees the Father. These three — substance, form, and goodness — cannot be separated.

But in money a greedy person sees only substance, form, and weight; he is not aware that it is a trace of the Son. Nor does he consider the use of the thing, that is, what purpose it should serve — chiefly, of course, the glory of God, then the benefit of one's neighbor. The ungodly do not discern the goodness of things, even though they look to some extent at the substance and the form. Thus the man who lacks affection does not see the use of wife or children.

Abraham, however, understood for what use Sarah was given to him — not for lust but as a help for managing the domestics and for begetting and bringing up children. Because the ungodly do not understand this, they are not affected by it; they are nothing but stones. Such insensibility and lack of affection is indeed an indication of their leprous nature.

Accordingly, these things are recorded in praise of Abraham and to have us learn that it is commendable to weep for one's friends, just as above (19:27) he wept for the Sodomites, although in vain. Because we are human beings, we should feel the affection created by the Creator and put into our hearts, lest we be like the beasts.

Therefore we should take careful note of this description of the patriarchs whom Holy Scripture has thus set before our eyes, namely, that they are like us, are moved by human feelings, and speak like human beings; for human speech, feelings, heart, and soul are creatures of God, although they have been tainted by original sin.

The Holy Spirit praises the natural feelings. In fact, He does so in the case of the greatest men — men noted for their virtue, piety, and deeds. They were not logs, blocks of wood, or dullards who are not affected by anything, whether joyful or sad. It is the mark of the godly to be affected by the misfortunes, the joys, and the lot of pious people and to grieve even when their adversaries are in danger. And the Holy Spirit directs these sentiments in the godly.

Accordingly, just as anyone else grieves over the loss of his wife, so the saints, too, mourned the death of their people; and their mourning is honorable and godly. Others, who do not mourn, boast of a certain manliness and firmness of character; but they are devoid of affection and are without knowledge of and indifferent toward things, that is, toward the creatures of God.

Abraham mourns because he has lost his wife Sarah, a godly and noble matron who managed the domestics and the entire rather large and extensive household. He lost the light of his home — the light that served as an example for the domestics in every kind of virtue. Sarah was a queen of queens and a mother of housemothers. This is what Abraham's example that is before us teaches concerning human emotions and mourning for the departed.

3. *And Abraham rose up from before his dead, and said to the Hittites:*

4. *I am a stranger and a sojourner among you; give me property among you for a burying place, that I may bury my dead out of my sight.*

The departed should be mourned, but in such a way that there is measure in things.[12] "Weep for your dead," says Sirach (Ecclus. 22: 10-11). "But weep with moderation," that is, set a limit to your grief, "because he has found rest." If you lose a brother, father, wife, or relative, there is a reason for your grieving and for your not being a log and a block of wood who would laugh when those who are very dear are being buried; for this it is not a time for laughing, and such an iron and stony attitude displeases God. Nevertheless, your weeping must be kept within bounds, lest you be consumed by excessive grief.

This being torn away from very dear parents, wife, or children is indeed painful; for they now lack the light, says Sirach (cf. Ecclus. 22:11), that is, they no longer enjoy this life and our association. But to this mourning there must be opposed what follows: "He has attained rest." The extinction of light is the reason for mourning, but rest is the reason for comfort. "Therefore let him rest in peace," should be your thought, "for I know that it is well with him. He is not in sorrow or distress; he is at rest. There he is sleeping and is waiting for a better life, just like us who are still living." Thus it is our comfort that wife, son, and parents are sleeping and are not affected by hardships and afflictions but are resting gently in peace.

But when those awful and tragic calamities occur — as when David loses his son Absalom, who dies in mortal sin and is condemned — this is the bitterest sorrow and grief of all. Yet what else should one

[12] Cf. Horace, *Satires,* I, 1, 106.

do than leave the matter to God? But where the passing is peaceful and quiet, those who die sleep in peace. And this is what Moses has in mind when he says: "Abraham rose up." He felt grief and sorrow as a result of his dearly beloved wife's death, but he overcame that very natural feeling and proceeded to think about the burial.

But this, too, is strange, that while all three — Sarah, Abraham himself, and their son — were still living, Abraham was never concerned about owning and acquiring property. Now that Sarah is dead, he is concerned about this. Concern about a place to sleep seems unnecessary when you are unable to get possession of it. Yet when Moses relates that Abraham bought a place for Sarah after she was dead, not while she was living, he does so with special application and uses more words than he is accustomed to employ.

Up to this time Abraham was an alien and was unable to change this rather difficult mode of life, but after the death of his wife he thinks about a burial place of his own. In the past, while he was in Canaan for 70 years more or less, several of his domestics, manservants or maidservants, undoubtedly died; but he was concerned about no one else as much as he was concerned about Sarah. Some he buried in Gerar, others in Egypt. Here he is seeking an undisputed place for her burial — a place that belongs to him.

To the Hebrews the word גֵּר denotes a stranger. In Ps. 39:12 we read: "I am a stranger with Thee, and a sojourner, like all my fathers." Thus Paul says in Eph. 2:19: "You are no longer strangers and sojourners." The word denotes an outsider and one who comes from a foreign place. Thus Abraham was a sojourner because he was not born in Canaan but had his origin in Chaldea.

A תּוֹשָׁב is a sojourner who is not a proprietor but is a stranger in the land in which he is living. He has nothing of his own. Christians are sojourners and guests in this world. Their native country and possession is in another place, because according to their physical birth they come into the world from nothing. Therefore they are sojourners and do not remain in the world but leave the world behind. Thus we are also גֵּרִים. We have been reborn by the Holy Spirit through Baptism and the Word, and we live on earth as strangers and sojourners.

Accordingly, Abraham is saying: "I come from a foreign land, and here I have nothing of my own. I am a sojourner in a twofold sense, and for this reason I have no place where I may bury my dead." In Ps. 39 David carefully ponders these words, and the matter deserves close attention. For so great a man with so numerous a household, namely, more than 400 men besides the women and children, wandered about and roamed for so long a time. If one computes it correctly, he had about 1,000 people; for where there are 400 men, they have with them the same number of women and children.

Therefore the management carried on by this patriarch was extraordinary. If you consider our times, it would be altogether impossible today. For it is a wonder of wonders that God supported him together with so large a household in a foreign land, and that Sarah had charge of all this. Accordingly, Abraham's administration or management of his household is no less remarkable than his church was. He is a stranger and sojourner together with all his household. But he undoubtedly encouraged and sustained himself with the promise.

Moreover, from this passage concerning the possession of the burial place a great sea of questions and opinions arises among teachers and for the Master of the *Sentences*.[13] For in scholastic theology the material for debating about simony was drawn from this passage, but they treat it in such an obscure and confused manner that it does not deserve to be brought to light and remembered. Two hundred years ago simony was a terrible crime; but as Julius boasts in a dialog written by Erasmus, the popes have barely retained the shadow of the word.[14]

Simony is the purchase or sale of something spiritual for money or when someone accepts money and gives a gift or something spiritual. Thus when Simon Magus (Acts 8:17 ff.) saw that the Holy Spirit was given through the laying on of the apostles' hands, he offered them money, saying: "Give me also this power, that anyone on whom I lay my hands may receive the Holy Spirit." He wanted the Holy Spirit, purchased with money, to be in his power and to do what pleased him. Then Peter sternly rebuked him. "Your money perish with you," he said, "because you thought that the gift of God is acquired with money."

[13] Peter Lombard, *Sententiae*, Book IV, Dist. 25, *Patrologia, Series Latina*, CXCII, 907.

[14] Luther is referring to an anonymous attack on Pope Julius II, published about 1514 under the title *Julius exclusus;* it was widely believed that Erasmus had written it, and most scholars still incline to this opinion.

From that Simon the crime is called simony. It occurs when, in accordance with Simon's example, someone thinks that the gifts of God are to be bought with or sold for money. Christ does not sell His gifts and grace, but He has redeemed us without charge.

This is the true definition. Later on the canonists distorted it in an astonishing manner; for that part of the definition, "the gift of God for money," they apply to everything men give to God. Thus they now call the revenues of the church "spiritual goods" [15] because they are gifts of God, not gifts that God has given but gifts that men have offered to God. Is this not monstrous blindness and stupidity?

Moreover, they drag in a text from Moses (Lev. 27:9): "All of such that any man gives to the Lord is holy." They maintain that such things — benefices, jewels, and other things originally contributed for the support of the ministers — are gifts offered to the church. But if one asks whether it is permitted to sell or buy them, their answer is: "By no means, because they are spiritual goods."

But Peter understands gifts given by God in a passive and not in an active sense. Hence it is a fallacy of division and composition, as the dialectician says, when they confuse and jumble them.[16] But how could they be teaching skillfully about this matter, since they are unconcerned about the gifts of the Holy Spirit and are submerged in simony and in gifts given to God, that is, things that are commonly called spiritual goods?

I have often deplored the misuse of these terms, "spiritual goods" and "spiritual persons," as they call their priests. I would gladly have retained them in their true and proper use, but they became lost to us because of their misuse; and now revenues, taxes, houses, towns, and lands — things that pertain most of all to the state — are called spiritual gifts by the papists. But a spiritual man is he who believes and has been baptized, whether he is a layman or is in an ecclesiastical office; it does not denote a priest who has been anointed, shaved, and ordained for sacrifices for the benefit of the dead.

I am telling you this in order that you may know that in canon law there is utterly perverse misuse and terrible blindness in discussions about simony. The purchase or sale, not of the gifts of the Holy Spirit in the active sense but of the gifts of men who have

[15] This practice is reflected in the use of the German adjective *geistlich* for the clergy: *ein Geistlicher* is a clergyman.

[16] See p. 168, note 72, for a similar reference.

given them to God or to the church, such as prebends, cities, and the like, is called simony by the canonists — for example, if someone sells a spiritual benefice, as they call it, a parish, or a benefice of an altar and a Mass; likewise if a bishop were to accept money and ordain a priest. Later they debate whether a simonist who has been ordained by a simonist is actually ordained or not. About these questions there are in existence wagonloads of books, yes, even oceans of them.[17]

But if this definition of theirs remains true, then all the papistic bishops and canons are simonists pure and simple, and all are condemned to hell and the devil. They condemn themselves by their own canon law, not by evangelical law. The Bishop of Mainz paid the pope 20,000 guldens for the pallium; the Bishop of Würzburg, 10,000.[18] Canons paid 100 guldens. Are not all these men simonists? Accordingly, the entire papacy has been plunged and condemned into hell, because they are all simonists, not by our law but by their own.

About this the canonists have nothing to say; nor do they tolerate our censure. But if the ministers and pastors of our churches marry, they condemn and kill them. What else is this than the height of iniquity?

If a bishop had branded someone with this crime 400 years ago, everybody would have avoided associating with that person. Indeed, he would have been excommunicated. But now everything is venal. Meanwhile they order us to observe canons and decrees from which they themselves are completely free. They bark at us that the decrees of the popes are being disregarded and that ecclesiastical rank is held in contempt and broken down. But why do they themselves not observe these things? Among them nobody sins but the Son of God; nobody is just but the devil.

But would that the pope had the wisdom to recognize this boon, that our doctrine frees him from his books and decrees, and absolves him from the crime of simony, because he seizes only temporal things, namely, gold and silver, which are not spiritual, as Baptism, the Gospel, and the ministry of the Word are! He seeks or seizes none of these, which are the true gifts of the Holy Spirit. To be sure,

[17] The appropriate sections in the *Corpus iuris canonici* are *Decretum Gratiani*, Part IIa, *causa* I; *Decretum Gregorii*, Book V, title 3.

[18] When Albert was appointed Archbishop of Mainz in 1517, he paid this fee but made arrangements with Rome and with the bankers of the House of Fugger that helped to precipitate the conflict over indulgences.

gold and silver are gifts of God; but they pertain to the state and to the household and are physical.

In conformity with the true definition, therefore, we absolve the pope from this crime in which he implicated himself by his own law. We do so because he does not sell things that are properly called spiritual, for he does not have them. No, he sells certain offices and seizes for himself the wealth of the world. He does not sell the ministry. Indeed, he is not concerned about the ministry of God and the church. For this reason the charge of simony should not be lodged against him; but he should be charged with the crime of Verres and Dionysius,[19] and he should be called robber of all robbers, thief of thieves, and brigand of brigands. For he is a man with a rapacious and insatiable gullet and a desire to devour and swallow material goods.

But simony, as Peter defines it, is the offense committed in the church when we accept money for the gifts of the Holy Spirit but not for material gifts. The canonists, who are out-and-out asses, confuse these two things. For there is no room for simony in the case of possessions of the household or of the state; it is committed only when the gifts of the Holy Spirit are involved.

But if the objection is made that those material goods have a connection with spiritual goods, the reply is: "This is certainly right; the household and the government have a connection with the church, because this present life cannot be sustained without food and drink. But that does not make all the things believers use spiritual, does it?"

It is simony when I sell for a price something spiritual that should be given gratis. But a church, a grave, and all other gifts given to the saints are not spiritual; they are simply material. They can be seized, divided, and sold. But we cannot steal, sell, or buy spiritual gifts; for they belong to the Holy Spirit, not to us.

But if a minister or pastor of a church were unwilling to give you instruction concerning the remission of sins and the blessings of the Gospel or refused you absolution unless you bought it from him for a hundred guldens, that would be simoniacal.

And in this sense the pope is a simonist, for he offers grace and remission of sins to all if they pay him a fixed sum of money. That is selling something spiritual and the grace of the Holy Spirit, although

19 Verres, who died in 43 B. C., was a governor of Sicily, notorious for his bribery, whom Cicero prosecuted in 70 B. C.; Dionysius the Elder, who died in 367 B. C., was a tyrant of Syracuse, famed for his ruthlessness in war.

these things cannot be sold even if you pay 1,000 or more guldens for one absolution. For in the first place, the pope does not have them, and in the second place, it is impossible to sell spiritual things. It is possible, however, to deceive those who are ignorant and to pretend that there is a sale.

But the gifts of the Holy Spirit and the blood of Christ are not for sale; nor is their sale possible except by deceit and some pretense in accordance with the choice and will of men. When the pope promises that he who brings five groschen will redeem a soul from purgatory,[20] then there is real simony; but it is based on falsehood, because no freeing of a soul follows, even though the price, the purchase, and the sale are there.

In this way the pope has concocted the fiction that he has the power to remit sins. He has usurped the Keys, sold remission of sins, and promised deliverance from hell and purgatory. But he merely carried off the money, while the wretched souls were left under the power of sin, hell, and the devil.

This is simony in the strict sense, namely, selling the gift of the Holy Spirit. But this gift is bestowed without charge. One can obtain it in no other way. To be sure, it can be put up for sale; but God is not purchased. Possession does not result from a simoniacal transaction. Therefore simony is factually impossible. As a matter of pretense, however, it is exceedingly common. For the name of the Lord is prostituted and sold. But simony itself is nothing but an empty sham.

Therefore the pope is a simonist in spiritual matters. He sells remission of sins and righteousness. In temporal matters he violates things that are sacred and is a robber who would sell Christ Himself if he had Him in his hands as the Jews had Him. The inclination to do so is certainly not wanting.

There was simony like this in the convents, both on the part of the seller and on the part of the buyer; anyone who paid a hundred guldens could have anniversaries celebrated.[21] Therefore the entire

[20] Technically the sale of indulgences was simony, although it was permissible to give or receive an offering in connection with an indulgence; as Luther had discovered in 1517, there were many people in the church who found this distinction too subtle.

[21] A reference to the anniversary Masses said in commemoration of the death of the faithful.

papacy is the church of Satan; it is full of robbery, sacrilege, and unspeakable abominations and blasphemies.

Here the question arises whether a minister of the Word may demand or receive support for his office.[22] My answer is: "He may by all means, just as a poor person can accept some gift." If I had such power that nobody could be absolved from sins unless he had paid me several guldens, I would rake together all the wealth of the world in a single day. But this is not permitted; and the pope, with satanic daring, has invented this way of making money. We are commanded to teach, comfort, and absolve all who accept it and believe; and they all receive this without pay, in accordance with the statement (Matt. 10:8): "You received without pay, give without pay."

But just as Christians enjoy the ministry of the Word without pay, so they, in turn, must without pay support and defend their ministers and provide them with food and clothing in conformity with a sense of duty. In Gal. 6:6 we read: "Let him who is taught the Word share all good things with him who teaches." 1 Tim. 5:17 states: "Let the elders who rule well be considered worthy of double honor, especially those who labor in preaching and teaching." And Christ Himself says (Matt. 10:10): "The laborer deserves his food." In Is. 49:22 the Lord says that princes and kings will give gifts to the church. But these gifts are not prices, purchases, or sales. We must have our daily sustenance, food and drink; but absolution is not paid for with these. For who would be able to pay it? What are 100 or 1,000 guldens in comparison with the incalculable gift of the forgiveness of sins?

Therefore when we receive sustenance from the church, it is not a price equivalent to this gift, which is worth so much that the wealth of the whole world cannot pay for it. But because this stupendous and incalculable gift cannot be administered except by men who need food and clothing, it is necessary to nourish and support them. This, however, is not payment for the gift; it is payment for the service and the work.

Among the canonists there is another question: "If a minister of the church has saved 200 guldens from his work, may he purchase a farm or an estate with that money?"[23] They say no, because it is

---

[22] This problem occupied Luther frequently in the reconstruction of the churches of the Reformation; see, for example, *Luther's Works*, 9, pp. 138—140.

[23] Cf. Peter Lombard, *Sententiae*, Book IV, Dist. 25, 5—8, *Patrologia, Series Latina*, CXCII, 907—908.

an ecclesiastical benefit. But I maintain that he may, because it is not a spiritual thing, even though the person administers spiritual things.

Hence the canonists err most disgracefully and do not know what simony is. They confuse spiritual and material goods, and according to their own law and their own conscience they are outstanding simonists. They rob and devour the property of pastors and churches, are worse than Verres and Dionysius, and distribute things that are truly spiritual for money, as though these things were spoils. Nevertheless, they take upon themselves the rule of the whole world and judgment concerning our doctrine and the Word of God; they order us to obey the pope, although they neither understand nor concern themselves about their own statutes and decrees.

Lyra touches on this discussion briefly and wants to slip away without further ado by stating that what Abraham bought was the location of the grave, not the grave.[24] But this is a sophistical way of speaking, as even they themselves must acknowledge. Of course, Abraham did not buy a grave, because there was no grave at that place; but he was at liberty to provide one where he wanted it to be.

Besides, this example teaches that the dead should be buried with special honor and respect because of the faith in and the hope of the future resurrection. Before the times of the martyrs people had graves in every field, garden, and house. Later on, however, there was greater respect. Then special places and cemeteries were designated for burial, just as among the heathen, too, there were dignified funeral ceremonies. Therefore there is all the more reason for some reverence among Christians, on account of the article of faith concerning the resurrection of the flesh, lest we seem to be deprived of life and buried like horses and mules.

What follows has largely to do with customs except that one passage: "Give me the possession or ownership." For what our translator renders with "the right of burial,"[25] is not in the Hebrew text. It is as though Abraham were saying: "I would not ask for even a footbreadth in this land during my life, but I am only seeking a place where I may dig a grave and set up a monument for my Sarah, who has died."

The entire land was promised to Abraham and belonged to him

24 Lyra *ad* Gen. 23:4.

25 Luther's Latin text (cf. p. 197) does not contain these words.

by every right as a gift of his own. Yet he does not have possession of a footbreadth but is an exile, and together with Sarah he dies as a sojourner in his own land.

These things the prophets and the apostles observed with spiritual eyes, and somewhat more profoundly than others; for because Abraham, who is the lord of this land by divine authority, is an exile in it with Sarah and his son Isaac, it is signified in the spirit that we are strangers on earth and are living as if we were in exile.

For St. Paul says 2 Cor. 5:6: "As long as we sojourn in the body." But if we are exiles in the body, which is ours in a very special sense, and our life in the body is nothing else than a sojourn, how much more are the things which we possess on account of the body, namely, fields, home, and money, nothing else than exiles and sojourns! The body is a gloomy prison, as it were, in which the soul is kept confined as in a prison and dungeon.[26] Therefore half of us is nothing, as it were, and a stinking cadaver in a grave.

Accordingly, it is sufficiently evident that the patriarchs extracted and examined the very kernel in the promises and did not concern themselves with the shell alone. Thus Abraham understood that the promise given to him included the true fatherland and the true life, namely, the future life and a life better than this one — a life which is not a servitude and captivity of the soul.

When David calls himself a sojourner (Ps. 39:12), one could wonder why he is saying this, since he was a most powerful king of Israel and was in possession of the Promised Land. But he regards these things as trivial and has in sight another and far better habitation, which is a matter of no concern to those who are busily engaged in robbery and usury in this life, as if there would be no future life.

But how empty and transitory it is to glory and take pride in the goods and riches of this world, since no human being can be sure of his life for a single moment! Thus we all feel, see, and realize that we carry about with us a body that is half like a corpse and dead. Nevertheless, very many have the conviction that this life is the best and will last forever. Their shameless eagerness and insatiable desire to grab by fair means or by foul [27] makes it clear that this

---

[26] The idea of the body as a prison is found in Plato, *Cratylus*, 400c, *Gorgias*, 493a, and other places; Luther may have known it through Augustine, *Against the Academics*, I, 3.9.

[27] An allusion to the Latin proverbial saying *per fas et nefas.*

is what they think. Why do they do this? Doubtless because they are in the devil's exile, are going astray, and are entangled in the cares and anxieties of this life.

Therefore the faith and patience of Abraham is praised. He is looking for another possession — an eternal possession beyond this Promised Land. He wants Sarah to be buried in this land in order that she may be raised with Christ when He rises from the dead. Meanwhile he himself sojourns in his own land as in a foreign country. God does not grant him a footbreadth, not even a grave; but he buys a place from the inhabitants for a price. Therefore he was not afflicted with that shameful greed to accumulate riches as though he had to remain in this life forever. But with his whole heart he was intent on the promised Christ. Him he beheld in the promise, and he waited joyfully for His coming to this earth. Next there are things that have to do with proper conduct. But they are altogether honorable and profitable.

5. *The Hittites answered Abraham:*

6. *Hear us, my lord; you are a mighty prince among us. Bury your dead in the choicest of our sepulchers; none of us will withhold from you his sepulcher or hinder you from burying your dead.*

In his description of this agreement Moses is very wordy. But the Holy Spirit is doing this first of all in honor of that most noble matron Sarah, who is the mother of all the patriarchs, prophets, and most distinguished leaders and kings. In no other historical accounts does one find men like these. For this reason no other funeral is described so magnificently in the Holy Scriptures as Sarah's. Doubtless Christ wanted His ancestress to be buried with honor, as her good qualities deserved. For she ruled the domestics with discipline and piety. She was a far more excellent abbess than ours are in external and domestic matters. The abbesses of the nuns should not only not be compared with her; they should be relegated to complete obscurity. For what are they in comparison with Sarah, the mother of most illustrious princes and kings, who managed her household in such a commendable manner during her lifetime? But what else are the works of the abbesses than horrible idolatry, no matter what they do?

But because this entire passage has to do with proper conduct, one should note first the example of courtesy and respect among this people. Remarkable politeness beams in their speech, manners, and actions. Surely it would be hard to find such politeness in our age either among the old or the young. For this is how they address Abraham: "My lord, you are a prince of God." This is extraordinary respect, and the very men who are lords of the land and possess it by divine right show this respect to Abraham.

In the second place, one should consider the extraordinary modesty in Abraham's request. I think that Ephron, about whom more will be said later on, was a prince in Hebron. Abraham does not approach him immediately but first addresses those who are beneath him. He ingratiates himself with the greatest humility.

The Holy Spirit did not want to pass over these facts; it was His purpose to point out that He demands these qualities and esteems them highly. For this reason He presents the examples of great men, in order that we may learn that mutual respect among men is necessary and pleasing to God, so that we may yield to one another and, as Paul teaches in Rom. 12:10: "Outdo one another in showing honor," and in Phil. 2:3: "In humility count others better than yourselves."

Thus this detailed description is by no means useless. For we were not born as swine, mules, blocks of wood, or logs but with faces turned upward toward the stars;[28] and God has put into the human being a rational soul, which understands what the difference is between things that are honorable and things that are shameful, so that it recognizes the good in others and shows them honor. Therefore that boorish and brutish life which is manifest in the rude and barbarian manners of our people is not becoming to Christians.

And our country in particular has produced men without any culture, discipline, and courtesy. Consequently, you could say that the peasants, burghers, and nobles of these regions are more like swine than like men; such strangers they are to every kind of good breeding. Therefore I am often wont to wonder why God revealed the light of the Gospel to such uncouth and rude people first.

The poets relate that Ulysses once lost his companions and that they were all changed into swine.[29] The same transformation seems to have happened to our people. Yet there is less danger among those who are uncultivated. But if this evil spreads to the teachers of the

---

28 An allusion to Ovid, *Metamorphoses*, Book I, lines 84 ff.

29 The companions of Ulysses were changed into swine by Circe, *Odyssey*, Book X, lines 210 ff.

church who, on account of their particular gifts, claim everything for themselves and, because of some silly and boorish arrogance, despise everybody else, for whom they should have friendliness and love — this is a great plague for the churches.

Therefore learn from this example to control your manners in such a way that you accustom yourself to courtesy, modesty, and respect toward all. It is for this reason that Moses so earnestly and with so many words sets before our eyes the example of Abraham, who requests with the utmost modesty and humility that a part of the land be sold to him and does not insist with any impudence or rudeness. Even though he seems to be doing this out of necessity, since he is a sojourner, nevertheless, since so many good qualities and gifts had been showered upon him, he had reason to be proud. But he forgets all these things and addresses the people of Hebron respectfully and courteously.

They, in turn, greet him as a lord, even though he is a sojourner, and in word and deed they show extraordinary courtesy and kindness. In their dealings with the sojourner and stranger they also forget their own right and sovereign power in the land.

These are truly good works. Even though they pertain to civil affairs, they should be contrasted with all the revolting activities of the monks, whose sole occupation is to accustom young men received into their order to a foolish and disgusting humility foreign to the conduct of honorable and saintly men. Young people should rather learn humility, courtesy, and respect from this account.

Nevertheless, the hypocrites, like the apostate Witzel,[30] who said that we stressed civil works too much in our teaching, reject these as ordinary; and if you should ask them what else should be done, they say that one should go into a church, bellow in a chorus, and mumble prayers. But this and similar examples clearly prove their hypocrisy, because the Holy Spirit does not disdain to relate and praise these civil works so painstakingly.

Moreover, it is evident that God endowed Abraham and his church with extraordinary influence and distinction among the heathen, just as above at the court of King Abimelech, who grants him the use of the land and esteems him highly, although he owned nothing of it and was compelled to leave after the king had died.

[30] George Witzel (1501—73) had joined the cause of the Reformation in 1525 but had reverted to Roman Catholicism and taken a Roman Catholic parish in 1533; he wrote violently polemical treatises against Luther and his supporters.

Thus the people of Hebron, a heathen nation, honor him and call him a prince of God; this shows that they heard Abraham's sermons and believed in the God of Abraham. For wherever the most saintly patriarch was, he produced very much fruit through the Word and Spirit by teaching, exhorting, and reproving; and through his preaching the heathen heard and saw the great deeds of God and therefore believed and were saved. Consequently, they properly respected him as a lord, just as Sarah addressed him as lord (Gen. 18:12), and they called him a prince of God.

It is great good fortune when princes have with them guests of this kind, recognize God and Christ in them, and treat them with respect, and when the guest and priest, in turn, does his duty by teaching in a godly and faithful manner. It is a very rare blessing for godly priests to have a safe and quiet place where they may teach. It is an extraordinary gift, which the devil, the most malevolent enemy of God and the salvation of man, often obstructs and disturbs.

But where there is such harmony that the princes of a land honor, protect, and support ministers for spreading abroad spiritual things, one may truly say that a paradise of the world is there.

But if ministers are despised, ridiculed, and treated with contempt, as happened to Isaiah and other prophets — Is. 57:4: "Against whom do you open your mouth wide and put out your tongue?" — although they were most excellent and most faithful teachers, it is the surest evidence of God's wrath and of impending disasters; for contempt of so great a blessing as is tendered to men by godly ministers has never gone unpunished.

On the other hand, the condition of ungodly and wicked priests is commonly better; for they have princes who are most obsequious and very ready to grant every favor, just as the pope made all the kings and princes of the world beholden to him and exceedingly lavish, not only with their properties and wealth but also with their bodies. But in return for such great favors he led them astray and gained them for the devil.

Today the ministry has been successfully cleansed of all error and idolatry. But how is it received and treated in the world? It is reviled, expelled, and trampled underfoot; and the ministers are killed.

Through His boundless favor God has granted us hospitality under Their Most Serene Highnesses the Princes of Saxony, Duke John

Frederick, the elector, and his brother Ernest.[31] But as great as are the benignity, the favor, and the goodwill of the princes, so great are the exceedingly savage hatred, the ill will, and the contempt among the nobles, officials, burghers, and peasants, who, if they could do what they desire, would long since have expelled us from these abodes.

Therefore the affection, respect, and courtesy of the Hebronites toward Abraham are amazing. They recognized that he was a guest who was making all the inhabitants and citizens of that place rich, not with wealth, with gold and silver, but with heavenly and spiritual gifts, since he pointed out the way of salvation and freed their souls from sin and hell through the Word, in short, that he abounded in every kind of blessing. Accordingly, they, in turn, have a high regard for him, love him, and gladly listen to him, just as above he encountered similar goodwill at the court of King Abimelech.

Furthermore, "prince of God" is the honorable and impressive title with which the Hebronites address Abraham, not because he ruled over them politically, but because he had a large number of domestics in his house, more than 1,000 men. On this account they call him a prince of God who rules the best and saintliest men in his house. It is as though they were saying: "We do not have such a faithful people, such saintly, obedient, and humble servants as you have. Your rule is godlike, and it makes men saintly."

And it is indeed an extraordinary gift of God when princes rule their subjects wisely and well, and the subjects, in turn, are obedient. For God makes both: a seeing eye, that is, a real teacher, bishop, or magistrate; and a hearing ear, that is, obedient subjects and listeners. Where either is lacking, there is anarchy and a very evil situation; for it is not enough if you are only a hearing ear without a seeing eye, and vice versa.

Among the Hebronites Abraham was the seeing eye by virtue of his teaching and his rule over his domestics, and the Hebronites were the hearing ear. There the Word bore abundant fruit.

But if the eye does not see — as the pope is a blind and accursed eye — and the ear nevertheless hears — as up to this time we have most eagerly heard and accepted his traditions — there one has the surest road to destruction.

Today we have the seeing eye, that is, the pure doctrine of the Word; but we do not find a hearing ear, because our doctrine is held

---

[31] Cf. *Luther's Works*, 13, pp. x—xi.

in contempt, yes, is horribly cursed. Where both are to be found, however, God has surely brought this about, and it is a divine miracle, in which God and the angels in heaven take pleasure.

The other evidence of their goodwill and courtesy toward Abraham is the fact that they point out a place. "Go," they say, "wherever you please, into the garden of the prince or of some counselor." For among them everyone customarily buried his dead at the place which pleased him. "Thus we are offering you not only the common burial place but one of the choicer spots."

Their deference is surely remarkable, and without a doubt they learned it in the church of Abraham, who trained and educated them with respect to the spirit and made them well mannered with respect to the flesh. And they make an additional statement. "There will be nobody who could hinder you," they say. "You will be free to choose whatever you wish."

7. *Abraham rose and bowed to the Hittites, the people of the land.*

8. *And he said to them: If you are willing that I should bury my dead out of my sight, hear me, and entreat for me Ephron the son of Zohar,*

9. *that he may give me the cave of Machpelah, which he owns; it is at the end of his field. For the full price let him give it to me in your presence as a possession for a burying place.*

In the first place, Abraham rises before the Hebronites as before men who are older and higher in rank; for he thought that honor should be shown them as the lords of the land. And this is proper and godly. God created us to accord honor to one another, not to be haughty, rude, devoid of feeling, and boorish.

Thus if I show honor to an officer of the state or to a pastor of the church, I am according honor to him as a person ordained by God, not as a brother from the midst of brothers.

In the same manner honorable matrons and virgins, but parents and teachers above all, should be honored, not so much on their own account but because they are creatures of God and God Himself is honored in them, as Augustine says: "Mutually honor God in yourselves." [32]

---

[32] Luther frequently quoted this saying from Augustine, cf. *Luther's Works,* 3, p. 187, note 11.

In the second place, Abraham bows to the people of the land. Here the kinds of bowing must be distinguished. In the first place, one bows by prostrating the face or body to the ground and taking hold of the feet of those to whom we are bowing. This extreme position is appropriate for kings and princes. Thus the Shunammite woman took hold of the feet of Elisha (2 Kings 4:27). Peter fell down at Jesus' knees (Luke 5:8). The second kind is to bend the knees or to fall on the knees. The third is to incline the head and to grasp both hands.[33]

Strictly speaking, therefore, the bowing referred to here denotes the posture of the body one assumes by inclining the head, by falling down on one's knees, or by prostrating one's face, in accordance with the custom of individual nations and men or as befits the rank of him to whom one bows. But it is not the worshiping in spirit of which Christ speaks in John 4:24.

Moreover, Abraham rose, not that he had prostrated himself or had bent his knees, but he bowed his head and perhaps grasped their hands and at the same time kissed them, a custom which that people had. These are commendable customs of humility, respect, and courtesy; they should be especially praised and presented to our youth, so that it may accustom itself to them and rid itself of its habitual boorishness.

But undoubtedly Abraham also had other reasons for this respect, not so much because they were the people of the land — that is, its lords and inhabitants — as on account of the godliness and the virtues of every kind he observed in them.

But no one knows how long they remained like this. It is well known that nearly all peoples of all lands preserve their discipline and virtuousness and foster decency for no longer than 20 years. All secular and sacred accounts bear witness of this.

Once men have been brought to the knowledge of God and moral respectability, they preserve their devotion to godliness and good morals for 20 years at most; for because of their indifference and their contempt for the prevailing situation they gradually become more and more corrupt, until they become involved in shameful deeds and horrible crimes. Read the accounts of David, of Solomon, of all the kings, and also of Augustine.[34] Indeed, consider our own age.

[33] On this entire problem cf. *Luther's Works*, 36, pp. 290 ff.

[34] Luther is probably thinking of passages like Augustine, *The City of God*, Book V, ch. 12.

Does experience not teach that when the heavenly doctrine was restored, it gave very great pleasure at first? Now, however, "this worthless food" (Num. 21:5) is causing more and more loathing and nausea.

Thus at the time of Abraham the Hebronites were rather godly and pious. Later on, however, at the time of Moses and Joshua, they were destroyed, evidently after the doctrine concerning God had been lost and discipline had become lax.

Above (Gen. 14) Moses related the same things about the Sodomites. When Abraham had freed them from great danger by repulsing their enemies, they were virtuous for a while; but after seven years such disgraceful deeds prevailed that they were burned and consumed by fire and brimstone from heaven.

After so great a light of the Gospel our Germany, too, seems all but possessed by the devil. Our young people are wild and unruly; they are intolerant of discipline. The old people are held in the clutches of greed, usury, and many other execrable sins. Doubtless this is how we thank God for the Word of grace and His only-begotten Son, as Moses complains in Deut. 32:6: "Do you thus requite the Lord, you foolish and senseless people?"

Accordingly, it is not at all surprising that punishments and misfortunes of every kind follow. But these are the ways of the times and the misfortunes of the world. "So then, as we have opportunity, let us do good" (Gen. 6:10),[35] each in his station by learning the Holy Scriptures and improving our ways, while the doctrine of the Gospel flourishes and shines, as Christ admonishes (John 12:36): "While you have the light, believe in the light." For the devil busies himself with the opposite and at all times foists his frauds and darkness upon the unwary.

10. *Now Ephron was sitting among the Hittites; and Ephron the Hittite answered Abraham in the hearing of the Hittites, of all who went in at the gate of his city:*

11. *No, my lord, hear me; I give you the field, and I give you the cave that is in it; in the presence of the sons of my people I give it to you; bury your dead.*

12. *Then Abraham bowed down before the people of the land.*

[35] The original has "Gal. 2."

13. *And he said to Ephron in the hearing of the people of the land: But if you will, hear me; I will give the price of the field; accept it from me, that I may bury my dead there.*

14. *Ephron answered Abraham:*

15. *My lord, listen to me; a piece of land worth four hundred shekels of silver, what is that between you and me? Bury your dead.*

16. *Abraham agreed with Ephron; and Abraham weighed out for Ephron the silver which he had named in the hearing of the Hittites, four hundred shekels of silver, according to the weights current among the merchants.*

17. *So the field of Ephron in Machpelah, which was to the east of Mamre, the field with the cave which was in it and all the trees that were in the field, throughout its whole area, was made over*

18. *to Abraham as a possession in the presence of the Hittites, before all who went in at the gate of his city.*

Ephron tries to persuade Abraham to take the field as a gift, without the payment of money. "What is it between me and you?" he says. "You are a prince of God; I am rich. What is it, even if I should sell it for 400 shekels?" This is godly and praiseworthy reverence toward the prophet and teacher. But Abraham modestly declines and wants to have it as his own and as purchased for a price.

For he thought or said: "I know that you are pious and honest people, but after experiencing the changeableness of others elsewhere I have learned to buy more cautiously. In Egypt and in Gerar I experienced the goodwill and respect of many, yet I was eventually expelled. Although I had done the Sodomites a great favor, in the end their remembrance of it and their gratitude were very small. Thus if I were to accept this field without cost, perhaps after your death your descendants, having forgotten your goodwill toward me and your gift, would again seize it and would disinter and remove my Sarah. For since we are sojourners and in a strange land, they would say, as the Sodomites said to Lot (Gen. 19:9): 'This fellow came to sojourn, and he would play the judge!' Therefore I shall buy it, in order that your descendants may not have any right at all to take it back."

Observe, I beg you, how prudently spiritual men do business even in civil and secular matters — not like the monks, who pretend to have spiritual interests only, even though all their works are completely carnal. But the true saints live in the world and carry on civil activities, and with remarkable prudence at that. They are respectful, courteous, prudent, and cautious; and they have an understanding of all civil obligations.

Moreover, Abraham bought the field in the sight and presence of all citizens — "all who went in at the gate of the city," says Moses. They all were present as witnesses that this field was the property of Abraham and of all his descendants forever. At that time written documents [36] and seals were not yet in use.

This is another virtue of Abraham, namely, the prudence with which he deals with men, whose descendants usually are changeable and fickle, as can commonly be observed in all families — of David, of Solomon, and of other outstanding men. Very rarely do children conform to the paternal character and virtue.

Abraham's request was also very modest; he wanted to be satisfied with some part in a very remote corner which would not be at the most convenient place but would be little suited for other purposes. Ephron, however, grants him the entire field, not merely a corner, then also the cave which is in the field. He himself withdraws to another estate or field, of which he undoubtedly had many.

But Abraham weighs out the 400 silver shekels according to the weights current among the merchants, for this is the Hebrew way of speaking. They call it money according to the weights current among the merchants, as we express it in German with *geng und geb, das auff dem marckt gilt.* The phrase "in the ears of the people" — that is, while the people heard, witnessed, and confirmed the contract — is repeated several times in the text.

This example reminds us that we should deal wisely and cautiously with people because of their descendants, who are changeable, but that we should conduct ourselves in a courteous, honorable, and humble manner with those who are present.

The shape and location of that double cave are uncertain. I think that there were two caves and that they were rather large, because Isaac, Jacob, and their wives were buried in the same place.

---

[36] In place of the meaningless *singraphae* in the Weimar text we have followed the Erlangen text and read the word *syngraphae,* familiar from its use by Cicero.

19. *After this, Abraham buried Sarah his wife in the cave of the field of Machpelah east of Mamre (that is, Hebron) in the land of Canaan.*

20. *The field and the cave that is in it were made over to Abraham as a possession for a burying place by the Hittites.*

Up to this point Moses has described the death and burial of Sarah in many words which contain excellent doctrine and outstanding examples of manners, because — in addition to Abraham's heroic qualities of faith, hope, and love — the Holy Spirit also praises in him those civil qualities, namely, reverence, humility, modesty, moderation, and justice. Accordingly, in the one Abraham there is a great number and host of all virtues, whether you are looking for those that pertain to the church and are spiritual or those that are civil and pertain to the household. Nothing surpasses his faith. Furthermore, how great his love toward the Sodomites was! How great his patience in exile was! Finally, how great his reverence, friendliness, and generosity were toward the lords of the land, because he does not want to take the field without cost and be a burden to the inhabitants! The whole doctrine of ethics could be gathered better from this source than Aristotle, the jurists, and the canonists have propounded it. Hence the words of this detailed description are not superfluous or unprofitable.

CHAPTER TWENTY-FOUR

1. *Now Abraham was old, well advanced in years; and the Lord had blessed Abraham in all things.*

2. *And Abraham said to his servant, the oldest of his house, who had charge of all that he had: Put your hand under my thigh,*

3. *and I will make you swear by the Lord, the God of heaven and of the earth, that you will not take a wife for my son from the daughters of the Canaanites, among whom I dwell,*

4. *but will go to my country and my kindred, and take a wife for my son Isaac.*

So far Moses has brought the account of Abraham's life up to that act which is customarily the last one in life, namely, his testament, which Abraham is now about to make. And the only care with which the father still concerns himself has to do with the marriage of his son and with the promised progeny. Consequently, this entire chapter pertains to Isaac, whose marriage is described.

Moreover, it is the first passage — and one that is completely clear — concerning the duty of parents toward their children and, on the other hand, concerning the proper and respectful attitude of parents toward their children when a marriage is contracted. As common as this discussion is at present, so very vexatious it is, since those mutual duties, imposed by divine and human right, have almost been done away with because of the depravity of men. Therefore when we attempt to restore them and to convince men by teaching that a betrothal entered into without the consent and will of parents can neither be lawful nor regarded as valid,[1] we incur the hatred and calumny of many.

The canonists of the pope oppose us very sharply. The professors of civil law are in complete agreement with them, and we surely have

1 See also p. 72, note 63.

them as our implacable and mortal enemies in the whole world. Therefore even though these efforts are thankless, yet the defense and confession of the truth must not for this reason be given up or thrust aside. For in this passage we have a clear example of our conviction, even though no law is being established. For elsewhere, of course, there is no lack of the authority of laws, not only of those that are divine but also of those that are drawn by sound inference from the fountainhead of natural right, as laws and civil rights are. On our side are the examples of Scripture, the written laws and the rights. Why, then, do the jurists and pettifoggers inveigh against us?

Accordingly, let us fortify ourselves with Holy Scripture against their stubborn spite. It is their habit to boast before their hearers that they cannot depart from their canons and pronounce a decision on the basis of our writings, which they contemptuously and shamefully call canonical,[2] as though we actually were inventing or sanctioning something new and out of our own heads. We have God's will, natural reason, the examples of the fathers, and civil law in our favor.

And they themselves know this, but they do not want to be admonished and rebuked. Yet it must not be tolerated that they corrupt and infect the hearts of young people with their outrageous opinions. We shall never tolerate it that their wicked, execrable, and vicious canons, which contradict the Word of God, prescribe anything to us; and on this account I am giving this warning, so that the godly may fortify themselves against their calumnies and blasphemies.

What a wickedness it is to know the truth and yet to say: "In my book I find it written differently; therefore a different decision must be made, without regard for laws, civil right, and the Word of God, which decree the opposite"! Should one delude and turn up one's nose[3] at people in such a way that they are forced to regard as settled whatever wicked pronouncements the canonists make in accordance with their canons?

[2] The word in the original is *Catonichen,* whose meaning remains a puzzle. It could perhaps be a reference to Cato (to whom the *Disticha Catonis* were attributed); but even if it is, the ending *chen* is a problem. Is it the German diminutive suffix, a copyist's error for the German adjectival suffix *schen,* or the Greek adjectival suffix χην? Because of the phrase *a canonibus recedere* earlier in the sentence, we have read *Canonischen.*

[3] An allusion to Horace, *Satires,* VI, 5, 6.

This senselessness is vicious, contrary to reason and common sense. They confess that they know that our opinion is godly and honorable; and yet, contrary to their conscience and the acknowledged truth, they render a different decision, obviously because their books prescribe otherwise.[4]

By the same reasoning I, too, might state: "I have been promoted to a doctorate in scholastic theology, but in the Bible I find very many things that conflict with this theology. Nevertheless, I shall follow the Cardinal of Cambrai, no matter how much the Holy Scriptures may teach the opposite."[5] Who would put up with this and not detest such teachers? But they show that they are nourishing in themselves a prodigious hatred of the Holy Spirit, because they carry the spirit of the pope imprinted on their hearts; and this wickedness of theirs comes close to downright blasphemy.

Let us strengthen ourselves with the Holy Spirit against that inhuman shamelessness and villainy, and let us hold those people in contempt with the utmost unconcern. Let him who up to this time has erred with them learn to have a better understanding, and let him follow those who have better things to tell. When you see canons that contain error, you should say: "Canon law, give way to the truth of the Holy Spirit!"

Therefore we are dealing with this passage, no matter how troublesome it is. It states that Isaac does not take a wife where it pleases him but is forbidden by his father to marry a Canaanite woman, that the father anxiously concerns himself about a wife for his son, and that the son obeys his father with the greatest willingness.

Daily experience teaches that those clandestine and stealthy betrothals are the cause of very great evils, of endless strife, of quarrels, of perjuries, and of murders, and, to the same degree, are a most hideous nuisance and disturbance for the church and for civil affairs.

Thus the canonists are doing nothing else than ruining the church and troubling the world on account of their foolish and unscholarly

---

[4] See the references cited in *Luther's Works*, 13, p. 353, notes 2 and 3.

[5] On the significance of Luther's doctorate cf. *Luther the Expositor*, pp. 46 to 47; by "the Cardinal of Cambrai" Luther probably means Pierre D'Ailly (1350—1420), who was created Archbishop of Cambrai in 1397 and made a cardinal by Pope John XXIII in 1412. According to Melanchthon's preface to the second volume of the Wittenberg edition of Luther's works (*Corpus Reformatorum*, VI, 159), Luther knew *Cameracencis*, as well as Gabriel Biel, practically by heart.

canons. But are we going to let them bring so many evils into our churches and states? The devil would tolerate this, nobody else. Indeed, I shall rather excommunicate all those teachers than have us tolerate their wicked opinions in our church.

Consider how worthless their argument is when they boastfully assert: "I cannot render a different decision, because it is not written otherwise in the canons." On the basis of similar reasoning some Turk or Mohammedan could argue: "I cannot accept the Gospel, because it is not in the Koran." Thus a Jew will not be converted to the Christian faith, because this faith is not taught in the Law of Moses. The Romans and the heathen would never have embraced the Gospel, since nothing like it was taught in their books. If all the statements that are contained in the books of the canonists are true — and indeed if they alone are true — but, on the other hand, if all the statements that are not handed down in them are false, we should throw away the other books.

Moreover, especially the dignity of matrimony should impel us to give instruction concerning matrimony in a sober and godly manner. For marriage is not a trifling matter; but it is the most serious and most important matter in the whole world, because it is the source of human society and of the human race. Life in its entirety has nothing that excels it in worth. Therefore one should discuss it with the utmost piety and on the basis of the weightiest arguments and reasons. For in other circumstances it has been dishonored enough by concupiscence of the flesh and by lust.

Accordingly, the will of God should be taken into consideration above all. This is the way God wanted it, and this is the way He ordained and instituted it. We are not at liberty to seek our own glory from this source, much less to inveigh against God's institution. Moreover, experience itself shows that marrying is no joke or laughing matter. During the first year, of course, everything is delightful and charming; that time is spent in laughter and caressing. But later — when the familiar line of the comic poet, "What misery have I not seen there?" [6] follows — the comfort derived from being sure about the will of God and about being joined by Him is necessary, so that you may positively maintain: "This girl is my wife, whom I have taken in marriage with God's own approving smile and with the assent of the angels." Next an invocation for divine help and for

---

[6] Terence, *The Brothers*, V, line 789.

protection from heaven should be added, and in this way you will overcome the most serious dangers and annoyances.

The canonists define wedlock in an exceedingly frigid manner. It is the union of male and female, they say, in accordance with the law of nature.[7] This is a very poor and weak definition. Therefore they are unfit to decide this dispute, because they give no attention to the importance of the matter.

Theology has a different definition. Marriage, it says, is the inseparable union of one man and one woman, not only according to the law of nature but also according to God's will and pleasure, if I may use this expression. For the will and approval and that favor of God cover the wretched depravity of lust and turn away God's wrath, which is in store for such lust and sins. In this way matrimony is treated with reverence.

The pope has no other understanding than that it is a marriage if two come together and say: "I am yours; you are mine." He has no thoughts of God's favor, of the consolation of spouses, and of how the man and the woman should be taught to keep the passion of lust in check, to govern the domestics, about the divine blessing, then about bearing weaknesses in one's wife, and about enduring dangers on account of one's children and wrongs from neighbors. He regards solely that shameful union of the flesh, which they call the link; but he disregards God's promise and ordinance.

Therefore the godly should be warned and fortified against those vipers who vaunt their canons in opposition to the divine truth. And that truly popish argument about a precept and about decrees of the canons should be utterly rejected.

Nevertheless, this is their unfailing procedure in judging our doctrine. They confess that they know that it is the pure and true Gospel, and yet they are unconcerned. Bishop Albert of Mainz was in the habit of saying that our doctrine was grounded in Holy Scripture and was the very truth, yet he neither wanted to nor was able to accept it. The canonists are exactly like him. They say that the statement which condemns clandestine marriages is true, but that it should be rejected because the canons decide otherwise.

These are horrible words, and I never thought that I would hear such things during my lifetime or that there would be anyone who would utter these awful blasphemies, namely, that he indeed hears

---

[7] See also *Luther's Works*, 3, p. 48, note 7.

and understands the truth and nevertheless denies it on account of the uncertain opinion of men. Is this proper for a pious and honest man? Indeed, it is not even proper for a Turk or for a heathen. A pious man can be deceived and fall when he is misled by the error of others; but if he is admonished, he acknowledges his error and comes to his senses, and he rejects and condemns his erroneous opinion. Hence I shall never approve of or defend the error and foolishness of the canonists; but I shall defecate all over the canons and the pope, since civil law itself has decreed differently and more honorably about this institution of God.

Therefore this account is noteworthy. When the lady of his house died, Abraham lost his right eye. He thinks of making other arrangements for managing the household; for an establishment of this kind needs a person like Sarah, or other arrangements must be made concerning its management. Therefore he entrusts the entire establishment to his oldest servant and appoints him as מֹשֵׁל, that is, as ruler (Ps. 8). Formerly the godly old man had placed the entire burden of management upon his dear wife. When he was forced to assume it himself after her death, he lays it upon his servant until he procures a housemother, namely, his son's wife.

Accordingly, Abraham gives up all managing after Sarah's death. He did not want such a great burden put upon himself in his very advanced age — although he took a wife later on — and it is for this reason that he is thinking of a person suitable for governing the domestics. Meanwhile, however, he makes use of the service of his senior servant, who was in charge of the household for three years.

For Sarah died when Isaac was 37 years old; he married Rebecca when he was 40. Those three years both the father and the son spent in mourning and sadness. For they did not have hearts of stone, and the remembrance of the very pleasant companionship and of the very beautiful virtues of his dearly beloved wife often renewed Abraham's grief. Nor could Isaac immediately forget his dearly beloved mother; for they were affectionate people. Therefore in order to comfort Isaac, his father seeks a lifemate for him.

Accordingly, what this passage teaches is that parents should concern themselves about an honorable marriage for their sons and daughters. Nevertheless, one should not fail to mention that it often occurs in life that parents misuse their right and authority and want to force their children to marry those whom they do not love. This often happens in large families of the nobility. Those people should be censured, because they have no fatherly feeling or affection but are blocks of wood and sticks and do not have the proper love for their offspring. In that case the pastor of the church or a civil magistrate should interpose his authority, because this is tyranny, not paternal power.

We are stressing the authority of parents so earnestly (1) on account of God's command and ordinance, the examples of Scripture and the civil laws; (2) on account of that extraordinary wickedness which has prevailed in the world in all ages and has been very painful for godly and respectable parents. When they brought up their children in a godly and decent manner to be the heirs of their paternal possessions, some were found later on who without their knowledge and against their will duped virgins or respectable young men by fraud and trickery into pledging their troth secretly to such as were not respectable enough, unworthy of them, and very offensive to their parents.

To these disgraceful deeds the pope has opened the window and the door, and has given procurers access, so that they can steal our sons and daughters from me, from you, and from every one of us. Are we going to think that this should be tolerated or defended? Yet they say that children should be watched over and that careful attention should be given to them. How can this be done when men are so wicked and perverse? How easily the sinful heart is corrupted and deceived!

Therefore let parents remember that the right and authority to give their children in marriage has been assigned to them by God and betrothals entered into without their consent are valid neither by divine nor by human right.

Next let children know that they owe their godly parents this reverence, that they seek their counsel and ascertain their wish. The young man who is old enough to marry should not shrink from making his desire known to his parents, to say that he loves a decent girl and is asking them to give her to him as his wife. Although this appears to be an indication of sensual desire that exceeds the bounds of modesty, they should nevertheless know that God's mercy covers it in marriage and has given a remedy for this malady.

Therefore let them humble themselves before their parents and frankly say: "My father, my mother, give me that young man or the virgin whom I love." If she is worthy of the alliance or the affinity with you or your parents, honorable parents will not refuse, even if the dowry or wealth does not meet their expectations.

Such marriages cannot but be happy and successful, and God blesses them according to His boundless goodness and overlooks and covers the ardor of desire as with the cover, as it were, of marriage. Yes, even Holy Scripture gives its approval and adduces the love and the voice of the bridegroom and the bride as an example.[8] Thus God overlooks the shamefulness in which we were born and that wretched desire. Indeed, He adorns and honors it with lawful marriage.

But let young people beware of that common disobedience to and contempt for their parents because of which some act altogether like madmen and on a blind impulse enter into a dishonorable marriage that is unworthy of themselves, their elders, and their parents. Here Holy Scripture presents a diametrically opposite and far more honorable example to imitate when Isaac takes Rebecca to wife in compliance with his father's wish, will, and advice.

Such is not the teaching of the pope and the canonists. Nor do they prescribe marrying wives; they prescribe snatching them by force, as though children were their own masters or so sacred a union should take place without the lawful order of God. Holy Scripture says (Prov. 19:14): "A prudent wife is from the Lord." Therefore the invocation for divine help should precede: "Lord God, Thou seest that I cannot remain unmarried without sin; counsel me, and give me a godly and virtuous wife."

Just as this servant, who is being sent by Abraham, prayed — and Abraham undoubtedly taught him to pray — Isaac, too, prayed. Then there should come the counsel, the will, and the consent of your parents; and you should undertake nothing contrary to their wish or opposition. Consider what great kindnesses have been heaped upon you, how much you owe them, and how unbecoming it is to trouble or offend the heart of those who have given you kindly care, reared you, and love you most ardently.

These things young people should point out to themselves and constantly recall, for in this way they will become accustomed to honoring their parents. And this is not only honorable and godly but is also in accord with the command and examples of Scripture and especially profitable throughout one's entire life.

---

[8] Luther is probably referring to the Song of Solomon; his commentary on this book had been published in 1539 (W XXXI-2, 586—769).

One must detest the popish canons, which do not teach these duties but, contrary to all this, implicate unwary hearts in secret and clandestine betrothals and bid them exchange their mutual pledges of marriage without the knowledge and against the will and opposition of their parents when a procuress or a procurer seduces them and an enemy or good-for-nothing ravishes them.

What sadder and more disgraceful thing can happen to a person than if a son or a daughter, brought up in a devout and virtuous way and instructed in the best manners, has to be given in marriage to a profligate and villainous fellow who is scheming to get your property and possessions? Of course, affinity has to be established with him, and he has to be regarded as a son and as heir of all the property. Is this not sadder than death itself?

Therefore it is not without purpose that I am so often stressing and warning in what way so important and so sacred a matter should be approached in order that the authority of parents and the reverence of children toward them may be preserved. A son or a daughter should seek advice from those who are both capable of giving advice and, because of the divine institution and blessing of God, are able to counsel. The parents, on the other hand, should not be unyielding and rude. They should not urge their children to contract marriage with those whom they do not love; nor should they rashly restrain them from loving decent people unless they have chosen persons who are not suited to them. Parents should keep in mind the natural affection and inclination which God has implanted and should put nothing in the way of honorable love.

Thus when Samson's parents became aware that he loved a Philistine woman and he asked that she be given to him as his wife, they permitted him to marry her, even though she was a heathen (Judges 14:1-4).

But I warn again that for entering into marriage it is above all necessary to call upon God that He may choose and bestow the wife or husband. If this is done, God's blessing and all good fortune in marriage follow. God gives the husband the grace to have patience and to take the weakness of his wife in good part, and that she, in turn, may be able to adjust herself to her husband's ways. On the other hand, where fear of God and prayer are not added, irritations very easily occur. From these originate hatred, quarrels, enmity, and perpetual dissension. I have often seen completely unhappy marriages of this kind, and they commonly happen to those who follow the pope and the canons.

But where people enter into marriage in a lawful and saintly manner in accordance with the ordinance and institution of God and are sure about the will of God and of their parents, the greatest disagreements and dangers are often overcome without any trouble and difficulty with the help of God and with a good conscience, which is certain that if anything unfortunate occurs, it does not happen by chance but in accord with the good will of God, at whose bidding they have entered into this kind of life. The papists see none of these things; they do not take into consideration the material, the efficient, or the final cause of marriage [9] but consider it to be the kind of copulation that takes place in fornication.

In the Law of Moses clandestine betrothals were so sternly forbidden and condemned that parents were permitted to declare them null and void even though intercourse had taken place (Ex. 22:16-17). Although we neither can nor must follow that law — for the forensic matters and the decisions of the Mosaic Law are not binding for us — nevertheless it is a Law which was written and proclaimed by God and our opinion is given powerful support by its example and testimony. Furthermore, we have on our side the civil law, which the canonists and all subjects of this empire are equally bound to obey.

When Moses states in the text that the Lord blessed Abraham in all things, he has in mind all the riches of marriage. They are called blessings. Whatever the head of the household possesses, all this Holy Scripture is in the habit of calling a blessing. If people knew and believed this, there would not be so much plundering and unlawful gain in the world. But the majority live without praying and therefore also without a blessing. And in this unconcern they enter into marriage; they seek and heap up wealth without the blessing about which they do not think even once during their life. How few peasants and burghers there are who have God's blessing and own their possessions without doing wrong to others! Everything is full of usury, greed, and covetousness.

But if you want to enter into a marriage with God's blessing seek the Lord's counsel first of all, and pray: "Lord God, give me a wife and daily bread." God regards those prayers with favor and

[9] Luther frequently uses the Aristotelian distinction of causes; see, for example, *Luther's Works,* 12, p. 400, note 35.

answers them. "I have made you man and woman," He says. "Why would I not support you? But refrain from the wrong of plunder and theft."

Therefore where a man and a woman are joined by God and in accordance with God's definite will, there is a marriage; and spouses who know this very easily bear and overcome whatever adversities befall them. Thus it is the first and greatest blessing if you know that you have entered into marriage in accordance with God's will and that you have taken a wife because you were compelled by necessity, in order to avoid sin.

Whatever God then bestows, to all those good things you should give their true name and say: "This son or daughter the Lord has given to me; this field, meadow, cow, and goat God has given to me, and it is a divine blessing."

That is truly a very beautiful and very happy marriage in which there is inscribed both on the table and on the bed: "The favor, will, and good pleasure of God." These are true and boundless riches, but such blessings you will not find in the canons. Thus the patriarch Jacob says below (Gen. 33:5): "These are the children whom God has given me," surely because of extraordinary favor and blessing. These people are aware of and know the Creator and His creature; they realize whence they originated and whence they receive everything.

But these things are taught neither in canonical and civil law nor in medical science; they are taught in Holy Scripture. Everybody hears that Abraham had much property and many successes, and that he acquired great wealth. But whence came that good fortune and wealth? Scripture gives the answer: "Because God's mercy gave the blessing; He who created him a man gave him his riches."

If we, too, were able to ponder and believe these things, we would be very happy with even a little good fortune; and in very great wealth our feeling would be no different from what it would be if we possessed nothing, because there is no difference between small and great wealth so far as God, who bestows the blessing, is concerned. He who has one cow or one child has the same Lord to bless him as the most powerful king has.

If in this manner we could give God credit for the enjoyment of every good thing, then everybody would be satisfied with his own lot. He who cannot do this turns to shameful gain and scrapes together by fair means or foul, in order that he may possess everything; and even if he has gained possession of it, his heart is nevertheless never quiet but struggles continually with an insatiable desire for riches and possessions.

But he would be far happier if these were his sentiments: "Lord God, whatever Thou wilt give me I shall receive with a glad and grateful heart; what Thou wilt not give me I shall cheerfully do without. I shall be satisfied with moderate means just the same as with great wealth."

But nobody follows this doctrine. Instead, people follow their inclination and the wisdom of the flesh. This is why we want to manage and arrange everything by reason. Meanwhile we are ungrateful and do not recognize the divine blessing of which Holy Scripture makes mention in this passage when Moses speaks of Abraham's means, silver, gold, herds, and cattle, which he had even as a stranger, and calls all these a blessing of God.

Next the instruction of the servant follows. From this it is clear that Abraham appointed this servant head of the household in his stead. If he was a truly godly man who knew God and believed in Him, it is the equivalent of a miracle and is a great blessing that he had a servant of the kind to whom he could entrust his house and his domestics, and could do so in such a way that he appointed him a lord, as Joseph was at the court of the king of Egypt.

It is a most excellent gift to have a faithful servant or handmaid in the household. In the entire world there is a common complaint about the dishonesty and wickedness of domestics, and it is a curse of God which increases from day to day, because we are smug, despise the Word of God, and do not pray. Therefore the wicked and ungodly are punished with this evil; but the pious are trained and plagued, as they are by other afflictions.

People who are truly blessed have all kinds of possessions and have some מֹשֵׁל and Eliezer who takes care of the affairs of the household faithfully and in the proper manner. Sirach says (Ecclus. 33:31): "If you have a faithful servant, let him be among his fellow servants as though you yourself were present; for you need him as your own life." Such a man was that Eliezer to whom the great patriarch entrusted the management of his household. He surely had to be a very saintly man full of the Holy Spirit, and perhaps he was later on set free; but in this passage he is still called a servant. Therefore God blessed this house with an unbelievable blessing: in the first place, with possessions and with riches; in the second place, with faithful servants and attendants. Now a third blessing follows: that of a bridegroom and a bride.

But at this point the question can be raised why Abraham, when he exacts an oath from his servant, bids him place the hand under his thigh or on the place of his thigh. Scripture says nothing about whether it was a rite observed by the fathers and handed down from father to son or recently instituted by Abraham for the servant to swear by placing his hand or fingers on his thigh. If there was an ancient custom of swearing in this manner, Abraham followed the usual and ancestral practice, and the servant, who was familiar with this custom, swore.

But it has a wonderful and grand meaning that he places his hand, not upon the breast, the head, or the hand of Abraham but on that place to which the begetting of children is ascribed in Holy Scriptures. In Gen. 46:26 we read: "All the souls who came into Egypt with Jacob came out of his thigh." Likewise: "Levi was in the loins of Abraham." David came out of Abraham's thigh; that is, Abraham was the source and origin, so to speak, of his offspring.

The Jews maintain that this was done on account of circumcision, which takes place near that part of the body;[10] but I prefer to believe that it originated from the understanding of the fathers, who understood from the very beginning that the Savior would come and be born from the human race.

Moreover, an oath is one of the most sacred acts, because it includes the name, the worship, the invocation of God, and everything that is divine. Accordingly, when an act so sacred and a worship of God so special is applied to this place, it follows that this place was regarded as sacrosanct and as much as divine.

One might have these thoughts if this custom had been handed down and adopted by the fathers; but because Holy Scripture is altogether silent, it is not our business to make any assertions or denials. What Holy Scripture teaches, denies, or affirms, that we can safely imitate and teach. Thus because it says nothing about Shem, does not describe his birth, his death, or his parents, we cannot know or relate anything about those matters; and this was done on purpose, in order that the figure of Christ might be set before our eyes.

[10] The source of this information about the rabbinic tradition is Lyra *ad* Gen. 24:2, 3.

Nevertheless, it is likely that Abraham was the first to introduce this rite and that he commanded his servant to place his hand under the thigh as under a most sacred object; for he could have found Mt. Moriah, an altar, heaven, earth, the sun, the moon, or any other creature toward which to raise his fingers, just as in our day they swear by the Gospel, while in the papacy they swear by the relics of the saints.[11] For an oath is always sworn by something holier and more sacred than we are (cf. Heb. 6:16). But since Abraham gives the order to touch his thigh, he undoubtedly regarded this as a sacred object.

But if it is true that Abraham was the originator of this rite of placing the fingers on the thigh, he understood the promise containing the words "in your Seed," not in a simple sense but in accordance with the Pauline explanation that the Savior of the world would come from his thigh.

This is how Paul expounds this passage in Gal. 3:16: "It does not say, 'And to offsprings,' referring to many; but, referring to one, 'And to your Offspring,' which is Christ." That meaning of the promise Abraham understood, especially since Isaac, his son and the heir of that land, had already been born. Therefore he regarded his thigh as a sacred object on which he bids the servant place his fingers when he is about to swear.

For this was the source and origin from which would come the Seed that would give life to and justify the entire human race.

This is in agreement with Holy Scripture, which, as I have stated before, frequently speaks highly of the loins and the thigh. To be sure, it appears to be a hideous object because of the lust and the horrible concupiscence which, in the human body, has its seat in the loins and the thigh; yet God regards as a most sacred object one which by its own nature is vile, indecent, and polluted by sin.

Thus God commands that circumcision be carried out in a most indecent place — in a place about which one can hardly think, much less speak, without offending decency. Yet it signifies not only that we wretched sinners were conceived and born in lust, but also that the Seed promised to Abraham would come and would not only be blessed and without sin and lust but would also bless all nations.

Therefore God concerns Himself with most unseemly things, and

[11] Cf. English oaths such as "by the rood" (*Hamlet*, III, iv, 14) or "God's blood" (*Henry V*, IV, viii, 10).

here Holy Scripture is wordier and more lavish in the description of marriage than when it is speaking of most important matters. Above (cf. 22:16) it disposes of the promise concerning the spiritual blessing in very few words: "By myself I have sworn. In your Seed shall all nations be blessed." This entire chapter contains nothing else than the description of Isaac's marriage, of how the servant is sent, and of how the bride is fetched.

Why is this done? Because God made us and we are His creatures and work, for this reason He concerns Himself about His work even in the midst of sin, death, hell, shame, and dishonor. God's salvation, life, and all instances of His help are in the midst of opposites. He preserves in death, bestows righteousness in sin, and gives peace and security in extreme perils.

These are divine works which carnal people, who do not have the Holy Spirit, do not understand. Therefore they turn their eyes solely to the lust and indecency in marriage. In concupiscence they do not see that most holy blessing of begetting children, because they are aware of nothing except the flames of extremely indecent concupiscence. Thus in death they discern nothing except death, and in hell no heaven. As they perceive, so they judge. But because we did not make ourselves — for "male and female He created them" — we should maintain that God cares for us as His creatures.

This, then, is the reason why Holy Scripture deals with this seemingly ignoble subject at such great length. Marriage is nothing new or unusual, and it also has the sanction and praise of the heathen, in accordance with the judgment of reason. But who has ever looked at it or thought of it in this way, that it is a creature of God, a blessing in a curse and chastity in lust? If you judge in accordance with reason and outward appearance, marital intercourse differs in no respect from harlotry. Yet the former is chaste and honorable under the forgiveness of sin and under the blessing, and is pleasing to God; the latter is shameful and condemned under the wrath of God, because in matrimony God preserves His institution and ordinance in the midst of lust and indecency.

Therefore Abraham understood this passage very well: "In your seed will all nations be blessed," which includes Christ. And because of Christ, who sprang from the loins of Abraham, from which the entire human race comes, everything should be regarded as pure, clean, and holy, because He is the same seed and the same flesh that we are. But He is truly holy and was conceived by a miracle, not like us, but without the passion, lust, lewdness, indecency, and vileness of a father, and was also born without the pain of a mother. Yet He is the Seed of Abraham.

This was indicated when Abraham commanded the servant to place his hand on his thigh, because Christ is in the thigh. Therefore for the sake of Christ marriage must be holy and pure; and sexual intercourse, which in itself is most indecent, must be chaste and honorable. And Abraham believed that his thigh was sacred, not on account of himself but on account of the promise of God, because the promise includes his thigh, and that promise is most holy. Therefore it sanctifies Abraham's thigh, so that those who come out of it through the lust and sexual intercourse of the flesh are also reckoned as chaste, not as unclean, and the marriage bed is regarded as undefiled and marriage as honorable (Heb. 13:4), solely on account of the Seed that is to come.

If Paul had not explained this passage in this manner, I would not have understood it. David, Isaiah, and Jeremiah saw the same things; but the great mass of the prophets, as well as the Jews, looked at them only in passing, just as we do. In women we seek that vile pleasure and nothing else than what we feel and what affects us carnally and agreeably and delights us. But this should be learned and painstakingly noted, that in the midst of death God sees life and in indecency sees honor.

The theologians of old assume a threefold chastity: of virgins, of widows, and of spouses.[12] But is it chastity when a husband begets children? It surely lies hidden, since it is covered by an astounding loathsomeness, so that nobody recognizes that it is chastity, because it differs in no wise in sensation and outward appearance from fornication. Thus no virgin is so chaste and pure that she does not feel a desire for a man. Young men have the same experience, and, what is more, indecent dreams and pollutions follow. Assuredly there is no true chastity in that case; it is only external, because lust is burning within the blood and in the innermost feelings. To such an extent has nature been corrupted. Therefore the papists flaunt their chastity and virginity in vain.

They are reluctant to admit that conjugal chastity exists or is called such. But they are compelled to do so by the authority of the theologians of old. For otherwise they call it uncleanness, just as

---

[12] Perhaps a reference to Augustine, *De virginitate*, 46.

they explain the statement of the prophet Isaiah, who says (52:11): "Purify yourselves, you who bear the vessels of the Lord." This, as they say, means: "Abstain from marriage if you want to serve the Lord and administer the sacred rites." [13]

Chastity is indeed a very fine gift, and it is most honorable to live with one's lawful spouse and to avoid fornication. Although the chastity of widows and virgins is on a higher plane, it is nowhere pure, and you will not find any virgin or widow in whom all feeling and desire are completely extinguished and dead. Therefore when they arrive at God's judgment, God declares: "You have been a very pure virgin, a chaste young man, perhaps also undefiled; but you have not been without passion and lust. Therefore the Law, which says: 'You shall not covet,' condemns you."

Thus chastity will remain in Christ alone, who was born from the thigh of Abraham without lust and sin. Through His chastity we, too, shall be chaste and saved.

And Abraham himself not only understood this and kept it shut up in his heart, but he also preached it in many sermons that were constantly based on this one statement: "In your Seed," etc. Inasmuch as he wanted to introduce that new rite into his church, he carefully inculcated the promise, in order to persuade the people about the certainty of the future Seed, just as we stress the doctrine of the deliverance and the raising of our bodies at the Last Judgment: "It is sown in weakness, in corruption, in dishonor" (1 Cor. 15:42-43). Therefore the godly should be exhorted to oppose faith to what the eyes see, and in the midst of corruption and dishonor to look at the glory which surpasses the brightness of the sun and the stars, and in the most horrible corruption, the consumption by worms, and the overpowering stench to look at the balsam and the eternal glory. Thus when faith sees a dead person placed into the earth, it does not see the corpse or the corruption; but it sees the unimpaired state of the body, immortal glory, and spiritual life.

Thus Abraham preached that in the lust and concupiscence which are apparent to our senses one should keep in mind the future Seed that would be without lust and blessed — the Seed that would save the entire world. And Abraham declared that he had been chosen to be the Seed's father. These words the godly, and especially the ser-

---

13 For the application of Is. 52:11 to the clergy of the Christian Church cf. Gregory the Great, *Cura pastoralis*, Part II, ch. 2.

vants in his house, believed; and for this reason they honored the thigh as a sacred object, yet not to the glory of Abraham, as we were once wont to accord to creatures the worship and honor owed to God, but on account of faith and their expectation of the future Seed.

If the pope had the glory that whoever kissed his feet was kissing a sacred object, good God, how overweening he would be! Yet by his downright lies he has brought this about among kings and monarchs.

Abraham had the promise which involved his thigh as the origin of the Seed. Therefore he regarded his thigh as a sacred object, but to God's glory and honor, not to his own. Thus he was justified, as a result not of the seed, the blood, and the will of a man or of the flesh but of God (John 1:13), that is, of the future Seed, which nevertheless was to come out of his thigh; and thus he found glory in the midst of shame and the utmost chastity and modesty in the midst of lust.

I am afraid, however, that sometime later there followed that horrible indecency of the heathen Ishmaelites. For human nature cannot keep within bounds or preserve in a sensible and godly manner what has been handed down correctly and scrupulously by the forefathers, but it turns aside at once either to the right or to the left. When the Midianites heard these grand promises, namely, that Abraham's thigh or the power of procreation enjoyed such great honor, they soon fell into the most indecent idolatry and not only defiled themselves with the indecency of lust, as though with extraordinary sanctity and righteousness, but even set up and worshiped a unique idol called Priapus.[14] Such is the custom of idolaters; they appropriate only the works of the ceremonies after they have abandoned the Word and the Spirit.

Thus others, too, because they overlooked the fact that Abraham had a special command to sacrifice his son, slaughtered their sons as an act of obedience to God. They did so without faith and a command of God. That is reasoning from the example of the fathers, not from their faith. Although they performed the same work, their faith and heart were different. In the case of Abraham there was the command of God; but they did not have a command, promise, and word. They were idolaters.

[14] Cf. *Luther's Works*, 22, p. 25.

Thus the adoration and worship of the sun undoubtedly originated from the traditions of Adam. For he taught his domestics and his children to bow their knees at sunrise and to give praise to the Lord of heaven and earth, and to acknowledge the countless benefits God bestows on the world through that most beautiful luminary. Although his decendants retained that rite and ceremony by bending their knees toward the sun, they forgot to give thanks for the goodness of God, who created the light and the sun; and later on they made an idol of the sun.[15]

All this originated from the godly traditions of the fathers; for wherever Christ builds a temple and gathers a church, Satan invariably has the habit of imitating Him like an ape and inventing idolatrous forms of worship and idolatrous traditions similar to the true doctrine and the true forms of worship.[16] But he belittles the promise and the spirit of the fathers, and meanwhile he introduces impressive pomp and magnificent pageantry. The result is that he overcomes and obscures true worship and the church by means of a semblance of religion and of saintliness.

Thus the pope has converted the Lord's Supper into horrible idolatry. Christ instituted it that we might eat and drink His body and blood, in order to buoy up our consciences and to strengthen our faith, as He says (1 Cor. 11:24): "Do this in remembrance of Me"; that is, "Proclaim Me, give thanks to Me, and awaken your faith." But the pope has kept the outward performance of the work,[17] and has completely done away with its true use in remembrance of Christ. Indeed, by means of a prohibition he has decreed that no one should read the words of institution in public. This is attested in a book titled *On the Secrets of Priests.*[18] No one was permitted to read the canon except the priest, and it would have been an infamous action and a crime to utter the words of the Supper in a loud voice.

15 On this view of the origins of idolatry see *Luther the Expositor,* pp. 238 to 239.

16 Luther frequently cites this proverb; cf. *Luther's Works,* 21, p. 212, note 2.

17 On various meanings of *opus operatum* see *Luther's Works,* 26, p. 122, note 38.

18 Luther is referring to a medieval manual of liturgical practice entitled *De secretis sacerdotum,* which deals with those parts of the Mass that are spoken silently by the priest. He had written a treatise against the canon of the Mass in 1525 (W XVIII, 22—36) and had discussed some of these manuals at table on February 2, 1538 (W, *Tischreden,* III, 563—565).

Later on the pope took away the second species [19] from the church and invented the fiction that in the Mass there is a sacrificial offering for the sins of the entire world. This business was by far the most productive; for from it came so many churches, altars, and convents, and that entire form of worship with its countless ceremonies, evidently for the purpose of stabilizing that abominable desecration.

In this manner the world always imitates the customs and rites of the fathers. But it cuts off their head; that is, it does away with faith, the promise, and the command of God and retains the deed itself or the outward performance of the work. Subsequently the unlearned are deceived, and wretched consciences are inveigled into the fraud by the magnificent pomp and splendor of works and outward ceremonies.

Thus mention was made above of Ur of the Chaldeans, where people worshiped *Orimasda,* that is, the sacred fire.[20] This form of worship arose from the fact that they had seen fire sent down from heaven consume the sacrificial animals that were offered. This was a sign of God's promise and intention to approve of the sacrifices of the fathers. Hence they appropriated these and similar sacrifices for their idolatry and worshiped light or the sacred fire. For this reason they called themselves חֲסִידִים, that is, saints.

For it is the devil's rule to build a chapel next to a church and temple of Christ, that is, to appropriate the works and examples of the fathers, disfigure them, and turn them into a work that is performed without regard for faith.

Thus the Jews are not very successful in imitating the ceremonies of the fathers. They make a work out of circumcision and pitifully torture their infants. Faith and the promise they have thrust aside, and they think that the work and the ceremony are of the utmost importance, not the Word and promise of God.

In this manner the Ishmaelites — since they knew that they were the sons of Abraham and had come out of his loins, but that the loins had the blessing on account of the Blessed Seed, who would be born from them — appropriated the outward performance of the work and the lust without the promise and faith, until eventually they worshiped the male organ, something that the Greeks and Romans later

[19] A reference to withholding the chalice from the laity, which became common in about the twelfth century in the Western church.

[20] See also *Luther's Works,* 2, pp. 234, 244.

on adopted. Indeed, Baal-peor (although I shudder at mentioning this) is nothing else than the indecency of the male organ with its lasciviousness.

Procreation is a blessing, and it is a work of God. For this reason the loins and the thigh of Abraham are blessed, but not as a result of the work that is performed; they are blessed because Christ, the divine Seed, is in the thigh. Then the blessing is there in the midst of lust and concupiscence, and the lust is covered and tolerated by divine forgiveness.

Abraham did not deny that concupiscence is a sin and that the thigh has been corrupted by the original disease, but he added saintliness and the remedy of marriage and of the divine ordinance. Thus we do not deny that the body is buried in the utmost dishonor; but we have a plaster with which it is covered and healed, because we know that the dishonor will be turned into very great glory.

In itself the dishonor is nothing else than the utmost uncleanness; but that it is turned into glory, this happens as a result of the pure grace of God. If, however, I wanted to accept the object and the work itself alone as glory, I would retain nothing but dishonor. But the work should be done as a result of the Spirit, faith, and the promise. Then the work is no longer dishonorable. No, it is illumined with a most glorious light that is brighter than the sun and gives off a more delightful odor than any balsam or incense. But this is not produced by the dishonor; it is produced by the grace of the Holy Spirit.

Thus the male or female organ is most indecent and does a very vile work; but because the promised Seed has come out of the thigh of Abraham, it covers that indecency and makes it a sacred object. The Ishmaelites, however, attributed purity, modesty, righteousness, and sanctity to the work in itself. For they said: "In what respect would the organ of a woman or of a man sin, inasmuch as Holy Scripture states that the thigh of Abraham was blessed?"

It is surely to be lamented and deplored that human nature has been so horribly corrupted. Therefore one should curb the sensual desires with all zeal, repress and detest concupiscence, and strive after modesty and chastity. And if it were impossible to cure and avoid altogether that evil which is implanted in our nature because of original sin, one should bemoan and deplore it, as Paul complains (1 Cor. 9:27): "I pommel my body and subdue it." "Yet," he says,

"I find nothing good in my flesh" (cf. Rom. 7:18). But afterwards one must apprehend and invoke the Seed on whose account God has blessed us, in order that the remnants of sin may not be charged against us.

"For there is no condemnation for those who are in Christ Jesus" (Rom. 8:1).[21] Paul does not say that there is no sin; he says that there is no condemnation. Otherwise we shall follow after the work of the flesh, fornication, and adultery, give free rein to lust, and thus apprehend the matter to the exclusion of the blessing, as happens in all superstition and idolatry, which for the most part take their beginning and have a very excellent origin from the fathers. But — to make use of the terminology of the dialecticians — the idolaters combine and divide improperly.[22] They separate the work from faith, the matter from its final cause. From the work they construct righteousness. This is devilish dialectic.

But Abraham, who knew how to distinguish these things properly, was a most excellent man. He was not addicted to the licentiousness of the flesh; yet he maintained that under lust and sin there was concealed a blessing on account of the future Seed from his loins — the Seed whose holiness and chastity are so great that He would bless the entire world, and that because of the blessing God would put up with that conjugal lust. Otherwise we would all have been condemned, because concupiscence inheres fixed in our bones and marrow and cannot be overcome and quenched by anyone, in accord with what is stated in Ps. 51:5: "In sin did my mother conceive me."

Therefore let this be the explanation of and the reason for that rite which Abraham introduced in his church, namely, that by his excellent spirit that wonderful mystery of the incarnation of Christ which he wanted to impress on his domestics was pointed out [23] not only by word but also by deed and by an external sign.

Then let the reader remember that it is always customary for horrible superstitions to follow from the religion of the fathers. Thus it is certain that the Ishmaelites boasted about the thigh of Abraham, that they were descended from that flesh which was considered worthy of having the name of God called upon over it; and after this

---

[21] The original has "Rom. 7."

[22] See *Luther's Works*, 27, p. 31, note 28.

[23] Both the Weimar and the Erlangen editions have *significatam* here, but we have read *significatum*.

they fell into horrible blindness and worshiped indecency itself, since they understood flesh in a material and not in a spiritual sense.

This disease has raged in human nature at all times, and it makes monkeys of us, so that we follow the deed and the examples of the fathers and abandon their spirit. This is especially worthy of mentioning and observing in this passage.

Thus the pope had very clear testimonies of Scripture and distinct signs of grace, and if one considers these, one will hardly believe that such a great abomination could have followed. What is clearer than the Sacrament of Baptism, the Eucharist, the use of the Keys, the voice of the Gospel, and the Passion of Christ preached, depicted, and represented in various ways? Yet among so great an abundance of sacraments, signs, words, and examples the Antichrist has been ruling for so many centuries with very great power.

By the grace of God we have cleansed that doctrine again, but I have no doubt that a little later there will follow men who will once more espouse works and human traditions after they have rejected the doctrine of godliness and have forsaken the source of righteousness. If Münzer and the Sacramentarians, although they heard that we were teaching the Spirit and rejecting works, were able to misuse this doctrine and, after despising the Word and the sacraments, to blare nothing else than the Spirit,[24] and that while we are still alive, teaching, and refuting, what will happen when our teaching has become silent?

They agree with us in thinking and preaching that the works of the pope do not justify, but that another righteousness of the spirit is necessary. But by this spirit they understand manias, revelations, and their own thoughts.

The antinomians have followed these people. They teach plainly that all sins have been removed and should not be censured, and that people should not be frightened with the Law, just as the Ishmaelites fancied that because the thigh of their father Abraham was holy, everything is holy. The antinomians, of course, carefully conceal this and try to disguise their doctrine; but secretly they support this absurdity and say that sin has been forgiven, that there is no condemnation, and that therefore sin is nothing or has been completely done away with (Rom. 8:1).[25]

[24] This is a frequent theme in Luther's polemics; see, for example, *Luther's Works,* 37, pp. 149, 150.

[25] See p. 49, note 48.

This error has its origin in the most glorious doctrine in the writings of the apostles (1 John 3:9): "No one born of God commits sin"; likewise in the statement [26] "I believe in the forgiveness of sins." For they do not understand that there is righteousness and forgiveness of sins in the midst of sins, but they imagine that sins have been done away with completely.

The Jews reason as follows: "If we are the seed and the sons of Abraham, we are holy and blessed, and we alone please God." Nor has it been possible for them to be disabused of this persuasion by the disasters they have suffered up to this time for so many centuries. But that Abraham's thigh is holy and his seed sanctified, this does not happen on account of his thigh in the flesh or on account of Abraham himself, in accordance with the statement in John 1:13: "Not of blood nor of the will of the flesh nor of the will of man, etc.," but because the holy Seed is enclosed in that thigh. This Seed they reject and blaspheme and believe that they themselves are the blessed Seed. For this reason they take and understand the thigh according to the flesh only, without the Spirit; and they become Ishmaelites, Epicureans, and antinomians, who, because of the remission of sins, deny that any sin remains.

But Paul has a different definition of the forgiveness of sins when he says (Rom. 7:25): "I serve the law of sin." Likewise (v. 19): "For I do not do the good I want"; that is, there adhere to me many wicked inclinations and emotions, smugness, doubt, and impatience in adversity. Therefore one should teach and believe the forgiveness of sins in this manner, that sin surely will not condemn us, because it has been forgiven — not through the righteousness of the flesh but through the Son of God, who put on our flesh — but that if you separate Him from the flesh, you are already condemned.

Therefore those who have been justified and have the forgiveness of sins are sinners, because they complain that they cannot do what they want. They fight, and they resist concupiscence and the inherent sickness; they crucify the flesh. Nevertheless, they cannot be completely set free, as Paul explains (Rom. 7:24): "Wretched man that I am! Who will deliver me from this body of death?"

The antinomians will obscure this doctrine, and they will stress grace so much that they will blot it out and bring people under the wrath of God, because they will make people altogether unconcerned

[26] This is, of course, a quotation from the Apostles' Creed.

about God's wrath and judgment, as though no sin remained and no fear of death and hell.

Accordingly, sin clings to the saints, and grace contends against it most vigorously. The struggle between the spirit and the flesh, between the serpent and the Seed, continues as long as this life lasts. The Seed crushes the head of the serpent, but the serpent lies in wait for the Seed and bites His heel (Gen. 3:15).

The Ishmaelites reject the Seed, and by taking the blessing in a material and carnal sense they glory that they are the children of the flesh. Therefore they are condemned sinners, even though they are descended from Abraham.

Thus we stated above that marriage is sacred, and Paul says (cf. 1 Tim. 2:15) that "women who bear children are holy if they continue in the faith"; that is, if they believe in Christ and contend with the serpent, which means that they are chaste or withstand the wicked impulses of their flesh. Otherwise a woman, so far as physical procreation without faith and without the Seed is concerned, will be condemned.

Accordingly, one must retain the holiness and the blessing of the thigh, or rather of the Seed which was born from that thigh, has blessed all nations, and has sanctified the chastity polluted in marriage, lest the uncleanness and the defilement of the flesh condemn us. If this is not done, we fall at once into the error of the Ishmaelites and into like condemnation, and nothing but the name of and the reputation for sanctity will be left.

Thus the pope taught holiness after he had thrust aside the Word and the Spirit. He taught that after Baptism, when they had grown up, Christians should enter monasteries, torment the body, and render satisfaction for their sins. Similarly, the Turks, too, have a variety of works and exercises on account of which they boast that they are saintly; but it is only the semblance and name of saintliness, under which horrible faults are hidden. Accordingly, when the doctrine concerning the Seed has been discarded, no salvation is left, because vices become virtues and turn into habits, as Seneca says.[27] What should be reproved as a fault is propounded as righteousness, wisdom, and salvation, just as pilgrimages, the cowl, and the distinction among foods and apparel were regarded as the height of righteousness, yes, as perfection.

27 Seneca, *Epistles,* 39, 6.

But if faults, that is, idolatry and error, are held up as righteousness, what and of what sort are sins that are openly manifest? There the Word of Christ is fulfilled (Matt. 6:23): "If, then, the light in you is darkness"; that is, if error and falsehood are your light, life, salvation, and perfect righteousness, "how great is the darkness!" This refers to the flesh itself, which is hidden and adorned and becomes a sevenfold sin.

Therefore I urge you to learn carefully and to meditate on the doctrine of justification. Together with us, false brethren condemn the works of the pope; yet they oppose us, because they strive for new, unusual works and do so while we are still living and contending against them.

The justification of Christians consists in this, that sin has been made weak and does not have dominion over us. If you take a wife, you will feel lust; but you will be able to live in a chaste and godly manner with her because you believe in Christ, for then sin has been made weak. On the other hand, if you enter into marriage with intense passion and with the expectation of sundry pleasures, when hardly one or two months have elapsed — often even before the wedding a dislike will develop — there will arise annoyances between you and your wife and a dislike greater than your love was at first. As a result, you will more eagerly desire to be separated from her than to be joined to her. You will wish for your wife's death, and any other woman will seem more beautiful and agreeable in her manners and character than your wife; for then sin has dominion.

Consequently, this passage presents an example of a marriage where grace reigns and sin is made weak. But if you do not begin so great an undertaking in a similar manner, namely, with humble prayer and faith, you will have a very sad marriage abounding in quarrels, contentions, and perpetual disagreements. Thus one encounters such common complaints as "I can live neither with you nor without you" and "Woman is a necessary evil." [28] These things generally happen to those who have in view nothing else than the wretched flesh and lust, and who picture to themselves pleasures of every sort. Why do they not call upon the Creator of both sexes, who is both the Author of marriage and the best Counselor in marriage? They have in mind solely the definition laid down in civil

[28] Cf. *Luther's Works*, 3, p. 48, note 6; the second aphorism is found in Menander, *Fragments*, No. 651.

law, namely, that marriage is the union of a man and a woman which maintains inseparable companionship. Here the true differences and duties have not been mentioned, for those people have no understanding of the matter. How, then, could they give a correct definition? Their definition is purely material.

But this is the true definition: Marriage is the divinely instituted and lawful union of a man and a woman in the hope of offspring, or at least for the sake of avoiding fornication and sin, to the glory of God. Its ultimate purpose is to obey God and to be a remedy for sin; to call upon God; to desire, love, and bring up children to the glory of God; to live with one's wife in the fear of the Lord; and to bear one's cross. But if no children result, you should nevertheless live content with your wife and avoid promiscuity.

Up to this point we have discussed the rite of taking an oath — the rite which Abraham instituted. Next let us consider the form of the oath. It was clearly a new rite when the servant who was about to swear placed a finger or his hands under Abraham's thigh. We raise two fingers because in every case two witnesses are required. Thus the two fingers which have been raised toward God and point out the true God take the place of two witnesses.

The form of the oath is this: "I shall make you swear; that is, I shall take an oath from you, or you will swear to me by the Lord, the Gods of the heavens and the Gods of the earth, that you will not take a wife for my son from the daughters of the Canaanites among whom I am living." Here Scripture bears witness clearly that the mystery of the Godhead was not unknown to the fathers, especially to Abraham, who would not have permitted the oath to be made in these words if he had not understood that the Seed is more than a human being.

Because the Son of God mixes Himself into flesh and is a divine leaven, as it were, that has been concealed in the dough which is full of sins and corruption, Abraham is speaking of one essence and yet continues with the plural "by the Lord, the Gods of the heavens and the Gods of the earth." Hence God is one altogether uncompounded essence and nevertheless more than one in respect to persons or hypostases.

But when we swear, we always give expression to two things: we invoke God's help and defense and call down His punishment. It is as though you were saying: "So help me God" or "May He punish me if I swear falsely. So help me God or not.[29] If I keep the oath, let Him be gracious toward me; if I am swearing falsely, let Him punish me."

This is a very beautiful way to worship God and to call upon Him; for he who is swearing confesses that he is imploring the mercy and favor of God, is expecting from Him the benefits of His defense and help, and is calling down upon himself God's vengeance if he should swear falsely. Therefore there is attached to the Second Commandment the threat which threatens perjurers: "For the Lord will not hold him guiltless who takes His name in vain" (Ex. 20:7).

For perjury is a denial and contempt of God. But if you keep your oath, you are rendering the highest form of worship to God; for to swear is to trust in God as your Protector and Deliverer. But if you swear falsely, you have already denied God and rejected His grace; and you have called down His displeasure and wrath upon your head.

Above, when Abimelech swears to Abraham, they did not make use of this form or of that rite; but here there is a new way to swear, because Abraham wants to include Christ in the oath, in accord with the statement in Ps. 63:11: "All who swear by Him shall glory." For he who swears in conformity with the truth worships and honors God and calls upon His name; he who swears falsely blasphemes and reviles the Divine Majesty and insults It. He despises It and regards It as nothing. Finally, he who swears unnecessarily sins, namely, when an officer of the state and the law of love do not demand it.

But why does Abraham forbid his servant to look for one of the daughters of the Canaanites? My answer is that Abraham, near death, had experienced many things in this land when he lived among the heathen people. It was necessary for him to observe their customs and way of life rather carefully, to associate with them, and to talk and confer with them about various matters, inasmuch as all his wealth and livelihood — almost as in the case of a shepherd — consisted in cattle and fields. From this source he not only fed and supported his domestics but also sold meat, butter, milk, cheese, and similar products. This could not be done without close association with the inhabitants and citizens. Consequently, as a result of that association and intimacy, some, possibly of the foremost families of

---

[29] Here the original has the German: *als mir Gott helff oder nicht.*

Ephron or others, were perhaps induced to desire Isaac, such a respectable and handsome young man, as a son-in-law or relative by marriage. And above it has been stated that because of God's blessing Abraham was wealthy. For this reason alone they surely wanted to be friends with him.

But Abraham had various reasons for refusing this. He was afraid of dangers either for his household or for his church. Perhaps he did not like the character and the conduct of the girls, because they were exceedingly proud if they were distinguished by wealth, beauty, or descent. For it is especially hard to be a son-in-law in the house of a powerful and rich man, and nothing is more unbearable than a rich and domineering woman; for the husband is forced to comply with his wife's command and authority, or by their blandishments the women at least prevail over and weaken the men who are in the clutches of love.

Therefore these dangers to his household came into his mind in order that he might not look for a beautiful or rich woman but might seek one who was honest and respectable, one who would be diligent and painstaking in managing the household. For to be subject to domineering wives is not only irksome but also disgraceful; and they should not lord it over their husbands but over oxen, sheep, and asses.

In addition to this reason, however, there was the more important one that concerned the church, inasmuch as this land was condemned by God, as God said above to Abraham: "I will give you this land" (Gen. 13:15); and "The iniquity of the Amorites is not yet complete" (Gen. 15:16). Therefore he regarded it as a land rejected and spurned by God — a land which God threatened with destruction. Meanwhile, however, he had intimate and friendly relations with them in business agreements and all sorts of transactions, and it was a wonder that he found that some saintly people were still dwelling in that place. Of these we have spoken above.

Abraham understood all these things, for he was a spiritual and intelligent man. Therefore he was unwilling to mix his seed with the blood of the Canaanites, lest his son become an idolater and the commingling of the seed lead at the same time to an intermingling of holy and idolatrous forms of worship. The worship of the saints is evidently plain and without show and splendor. On the other hand, the ungodly are puffed up with their righteousness, and by their show they very easily deceive the weak. Therefore Abraham saw that his son would nevertheless be in grave danger, even though he might not be led astray.

Therefore Abraham is concerned about his son and about the bride and the family of his son. And this is a matter of divine right and has to do with the definition of marriage over against the pope, who makes a brothel of marriage and does not see any difference between the coition of beasts and that of human beings.

I do not doubt that very many girls were offered to Isaac and that among them there were some who were beautiful, rich, and of noble birth. But Abraham closes his eyes and forbids his son to marry any one of them, not because he opposes the honorable desire of his son, who, because of his age, was now ready for marriage, but because he wants by all means to give him a respectable girl in marriage, not one who would be his son's ruin and an offense to the entire church.

Moreover, Isaac does not oppose his father but takes his advice with the utmost goodwill.

Therefore let all young people remember this example, and let them learn to respect the authority of their parents and the sanctity of the divine ordinance. Let them not think that intercourse is bestial, as the pope supposes it to be. But above all they should call upon their true Father and the Author of all things, in order that they may start without sin: "Lord God, Thou hast created me a man. Thou seest that I cannot be continent. I am calling upon Thee. Direct and bless my undertaking. Give me counsel and help. Choose for me a woman with whom I may be able to live honorably and to serve Thee, and by faith and prayer to overcome the inconveniences and difficulties of marriage." Those who disdain these admonitions and are carried away by a blind impulse, without faith and prayer, will eventually experience, and be overwhelmed by, all kinds of misfortunes.

What is more desirable than a happy and peaceful marriage, where mutual love reigns and there is a most delightful union of the hearts? A marriage of this kind is praised everywhere as a miracle. When I, as a young man, heard such commendations and praise of an honorable and happy marriage — likewise, when I read in Paul (Eph. 5:25): "Husbands, love your wives" — I used to wonder why this happened and what purpose it served to give exhortations and precepts about the love of spouses among whom one could often find not only love but even passion.

But experience has taught me that out of many marriages hardly one merits praise. From this fact stem those common disparaging statements: "The bed in which a wife lies is never free from wranglings and mutual bickerings." [30] On this account many men are most vehemently averse to marriage.

But one should not feel or think about this kind of life after the fashion of the heathen. No, one should acknowledge God as the Creator, and one should bend the knee in humility and implore Him in faith to bestow a companion and bedmate. When this spirit and faith are associated with the invocation, then one will be able to take care of everything else in a reasonable manner, to deal with one's parents, and to listen to their advice. Later on, if everything does not turn out according to your wish, you nevertheless have this comfort: "I have prayed. I have asked God, my parents, and my relatives for advice. If anything untoward happens, I shall bear it calmly." For it is a great comfort to have God as a Witness and Supporter, and one's parents and relatives as confidants and advisers.

On the other hand, if you have entered into a marriage at your own risk and without the knowledge of your parents, it will everlastingly trouble and distress your heart. You will say: "Behold, I am being punished for my foolishness and obstinacy. I have displeased my parents; and I, in turn, am being burdened with every kind of misfortune." That is an unbearable cross.

Accordingly, this is a very fine chapter not only for doing honor to marriage but also for comforting the consciences of those who experience the inconveniences of marriage.

Inexperienced young people do not see the annoyances and burdens of marriage beforehand. Nor do they consider that they have the devil as their enemy. He hates the begetting of children as well as the respect, the mutual love, and the harmony of spouses. The bridegroom and the bride do not trouble themselves about these things. Therefore they should be taught to bring this trust with them: "Lord God, I have entered into this kind of life in accordance with Thy will and with an appeal for Thy help. Thou wilt give the grace and the blessing, that I may be able to bear the burdens that lie ahead." To this prayer God undoubtedly gives assent and answers: "Let what is being asked for be done."

But the ungodly give consideration to the vituperations and the

[30] Juvenal, *Satires*, VI, lines 268, 269.

inconveniences of marriage and therefore shun it and fall into the works of the flesh: uncleanness, fornication, and adultery, of which Paul says in Gal. 5:21: "Those who do such things shall not inherit the kingdom of God."

I am discussing these matters rather carefully and extensively because I see that the Holy Spirit did not disdain to describe His own work at such great length. Ungodly and wicked men, who suppose that everything happens by chance, understand nothing in the Holy Scriptures and the creatures of God. But it is our duty to read and to instruct others, in order that from Holy Scripture we may gain knowledge of the creatures, and from the creatures of the Creator.

Scripture points out that God's creature has been blinded and marred. For this reason it praises the dignity of marriage at such great length. We are to learn, and to teach others that marriage is not to be held in slight esteem, as the flesh and the world are in the habit of doing. They do not consider what marriage is but take into account only concupiscence, lust, and sensual pleasure. They strive for ease and riches, which are original sin itself, by which our wretched nature is horribly contaminated. Therefore instead of the pleasure and enjoyment hoped for, they eventually find vexation, grief, and trouble.

Accordingly, a happy and joyous marriage is very rare; for people do not distinguish the work of God from original sin. But Holy Scripture honors marriage with true and most ample praises and shows how it is the source and origin of the household, the state, and the church, which derive their origin and growth from it so far as their substance is concerned. In the church one seeks the glory of God; in the state, peace; and in the household, the rearing of children. In addition, marriage comprises a huge number of good works and fruits.

Hence God, Abraham, and those who are truly godly regard marriage in a manner that is far different from the view held by the pope, who considers only the lust and the pleasure, that is, original sin, and then also the cross and the afflictions in marriage.

Meanwhile, however, God, in His accustomed mercy, bears with the faults and the punishments of the original evil, because they are hidden, being covered by the blessing and the marvelous abundance of good works. These fruits the papists do not see but call them civil, secular, and carnal works. Consequently, they look at them as a horse and a mule does (Ps. 32:9). Their judgment is not in accord with Scripture, which points out the fruits and good works of marriage. Indeed, the heathen, too, approved of marriage and wanted to compel their youth to marry, in order that human society might be preserved. But those who, like the papists and the monks, avoided the accustomed troubles and vexations have devised unusual endeavors, works, and orders designed to please themselves and God. Thus even though they saw, they did not see the things that have been mentioned.

Even if these things are commonly disregarded, the bishops and teachers of the church should nevertheless learn them and teach them to others. For God has not revealed His Word that it should be despised but that we should hear and ponder it, and learn the things that are unknown to us by nature.

The other sciences, namely, medicine, jurisprudence, and philosophy, have more students. But because we disregard this doctrine, we deserve the punishments and the deplorable blindness that follow. We have Scripture and what God has created; if we do not search these sources, we are deprived by our own fault, and deservedly so, of the blessings offered there.

Lastly Abraham commands his servant to journey to his native country and to fetch a bride from there. Abraham and Sarah were born in Babylon; they were Babylonian citizens, that is, Chaldeans, as Moses related above in Gen. 11:31, namely, that Terah took his son Abraham and his daughter-in-law Sarah and brought them out of Ur of the Chaldeans. Abraham was not born in Haran, as some suppose and attempt to prove from this passage.[31]

5. *The servant said to him: Perhaps the woman may not be willing to follow me to this land; must I, then, take your son back to the land from which you came?*

6. *Abraham said to him: See to it that you do not take my son back there.*

7. *The Lord, the God of heaven, who took me from my father's house and from the land of my birth, and who spoke to me and swore to me: To your descendants I will give this land, He will send His angel before you, and you shall take a wife for my son from there.*

---

[31] On the question of Abraham's birth cf. *Luther's Works*, 2, pp. 276—278.

All this is described, not because of Abraham, Isaac, and the servant, but because of us and of all human beings to the end of the world. For God wanted to set before us the excellent example of the faith of Abraham — the faith which shines and reigns in his entire life. For he lives and is dependent wholly on the Word of God, who gives him the promise, and according to that Word he arranges all his plans and actions. He does not rely on his own wisdom or on the judgment of reason.

Then he does his duty with diligence. He does not wait idly for an angel to descend from heaven and bring a bride for his son; nor does he neglect any of the things about which a father must be concerned. It is his purpose not to appear to be tempting God. Therefore it is necessary for parents to provide for an honorable and godly marriage for their children, to look for and obtain a bride. They should not suppose that she will come from somewhere by chance or in a novel and unusual manner.

Nor is it a sin if a young man or a girl thinks about a future bride or bridegroom. Indeed, to this end banquets are arranged, decent social gatherings and dances, which should by no means be condemned if they are modest and temperate.

Because we have not been created for fornication but for marriage, it is not only permitted, but it is both godly and honorable to desire and to try to get a wife. But this should be done in faith and with prayer in the manner discussed above, and in accordance with the advice of parents or whoever may be in their place.

Thus Abraham sends out his servant with money and with gifts for the betrothal, because these things belong to contracting a marriage. And let us not think that they are displeasing to God. On the contrary, they are very much approved of by Him, provided that they are done in the fear and reverence of God.

Moreover, the instructions with which Abraham provides his servant abound in faith. "Beware, I beg you," he says, "of taking my son to that land from which I departed; for God has forbidden me to return there. I was led out by the Lord, the God of heaven; He has more dwelling places and lodgings than that region and my native country. He is the Lord of the heavens. Consequently, He has destined for me another kingdom than my native country. Nor do I want you to obtain anyone from this land in which I am now dwelling, because the Canaanites must be destroyed on account of the idolatry with which they have been polluted." The same thing is also indicated below (Gen. 34) in the account of Dinah.

Furthermore, for the purpose of strengthening his servant Abraham adds that God not only spoke to him but also gave him an oath. Thus he lives or speaks nothing else than God. He believes God's promise, and in this faith he does all things successfully in the state and in the household. In full and firm faith he performs not only those sublime deeds, such as the sacrifice of his son and the victory over the kings, but also common and everyday deeds. "Because," he says, "God has spoken to me, has promised me, and has sworn to me: 'I will give you this land,' you shall not take my son to that place, because this would be contrary to the promise and the Bible, or to my Scripture and faith."

Thus Abraham lives completely in faith, even in those most trivial matters which the pope calls carnal, secular, and worldly. But that which is done according to the flesh is truly carnal, such as "concupiscence, lust, and the like" (Gal. 5:19). To seek a wife, however, is not carnal; but whatever remains of the flesh is devoured by faith. Therefore it is spiritual, for the Spirit sets us free from the corruption and the blemish of original sin.

Accordingly, Abraham relies on the promise and teaches that all things, great or small, should be done in the full assurance of faith. Thus we, too, should learn that all things, extraordinary or usual, the highest and the lowest, must be submitted to God and committed to Him, in order that we may rejoice and be strong in the Lord, casting all our care on Him. To arrange a wedding for a son appears to be a sordid and almost indecent business. But what great value and dignity it has in Abraham's eyes — so much so that he has no doubt about the presence, the solicitude, and the help of the angels!

Abraham lays stress on his Bible, that is, on the promise which he had in place of the Bible which we have. "The God of heaven, who has spoken to me," he says, "will send His angel before you." For this is how he reasons: "The angels and all creatures will minister to anyone to whom God speaks. God has spoken to me. Therefore the angels will minister to me."

This very excellent conclusion, by which he establishes with certainty that angels will be with his servant, is based on God's promises: "I have a God who has angels; He will send an angel to accompany and help you." This is an altogether marvelous statement and trust which leads him to believe that this work has already been entrusted to the angels in order that they may be present with his servant. He thought: "I shall do my part; I shall give my servant gifts to bring to the bride. God will add an angel to take care of the rest."

Thus he commits the matter to God and the angels in complete and perfect faith. He thinks that those heavenly spirits and princes are engaged in this seemingly insignificant, carnal, and foolish work. And so sure is he about their service that he knows and believes not only that he has the angels at home, but that they are also present wherever he sends his servant. Because we have the God of heaven and earth, the angels are our protectors, guardians, yes, our attendants, wherever we are.

From this passage originated the most delightful words in the psalms, such as "The angel of the Lord encamps around those who fear Him" (Ps. 34:7) and "He will give His angels charge of you" (Ps. 91:11). David looked a little more deeply into these accounts than the pope and we are in the habit of doing. We suppose that the angels are not concerned about us but are at leisure playing in heaven. We all think this way by nature, and to this fault of original sin comes the custom of teaching and thinking that they are a very great distance away from us, although we see that whatever we have is preserved and protected because of their defense and service, and that people often perish horribly when deprived of their service. Abraham thinks far differently and more correctly: "The angel of God, who has created me, has given me a promise, and has sworn to me, will concern himself about a bride and fetch her." He does not say: "My cousins and kinsmen will consider how my son will get a bride." No, he says: "An angel will be the spokesman and ambassador who will persuade the bride to follow."

Who has ever heard of or had a like faith — a faith that would give him such a firm conviction about what Abraham promises himself? Ambrose, Augustine, or men like them are nothing when compared with him. And you see what his works are. He is a householder and shepherd; he lives among people according to the common and ordinary way of life; and he does what is usual among all parents, namely, that they take care of and are concerned about the marriage of their children. Here nothing spiritual is evident, no cowl, tonsure, or similar nonsense.

Consequently, these things tend to spur us on to faith and to pray that he who is about to enter into a marriage may call upon God and believe that God will grant the wife he is asking for — the wife who is suited to his character. Therefore you should maintain with confidence: "O Lord, I know that Thou wilt send an angel along with me to manage everything. I shall provide the hand and the tongue, and I shall do my share; the rest will be Thy concern."

These should also be our thoughts when we are about to assume functions in the church or in the government. Because I am being called to the office of pastor or teacher, I shall do what I can. An angel will be at hand to direct everything. Peace, security, and joy of spirit follow this faith in any trial whatever, because I am sure that even if many evils beset me, angels nevertheless watch over and guard me. Therefore let them provide for a happy outcome and for my deliverance.

Anyone who believes this we shall declare truly blessed. But the unbelief and blindness which neither recognizes such great benefits nor believes that they exist is a most disgraceful fault. On this account we are also so ungrateful, rude, and unfeeling that the services which the angels perform for people are completely disregarded among us. Nor does one person promote the advantages of the other with the same zeal with which those heavenly spirits most assiduously perform their services daily and every moment. Therefore we shall eventually pay the penalty for this ingratitude.

And yet the presence of the angels is an assured fact — a fact about which we should not have even one doubt. It is certain that they are not only waiting for our arrival in our future fatherland, but that they are actually abiding with us in this life, concerning themselves with and directing our affairs, if only we believe this with a firm faith.

But if any misfortune happens in your life, think as follows: "The God of heaven has promised and has sworn an oath that He wants to be my God. Therefore I shall not despair of His help and defense; for I hear that those great princes in heaven have nothing else to do than to be groomsmen at the wedding, to join the bridegroom and the bride, to take care of the wedding, and to watch over the children and the household."

This care has been committed to them; and if we believe, every one of us will have this same experience. For thus we see Abraham fully convinced that angels are with him and are serving him in no other way than if they were standing before his eyes, even though they are invisible. So great is his faith. And he who has the same confidence that the angels are among us and are managing everything sees the angels most certainly; but he sees them with spiritual eyes, not with eyes that are carnal.

But this is extraordinary praise of the heavenly spirits, that they allow themselves to be made use of for such humble services, which, as it seems, are unworthy of them. Surely, our pride being what it is, we justly give thanks to God that we were not created as angels; for we would not have been able to put up with so lowly a service and would all have followed Lucifer. Is it not a lowly and sordid business to fetch a bride for Isaac? For in addition to the fact that human nature has been corrupted and horribly marred by sins and punishments, this sex, in comparison with men, bears special misfortunes and a cross. Accordingly, will an angel so holy allow himself to be sent to a woman? It is altogether beneath the dignity of the angelic majesty.

We, who are nothing else than filth, corruption, and worms, are in the habit of acting like this: If some surpass others by reason of the gifts of eloquence, wisdom, talent, yes, even wealth or beauty, with what arrogance they exalt themselves above those who lack these things! Yet they are their equals in sins and misfortunes.

Thus the devil considered it beneath the dignity of the angelic majesty to serve Rebecca, not in response to Abraham's request but merely in response to his wish when he says: "Go, the angel of the Lord will be with you." This seems to be a very just reason for his arrogance and anger.

It is also clear from this passage what the nature of the good angels is, how humble, pleasant, and kindly their nature is. It does not regard it beneath its dignity to serve the most wretched sinners, men as well as women; for they burn with the light and the knowledge of the goodness of God and realize that whatever God commands is excellent and best because it pleases God.

Thus Gabriel does not refuse to be sent to a virgin far beneath him and to bring the message committed by God (Luke 1:26-27). He does not delay at all; for he knows that it pleases God, no matter whether the commission is unusual or ordinary. The evil spirits despise not only such service but even the Lord and God Himself.

Consequently, since we know that we are enjoying the companionship, protection, and friendship of the angels, let us give thanks to God, and let us imitate their virtues and services of love and of mutual goodwill. No human being is so benign and ready for any good turn and kindness as the angels. But we do not believe this. Nor do we attribute these virtues to them. It is certain, however, that Rebecca and Isaac had a friend and guardian angel more faithful than their servant and relatives were. The faithfulness of their servant was evident enough to them, but it was nothing in comparison with the faithfulness and the goodwill of the angel.

Therefore let us learn that our best and most steadfast friends are invisible, namely, the angels, who in their faithfulness, goodwill, and friendly services far surpass our visible friends, just as the invisible wicked angels and devils are enemies more dangerous than those who are visible. Whatever mischief is done springs from the former rather than from the latter, whom we see with our eyes. On the other hand, if anything good happens, it is performed entirely by the good angels.

Therefore if we believe and are godly, the good angels are our best friends, just as they were the best friends of Isaac and Rebecca, who were sinners and undeserving of such great assistance. But because they believed, they had angels joined to them as their servants. Thus we, too, should maintain that we are enjoying the companionship of the heavenly spirits, no matter how greatly we are marred by sins and how unworthy we are of the service of such excellent creatures.

About the fall of the wicked angels there is a statement of Bernard, who, as the poets do, invents the story that Satan fell from heaven because he saw that the Son of God was to become man and would take on this wretched mass of the human race, and that then the service and care of the human nature, which was far more wretched than they, would be entrusted to the angels. Therefore since, as Bernard says, he was irritated by the disgracefulness of the situation, he despised the Son of God and for this reason fell from heaven.[32]

The thought is excellent and pious enough, and we see that through sin Satan, too, has put this evil into all men, that the richer, the more learned, and the more beautiful one is, the more arrogant one becomes, just as the heathen poet asserts: "A man who is proud because of his good fortune does not observe moderation." [33]

Therefore people should be warned to shun this devilish arrogance

[32] Cf. Bernard of Clairvaux, *Sermones in Canticum Canticorum, Patrologia, Series Latina,* CLXXXIII, 857.

[33] Lucan, *The Civil War (Pharsalia),* II, 381.

and to recognize their own wretched state. If angels fell because of the pride they took in the greatness and excellence of their gifts, it will also be the ruin of human beings, and especially of those who rashly arrogate to themselves a judgment about God's affairs and when they have barely an ounce of wisdom imagine that they possess a hundredweight.

By means of this solicitude and friendship of the angels God wanted to indicate how highly He regards us, who believe in Him, and how ardently He loves us. Would that for the sake of our corruption and that horrible depravity we could know God and love Him in return! He shows Himself so benign and propitious that He dwells with us and associates with us, albeit invisibly. Yet He does not do so imperceptibly, if I may use this expression. He has given us His Son as a pledge of this love and intimate association (John 3:16). But those who are smug and irreligious have ears and do not hear. Their hearts have been blinded, and their ears have become obtuse (cf. Is. 6:10).

But if we believed, we would be blessed and in heaven itself; for faith is the restoration of all things (Acts 3:21). We have the association of the angels and of the heavenly spirits, who take pleasure in being solicitous about our life and our affairs. But the devil opened our eyes in Paradise (Gen. 3:7). As a result, we consider ourselves wiser and greater than God and the angels. But let us acknowledge our feebleness, and let us exercise our faith in contemplation based on the expectation of the great benefits we enjoy because of the protection of the angels in the presence of the Son of God Himself.

This, too, serves to confirm our doctrine about marriage — namely, that it is a matter of concern to God — over against the satanic blasphemies of the pope, who calls it uncleanness. We know from the New Testament (John 2:1-11) that Christ came to a wedding, and in this passage the angels are said to be the bridesmen whom God assigns to His saints. Therefore let parents hold fast to this comfort. Let them pray, believe, and do their duty. Let them send a servant, look for a bride, and obtain her. And the angel of the Lord will be present, and God Himself, who will manage and accomplish everything.

8. *But if the woman is not willing to follow you, then you will be free from this oath of mine; only you must not take my son back there.*

9. *So the servant put his hand under the thigh of Abraham his master,*
and swore to him concerning this matter.

Abraham's extraordinary anxiety is described. He does not want
the servant to take his son back to his native country, to Chaldea.
For this reason he orders the servant to return without further ado
if he does not find a woman who will follow him. And he himself
did his duty; he sent the servant to look for and obtain a girl, and
he added: "The angel of the Lord will provide a wife if there is one
at that place who has been assigned to him by God; but if no girl
follows, it is sure that they are unworthy and please neither God
nor the angels." Nevertheless, he hopes that God will incline the girl
to follow him. But if it should turn out otherwise, he releases the
servant from his oath.

All this springs from the amazing strength and the full assurance
of faith; for Abraham was sure that if he did not find a daughter-in-law
among his relatives, God would raise up a bride either from stones
or from a clod or a rib; for he is arranging the wedding for his son
even though it is uncertain whether the servant will fetch a bride.
But the earlier favors and miracles, such as the deliverance of his
son when he was already about to be killed as a sacrifice, increased
his confidence and hope.

Accordingly, Abraham thought: "If I find no one in Syria, in
Babylon, or in the entire world to marry my son, God will nevertheless provide a wife for my son."

Therefore let us learn from this example to believe the promises,
to look for God's favors, and to endure if any misfortune has to be
borne; for Abraham was endowed with a heart fully prepared for any
outcome. He occupied himself even with external and seemingly
absurd matters in true obedience and firm faith. Consequently, he
hoped for good things from God and calmly bore the inconveniences
that occurred. A disposition of this kind is truly Christian and altogether free. "If you find a bride," he says, "fetch her; but if not,
it is certain that there was none worthy of following you or was
intended by God for my son."

About that rite of swearing it has been stated above that by it
not only the descendants but also the Son of God, who would come
from the loins of Abraham, is being honored. One may swear by
Him, but by nobody else. Moreover, by the very fact that Abraham

commands him who swears to place his hands under his thigh Holy Scripture indicates that the Fruit from his loins is true God.

The question whether Christians may swear has been adequately dealt with and explained elsewhere. It has been shown that they are permitted to require and to swear an oath.[34]

10. *Then the servant took ten of his master's camels and departed, taking all sorts of choice gifts from his master; and he arose, and went to Mesopotamia, to the city of Nahor.*

11. *And he made the camels kneel down outside the city by the well of water at the time of evening, the time when women go out to draw water.*

This matter seems to be without purpose and of no importance, or, as the papists think, secular and carnal. Does the Holy Spirit have nothing else to relate, or to write about, than camels? My answer is: God is bearing witness that the godly and the believers are the objects of His concern even in the case of trial and very insignificant matters, and He indicates that whatever they do has His approval.

In the second place, Moses wanted to give a description of the pomp and the preparation connected with the wedding when he related that the servant took 10 camels along. The pomp was not wholly magnificent, since no horsemen were present; and perhaps the camels were used to carry the garments and the finery of the women. For Abraham wanted the bride to be fetched in a manner that would do her honor.

Therefore preparation in a matter like this should not be censured if it is moderate and without excessive expense, so that attention is given to respectability and propriety, and all things are done in the fear and reverence of God. The monks condemn all this, even the wedding itself, which nevertheless is celebrated not so much because of custom and enjoyment as on account of the purpose and benefit, namely, on account of the household, the government, and the church, which derive their existence from this source. The wedding is their prerequisite,[35] so to speak. For this reason Abraham adds camels and other gifts to be presented to the bride and her parents.

[34] See Luther's discussion of this question, *Luther's Works*, 21, pp. 99 ff.

[35] The Latin term is *antepraedicamenta*. In medieval Latin the *praedicamenta* were the ten categories of Aristotle's *Organon;* cf. Augustine, *Confessions*, IV, 16.29.

The additional statement — that the servant had all the wealth of Abraham in his hand — the Jews, as Lyra relates, understand of the account books in which the possessions and riches of Abraham were described and which were given to the servant that he might show them to the bride and her relatives for the purpose of winning their affection and goodwill.[36]

But it is more in accordance with the truth to conclude that this should be understood of the various gifts which the servant took from all the possessions of Abraham and had in his hand, that is, in his power. It is the custom among all nations to win mutual goodwill and friendship by exchanging gifts. Thus the servant took along gold, silver, spices, and the like, to present them to the parents, sisters, and brothers of the girl, just as today we are in the habit of giving gifts to the bridegroom or bride when we are invited to a wedding. This is not at all to be censured, the way the monks have declared it to be a sin; for Scripture asserts that the same thing was done by eminent and saintly men.

Finally Moses also adds particulars about the place, the time, the city, and the persons; so exact is he in this description. This happens in order that we may unhesitatingly maintain that God directs and concerns Himself about our individual affairs and actions as assiduously as possible. The angel, who is the suitor, was given to the servant by God, and he directs the journey and all the plans. The servant had no order to go chiefly to the city of Nahor; Abraham merely told him: "Go to my land, or my native country." But because the angel advises and impels him to do so, he arrives at the city of Nahor. There — because he is not sure where he should turn — he offers a prayer to God.

12. *And he said: O Lord, God of my master Abraham, grant me success today, I pray Thee, and show steadfast love to my master Abraham.*

13. *Behold, I am standing by the spring of water, and the daughters of the men of the city are coming out to draw water.*

14. *Let the maiden to whom I shall say: Pray let down your jar that I may drink, and who shall say: Drink, and I will water your camels — let her be the one whom Thou hast appointed for Thy servant Isaac. By this I shall know that Thou hast shown steadfast love to my master.*

---

[36] Lyra cites this interpretation in his comments on Gen. 24:10.

As a result of this prayer there arises the question whether one may prescribe to God a time, a place, a person, and a measure of the thing for which we are asking; for since God is very free, one should pray in such a manner that we do not bind God to any circumstance but simply say: "Thy will be done" (Matt. 6:10).

Thus in the story of Judith, when Uzziah had said: "Let us wait these five days for mercy from the Lord" (Judith 7:23), Judith censured this severely and said: "You have set a time for the mercy of the Lord, and you have appointed Him a day according to your pleasure. This is not a word that may draw down mercy, but rather that may stir up wrath and enkindle indignation." (Judith 8:13, 12.)

Therefore the question is asked whether this servant sinned by prescribing to God the manner in which He should act, or whether he was putting Him to the test. Hezekiah's petition is similar when he requires a sign that he will recover and that he will go up into the temple (2 Kings 20:8); likewise Gideon's when he asked for a sign on the fleece that he would be victorious (Judg. 6:36-37).

My answer is brief. According to the Law, one may not prescribe anything to God; but according to the Gospel, the godly, who are without the Law, may do so, while the ungodly may not. Therefore this request is granted to the servant because he has a command from God. Thus one could give a brief answer, but we do not want to take advantage of this evangelical freedom.

Let us rather explain this question in accordance with the Law. In the first place, one should note that the examples of the saints and of the children of God must not be understood as something to imitate and as a rule except when they follow the rule laid down in the Word.

In the second place, one can answer by saying that the servant did not specify anything when he spoke, but that he expressed a wish; and it is likely that he did not utter these words clearly and distinctly, but that they were a sigh and desire of his heart. Moreover, Scripture also commonly speaks of one's thoughts as words, as in Ps. 14:1: "The fool says in his heart." And in Matt. 9:21 the woman who was suffering from a hermorrhage kept saying within herself; that is, she kept thinking: "If I only touch His garment, I shall be made well."

The servant's thoughts were these: "Behold, I have arrived in Mesopotamia. I am uncertain about what I shall do now. My orders say nothing about where I should turn and whom of the relatives I should approach. Lord God, bring help." And he adds the wish:

"O that the virgin who is to be the bride of the son of my lord would come!" He prescribes nothing to God in the indicative or in the imperative mood, as is done in the account of Judith; but he merely expresses a wish, just as if I were silently wishing for the arrival of a prince or of some friend contrary to everybody's hope and expectation.

This serves to comfort us and to strengthen our faith when we pray, because in this passage Holy Scripture points out that God is so near to the godly that He not only hears prayers that specify something, if I may use this expression, but also those that express a wish, just as anyone, if he examines his entire life, has experienced this and will bear witness that oftentimes many things have happened contrary to his hope when he merely expressed a wish.

Therefore it is not necessary to explain this question by means of evangelical freedom; for the sense is no other than that the servant wishes silently: "O that the girl who has been chosen to marry Isaac would come to the spring now and would carry a jar to draw water!"

The Jews advance nothing but nonsense. But this is the simple intention of the servant who is wishing for the arrival of the girl; and when he sees her coming toward him after she has made herself known by those very signs, he is very much afraid, because what is happening so suddenly and unexpectedly corresponds to his wishes. Therefore it is an indication of some ardent desire, not a tempting, just as if a young man were to come to a place where girls were dancing and were to think: "Would that I might see her who will be my wife!" and [37] by chance were to see someone who later on would be joined to him in marriage.

There are countless examples of this kind even among the ungodly, who sometimes attain their wish contrary to their expectation. But this is the great comfort for the godly, that even when they express their wish, they are praying to and calling upon God. Besides, the disposition of this servant was such that even if Rebecca had not presented herself, he would have submitted to the will of God; otherwise it would have been correct to call it a tempting. But for the previously mentioned reason it is not a tempting or a request for a sign.

[37] Although the original text has *aut* here, we have followed the suggestion of the Weimar editors and read *et*.

But if these statements do not satisfy a contentious person, he should be answered in the same manner in which we answer in the case of the example of Hezekiah and of Gideon. For they pray humbly for forgiveness and beg to be forgiven for asking for a sign. Nor do they ask for this because they are prompted by some lack of trust. No, what has been promised is so great that they can hardly comprehend it; and since they are stunned, as it were, by their joy and surprise, they feel compelled to request a sign of something so great.

Gideon did not doubt that God had sent and called him to serve Him in war; but because of some joy and spiritual amazement he asked for a sign, in order that others, too, who would hear this promise might be strengthened by the sign. Thus the servant could have asked silently for a sign, not for his own sake but in order to strengthen his heart and the girl's love. This is not an inappropriate answer; but what we have said about the optative mood pleases me more, because it is in agreement with the common experience of the godly as well as of the ungodly.

Let us also look at the words of his prayer. "Make it occur," he says; that is, "Make it happen. I beg Thee to let it happen. *Lieber, lass mir's widerfaren, begegnen. Let her be the one whom Thou hast provided.*" The Hebrew verb נכח means "You have chided" or "You have reproved." The Jews deserve our disgust; for they obscure the proper force of words, weaken it, as it were, and make the words ambiguous. But let us learn to understand and translate them in their proper meaning. For instance, when Scripture states (Gen. 2:21): "He built a woman from the rib of the man," the Jews explain it by saying: "He formed." [38] And this is not an inappropriate interpretation, but the sense and proper meaning of the word is not completely reproduced.

Thus since it is likely that the servant did not bring out this meaning in these words but merely in his mind and thoughts, it seems that Moses wanted to express it in special and meaningful words worthy of the Mosaic spirit; and he was undoubtedly mindful of the various obstacles which the devil puts in the way of people in everything that must be undertaken and done. And for this reason it is necessary to pray God to ward off these obstacles and to grant a favorable outcome. Unless He Himself builds and protects the city,

[38] See Luther's earlier discussion of this, *Luther's Works*, 1, pp. 131, 132.

the home, and the church, every human endeavor will be of no avail (cf. Ps. 127:1).

These were the servant's thoughts; for he had an experienced teacher whom he often heard giving the warning that all our activities and plans have a most malevolent and bitter adversary, the devil. Therefore he prays that the plots and obstacles of the devil may be thwarted and that a happy issue and a favorable outcome may be granted. This he has in mind when he says: "Make it occur"; that is, "Grant that the parents and the daughter may accede to my request."

It is true that he had a definite command and was not in doubt concerning the presence of the angel — although he did not see him with his eyes — but as a pupil in the church of Abraham he knew that Satan does not rest but turns every stone in order to throw pious undertakings into confusion. He thought: "What if I am not admitted into the city, or at least into the house of Laban? What if the girl does not give her consent? Therefore give me Thy help, in order that everything may go well and be accomplished."

There is a similar expression in Is. 64:5: "Thou hast met him who rejoices"; that is, "Thou wast at hand for those who are Thine, and Thou didst deliver them." But at hand for whom? For him who works righteousness; that is, "No matter how the devil and the enemies stood in the way, Thou nevertheless didst deliver Thy people."

Accordingly, Moses has used an exceedingly meaningful word and has pointed out that the servant was a very excellent theologian who had an outstandingly clear understanding of the plots of the devil, namely, that on all occasions he is in the habit of being intent on interfering with and resisting all good works. Thus it is stated in Dan. 10:13: "The prince of the kingdom of Persia withstood me, and behold, Michael, one of the chief princes, came to help me," and in Zech. 3:1: "Satan was standing at his right hand to accuse him."

These great and diverse perils should dispel our smugness and incite us to pray God to meet us and to grant favorable progress to all our affairs. The obstacles and perils in marriage are countless, but prayer and the angel put an end to them and easily overcome them. Similarly, in all duties, whether you hold a position in the government or assume an office of teaching in the church, you should learn to pray and, in accord with the example of this servant, to entreat God: "Make it occur. Grant that all things will come about of themselves." The servant could never have wished or asked for this if he had not been well instructed in the knowledge and experience of spiritual things and of the plots of Satan. Therefore let the beginning of all our affairs be prayer to God and next the thought of the care of the angels.

Here also belongs the proper meaning of the other word: "Thou hast appointed her." The Jews interpret this as "Thou hast prepared, hast contended to the end." [39] Not bad really, but they do not bring out the force of the Hebrew word and the spiritual meaning. The same verb occurs in Ps. 6:1, Ps. 50:8, and above, in Gen. 20:16: "And Sarah was reproved." Therefore my own explanation is this: The servant was in the greatest distress, although the angel was very close at hand; for he did not feel or believe so firmly that the heavenly spirit was present as surely as he himself was there. Even though we know that we have guardian angels, nevertheless we are often in doubt, and therefore we fear and tremble; for the curse and unbelief are the reason for our doubting and are an obstacle in us to faith.

Consequently, I think that the word הוֹכַחְתָּ, that is, you have rebuked, should be referred to the devil, so that the sense is: "Lord God, refute the devil and prove him wrong for Rebecca, in order that she may become Isaac's wife and the mother of the church and of the Promised Seed."

But Moses points out that there is an amazing conflict and struggle in all the works of God and that God brings everything to pass through angels as in a conflict with Satan. The example from Dan. 10:13, mentioned earlier, makes this clear. We have angels associated with us, but they are perpetually engaged in disputing with and refuting the devil, who endeavors to hinder the work the angels desire to accomplish.

The devil saw that Rebecca was a godly, virtuous, and very properly brought up girl, and that she would be the wife of Isaac and a mother of the Blessed Seed; for on this account the servant was there with orders to bring her back with him. This the devil tried to prevent. Consequently, it was necessary for the good angel who was with the servant to dispute with the devil and to refute him; and the servant wished and prayed for this one thing alone, that through the good angels the Lord would eventually prevail in His conflict with the devil.

[39] These philological opinions are from Lyra *ad* Gen. 24:14.

This is the proper meaning of the verb and the real sense of this passage, namely, that there was a dispute over the girl, if I may use this expression; that is, she was acquired by disputing, because there is continual disputing between the good angels and the demons. The good angels propose and promote what is good; the evil angels oppose to it what is evil, and the godly weaken the wicked objections of the latter and reprove the counsels and efforts of the hostile spirits. In this way Moses wanted to express the prayer of the servant in a poetic manner, as it were, and in figurative words.

15. *Before he had done speaking, behold, Rebecca, who was born to Bethuel the son of Milcah, the wife of Nahor, Abraham's brother, came out with her water jar upon her shoulder.*

From this passage one can get the explanation of the previous question in the servant's prayer, which included nearly all circumstances and prescribed to God. This conflicts with the doctrine of Christians and with the Word of God, which teaches that the time, place, and manner of doing something must be left to God, and that only the thing itself should be asked for, with the confidence that He will give it in His own time and place.

But if help is delayed, one should not for this reason stop praying. Nevertheless, a time or something similar can be suggested, with a condition: "Lord God, if at this time or at this place it could [40] be done as I would want it, I pray Thee not to fail me now," just as we are now praying for Philip, who is away from us and lies seriously ill at Weimar, that God would restore to him his strength and health and preserve him longer for the church and the university.[41]

Furthermore, it is believable that the servant prayed in this manner not only at this hour, when he was standing at the spring, but during the entire journey; and when he had been commanded to journey to this region and Abraham had assured him that an angel would be his companion, it was necessary for him to specify the place and the time in accordance with the command and promise of his master. Nevertheless, because Abraham had released him from the obligation of the oath if he did not find a suitable wife for his

[40] The Weimar text reads *posse* here, but the reading *posset* in the Erlangen edition is necessary grammatically.

[41] On June 14, 1540, Melanchthon wrote to Luther from Weimar: "I am still in doubt about my journey. My weakness of body and of health is growing worse each day" (W, *Briefe,* IX, 137).

son, he no doubt committed the entire affair to God's care. If God did not want to give her from this land, city, or house, He would give a much more suitable wife from another place or in another manner.

In addition, this passage presents a clear example of God's mercy and kindness in hearing the prayers of the godly. By means of this example we are invited to pray, and our faith is marvelously strengthened against mistrust and doubt. For these events have been recorded, not for the sake of the servant but for your sake and mine. Before he had stopped speaking, behold, his prayer was heard; while he was speaking, God said yes to his prayer.

Therefore let us persuade ourselves without any hesitation that God is ever so ready and prompt to hear our prayer and to grant what we ask for, as Ps. 66:20 praises Him: "Blessed be God, because He has not rejected my prayer or removed His steadfast love from me!" And the name of God that is suitable to the highest degree and proper is Hearer of Prayer. Indeed, it is just as proper as the familiar name Creator of Heaven and Earth.

And God not only hears a prayer that is offered without specifying particulars; but let us maintain that even at the very moment a prayer is uttered that which is asked for is being done or has been done, just as very many ever so pleasing words of the psalms testify, such as "To Thee they cried, and were saved" (Ps. 22:5), where simply no particular at all is added.

Consequently, the one who cries out is here; God, who hears is there. Just cry out, and you will be heard, as Ps. 34:5 urges: "Look to Him, and be radiant; so your faces shall never be ashamed." And from this source Isaiah has taken the very beautiful promise (65:24): "Before they call, I will answer; while they are yet speaking, I will hear." Thus in one place Bernard has stated excellently and piously: "Brethren, do not despise your prayers; but know that as soon as you begin to pray, your prayer is read and written down at once in the presence of the Divine Majesty." [42]

Of this way of praying all the monks have no knowledge, for they merely mumble their prayers on account of obedience to the church or to their own rule. Accordingly, you should pray with such trust and full assurance that you maintain that your prayer has been

[42] Cf. Bernard of Clairvaux, *Sermones de diversis*, XXV, 8, *Patrologia, Series Latina*, CLXXXIII, 609.

heard before it leaves your mouth. But if what you are asking for is not granted so quickly, your prayer will not on this account be in vain. It will be granted in His time, and what you wish will be granted, or something far better and more desirable.

Therefore let there be no doubt whatever about being heard. Indeed, when I ask God to hallow His name against the pope and against the Turk, I know that my prayer has certainly been heard before I add the amen; for before I have begun to pray, God has seen the motion and the desire of my heart, and this He sees and hears far sooner than my lips utter the words.

But hindrances of many kinds are put in the way, for the devil resists and disturbs this confidence in whatever way he can. Our flesh and hearts do not burn with faith; nor are they stirred by constantly meditating on and dealing with the statements and examples of this kind that should be reflected on by the heart and often repeated for the purpose of stirring us up to prayer against the pope and all potentates who persecute sound doctrine. But if the desired effect or result does not follow this year, it will surely follow in another year.

But among all the examples of prayers the one described in Dan. 9:20-21 is outstanding and a jewel, so to speak. I earnestly commend it to all godly people. Daniel says: "While I was still speaking and praying, etc., behold, the man Gabriel, etc." All this is described, not in order that we should read it only once in passing, the way we are accustomed to become acquainted with secular examples, but that we may be instructed, and in such a manner that we maintain that it pertains to us. Nor should we have any doubt about being heard; but we should leave the place, the time, and all particulars to the will and counsel of God.

Whoever does this will experience through the actual result how wonderful the power and efficacy of prayer is. For "likewise the Spirit also helps us in our weakness . . . and intercedes for us with sighs too deep for words" (Rom. 8:26). And Eph. 3:20 states: "Who is able to do far more abundantly than all that we ask or think." We ask solely for these outward blessings: peace, quiet, good health, and the things necessary for this life. But God's power surpasses all our understanding, hope, and asking. Consequently, God bestows on those who call upon Him more and greater things than the human heart can comprehend or request; for we worship Him whose power and beneficence are boundless. Indeed, He also determines all the particulars, the place, the time, and the person far better and more successfully than we would prescribe with our thinking. Therefore let us habituate and stir up our hearts to prayer, in order that many may pray together; for the greater the number of those who will pray, the more quickly and more abundantly they will get what they ask for. But one must pray in the name of Christ, not of Mary, Peter, or other saints, as the papists are in the habit of doing. But of this we have often spoken elsewhere.

Up to this point Moses has described the faith and prayer of the servant; for faith must precede in all our works and activities, even in the smallest. Whether we eat, sleep, or engage in domestic or civic services, everything should proceed from faith, prayer, and thanksgiving, since the works of the godly should be good and pleasing to God. This cannot be the case unless fervent faith and prayer to do and direct everything are present. Paul suggests the same thing in Col. 3:17: "Whatever you do, in word or deed, do everything in the name of the Lord Jesus, giving thanks to God the Father through Him."

This eulogy of faith, which makes everything pleasing and acceptable to God, is followed by a description of hospitality, which is often praised elsewhere in Holy Scripture. Moses relates an example of this in this whole wordy chapter. To irreligious minds or hypocrites his words will seem to be unprofitable, boorish, and vulgar; and if, as they think, he is speaking in this way, what he is saying is without God, faith, and prayer. But with God everything is excellent and magnificent.

16. *The maiden was very fair to look upon, a virgin, whom no man had known. She went down to the spring and filled her jar, and came up.*

17. *Then the servant ran to meet her, and said: Pray give me a little water to drink from your jar.*

18. *She said: Drink, my lord; and she quickly let down her jar upon her hand and gave him a drink.*

Holy Scripture also praises Rebecca's beauty, for beauty is something good created by God and should by no means be despised. A little drop of external pleasure is granted to the flesh, since our nature has been either so corrupted or so created that we have a greater fondness for women who are beautiful, especially for those who are respectable, well-mannered, and endowed with fine talents, those who show some promise that they will make good housewives. Such women are very excellent gifts of God.

Moreover, this, too, is intended for our instruction, when Moses relates in such detail that Rebecca was endowed with beauty, a very fine disposition, and outstanding virtues, and, in addition, was born of pious and respectable parents; but there is no mention of wealth, because it is nothing compared with those gifts.

Nowadays, of course, people strive for and seek to get almost nothing but riches. But Holy Scripture describes Isaac's bride in this manner, that she was a beautiful virgin, chaste and modest, endowed with good manners, intelligent, sensible, and obedient to her parents. A woman like this certainly does not need great treasures, but through her God grants an exceedingly great treasure. On the other hand, a woman who has crude manners, is stupid, lacking in good sense, not alert, and, in addition, is suspect as to her chastity will bring with her all faults, misfortunes, and afflictions, no matter how rich she is. In short, let him who desires to have a good wife call upon God. He will hear him when he prays and will grant one who, if not endowed with all virtues as Rebecca was, is nevertheless suitable and respectable.

Rebecca's manners and upbringing are also depicted when Moses relates that she went out to the spring and carried a jar to draw water. From this it is evident that she was not a lazy virgin accustomed to leisure and luxury. No, her mother taught her and accustomed her to the usual works in the household, no matter how mean or irksome they were. She used her as a servant or handmaid. For this reason she sent her to fetch water. Rebecca herself serves her mother in sincerity and obedience. She concerns herself with nothing else than the performance of her duty in those things which the mother of the house commands. And she was destined to be the mother of prophets, of patriarchs, and of Christ!

The only thing our girls know is how to dress gorgeously in purple and fine linen. But of the other adornment, that of good manners, they have no knowledge. This girl, however, you see adorned in such a manner that she is suitable and useful for the saintly man and worthy of becoming a mother so glorious that her

womb will produce that divine fruit. I am not at all disparaging
the praises of others; but even if they are, or at some time were,
rich and beautiful, they must not be compared to Rebecca.

Moreover, hospitality is added to the other virtues. For when
Rebecca comes up again from the well — which evidently was in
a deep place, so that one had to go down on steps — the servant says
to her: "Give me a little water." And now observe what good order
there was among those nations. The servant watches Rebecca returning from the spring and runs to meet her. But he asks modestly
and bashfully: "Pray give me a little water to sip from your jar."
Thus in Acts 20:11 [43] Luke says about Paul that he broke the bread
and tasted it, but he does not say that he ate it. Great humility and
bashfulness are evident in the servant, just as the virgin shows remarkable kindheartedness and hospitality; for she hastens to offer him
a drink at once and tells him not only to sip but to drink enough;
and she hands him the drink.

Great praise is due this nation because of its extraordinary modesty
and kindheartedness, which had their origin in the religion of the
fathers and in their knowledge of God. Rebecca addresses the servant
most respectfully and calls him lord. Peter makes very much of this
word when he says (1 Peter 3:6) that Sarah honored Abraham, not
as her equal or husband but as her lord. Thus Rebecca treats the
stranger and foreigner with respect and calls him lord.

This discipline originated with the fathers, who accustomed their
young people to hospitality, so that they washed the feet of strangers
and gave them food and drink as though they had been intimately
known to them. Thus Paul says about widows in 1 Tim. 5:10: "As
one who has brought up children, shown hospitality, washed the feet
of the saints, relieved the afflicted."

Among us examples of these virtues are rare, for here we are not
living with human beings but with swine. They have no sense at all;
nor do they learn anything either about faith or about good manners.
Therefore we need patience on account of the glory of God, who
has put us in this place. But Rebecca has learned kindheartedness,
politeness, and pleasantness in manners from her parents. Therefore
she offers a drink to the servant with respect. "Drink, my lord,"
she says. Among other rather polite nations you will still find similar

[43] The original has "Acts 2" here.

urbanity. The Italians say: *Mi ser si* ("Yes, my lord").[44] Germans whose upbringing is a little better and who are more civil say: "*Lieber freund, lieber knab.*" In this barbarian land you will hear nothing like this. Therefore let us shun those faults and such rudeness of manners, and as a result of these examples let us learn to improve our manners.

19. *When she had finished giving him a drink, she said: I will draw for your camels also, until they have done drinking.*

20. *So she quickly emptied her jar into the trough and ran again to the well to draw, and she drew for all his camels.*

It is not hospitable enough to have given him a drink; she also gives a drink to the camels and the rest of the servants. She is so obliging and godly that she does not consider it beneath her dignity to be the maidservant of the stranger and his camels. For this reason she is later on raised to such a high position of honor that she becomes a matriarch. These were evidently the customs of the most ancient fathers, who accustomed their children to the ordinary duties of kindheartedness and respect toward any people whatever, in order that they might be ready to serve others and to converse with them in a pleasant and friendly manner.

These virtues the Holy Spirit commends in this passage. He even describes every particular and motion, in order to indicate that all the works of the godly which proceed from a pure and believing heart are most pleasing to Him. And Moses adds once more that Rebecca was quick, because nimbleness and speed have always been praised. And Paul requires it in Rom. 12:11: "Never flag in zeal." Because a favor granted tardily is no favor, he who gives quickly gives twice.[45] Hence we should be prompt and ready to perform our mutual duties of hospitality and friendship, since we see that they are inculcated in this chapter so copiously and carefully. Above (Gen. 19) we heard the same thing about Lot, how he entertained the angels; but it should not annoy us to read and hear the same things more frequently, since the Holy Spirit does not disdain to describe and relate these facts with so many words.

44 This may be a reminiscence of Luther's journey to Rome; cf. also *Luther's Works*, 27, p. 384, note 5.

45 A proverb attributed to Publilius Syrus; cf. also p. 61, note 54.

Throughout the entire narrative are scattered most beautiful incidents pertaining to manners that must also be traced back to God, because they are gifts of God put into practice not only in the spirit but also on the outside and toward people; for God is also the God of the bodies. Therefore He provides us with bodily gifts, and He wants us to enjoy these gifts with gladness.

These gifts seem secular and profane. A Stoic or a Pharisee would ask whether they are lawful. People of this kind are exceedingly disgusting. They allow the body no delight and joy at all. It is their religion which Paul describes in Col. 2:23, namely, not to spare the body but to torture and kill it until it is reduced to nothing. Thus it is said of Bernard that in order to overcome his lust he tormented his body to such an extent that eventually the brothers could not associate with him because of his stinking breath.[46] God created body and soul, and He wants recreation allowed to both, but in a definite amount and manner.

21. *The man gazed at her in silence to learn whether the Lord had prospered his journey or not.*

The servant was amazed at such quickness and dispatch on the part of the girl, who is so prompt and eager to serve him and his camels in such a kindly manner. And instantly it entered his mind that his prayer had been heard. Hence such surprise and amazement. For he thought: "This is not the bride, is it, who is so suddenly appearing to me when I am not yet expecting her? Surely it is."

All this belongs to the previous comfort concerning the hearing of prayers, namely, that God grants more than we understand and ask for. Thus I never thought or hoped that the Gospel would be spread abroad so widely in so short a time as has happened thus far through the boundless kindness of God. I did not dream anything of that kind when I began to teach. Therefore it is amazing and deserving of our wonder, and it should give us proof of the boundless goodness of God. Thus the servant no longer has any doubt about the girl but is sure that she will be the bride. And now he is thinking about approaching her parents, and he explains to the girl his intention and the purpose of his journey.

---

[46] Cf. the *Vita Prima* of Bernard, *S. Bernardi vita et res gestae*, 22, *Patrologia, Series Latina*, CLXXXV-1, 239, 240.

22. *When the camels had done drinking, the man took a gold ring*
weighing a half shekel, and two bracelets for her arms weighing
ten gold shekels.

What is related in this passage seems completely carnal and
worldly to reason, and I myself wonder why Moses has so much to
say about such unimportant matters when above he has been very
concise in the case of matters that are far more sublime. There is
no doubt, however, that the Holy Spirit wanted these things to be
written and to stand out for our instruction; for in Holy Scripture
nothing unimportant is put before us, and nothing unprofitable. But
"whatever was written . . . was written for our instruction" (Rom.
15:4). God wants to be acknowledged in all things, the greatest and
the smallest.

Above (Gen. 19:24) Moses uses only a few words to tell about
the burning of Sodom and about the trial Abraham underwent when
he was ordered to sacrifice his son (Gen. 22:2 ff.), for these are lofty
matters. Unless a man is spiritual, he does not easily understand them.
But things that are external, on the body, we grasp somewhat more
easily. For this reason God speaks with us about these at some
length. Therefore let it not annoy us to read or ponder the things
that are described rather wordily in this chapter. Although the
article of faith and justification is not taught, nevertheless matters
pertaining to good manners are dealt with, just as examples of kindheartedness and beneficence toward strangers will follow. This chapter
has invited us to Rebecca's marriage. Therefore let us hear the
nuptial song as an example for young people, in order that they
may learn to have honorable sentiments about marriage and both
sexes, matters that are disparaged among the heathen, as can be
observed in the Greek and Latin poets; for young people consider
solely the flesh and thus insult God the Creator. We should put the
text of Holy Scripture before their eyes.

The word נֶזֶם occurs often in the Holy Scriptures, and I believe
that through careful observation I have discovered its real meaning.
The Latin text has *inauris,* "earring," which is a jewel that is hung on
the ears, as the historical accounts relate about the Ethiopians and
about Cleopatra, among whom this ornament was in common use.
But this is not the real force of the word; as Jerome, too, believes,
it really means a small crescent or frontlet, a kind of semicircle from

one ear to the other.[47] Our virgins use pearls and gold braids in place of this ornament. But the one mentioned here was solid gold.

Thus in Prov. 11:22 it is stated: "Like a gold ring in a swine's snout is a beautiful woman without discretion." This is the same as if one said in our proverb that beauty in a doltish woman is like a crown on the head of a sow. Thus Aaron made a calf from earrings (Ex. 32:2 ff.),[48] which were ornaments not only of the women but of men, virgins, and matrons, the way women wear their gold braid under their veils.

From this came the plate on the forehead of the high priest. It was a kind of semicircle. He had a miter of fine linen and on his forehead a semicircle of gold. From this came the diadem of kings, who wore miters. The orientals wore white ones, as the Turks do today; but the Romans wore purple ones, a beautiful red cap surrounded by a golden ornament. Later crowns of solid gold were worn, just as the pope wears a triple crown. The emperor of Turkey, as I hear, has a sextuple crown; but this is because of the degeneration from the simplicity of antiquity.

The servant gives Rebecca a golden ornament of this kind, a small headband or golden crescent, that is, a golden fillet or braid around the hair, and two צְמִידִים, "arm rings." Our German word *geschmeid,* or *armgeschmeid,* corresponds to the Hebrew. Matrons in particular adorned one arm with gold or gems. The servant adorns both. But, as I stated before, this seems altogether worldly and like luxury. A Franciscan would undoubtedly condemn this; for it is a religious obligation of the Franciscans not to touch gold and silver with their hands, although in their hearts they foster ravenous hunger that is insatiable. Because of this hunger[49] they long for and consume the wealth of the entire world. Hence these things are pointed out in opposition to the hypocrites, in order that we may hold to a middle course. For God does not want those things to be condemned. No, He wants weddings to be regarded with honor, in order to attract young people to an honorable marriage in contrast with pollutions of every kind and with promiscuity.

[47] Jerome, *Liber hebraicarum quaestionum in Genesin, Patrologia, Series Latina,* XXIII, 1023.

[48] The original has "Ex. 23."

[49] We have followed the Erlangen edition's reading, *qua,* in preference to *quae,* which appears in the Weimar text; for "insatiable hunger" Luther uses the Greek word βουλιμία.

Therefore He praises this moderate and honorable display and wanted it recorded. In the eyes of the monks it appears to be luxury. But it was His purpose to bear witness that the finery, the banquets, and the merriment connected with the wedding meet with His approval because of the final cause of marriage, which is the begetting and upbringing of children and the governing of the household, the state, and the church.

This should be stressed in opposition to the gloomy hypocrites, who consider it piety and saintliness to abstain from gold, silver, food, clothing, or the like. Such abstinence does not please God. Indeed, He has appointed us lords and rulers of all things, over sheep and oxen and the entire earth (Ps. 8:7-8; Gen. 1:29-30). He assigns to us not only the possession of and the dominion over things but also their use.[50] He wants us to preserve our bodies, not to kill them. Therefore He has given us food, drink, clothing, the sun, and the moon; and in this way He permits display and finery at a wedding.

Let those who have been delivered from the condition human beings have in common be so; and let them delight in their gift of chastity. But this does not mean that the others sin when they marry and make merry in the manner customary at marriages. Indeed, God praises this and has much to say about married couples. Here the Holy Spirit adorns the bride in a wonderful way, as though nothing else were left for Him to concern Himself about or to teach.

But it is not our intention to provide a defense for the wicked Epicureans and antinomians in this way. If they hear this, they look for nothing but excessive luxury and gluttony, in which they exceed all bounds and transgress the laws of godliness and respectability. Thus in our customs too one sees horrible licentiousness in dress, finery, and banquets. Everyone supposes that he is allowed to do what he pleases without giving any consideration either to his station or to respectability. The burghers want to outdo the nobles with their expenditures and splendor; the nobles want to equal the princes and kings. This is departing too far to the right.

We condemn the Stoics and the monks, who believe that these worldly things, as they call them, are condemned by God. They praise their own works as heavenly and spiritual and refrain from

---

[50] A reference to the distinction in feudal law between the *dominium* over a fief, which was retained by the suzerain, and the *usus*, which was the right of the vassal.

these permissible joys with the most impious aim, as though they had a unique way of worshiping God which earns for them and others the remission of sins. Therefore let him who is able adorn himself, and let him even wear a golden garment in order to contradict their superstition and to tread it underfoot. For God has given us physical gifts that we may make use of them. But we should do so with thanksgiving.

On the other hand, we also condemn the excess and luxury of those who want to adorn themselves, to dress, and to revel in an extravagant manner without any fear of God. These people — Rebecca and her parents, likewise Abraham and Isaac — lived in great humility and godliness, and they used this display (1) to honor marriage and (2) on account of the future generation, the church, and the state. And they did so in the fear of God, in faith, and with thanksgiving.

Hypocrites do not do this. They imagine that they are showing deference to God if they abstain. Nor do gluttons, who imagine that it is godly and permitted to stuff themselves and to misuse the creatures of God, observe moderation. Thus neither hypocrites nor gluttons have a correct understanding of Scripture. There is a time for feasting, fasting, mourning, and rejoicing. It is proper to mourn with those who are mourning, and God says (Is. 66:2) that He will dwell with the humble and contrite heart that trembles at His words. On the other hand, He does not hinder an upright and believing heart when it rejoices in the Lord. As a matter of fact, He praises it. One should live a spiritual life, but in such a manner that the physical life, too, has its recreation, especially among those who are in great troubles or trials and are plagued by sleeplessness. They should drink more plentifully, in order to induce sleep; for Holy Scripture says (Ps. 104:15) that wine was created to gladden man's sad and afflicted heart. Let him eat and drink, in order that body and soul may come together again.

Hence we ought to steer a middle course,[51] lest we become either Epicureans and dissolute or hypocrites and gloomy monks. Weddings should not be stripped of respectable displays and of respectable pleasures; but excesses by day and by night, extravagance in clothing, or unseemly pranks should in no wise be tolerated, because they are condemned in Holy Scripture.

[51] Luther's Latin is *regia via*, which he sometimes uses to refer to the idea of the golden mean.

Besides, God dislikes gloominess and is fond of a cheerful and upright heart; for there is enough other affliction and sorrow which the devil inflicts. The body must receive its honor and care, yet in such a way that it does not become wanton and addicted to every kind of depravity. Therefore a godly husband who carries heavy burdens in the government, in the church, or in the household should seek refreshment for his spirit. But if he is idle and devotes himself solely to swilling and gormandizing, he is committing a grave sin.

25. *She added: We have both straw and provender enough, and room to lodge in.*

The Holy Spirit is delighted by this example of hospitality. Therefore He uses many words to bestow rich praise on it. But the girl promises something which is not in her power; she invites the servant into her father's house, although she is only her mother's maid. From this it is clear what was customary in the families of the saints and what the training was. Thus it was stated above about Abraham (Gen. 18:1) and Lot (Gen. 19:1) that they were always ready and sat at their doors and looked for guests. For this reason Rebecca has no doubt that her parents will receive the servant with the greatest goodwill. These words are high praise of kindness, affection, and hospitality, virtues in which the saints trained their children so that they would be generous and hospitable, especially toward patriarchs, prophets, and those who were disseminating the Word and the heavenly doctrine. Let us, too, strive to follow and imitate this.

26. *The man bowed his head and worshiped the Lord,*

27. *and said: Blessed be the Lord, the God of my master Abraham, who has not forsaken His steadfast love and His faithfulness toward my master. As for me, the Lord has led me in the way to the house of my master's kinsmen.*

28. *Then the maiden ran and told her mother's household about these things.*

Now that the servant has obtained his request and is glad because the bride has presented herself, he is mindful of God's beneficence and kindness and his own gratitude. Here, therefore, the proper measure of joy and display is prescribed, namely, that they should be of such a nature as not to offend the conscience or burden it with sins but to preserve the fear of God, faith, prayer, and thanksgiving.

The servant bows and gives thanks for the successful completion of the journey. Even though this is a small and worldly matter, he nevertheless praises God. Thus nothing is so paltry and inconsequential that it cannot be turned into a sacrifice and into worship of God; and in everything that is said and done God should be kept constantly in mind, in order that people may discern the gifts that have been bestowed by God and may be grateful. It is a trifling matter to look at a girl and to give her earrings. Nevertheless, they are all gifts of God, even though they are not great but are small; for the same God dispenses both kinds. Therefore one owes God worship, thanksgiving, and gratitude in very small matters just as in matters that are great. May the reverence and remembrance of God as the Author and Preserver of all things never disappear from the hearts of the godly!

"Thus a man will be perfect and equipped for every good work" (2 Tim. 3:17), because he has been so trained that he maintains that God graciously bestows all good things, the smallest and the greatest, and says with this servant: "Blessed be the Lord, the God of heaven and earth." The life of such people is truly holy and is pleasing [52] to God in all their activities, whether they eat, drink, sleep, or are awake.

In this passage Moses, as he frequently does elsewhere, hints at the Trinity in the Godhead when he says: "Lord Gods." [53] Thus also in Deut. 6:4: "Hear, O Israel: The Lord our God is one Gods." In all things God is one God, and He is to be worshiped by us in this way if we follow the Word; but when another manner of calling upon or worshiping God is adopted without the Word, then He is not one Gods. Evidences of this kind should be noted, because they bear witness that the saintly fathers understood the mystery of the Trinity, which is preached to us in clear and plain language.

The servant repeats and counts up in his mind the kindnesses which God has shown to his master in accordance with the promise made to him by Abraham, namely, that the Lord would send His angel; and he feels that this promise has now been fulfilled. It is

[52] We have followed the Erlangen edition's reading, *grata,* in preference to *gratis,* which appears in the Weimar edition.

[53] Cf. also *Luther's Works,* 1, pp. 57—59.

as though he were saying: "God has shown my master many kindnesses, and He is keeping the promise made to him; He is truthful. Thus He has brought me here through the hand of the angel. I was on my journey; but I did not know the way, and I was unable to be my own guide. But the Lord God led me, just as a shepherd goes ahead of his flock and leads it (John 10:4). His angel went before me in accordance with His promise and truthfulness and has brought me to the house of my master's brothers."

The girl heard this giving of thanks and at the same time the name of Abraham, her blood relative. But up to this point nothing has been said by the servant about a marriage; only small gifts have been presented. Now she hastens home and reports to her mother in accordance with these words; that is, that Abraham, her great-uncle, had sent this servant. And once more, just as above, it is stated in the text that she ran. It is Moses' purpose to indicate the earnestness and the diligence of the girl.

Moreover, the girl runs to her mother's house. It is not that there were two or entirely different houses. No, there were separate quarters for the men and for the women. The mother of the household lived separately with her daughters and the maidservants, and there they busied themselves with the tasks of women. The men had their own place, which was suited for work done by men. Thus in our time it is customary for some spouses to have separate bedrooms. Consequently, the girl runs to the house of her mother, whose quarters she was sharing. But Milcah and Laban occupied the same house.

The Jews debate whether Bethuel was dead.[54] They disregard Scripture and talk nonsense of various kinds. But the text that follows makes it clear that Laban and Bethuel were brothers. The former was the first-born; the latter was born second.

29. *Rebecca had a brother whose name was Laban; and Laban ran out to the man, to the spring.*

30. *When he saw the ring, and the bracelets on his sister's arms, and when he heard the words of Rebecca his sister: Thus the man spoke to me, he went to the man; and behold, he was standing by the camels at the spring.*

31. *He said: Come in, O blessed of the Lord; why do you stand outside? For I have prepared the house and a place for the camels.*

---

[54] Lyra *ad locum* alludes to these arguments.

32. *So the man came into the house; and Laban ungirded the camels, and gave him straw and provender for the camels, and water to wash his feet and the feet of the men who were with him.*

33. *Then food was set before him to eat.*

Another example and commendation of hospitality, and one that is no shorter. Laban knows nothing about the man except what he hears from his sister; and as soon as he realizes that a stranger is standing outside, he hastens toward him to invite him into his house. From those most eminent patriarchs Shem, Nahor, and Terah they learned that guests should be received with a ready and willing heart, especially godly brethren. Thus it is stated above (Gen. 19:2-3) that Lot compels the angels to turn aside and enter his house. Abraham runs to meet the three men. And Peter [55] (1 Peter 4:9) enjoins us to be hospitable and to do this without grumbling and with a ready and cheerful heart.

Nevertheless, in this wretched and corrupt age of ours no one should be admitted rashly. He must bring along testimonials of pious men. At this time Germany is flooded by very many rascals and incendiaries who have savagely destroyed many towns and villages because among governments the laws concerning judicial investigations and the maintenance of discipline are altogether disregarded.[56] Therefore it often happens that those who have received great kindnesses from us heap insults and abuses on us later on.

But if in spite of this some come provided with testimonials worthy of consideration, we should invite them, take care of them in a kind and generous manner, and compel them to come into our house; for we have been instructed by the example of the patriarchs and the teaching of Christ that we are receiving with hospitality not human beings but angels, yes, even Christ the Son, and the eternal Father, in accordance with the statement (Matt. 10:40): "He who receives you receives Me." And thus your house will become a temple, yes, even a paradise and the kingdom of heaven; for where God dwells, there His temple is.

[55] The original has "Paul" here, but we have changed it to "Peter" because of the reference to 1 Peter 4:9.

[56] On June 12, 1541, Luther wrote to Melanchthon that the prince of Saxony had arrested 25 arsonists (W, *Briefe*, IX, 446); on July 8, 1541, he wrote to Wenceslaus Link that 170 had been captured in Prussia and more than 60 in Pomerania (W, *Briefe*, IX, 466).

Prompted by these promises and examples, the fathers received saintly and pious guests with the certainty that they were receiving God Himself; and in this manner they made of their houses a heaven and a dwelling place of God. This they also taught their children and accustomed them to hospitality. But at that time there was better discipline, and governments were stricter than they are in our age. Now there is danger from people we do not know that they will poison our food or pastures, for we have arrived at the last times — times that are most productive of crimes.

But if harm were to result for anyone who kindheartedly shows hospitality to a wicked guest, he should nevertheless hold fast to this comfort, that he did it to the honor of God and with the intention of doing good. But let the heads of households be cautious, lest through lack of discretion they invite dangers for themselves.

Laban addresses his guest most courteously and respectfully and calls him "blessed of the Lord." Consequently, he receives him as a saint or as some prophet, and this is a fine example of that statement in Matt. 10:40: "He who receives you receives Me."

And Laban adds: "I have prepared the house and a place for the camels." In the Hebrew the verb is very graphic: "I have cleared all corners *(Ich hab ausgeraumpt auss allen winckeln).* There is no corner that is not open to you." The Holy Spirit seems to delight in recounting this. Therefore He used such clear words, for He wanted to indicate a heart that was prompt and joyful in showing hospitality.

Yes, Laban performs even the menial services; he unharnesses the camels and washes the servant's feet. This was customary among that people and is a praiseworthy practice which St. Paul commends in 1 Tim. 5:10. Our bishops and papists imitate it on Maundy Thursday,[57] but they merely amuse themselves with their pretense of humility. Afterwards they wash their hands in the blood of the saints and of those who profess sound doctrine.

But he said: I will not eat until I have told my errand. He said: Speak on.

This entire chapter presents an example of a faithful servant and a godly and saintly deputy. The servant abounded in faith, in saintliness, and in virtues of every kind. In him are missing none of those

[57] On this practice see also *Luther's Works,* 13, p. 54, note 19.

qualities that are required in a faithful servant. He has found magnificent lodging, a generous and friendly host, and very splendid furnishings; but all these things do not keep him from carrying out his orders first of all.

Consequently, this Eliezer is an example for all who are in the office and state of a servant. Our age has no example to equal this one. But everybody is complaining about the malevolence and the unheard-of insolence of domestics who do not serve their masters but give them orders. The Holy Spirit does not approve of such servants; they are an abomination in the sight of God and slaves of the devil, whom they serve and obey. We have Paul's admonition in Col. 3:22: "Slaves, obey in everything those who are your earthly masters, not with eyeservice, as men-pleasers, but in singleness of heart, fearing the Lord." But among thousands one would hardly find one who would pay attention to this. Nevertheless, these facts must be taught and impressed, and the insolence of domestics must be condemned.

This godly and saintly servant, who first of all wants to carry out his master's command, however trivial, with regard to seeking a wife, is praised because he esteems his master's command highly and knows that he is serving God in any duty. Therefore he was full of faith and of the Holy Spirit. Thus Joseph, too, faithfully served his master in Egypt and for this faithfulness received the outstanding reward of being elevated to royal rank; and I have no doubt that later on the lot and rank of this servant was improved.

For the servant observed Paul's admonition — "not with eyeservice" — in an excellent manner when the master was watching. But he is just as faithful and diligent when his master is absent as he is when he is present. Indeed, so far as he himself was concerned, the proverbs that say: "The master's eye fattens the horse," "The best manure is that which falls on the field from the master's sole," and "The forehead is in front of the back part of the head" lost their force. All these proverbial statements find fault with and make accusations against the deceit and the laziness of servants. Thus in comedies one finds again and again exceedingly familiar complaints about the wickedness of servants; for on the basis of experience we are forced [58] to admit what is stated in the Greek proverb: "In every house the master is the only servant." Eliezer's faithfulness

[58] With the Erlangen edition we have read *cogimur* rather than *coguntur*.

and diligence invalidate all these statements; for he is Abraham's eye, and from his sole falls the manure.

These examples of godliness are praised by the words and writings of the Holy Spirit. They are trivial, of course, and pertain to the household; for the servant does nothing else than proceed with camels and carry gold. All these are human, worldly, and carnal works; but they are very good and very saintly because they spring from his utmost godliness and faith toward God, and surely from obedience and faithfulness to his master.

These facts had to be pointed out to servants and domestics. Indeed, it was necessary to set them against the works of the monks that are so well known. For Holy Scripture praises these menial works in the household and in civil life and extols them most abundantly, because they are good for the establishment and preservation of the household and the state, yes, even of godliness and religion.

34. *So he said: I am Abraham's servant.*

This pride of the servant is beautiful and godly, for he boasts of his master and puts on airs because he is the servant of a man as great as Abraham. It is as though he were saying: "I am the ambassador of a king, a prince, or some monarch." To us it appears insignificant and trivial that he boasts of being the servant of Abraham, but he himself regards this as very important. In this way he seeks to gain their goodwill. Indeed, he wrests this from the Syrians. "Has the name Abraham ever come to your ears?" he asks. "I am his ambassador."

But with this pride the servant combines the utmost courtesy and modesty, for he says nothing else about himself than that he is a servant. Yet he is a prince in Abraham's house. The management of the household had been entrusted to him.

Therefore this is honoring his master as Paul admonishes (Col. 3:23): "Whatever your task, work heartily, as serving the Lord and not men." This man read and fulfilled the letters of Paul before Paul was born, and he concludes very correctly that he is serving Abraham, not as a human being but as a prophet and patriarch of God.

Consequently, the servant does not say in vain: "I am Abraham's servant; of this I am boasting even though I am not worthy of this honor. But I am serving him gladly and heartily, because I know that he is a son and man of God. Who would not gladly serve such a man?" For he is convinced that his master is held in such high esteem by God that on his account He sends an angel as a companion for the servant.

Therefore this is an outstanding example of proper conduct. It confirms the injunction of St. Paul and teaches that servants should serve gladly because they are sure that, when they serve their masters faithfully either in their absence or in their presence, they are serving the Divine Majesty. And if we were not so blind and insane, we would thank God for the certain knowledge that we are serving God, not men, and that He so richly overwhelms us with good works and with His services. For whatever household tasks a servant performs in the house, even if he sweeps the house, he should be sure that he is performing this service for God.

But such is our foolishness that we think: "If I were able to serve the Lord God in heaven, then I would be willing to boast. These tasks are trivial and ordinary." It is then that our flesh betrays itself; it does not believe it to be true that a servant who obeys his master is serving God — likewise a son, a daughter, a maid, or a pupil who obeys his teacher. For if we believe this, then all our works would be done with pride, joy, and gratitude. But because we do not have the Holy Spirit and do not believe that master, mistress, pastor, teacher, and the like are a divine ordinance, our obedience flags completely. Otherwise we would submit with joy.

If God were to order you with a new and unusual command to go for the purpose of bringing greetings to some friend or prince, you would do so with the utmost eagerness and without any delay. Why do you not do the same thing when your master or your parents give you an order? For God is giving you the same command and order through your master or parents, as Paul attests (Col. 3:24): "You are serving the Lord Christ."

But who acknowledges or believes this? How much complaining there is in our day on the part of magistrates, masters, parents, and teachers! Men seem to be altogether frantic and to be driven by madness, yes, even filled with horrible murder. For children kill their parents — not with the sword; but through sadness of heart and sorrow they sap the strength of their parents, who are consumed by love and affection for their children, although they should be gladdened and refreshed by their children's obedience. Domestics cause their masters to waste away solely because of the grief that is felt as the result of the insolence of the domestics. And thus all the lower classes grieve the Holy Spirit. This is worst, as is stated in the Epistle to the Hebrews (13:17): "Let them do this joyfully, and not sadly, for that would be of no advantage to you."

Therefore examples of this kind should be carefully noted, in order that we may learn how important a matter it is faithfully to serve the masters who are set over us; for however contemptible and trivial our service or obedience may appear, they are nevertheless set over us by divine ordinance, whether in the household or in the government. But if you show the obedience you owe, you have a gracious God, a quiet heart, and a master who blesses you. If not, God is offended, and on account of your obstinate disobedience you cannot have a quiet conscience; you have lost the Lord God from your heart, a good conscience, and every blessing.

35. *The Lord has greatly blessed my master, and he has become great; He has given him flocks and herds, silver and gold, menservants and maidservants, camels and asses.*

36. *And Sarah, my master's wife, bore a son to my master when he was old; and to him he has given all that he has.*

37. *My master made me swear, saying: You shall not take a wife for my son from the daughters of the Canaanites, in whose land I dwell;*

38. *but you shall go to my father's house and to my kindred, and take a wife for my son.*

39. *I said to my master: Perhaps the woman will not follow me.*

40. *But he said to me: The Lord, before whom I walk, will send His angel with you and prosper your way; and you shall take a wife for my son from my kindred and from my father's house;*

41. *then you will be free from my oath, when you come to my kindred; and if they will not give her to you, you will be free from my oath.*

42. *I came today to the spring and said: O Lord, the God of my master Abraham, if now Thou wilt prosper the way which I go,*

43. *behold, I am standing by the spring of water; let the young woman who comes out to draw, to whom I shall say: Pray give me a little water from your jar to drink,*

44. *and who will say to me: Drink, and I will draw for your camels also — let her be the woman whom the Lord has appointed for my master's son.*

This is a lengthy repetition of what was said above and it is proof of the faith and diligence of the servant. Now, however, the servant is praising his master. "I am not the only one who is serving this master of mine; the angels, too, are serving him. Besides, he is an important man who has been greatly and richly blessed by God. Indeed, he is famous not only on account of his wisdom, devotion, and godliness in the church and in the state, even among kings" — as has been related above in the account about him — "but also in his household, on account of the physical blessing: the gold, the silver, the servants, etc."

The servant puts primary emphasis on the fact that Abraham owes all the great wealth he has in such abundance to the blessing of God, for he regards all this in faith. The gifts themselves, of course, he considers of less value. It is most important by far that whatever he has is a gift of God, and that whatever is under his management is from God. "But I have been appointed," he says, "to guard these things and to manage his household. Therefore you do not have an ordinary guest; you have an ambassador of God."

Surely one could not blame anyone who understands this for wishing that in preference to all other honors in this life he, too, were a servant of this master. But nobody gives thought to these things and traces them back to God as the Author and the Bestower, as this servant does. It is true especially of avaricious persons and of those who devote themselves to unlawful gain that they do not discern the gifts of God.

Then the servant goes on to add: "I shall recount not only those great and excellent gifts of God but also the miracles which prove that God is with my master Abraham. Sarah, his wife, was barren and was exhausted by age. She was incapable of giving birth to children. But she bore a son, whose name is Isaac, for my master." He undoubtedly enlarged on the fact that Isaac was born of an aged and barren mother, and related in greater detail what is described here in few words.

And this is praise of godly and Christian service. Those who are in a lower class should know that their calling carries with it the same honor and lofty spirit that their masters or other, higher classes have; for whatever prestige or distinction attaches to their superiors, this the servants have in common with them, and the servants share in the honor for which they praise their masters.

"But what is the purpose," you will ask, "of this lengthy repetition?" In the first place, its purpose is to honor and commend betrothals, which should not be clandestine. It is altogether civil for the servant to speak highly of the riches of the master and his son, but this is repeated in order that we may know that it is not only not a sin or condemned by God but even honorable and praiseworthy before God to praise a suitor. Nor does this lengthy narration deal only with Abraham or the servant; it is praise of the suitor, whom it is proper to honor in words and to commend to the girl because of his respectability, fine appearance, wealth, and parents. On the other hand, words of praise for the girl — that she is chaste, well brought up, and born of pious parents — are also necessary. All these things belong to marriage and to preparing for a wedding. They are pleasing to God. In addition, therefore, to carrying out the other instructions with regard to finding a bride, the servant praises Isaac for his good qualities and because of the wealth his father has given him.

In the second place, these words serve to confirm our conviction that secret betrothals by which some worthless fellow secretly steals a son or a daughter from respectable parents should not be permitted. Therefore we are fighting with all our might against these devilish deceptions, since in this passage the Holy Spirit lays such careful stress on the wish and the consent of the parents and also of the groom and the bride.

And this praise of Isaac is introduced, and all particulars are gathered together, in order that the heart of the girl may be explored, lest it seem that she is being compelled to marry a man whom she dislikes. Therefore the servant reports that Isaac is a decent and virtuous young man, that his parents are godly, and that his religion and doctrine are in the entire household.

In his decrees the pope declares that an error and a condition dissolve a marriage which has not only been entered into through the exchange of vows but is fully valid and ratified. He lists 15 impediments to contracting a marriage. But he says that those two dissolve a marriage that has been contracted and consummated.[59] According to his laws, Jacob and Leah can separate, because Jacob had not chosen Leah but was deceived in respect to her person through some error and in a fraudulent manner.

Should fraudulent acts, then, not dissolve a secret betrothal when some imposter surreptitiously carries off my [60] daughter against my will or without my knowledge? In order, therefore, to guard beforehand against tricks and mistakes, there should be mutual consent of the parents on both sides, and the mutual personal acquaintance of the groom and the bride to make the marriage truly valid and ratified and to avoid the necessity of dissolving it because of some condition or mistake.

Therefore secret betrothals must be condemned as a Lerna [61] of countless evils, and in order that we may be able to beware of all these evils God has pointed out a very excellent arrangement, namely, that marriages should be entered into with the advice and consent of the parents and also of the groom and the bride. Furthermore, we warned above that parents should not misuse their right and should not tyrannize their children.

Then, because this entire repetition pertains to the description of the display connected with a marriage and a betrothal, it should be referred to the commonplace — also treated of above — concerning the dignity of marriage, namely, that this kind of life is pleasing to God, because the entire world has been blinded to such an extent by original sin that it cannot become aware of the works of God or recognize the glory of God in them. Again and again the writings of Latin and Greek authors disparage marriage. They pick out what is bad in it, but what is good in it they conceal.

[59] The number and classification of impediments and diriments to marriage varied throughout the history of medieval canon law, but Luther may have been thinking here of the mnemonic verse (from the *Gloss* of the *Decree, Causa* xxvii, q. 1, *Quidam, etc.*) that enumerated them:

> *Votum, conditio, violentia spiritualis,*
> *Proximitas, error, dissimilisque fides,*
> *Culpa, dies vetitus, honor, ordo, ligatio, sanguis,*
> *Quae sit et affinis, quique coire nequibit,*
> *Additur hic aetas, habitum conjunge furoris;*
> *His interdictum subditur Ecclesiae.*
> *Haec, si canonico vis consentire rigori*
> *Te de jure vetant jura subire tori.*

[60] We have read *meam* rather than *eam*, the reading in the Weimar text.

[61] The Lerna is the forest mentioned in Vergil, *Aeneid*, VI, line 287.

But in marriage there are two evils which sin and the devil have inflicted. The one is sin and imperfection; the other is death. Those two evils have so marred and corrupted our entire nature that reason can see nothing in the female sex but weakness and annoyances. In addition, there are pains, sicknesses, and endless misfortunes, which are offensive to people and make important men even more hostile to this ordinance, as though these two evils adhered to women alone, when in fact we men have faults that are far more disgraceful: pride, avarice, and the like, because of which we create upheaval in governments and churches. Add pains and sicknesses of every kind.

Therefore if these facts had to be compared with one another and entered into a list or a book, far greater evils would be discovered in men than in women. But such is our wretched condition and foolishness that we cannot discover and see anything good but see only those things that the devil has put into our senses and into the powers of soul and body. This has led to so many more insults of the female sex than of the male.

Accordingly, we should put forth as much effort to make clear and to praise God's work and the divine glory in the divine ordinance as the devil has put forth to becloud what God has ordained.

For everyone will have to agree that this sex [62] is a creature of God. Moreover, Scripture states (Gen. 1:31): "God saw, and they were very good." The devil conceals those good things by means of his insults, and he is in the habit of mentioning and pointing out the things that are bad. We, on the other hand, should consider the use and the good things; for these good things surpass the faults and the evils to the extent that the kindness of God is greater than the devil's malice. But if we were able to see clearly the excellence of nature as it has been created, then we would be blessed, just as we shall understand perfectly in eternal life.

As I have stated before, this sex has faults that are certain: death, that is, all kinds of punishments, sicknesses, and discomforts which pertain to death not only in the case of the mother but also in the case of the offspring. She is morose, the children are unruly and unrestrained, and the neighbors are mischievous and malevolent. But we are speaking about the faults that are within the bounds of marriage and do not separate spouses as adultery does.

But all these faults should be buried by the good things and the

[62] That is, the female sex.

advantages that have been mentioned in opposition. For even though the female sex is the weaker and carries around with it very many faults in the mind as well as in the body, nevertheless that one good thing, the womb and childbearing, covers and buries them all. This dialectic argument and proof is very strong; it penetrates and prevails. Nothing could argue and convince as powerfully as it does — not beauty, not morals, not wealth, or whatever other endowments women have.

With this boon Adam, too, covered all faults and disadvantages when he gave his wife the name Eve, which means life. Life overcomes all other things, whether bad or good, and has its origin from woman. For nothing lives without the womb, birth, milk, and breasts. All kingdoms, empires, prophets, and fathers have had their origin from this source.

Consequently, God has placed in woman His creation of all human beings. Likewise the use of creation, that is, conceiving; giving birth to, nourishing, and bringing up children; and serving her husband and managing the home. Thus among all the exceedingly bad faults and evils this indescribable good shines forth. This very brief eulogy includes everything Adam summed up in one word by calling his wife Eve.

Thus woman is the mother of all human beings. She carries human beings in her womb, brings them forth into this world, nourishes them with milk, and takes care of them by bathing them and performing other services. What would kings, princes, prophets, and all the saints be if there had been no Eve? For God does not make human beings from stones; He makes them from man and woman.

This argument should be advanced in opposition to the papists, to those who fight against God, and to all who despise the female sex. At the same time the examples of the fathers and the saints who were married should be presented. These examples bestow honor on marriage, which the entire world considers of little value and disparages, as can be seen in the poets Juvenal and Martial.[63]

But why do they confine their complaining to the inconveniences and not also give consideration to life in death and in punishments, namely, that human beings are born, nourished, and preserved for this life and for eternal life? They should by no means lose sight of this incalculable, incomprehensible, and truly divine good. If they

---

[63] See, for example, Juvenal, *Satires*, VI, lines 28 ff.

kept it in mind, their opinion about this sex would be more in accordance with what is right.

In Gellius there are memorable words from the speech of Metellus, who had urged Roman citizens to marry.[64] Since he knew that they were avoiding all the common discomforts of sin and death, he began his exhortation in the following manner: "Citizens, if we could exist without wives, we would not have all these discomforts; but seeing that nature has so ordained it that one cannot live conveniently enough with them or live at all without them, one should have regard for lasting welfare rather than for brief pleasure."

At that time these words offended wise men, who thought that the discomforts should have been concealed and covered. And surely you would have good reason for saying that he dissuaded by persuading. But this is the same argument that Adam had. Metellus does not deny the discomfort, but he opposes to it what is good: "If you do not marry, you will be free from great discomfort; but if you want to rule the world, wage wars, and extend the borders of the empire, there must be human beings who are living. Consequently, one must think first of all about life; for human beings who are not living will not rule and will not vanquish other nations."

Hence life is the highest good of the female sex. Life alone utterly rejects and refutes those abusive words of Juvenal and others. In order to fill a city with children and citizens, it will be necessary for people to marry. This is in excellent agreement with that one name given by our first parent — the name by which he called Eve the mother of the living, the mother who would bear children who later on would govern the state, the church, and the home, who would know God and would be saved in eternal life.

Even the patriarchs experienced the discomforts and troubles of marriage. Abraham, Lot, and the others were strangers in the land. They were tossed about by many great hardships and misfortunes; but they bore and swallowed all this calmly, mindful of that very great comfort that Eve is the mother of the living who bears and brings up children.

Therefore we must wrestle with these discomforts, because the present evils strike our eyes and senses too much. For we are not yet in that blessed life for which we are looking; we are in the life in which we wrestle and contend with many evils. But we should

[64] Gellius, *Attic Nights*, I, vi, 2.

learn to overcome these through our knowledge of God, His creation, and His good and divine ordinance. And young people should become accustomed to true and godly opinions about the female sex and marriage.

"But," you will say, "the entire world and many wise people detest this kind of life." I answer that by that very attitude they betray their foolishness, for they direct their attention only to the faults and do not open their eyes to take motherhood into consideration. Motherhood reduces all evils to nothing. Besides, in the Fourth Commandment God Himself bestows praise and honor on marriage. "Honor your father and mother," He says (Ex. 20:12). But whatever He has established and ordained in His Commandments should in no wise be disparaged or spoken of irreverently. Let him who is able to be continent, be continent. Nevertheless, let him think and speak respectfully about marriage and about motherhood, which is a divine blessing and ordinance by which God preserves the entire human race in this life. I wanted to repeat these statements about the praises of marriage because Rebecca gives the Holy Spirit occasion to say so much about marriage and betrothal, evidently for our instruction and as an example for us.

45. *Before I had done speaking in my heart, behold, Rebecca came out with her water jar on her shoulder; and she went down to the spring and drew. I said to her: Pray let me drink.*

46. *She quickly let down her jar from her shoulder and said: Drink, and I will give your camels drink also. So I drank and she gave the camels drink also.*

47. *Then I asked her: Whose daughter are you? She said: The daughter of Bethuel, Nahor's son whom Milcah bore to him. So I put the ring on her nose, and the bracelets on her arms.*

48. *Then I bowed my head and worshiped the Lord, and blessed the Lord, the God of my master Abraham, who had led me by the right way to take the daughter of my master's kinsman for his son.*

Here the servant explains that he has not spoken the words of his prayer clearly but has turned them over silently in his mind; and he attests again that before he finished his prayer, God heard him as he was calling upon Him. But everything he says — which repeats each particular, how he came to the girl and asked her for a drink and other things — has been dealt with above.

49. *Now then, if you will deal loyally and truly with my master, tell me; and if not, tell me, that I may turn to the right hand or to the left.*

This is the request. After finishing his story the servant adds: "If you are such people as are worthy of showing my master affection, kindness, and good faith." For this is the meaning in the Hebrew. In German we say: *Seid yr solch leut, die yr werdt seid, das yr meinem herrn freundschafft und treu beweyset.* "Mercy" in this passage is kindness or goodwill; "truth" means to satisfy the expectation and hope of someone. But again the Holy Spirit employs striking words. The servant calls giving the daughter in marriage to his master's son "mercy and truth." Everything is aimed at erasing from the hearts of people those pernicious opinions about marriage which Satan and the enemies of marriage have put into the flesh. In this passage Scripture regards it as a very great gift and kindness to give the girl to Isaac as his wife in order that the troubles and discomforts of marriage may be removed from sight and that Eve, the womb, birth, and motherhood may be presented to the hearts of people. Up to this point the servant has asked for Rebecca. Now the answer follows.

50. *Then Laban and Bethuel answered: The thing comes from the Lord; we cannot speak to you bad or good.*

51. *Behold, Rebecca is before you, take her and go, and let her be the wife of your master's son, as the Lord has spoken.*

52. *When Abraham's servant heard their words, he bowed himself to the earth before the Lord.*

This entire affair succeeds so easily and auspiciously because God and the angels are there to support and promote it. Besides, the Word of God finds room in Laban and Bethuel. Therefore they answer: "We gather from your words that you are the servant of Abraham and that Abraham is a servant of God." For they understand and accept those words in no other way than as if God Himself had spoken them. We would be fortunate indeed if we had the same conviction, namely, that when we hear one of the brethren or of the ministers proclaiming the Word of God, we are hearing God Himself. If we believed this, we would be truly blessed, and it would do very much to increase and strengthen our faith and to stir up hope and all other virtues.

Certainly we should receive the spoken word of a human being as the voice of God sounding from heaven. This word of the servant is also a spoken word, just as in the ministry. Nevertheless, these saintly men conclude and declare that it is from God. Therefore this answer is very excellent and striking; it teaches and encourages us, too, that whenever we hear a pastor or a minister or servant of the church, we are hearing the Word of God.

Moreover, this must be carefully noted on account of the usual temptation; for in the entire world there is not a more submissive pupil who would put up with more masters and teachers than the wisdom of God, as Christ says in Matt. 11:19: "Yet wisdom is justified by her children." Whatever God says or does finds countless judges, correctors, and critics, when one should rather say with these men: "These words have come from God. Therefore let Him change and correct what will seem to need changing, adding, or taking away. I am in no wise permitted to do this." But in this matter the papists, the Turks, the Jews, the Sacramentarians, and all sectarians are sinning. God grant that we may preserve the true and sound understanding of His Word.

Now this marriage was arranged and confirmed by the Lord, who brought Rebecca to Isaac, just as He had brought Eve to Adam. The Holy Spirit has given this description that we may know that the union of a man and a woman is from the Lord, especially if it takes place with the consent of the parents and the girl, as happened here. Therefore the servant adds words of thanks for the bride bestowed by God. To that extent godliness abounds in all his activities, for in small matters as well as in great thanks should be given to God.

53. *And the servant brought forth jewelry of silver and of gold, and raiment, and gave them to Rebecca; he also gave to her brother and to her mother costly ornaments.*

54. *And he and the men who were with him ate and drank, and they spent the night there.*

Two things are described in this passage: that gifts were presented to the bride and her friends, and that a banquet was prepared. Let us not suppose that these things are forbidden or condemned by God; they are proper and are approved by God, provided, however, that they are done with moderation. The jewels of gold were not golden goblets; they were ornaments and attire for women: a fillet, a jacket, a stomacher, a veil, and a cap.[65] The small gifts which he gives to her brother and mother are rarer and precious products, such as pomegranates, spices, myrrh, balsam, and the like, as are enumerated in the blessing of Joseph (Deut. 33:13 ff.): "The choicest gifts of heaven above, and of the deep that couches beneath, with the choicest fruits of the sun, and the rich yield of the months . . . with the best gifts of the earth." He has no money, but he brings ornaments suited for the bride. For the mother and the friends he brings gifts that seemed to be appropriate for them. These things are necessary in accordance with the practices and the custom of everyday life. Christians should not disregard them. Nor does Holy Scripture forbid them; it praises them.

When they arose in the morning, he said: Send me back to my master.

55. *Her brother and her mother said: Let the maiden remain with us a while, at least ten days; after that she may go.*

56. *But he said to them: Do not delay me, since the Lord has prospered my way; let me go that I may go to my master.*

57. *They said: We will call the maiden, and ask her.*

58. *And they called Rebecca and said to her: Will you go with this man? She said: I will go.*

59. *So they sent away Rebecca their sister and her nurse, and Abraham's servant and his men.*

60. *And they blessed Rebecca and said to her: Our sister, be the mother of thousands of ten thousands; and may your descendants possess the gate of those who hate them!*

61. *Then Rebecca and her maids arose and rode upon the camels and followed the man; thus the servant took Rebecca and went his way.*

This is the memorable example of the servant who is hastening to bring the bride to his master. It admonishes us never to hesitate

---

[65] In the original the names of these garments are given in German.

or delay in the works of God but to remove all obstacles and whatever can hold us back in the work we have undertaken. The writings of the heathen contain the same admonition, namely, that after a matter has been carefully considered, one should hasten to carry it out, as Sallust says: "When you have deliberated, you must act quickly." [66] Likewise: "Opportunity, though she has hair in front, is bald behind." [67] And Bonaventure's excellent maxim is "He who abandons opportunity will be abandoned by opportunity." [68]

Much less, then, should procrastination have a place on the way of God; for it does exceedingly great harm, as the bride complains in the Song of Solomon (5:2-6) that, while she was promising that she would open, the bridegroom waited only a little while and meanwhile turned aside and passed by. Why did she not go at once to open without deliberation or delay when she heard his voice?

He who does not rise for the Holy Spirit in the very hour or at the very moment He calls will never take hold of Him, for the Holy Spirit does not return when He has once gone away. Thus daily experience teaches that those who delay never acquire riches and resources. Therefore they will never be learned or great men in the church. For even though it was a poet who said: "He who is not ready today will be less ready tomorrow," [69] his words apply everywhere. I have learned from my own experience that whenever it was necessary to pray, to read, or to partake of the Lord's Supper, the longer I delayed, the more disinclined I was. Then I felt least fit.

Procrastination is a hidden evil, but it is horribly injurious. The Holy Spirit does not bestow His gifts on procrastinators; He bestows them on those who are prompt, ready, and alert, as the psalmist says: "I am ready, or I have hastened, and have not delayed, have not put off to keep Thy commandments" (cf. Ps. 119:60). Thus in the case of Rebecca the Holy Spirit has commended her speed: "She quickly let down her jar" (Gen. 24:18), and "she ran to tell her mother's household" (Gen. 24:28).

Consequently, the example of the servant should impel us to learn to guard against and hate this fault. Often one little hour is

[66] Sallust, *Bellum Catilinae,* I, 6.

[67] *Disticha Catonis,* I, 2.

[68] The epigram attributed to Bonaventure is *Qui deserit occasionem, deseretur ab occasione.*

[69] Quoted from Ovid, *Remedia amoris,* line 93.

of greater importance for doing something very well than a month or a year would be at other times. Soldiers are of the same opinion, and the devil is attentive to every opportunity. This is why he overcomes.

The last passage deals with the girl's consent; for before the servant departs, they call her and ask: "Do you want to go with that man?" Therefore a marriage should be brought about in such a way that we have God present. He established marriage for countless good purposes, and He Himself joins the spouses. Nor does He only join them; He also blesses them. But He requires the consent of the parents as well as of the girl, in order that there may be a lawful and truly divine union.

62. *Now Isaac had come from Beer-lahai-roi, and was dwelling in the Negeb.*

63. *And Isaac went out to meditate in the field in the evening; and he lifted up his eyes and looked, and behold, there were camels coming.*

64. *And Rebecca lifted up her eyes, and when she saw Isaac, she alighted from the camel*

65. *and said to the servant: Who is the man yonder, walking in the field to meet us? The servant said: It is my master. So she took her veil and covered herself.*

66. *And the servant told Isaac all the things that he had done.*

67. *Then Isaac brought her into the tent, and took Rebecca, and she became his wife; and he loved her. So Isaac was comforted after his mother's death.*

Mesopotamia, the land from which the servant brought the bride, is situated toward the north; but Isaac lived in a southern land. And it is evident that Abraham had given Isaac a house of his own and domestics to be in charge of where the Well of the Living and the Seeing was. Abraham remained in Hebron. Consequently, Isaac went forth either to his father in Hebron or to some other place.

The Latin text states that "Isaac went out to meditate." The Hebrew has "to pray." But the former pleases me more. For the word שִׂיחַ has two meanings. Sometimes it denotes a bush or a shrub, as above in chapter 2:5;[70] sometimes Holy Scripture uses it for speaking, as when someone converses either with himself or with another, as in the heading of Ps. 102: "When he poured out his speech." It denotes the private and secret conversation when two who are walking together converse. At that time Isaac did not think of his bride but went out with a friend, with whom, during their walk, he conversed about God's promises, about marriage, or about the management of the household. He conducted himself as becomes the head of the household; he talked about God and God's blessing, about managing the domestics, or about agriculture.

Finally Moses points out that Isaac received with joy the bride who was brought to him, and that he loved her. After his mother's death he spent three whole years mourning and grieving, as has been related above. But when his bride was brought to him, his grief was assuaged. The affection with which we love our wives pleases God, although this is difficult for our depraved nature, which looks only at the evil of sin and punishment and at the discomforts on the inside and on the outside. But one should rather consider that this sex has the gift of motherhood. This should be borne in mind. But many have no desire for children. The only thing they look for is the pleasure of the flesh. Later on, therefore, when they have had their fill, they begin to loathe, hate, and detest that union. But there is a difference between loving a wife and being lustful. To love a wife is not characteristic of our corrupt nature, but it is characteristic of our renewed and restored nature.

Next Rebecca's modesty is praised, because she covers herself with a veil when she sees Isaac. This conduct is a sign of a most excellent upbringing and of a virgin who has been reared chastely and modestly, who shrinks from looking at men, even at her bridegroom.

[70] The word occurs also in chapter 21:15, p. 40.

CHAPTER TWENTY-FIVE

1. *Abraham took another wife, whose name was Keturah.*

2. *She bore him Zimran, Jokshan, Medan, Midian, Ishbak, and Shuah.*

3. *Jokshan was the father of Sheba and Dedan. The sons of Dedan were Asshurim, Letushim, Leummim.*

4. *The sons of Midian were Ephah, Epher, Hanoch, Abida, and Eldaah. All these were the children of Keturah.*

LET us bury the most saintly patriarch Abraham, whose example very much deserves to be preserved forever in the church of God. But this chapter presents a matter and a seemingly very bad example that gravely offends everybody. For Abraham, an old man, decrepit, near the grave, and altogether moribund, before whose eyes and mind there can be nothing more than death, marries a young girl and begets more children.

In the previous chapter Abraham concluded his span of life, drew up his testament, and made Isaac the heir of all his goods. Now however, after his son's wedding, he himself also takes a wife. It is not sufficiently evident what one's reaction should be, and I am altogether uncertain whether there is a hysteron proteron or, on the other hand, a proteron hysteron.[1] But if we follow the order of the text, a strange question arises. Paul himself explains in Rom. 4:19 that "Abraham's body was as good as dead and unfit to procreate, because he was now 100 years old." Hence it seems somehow that this part of the chapter should have been inserted earlier and that Abraham married the girl Keturah before he begot Isaac. Perhaps it would be possible to answer that pressing question in this manner. But I am not making a positive statement.

For even though we assume that Abraham married Keturah after he had driven out Hagar, yet at that time he was not far from 100

[1] In his *Computation of the Years of the World* (W, LIII, 69) Luther considered the possibility that many of the accounts in the Pentateuch had been written *per hysteron proteron*, but he was inclined to reject it.

years old; for Hagar gave birth to Ishmael when Abraham was 86 and Sarah 100 years old. Therefore this answer does not yet satisfy, but the question is still left in doubt.

But let us follow the familiar and common procedure in conformity with the description in the text. Paul says that Abraham's body was as good as dead after he begot Isaac, and he is 140 years old when Isaac marries Rebecca. Perhaps one or two years intervened between his own marriage and that of his son. Therefore what answer should one give? Some maintain that Keturah is Hagar herself, whom he again received into favor after the death of his wife Sarah and later on took to wife, since she had now humbled herself and repented.[2] This is a very fine thought. It abounds in kindheartedness, and I would gladly believe and agree that Abraham had taken Hagar and her son back into his home and had provided for her in this manner. But there is no certainty.

St. Jerome is greatly offended and would gladly speak irreverently of so great a man if he dared. But he keeps his resentment in check and says: "The age of Abraham, who is now decrepit, seems to be a reason for excusing him, lest the old man be charged with having been lascivious because of his marriage after the death of his aged wife." [3] But the most general opinion, of which Lyra, too, approves, is that Keturah is Hagar, although he sees that contrary to this the text states that gifts were given to the children of the concubines, of whom Hagar has to be one and Keturah has to be the other.[4]

It is my opinion that Keturah was not Hagar, and the reason that induces me most of all to hold to this view is to be found in the fact that the computation of the years does not agree with the notion that has been mentioned. For Hagar bore Ishmael when Abraham was 86, and she was married to him when she was about 30. Since her fifteenth year she had been reared by Sarah, who then took her into the house for the first time. There she remained until she was 30, when she became the mother of Ishmael. But Isaac is born 14 years after Ishmael's birth. When these years are added up, they make 44 years, or at least 40. To these should further be added the 40 years of Isaac, who marries Rebecca in his fortieth year. Conse-

---

[2] See p. 43, note 41.

[3] Jerome, *Liber hebraicarum quaestionum in Genesin, Patrologia, Series Latina,* XXIII, 1025, 1026.

[4] Lyra *ad* Gen. 25:1-2, where he suggests that the name Keturah means *thurificata,* "one who offers incense."

quently, Hagar's age adds up to 84 years, more or less, when she, too, in accordance with nature, had to be exhausted. And it is impossible to conclude that she bore six sons at that age.

Therefore I hold that Hagar cannot be Keturah, unless it is recorded by a hysteron proteron that Abraham took Keturah when, as has been related above, Hagar was joined to him. Furthermore, the text mentions concubines in the plural number. Consequently, Keturah is another woman. She is not Hagar. Besides, Abraham had two concubines: the one, who is called a mistress, in addition to his wife; the other, after his wife had died. Thus there still remains that very serious offense that Abraham, 140 years old, when his body was already as good as dead, married a young girl and begot six sons, although previously he had no offspring from Sarah except Isaac.

In the first place, one asks whether this was not impossible because Abraham's body was as good as dead. In the second place, one asks why offense was taken. To the first question I reply that old men can beget children and now and then are wont to do so. Therefore it was possible, even natural, for Abraham to beget children when he was 140 years old, because his was a healthy old age and not at all burdensome and annoying. Nor was he like our people, most of whom are completely exhausted when they have barely reached their fiftieth year. But he undoubtedly had a strong and vigorous body, just as today some men are so strong and healthy in their old age that they are able to bear huge burdens in managing a state or a household.

Furthermore, it is likely that God had given Abraham strength beyond what is natural and that he gained much vigor both of mind and body after the birth of Isaac, the son and heir of the promise.

The second question concerns the offense that is taken because Abraham marries a young girl. Lyra advances this reason: that girls conceive more easily from old men than do women of a more advanced age.[5] But the offense will be removed more properly if we distinguish the times and the customs of the fathers from the present times and customs. Many are offended by the fact that in this first book Moses relates so much about the procreation of the fathers.[6] But they do not consider the difference in customs in different ages. At that time faith ruled in the fathers, and also faith in this article

[5] Lyra *ad* Gen. 25:1-2.

[6] See *Luther's Works,* 1, p. 240.

(Gen. 1:28): "Be fruitful and multiply." In our age, especially after those papistic monstrosities of celibacy, marriage has been deprived of its prestige and due honor, and true knowledge of the Word and ordinance of God has become extinct. Among the fathers this knowledge was pure and proper. For this reason they had a very high regard for the begetting of children.

Therefore one should not suppose that Abraham married Keturah because he was prompted by lasciviousness, for previously indeed, while the barren Sarah was living, he waited long enough for the blessing of God, and there was never any suspicion of lust in him. Therefore he did this because of his eager desire to obtain offspring, especially since he had heard in the promise (Gen. 17:4): "You shall be the father of many" — not only of Isaac but of many nations, through which God would multiply him not only spiritually but also physically.

Furthermore, Shem, Eber, and Shelah were still living. Abraham and Noah were contemporaries for 58 years. Noah heard Shem before and after the Flood. But Shem outlived Abraham by 31 years. Hence it was a magnificent age, and it produced most illustrious men, none of whom would have permitted Abraham to perpetrate anything unseemly. Indeed, it seems that he did this at their bidding and at their advice. Others, who are indecent, do not have advisers and mentors of this kind. They are more like swine than like Abraham. Therefore they pursue in marriage a purpose different from what Abraham sought. But one should not rush into it as such people and the papists also do. Their sole aim is lust, shamelessness, and the pleasure of the flesh, in which they are not only submerged but almost swallowed up.

Here, therefore, one must consider the time of the very saintly patriarchs, to whom Abraham undoubtedly listened. Thus there is a subsequent account of how Rebecca sought the advice of the patriarch Shem.[7] Therefore it is an honorable marriage, and to it applies the statement in Mal. 2:15: "And what does He desire? Godly offspring." Abraham was not a lustful old man; but whatever he did, he did because of his love and desire for offspring and at God's command, and finally at the advice and urging of the most saintly fathers, who said: "Marry a second wife, in order that your church may be extended and spread out over the world."

Jerome had the same thoughts I had when I was still a monk.

[7] Cf. p. 359, note 53; *Luther's Works*, 2, p. 231; and *Luther the Expositor*, p. 104.

But one should form a different opinion about such great men. They were most saintly, full of the Holy Spirit and faith; and they were directed by very great patriarchs, by Shem and the others. I am saying this in order to excuse the most saintly man Abraham, lest someone interpret this action of his as rashness, lasciviousness, or shamelessness and fail to realize that his obedience and his love for offspring led him to marry Keturah.

Furthermore, God's special counsel is apparent in this passage. For the Holy Spirit, who is on the lookout for future errors and foresees them far in advance, is at pains to guard against them beforehand and to refute them, in order that the heretics who someday would condemn a second marriage may blush with shame. Jerome is one of these. He finds a second marriage so reprehensible that he regards it as adultery.[8]

In this passage, therefore, God has set before us an example and a striking evidence of His will. He does not condemn a second marriage that takes place after the first wife's death. Indeed, through His patriarch Shem He ordered the decrepit old man to take a wife.

And it seems that God wanted to teach and attest that the begetting of children is wonderfully pleasing to Him, in order that we might realize that He upholds and defends His Word when He says: "Be fruitful." He is not hostile to children, as we are. Many of us do not seek to have offspring. But God emphasizes His Word to such an extent that He sometimes gives offspring even to those who do not desire it, yes, even hate it. Occasionally, of course, He does not give it to some who earnestly desire it. It is His purpose to test them. And, what is more, He seems to emphasize procreation to such an extent that children are born even to adulterers and fornicators contrary to their wish.

How great, therefore, the wickedness of human nature is! How many girls there are who prevent conception and kill and expel tender fetuses, although procreation is the work of God! Indeed, some spouses who marry and live together in a respectable manner have various ends in mind, but rarely children.

The first class of spouses consists of those who seek to have offspring and have a desire for this kind of life in order that they may become parents. Although original sin is there too, nevertheless procreation is the main cause. These people are really angels in

8 Perhaps a reference to Jerome, Contra Jovinianum, Book I, ch. 14; but cf. Augustine, The City of God, Book XVI, ch. 34.

comparison with the others, because they desire to make use of marriage for procreation. But their number is very small, and I simply count them among the angels and not among human beings. For it is a great gift of God if I look for and desire only offspring from a woman, especially if I am aware of the discomforts of marriage, of the vexing and the darts of the devil (Eph. 6:16). Such a man was Abraham, whom I count among the angelic husbands who desire "godly offspring," as Malachi (2:15) says.

The second class consists of those who marry for the sake of avoiding fornication. They do not turn away from or hate children, but it is their main purpose to live chastely and modestly. These, too, are pious people, but they are not on a par with the former. If God grants children, they are delighted. They love their wives and their offspring, and they diligently perform the duties of their calling.

The third class consists of those who desire wives solely for the sake of pleasure. These are not concerned about children but want to lead a soft and pleasant life and to have a pretty girl to give them pleasure.

The fourth class consists of those who marry old ladies for the sake of wealth or honor. May God give them the cup of suffering, as Bernard says;[9] for they seek only wealth and honor, not the begetting of children! Nevertheless, because of the respect for and the honor of marriage they should not be condemned.

But people must be diligently warned that such examples of the fathers should not be taken as a pattern to be imitated, since there is a great difference between Abraham's desire and that of an old woman who marries a young man. For although Abraham is under the sin of lust to the same extent as others are, he is nevertheless the master and not the slave of lust. Indeed, there is purity in him and sincere love for offspring. The love for offspring and seed prevails, just as among the heathen as well as among Christians many have for various reasons had an intense longing for children.

In the first place, therefore, I am of the opinion that Keturah is not Hagar. In the second place, I hold that Abraham should by no means be censured, but that the chasteness of his marriage should be discussed in the most respectable manner, and that the love he has for offspring should be commended because it increases the household,

---

[9] The idea of a *calix passionis*, though not with this meaning, occurs in Bernard of Clairvaux, *Vitis mystica*, XIII, 44, 45, *Patrologia, Series Latina*, CLXXXIV, 662, 663.

the state, and the church. But if in addition to this some weaknesses make their appearance at the same time; they are nevertheless not matters of primary importance.

I believe that Keturah was the daughter of some pious and faithful servant like Eliezer. She was not an Egyptian or a Canaanite. For the word has the same meaning as if one said "bound," "joined," or "associated"; for she was related to Abraham by affinity, either through his servants or from the family of Lot.

But why is Keturah called Abraham's wife in this passage, although it is stated later on that Abraham gave gifts to his concubines? If she was a concubine, why is she called his wife? Above there is a similar expression: "Sarah gave Hagar to Abram her husband as a wife" (Gen. 16:3). I am leaving the disputes about grammatical matters to the grammarians themselves. The Latins give the name *pellex* to a woman joined to a man who has a wife. They themselves had many *pellices*. A concubine is a woman whom an unmarried man has outside wedlock, with whom he has intercourse. She is neither a *pellex* nor a wife. Augustine had such a concubine.[10]

But the times change laws and customs. Therefore one should note how in this passage and before the Law of Moses these terms must be distinguished, for there is a difference between wife and wife. Abraham never had two wives. Lamech (Gen. 4:19) was the first to marry two women. Of Abraham, however, it is stated that he had only one wife. Yet there were two.

The term "wife," in only one meaning and in only one way, is applied to a woman who is free and who bears the heir of all goods. Such a one is Sarah. In another way a female slave who bears a child, but not an heir, is improperly called a wife. Later on Moses changed everything. Jacob had four wives, and the two female slaves or maids also gave birth to heirs.

Here a woman who is free and bears children is properly called a wife. A slave woman who bears children, but no heirs is also called a wife. Keturah is a wife. Nevertheless, she is a *pellex*, as is stated later in the text. And in 1 Chron. 1:32 the sons of Keturah, the פִּילֶגֶשׁ of Abraham, that is, the concubine or *pellex* of Abraham, are enumerated. The Latin word is derived from the Hebrew.[11]

---

10 Cf. Augustine, *Confessions*, Book IV, ch. 2.2.

11 Although many of Luther's etymologies are highly questionable, especially when they connect Semitic words with Latin, Greek, or German ones, this explanation of the Latin *pellex* (more correctly *paelex*) is still shared by philologists.

Thus that woman Keturah seems to have been a slave woman, because she is numbered among the concubines. She is not considered the lady of the house or as an heiress; she was taken only for the purpose of becoming the mother of offspring and bearing children. Such wives are not free or ladies of the house.

For the most part the names of Keturah's sons have disappeared. Midian was praised later in the Holy Scriptures; but the others vanished, and no mention is made of them. Thus Scripture indicates that the sons of the maidservant are servants who do not remain in the house. In Is. 60:6 mention is made of Midian and Ephah, who lived in Arabia Petraea toward Egypt and occupied a large part of Arabia Felix. Midian is situated toward the Red Sea. Ephah is part of Arabia Felix and got its name from that forefather.[12]

This, then, is the new and second marriage of the very saintly man Abraham. Concerning it one should note above all that God praises the work of procreation and counteracts the offense of the heretics who condemn a second marriage. For everything is recorded for the purpose of honoring and showing respect for marriage, in which God regards the offspring and then also chastity, the two adornments of marriage. For where children are brought into the world, there the highest blessing is; but if no offspring results, conjugal chastity should nevertheless be praised. This is profitable and necessary instruction over against the heretics who approve only of a first marriage or of one that is always fertile. They want like to be joined to like — an old man, for example, to an old woman. Let us pay heed to the two things I have mentioned and to whether a husband is content with his wife, of whatever kind she may be, and lives with her decently and chastely.

5. *Abraham gave all he had to Isaac.*

6. *But to the sons of his concubines Abraham gave gifts; and while he was still living, he sent them away from his son Isaac, eastward to the east country.*

The saintly father now bids the world farewell and makes his testament with a cheerful and serene heart, for to him death and life are alike. This example teaches us that we should take care diligently that our passing out of this life is serene and in peace, lest opportunities and seeds for disputes, quarrels, and disagreements about our

---

[12] Cf. *Luther's Works*, 1, p. 101, note 31.

fortune and possessions be left behind. But while the father is still living, the children or heirs should be informed how much will be coming to each one according to the wish of the testator or according to the laws.

Thus Abraham dismisses the sons of the concubines with his gifts and sends them away to the Orient. Some reached India, but the names that are mentioned here are those of Arabia Petraea and Arabia Felix. Abraham sends them into that waste and still uncultivated place after he has bestowed on each one his gift. But he appoints Isaac as the sole heir.

This, too, should be noted on account of the heretics who either confuse or condemn these duties of everyday life. While Abraham was alive, he made these arrangements with the good intention that after his death no occasion for quarreling should remain.

Moreover, Abraham has shown us, too, very many most excellent kindnesses; for from him we have the entire Holy Scripture. Indeed, in the beginning Adam transmitted to the patriarch Noah the doctrine of God and of the true forms of worship by word of mouth. Noah then transmitted this to Abraham as if from hand to hand. But I think that Abraham composed a little book or a brief account from Adam up to his own times. Finally, when he has left behind his son Isaac, from whom Christ would be born, and then a well-established church and household, he departs this life and bids the world farewell.

7. *These are the days of the years of Abraham's life, a hundred and seventy-five years.*

8. *Abraham breathed his last and died at a good old age, an old man and full of years, and was gathered to his people.*

9. *Isaac and Ishmael, his sons, buried him in the cave of Machpelah, in the field of Ephron, the son of Zohar the Hittite, east of Mamre,*

10. *the field which Abraham purchased from the Hittites. There Abraham was buried, with Sarah, his wife.*

Abraham sojourned for 100 years in the land of Canaan after he had gone out from Ur of Chaldeans when he was 75 years old. But what the Lord said to Abraham above (Gen. 15:15) — "As for yourself, you shall go to your fathers in peace; you shall be buried in a good old age" — is recorded in this passage as having been fulfilled. He breathed his last. He departed. Nevertheless, he died. This is intended to comfort us, for it was not written for the sake of oxen or other irrational creatures. Abraham departed like any other human being, and Moses says that he died. Such a great man, a man abounding in all virtues, the father of the promise, of faith, of the children of God, and of all nations — this man dies just as we do; but he dies in a pleasant and agreeable old age, an old man and full of years.

In all Holy Scripture this is the first passage which declares that the death of the saints is peaceful and precious in the sight of God (Ps. 116:15) and that the saints do not taste death but most pleasantly fall asleep. Isaiah read and carefully expounded this passage, for from it there originated those striking statements he made: "The righteous man is taken away from calamity, he enters into peace; they rest in their beds" (57:1-2)[13] and "Come, my people, enter your chambers, and shut your doors behind you; hide yourselves for a little while until the wrath is past" (26:20).

In the eyes of the world the righteous are despised, spurned, and thrust aside. Their death seems exceedingly sad. But they are sleeping a most pleasant sleep. When they lie down in their beds and breathe their last, they die just as if sleep were gradually falling upon their limbs and senses. For previously they have been humbled by various trials, and they have become peaceful and quiet, so that they say: "Lord God, I shall die gladly if this seems best to Thee." They do not dread death as do the ungodly, who tremble and are horribly afraid. This they do to awaken us, in order that we may learn to obey God when He calls us out of this wretched state and may be able to say: "I do not want one hour to be added to my life, Lord Jesus Christ. Come when Thou wilt." In this way Abraham dies full of days, when he was well content.[14]

But where did Abraham go? Moses says: "He was gathered to his people." Do people, then, still remain after this life? For the words sound as though he had gone from one people to another or from one city to another. This is truly an outstanding and notable evidence of the resurrection and the future life. It should be set forth for the comfort of all who believe in God. Although more excellent and clearer evidences are presented to us in the New

---

13 The original has "Is. 56."

14 These last words appear in German: *da er wol zufrieden war.*

Testament, it is nevertheless worthwhile to see what the saintly fathers in the Old Testament had and believed.

We have the grace and the gift. In addition, we have a clear and extensive knowledge about death and life, since we are sure that our Savior Christ Jesus is sitting at the right hand of God the Father and is waiting for us when we depart this life. Therefore when we depart from the living, we go forth to the Guardian of our souls (1 Peter 2:25), who receives us into His hands. He is our Abraham in whose embrace we take delight. He lives. Indeed, He rules forever.

About the fathers one must speak in a different manner, and our comfort is far more glorious and far greater, although they had the same evidence and solace concerning eternal life and the resurrection of the dead. Thus Moses attests in this passage that Abraham was gathered to his people. Above (Gen. 15:15) Abraham heard in the promise that he would go to his fathers. And these two are the first passages in all Holy Scripture that speak of the dead after this life. In the fifth chapter the statement "He died" is made about all except about Enoch alone (v. 24), who was translated by the Lord. Concerning Abraham it is stated that he would go to his fathers and that he was gathered to his people.

These words of the Holy Spirit are by no means useless. Nor are they spoken to beasts, which do not go to their fathers and their people. No, they are spoken to human beings, and they bear witness that after this life another and better life remains, yes, that even before the coming of Christ there was a people of the living which dwelt in the land of the living. To them the godly went away. Therefore from then on the fathers had an understanding of the resurrection and of eternal life, and the words of each passage are used in their proper and clear sense. "You will be gathered to the rest of the saints," they say, "who have died before you. Therefore the fathers are living and are a people." This is not said about the ungodly, but the discussion is about the righteous and the saints.

In the Books of Kings (1 Kings 2:2) David makes use of another figure when he says: "Behold, I am about to go the way of all the earth." But later on Moses retains the same expression in connection with Ishmael, Isaac, and Jacob: "He breathed his last and was gathered to his people." Therefore the fathers concluded from these passages that another life remains and that the saints do not perish like cattle but are gathered to the people in the land of the living. And this is the reason why they are buried by their sons with such respect and honor — which it is not customary to do in the case of beasts — doubtless because of the certain expectation of another life.

Accordingly this serves to comfort us, lest we, like others, who have no hope (1 Thess. 4:13), be frightened by or shudder at death. For in Christ death is not bitter, as it is for the ungodly, but it is a change of this wretched and unhappy life into a life that is quiet and blessed. This statement should convince us fully that we do not pass from a pleasant life into a life that is unhappy, but that we pass from afflictions into tranquillity. For since the fathers had this comfort from these few passages long before Christ, how much more reasonable it is for us to guard and preserve the same comfort! We have it in far greater abundance.

Later on, in the Gospel, Christ called the place into which Lazarus and all the other saints have been gathered the bosom of Abraham (Luke 16:22). But how to explain or define this I leave to the judgment of anybody in accordance with each one's understanding. Nor shall I make positive statement, since even Augustine says that he does not know.[15] But we are not doing the right thing if we retain "the bosom of Abraham" in the New Testament. For just as before Abraham's death there was no bosom of Abraham, so there is no longer a bosom of Abraham after Christ's coming. Consequently, I am not making a bosom of Abraham at this time. Nor do I think that there is any place where Abraham embraces us on his lap, so to speak. But the bosom of Abraham where he holds and has embraced all the saints who died up to the death of Christ is the promise made to Abraham (Gen. 22:18): "In your Seed all the nations shall be blessed." Thus the bosom of Adam was the promise given in Paradise (Gen. 3:15): "The Seed of the woman shall crush the head of the serpent"; and those who departed with faith in that promise were saved, because the Word of God is greater and more extensive than heaven and earth.

Therefore the bosom of Abraham is the promise concerning the Christ who would come; and the father of this promise is Abraham. But today it is changed to the Word concerning the Christ who has been manifested in the flesh; and he who would believe otherwise would be a Jew and condemned, because Abraham's bosom was done away with after the resurrection of Christ, and a better bosom, namely, that of Christ, has taken its place. For when we depart this life,

---

[15] Perhaps a reference to Augustine, *De cura pro mortuis*, chs. 17, 18.

we are carried into the bosom of Christ. And just as the fathers died in faith in the Christ who would come and were thus gathered into Abraham's bosom, that is, in the expectation of the future Savior, so we must die in faith in Christ, the Savior who has appeared; and after this life we are gathered into the bosom of the Christ who was born, suffered, was crucified, and rose again for us. We are not worried at all anymore about Abraham's bosom.

Furthermore, at this point one can be concerned about the state of the souls after this life. The body is destroyed by putrefaction and worms. But what, it is asked, becomes of the soul before that Day of Judgment? I am touching on this controversy, of course, in order to forestall and put an end to the prying questions and discussions of others. But the answer which Christ prescribes is simple when He says in Matt. 22:32: "God is not God of the dead, but of the living." This makes us sure that our souls are living and are sleeping in peace, and that they are not being racked by any tortures.

And many passages of Holy Scripture confirm that we do not die after death but are plainly alive, as very clear statements from the Book of Isaiah (57:1-2) prove: "Devout men are taken away while no one understands. For the righteous man is taken away from calamity; he enters into peace; they rest in their beds." These are most extraordinary words. They clearly indicate the state and condition of the dead after this life. "They enter," he says, "not into death, purgatory, or hell; they enter into peace." And it is a great comfort when he says that the righteous are called away before calamity comes. Thus we ourselves shall die in peace before evil and calamity come over Germany.

Consequently, the testimonies of the prophet are in agreement with that passage of Genesis where Moses says that Abraham was gathered to his people; and we should have no doubt about the importance of these testimonies, for Holy Scripture does not lie or deceive. The saints repose gently and peacefully, just as in the Book of Revelation (14:13) the voice from heaven bears witness to this: "Henceforth, says the Spirit, that they may rest from their labors."

At that time this rest was called the bosom of Abraham; and from the beginning, before Abraham, it was called the bosom of Adam. For the saints who believed the promise concerning Christ died in such a manner that after they had been called away from the troubles and hardships of this life, they entered their chamber, slept there, and rested in peace. This is true and clear. It is in agreement with Scripture and the statement of Christ (Matt. 22:32) that God is not God of the dead but of the living.

But now another question arises. Since it is certain that the souls are living and are in peace, what kind of life or rest is this? But this question is too lofty and too difficult for us to be able to define it. For God did not want us to know this in this life. Thus it is enough for us to know that souls do not go out of their bodies into the danger of tortures [16] and punishments of hell, but that there is ready for them a chamber in which they may sleep in peace.

Nevertheless, there is a difference between the sleep or rest of this life and that of the future life. For toward night a person who has become exhausted by his daily labor in this life enters into his chamber in peace, as it were, to sleep there; and during this night he enjoys rest and has no knowledge whatever of any evil caused either by fire or by murder. But the soul does not sleep in the same manner. It is awake. It experiences visions and the discourses of the angels and of God. Therefore the sleep in the future life is deeper than it is in this life. Nevertheless, the soul lives before God. With this analogy, which I have from the sleep of a living person, I am satisfied; for in him there is peace and quiet. He thinks that he has slept barely one or two hours, and yet he sees that the soul sleeps in such a manner that it also is awake.

Thus after death the soul enters its chamber and is at peace; and while it sleeps, it is not aware of its sleep. Nevertheless, God preserves the waking soul. Thus God is able to awaken Elijah, Moses, etc., and so to control them that they live. But how? We do not know. The resemblance to physical sleep — namely, that God declares that there is sleep, rest, and peace — is enough. He who sleeps a natural sleep has no knowledge of the things that are happening in his neighbor's house. Nevertheless, he is alive, even though, contrary to the nature of life, he feels nothing in his sleep. The same thing will happen in that life, but in a different and better way.

Just as a mother brings an infant into the bedchamber and puts it into a cradle — not that it may die, but that it may have a pleasant sleep and rest — so before the coming of Christ and much more after the coming of Christ all the souls of believers have entered and are entering the bosom of Christ.

[16] Instead of *cruciarum* in the Weimar text, we have followed the Erlangen text and read *cruciatuum*.

There have also been discussions about where the souls are. In his *Enchiridion to Laurence* Augustine states that their whereabouts is concealed. He says: "But the time that elapses between man's death and the final resurrection keeps the souls in hidden places, inasmuch as each one deserves either rest or distress, depending on what its lot was in the flesh while it was living." [17]

Here one discovers the weakness of the human intellect. But one must consider the Word and the omnipotence of God; for if God weighs heaven and earth with three fingers, as is stated in Is. 40:12, His Word is surely far greater and far more extensive. Therefore the whereabouts of the souls is the Word of God or the promises in which we fall asleep. To be sure, it appears to be of no consequence and feeble when it is uttered through the mouth of man; but when we take hold of it in faith and fall asleep in the Word, the soul comes into infinite space.

I have said this in order to curb unprofitable and idle thoughts about these questions. For it is more than enough to know that we depart safely and quietly into the bosom of Christ; that is, that those who rely on the Word and the promise escape afflictions and tribulations and enjoy everlasting peace and safety, in accordance with Christ's statement in John 8:51: "Truly, truly, I say to you, if anyone keeps My Word, he will never see death." Consequently, he will live in an eternal life.

But here one must also censure the foolishness of the papists, who have devised five places after death: (1) the hell of the damned; (2) the hell of infants who were not baptized; (3) purgatory; (4) the limbo of the fathers (in the New Testament they added Paradise on account of Christ's statement in Luke 23:43: "Today you will be with Me in Paradise"); and (5) the open heaven.[18]

They say that the first place, which is torment by eternal fire, is for the damned. But whether the souls of the ungodly are tortured immediately after death I am unable to affirm, although the example of the rich glutton applies here. But there is a passage to the opposite effect in 2 Peter 2:4. It deals with the wicked angels who are being kept until the judgment. And in 2 Cor. 5:10 Paul says: "For we must

---

17 Augustine, *Enchiridion*, ch. 29, par. 109.

18 This doctrine had been promulgated in the bull *Laetentur coeli* of Pope Eugenius IV on July 6, 1439, *Concilium Florentinum. Documenta et Scriptores.* Series A, edited by G. Hoffmann, II (Rome, 1944), 68—79.

all appear before the judgment seat of Christ, so that each one may receive good or evil, according to what he has done in the body." It seems that they, too, are sleeping and resting; but I am making no positive statement.

The second place is that of infants who were not baptized. They maintain that while those infants are damned, they are not suffering punishment by fire or by worms but are merely without the vision of God. They do not have the light which would enable them to see God and the angels. Nevertheless, they are not tormented.

The third sphere is that of purgatory, into which neither the damned nor infants enter; it is for those who, while they believe, yet have not rendered satisfaction for their sins. The souls of these are ransomed by means of indulgences. From this source comes the hogwash of indulgences and the entire papistic religion.

The fourth place is the limbo of the fathers. They say that Christ descended to this place, broke it open, and set free — not from hell but from the limbo — the fathers who were troubled by the longing and waiting for Christ but were not enduring punishment or torments.

With these silly ideas the papists have filled the church and the world. We have overturned all this completely and maintain that unbaptized infants do not have such a sphere. But in what state they are or what becomes of them we commend to the goodness of God. They do not have faith or Baptism; but whether God receives them in an extraordinary manner and gives them faith is not stated in the Word, and we dare not set down anything as certain. To be deprived of the vision of God is hell itself. They admit that they have will and intellect, especially concerning the vision of God and life; but these are falsehoods. And purgatory is the greatest falsehood, because it is based on ungodliness and unbelief; for they deny that faith saves, and they maintain that satisfaction for sins is the cause of salvation. Therefore he who is in purgatory is in hell itself; for these are his thoughts: "I am a sinner and must render satisfaction for my sins; therefore I shall make a will and shall bequeath a definite amount of money for building churches and for buying prayers and sacrifices for the dead by the monks and priests." Such people die in a faith in works and have no knowledge of Christ. Indeed, they hate Him. We die in faith in Christ, who died for our sins and rendered satisfaction for us. He is my Bosom, my Paradise, my Comfort, and my Hope.

Their talk about a limbo of the fathers is inappropriate. It would have been better if they had called it the bosom of Abraham; for those who died before Christ were saved in the promise of the Word in which they lived in this life, and when they died, they entered into life and were truly alive.

The meaning of the words of Christ to the criminal (Luke 23:43) is this: "Today you will be with Me in Paradise"; that is, in My bosom; where I am, you likewise shall be. There heaven and Paradise are the same thing, except that as yet there is rest and peace among the saints, but not the kingdom. Christ is in heaven or Paradise to direct, judge, and rule His church, to send angels to minister to His church, to distribute gifts to men, to exalt the humble, etc. For He is always working and does not rest as do the saints who sleep, about whom it is stated in Is. 63:16: "Abraham does not know us, and Israel does not acknowledge us."

Therefore there is a great difference between the sleeping saints and the ruling Christ. The former sleep and do not know what is going on. Nevertheless, they are resting. But when the ungodly die, whether they have departed long ago, before the coming of Christ, or today, after Christ has been revealed, they go simply to damnation. But we do not know whether their damnation begins immediately after death; for it is written (Rom. 14:10) that all will have to stand before the judgment seat, and John 5:29 states: "Those who have done good will come forth to the resurrection of life, and those who have done evil, to the resurrection of judgment."

Accordingly, we should remember that after Christ the bosom of Abraham has come to an end and that all the promises about the coming Seed have been fulfilled. We have other and far more glorious promises that were given us by the Son of God, who became incarnate, suffered, and was raised again. If we do not believe these, we are condemned forever. But I am unable to say positively in what state those are who are condemned in the New Testament. I leave this undecided. Concerning the godly it is most certain that they live and enter into peace. About this matter we indeed have far more and far clearer examples and evidences in the New Testament from the addresses of Christ and of the apostles than did the fathers, who had only a few passages which clearly indicated the resurrection and eternal life. The passages in The Wisdom of Solomon (3:1) — "The souls of the righteous are in the hand of God, and no torment of death will touch them" — was taken from Isaiah.

But this faith — both that of the fathers and our own — is one and the same, namely, that there remains another and better life after this one. It would be most shameful indeed for Christians to have any doubt concerning it when they have such great light. Let us, therefore, receive and with firm assent of the heart preserve this doctrine which has been revealed to us through God's boundless favor by means of many clear evidences. For a most pestilential age is now arising, and the Epicureans are increasing in number. This is most certain proof of the confusion of everything and of the approaching judgment. For if I do not believe in a future life and a resurrection, why do I have need of God and a knowledge of Christ? Or how can I maintain that there is a God who punishes the wicked and does good to the pious? The denial of a future life completely does away with God, and thus we shall be altogether like horses and mules (Ps. 32:9), which do not trouble themselves at all either about death or about life. And this can surely be observed in the case of the Epicureans. Whatever they hear about God, either when He is promising or when He is threatening, is now ridiculous to them and an empty tale. But let us Christians shun that horrible smugness, and let us firmly hold fast to the evidences of eternal life and of the resurrection that have been handed down from the beginning of the world.

Moses describes the death of Abraham with two words, both of which mean "to die." "He breathed his last, or departed," he says, "and died." Above (Gen. 7:21) we read about the Flood that all flesh departed, or died, whether it lived in the water or on land. There Moses employed the first word: גָּוַע. Below (Gen. 49:33), in the account of Jacob only the other word appears: "He breathed his last and was gathered to his people." But here Moses combines the two words, and I think that this is the difference: With the first word he wanted to point out the well-known demeanor or agony of a dying person, as though he were saying: "He became sick, lay down, and was at the point of death, so that no hope of life remained. Nevertheless, he was not yet dead." Therefore I explain the former as the imperfect tense but the latter as the perfect: Abraham was dying, and he died; that is, he was struggling with death and was at the point of death; then he died and passed over into eternal life.

These facts are related by Moses so carefully for our comfort, in order that we may know that Abraham departed this life in the manner of other human beings and that he did not have any particular advantage over others but underwent the death that is common to all men. Since this is said about those most excellent and most saintly men, we, too, should bear calmly the common lot of mortals and should prepare ourselves with the same patience, faith, and hope of a better life for our departure from the troubles of the present life and for our future immortality.

Now, therefore, we have buried the saintly patriarch Abraham, and it is most beneficial that his memory be in honor and remain in the church on account of the promise concerning the coming Seed — the promise which was repeated and explained — and on account of the faith of Abraham himself and the various most excellent examples of his very many virtues. And may Christ — the Son of God, who sits at the right hand of the Father and gives gifts to men (Eph. 4:8) that they may gather and preserve a church for Him — may Christ grant that we may be able to remember gratefully, to follow, and to imitate all these. To Him be praise and honor with the Father and the Holy Spirit forever. Amen.[19]

Up to this point we have expounded three books of Genesis as we divided it above.[20] The first presents the account of Adam, our first parent. The second praises Noah, the preacher of righteousness, and tells about the horrible punishment of the Flood, by which the original world was destroyed. Noah alone, together with his family, was saved. The third is devoted to Abraham, whose history is memorable above all because of the repeated promise concerning the Seed who would bless all nations, and because of various examples of faith and other virtues. And surely if someone thinks this over carefully, he will understand that it is a great and indescribable kindness of God that the accounts of such great men have been related in the Holy Scriptures and in records and have been preserved to this day. For the writings of the heathen have no knowledge at all of these accounts. The church alone enjoys this blessing and has the sure knowledge and divine evidence about the true beginnings and the wonderful dissemination of the doctrine which the church itself preserves, which in the beginning God gave with His own voice to our first parents, and the profession and

---

[19] In the original Wittenberg edition this was the end of the second volume (Nürnberg, 1550).

[20] On these divisions of Genesis cf. *Luther's Works*, 2, p. 3.

evidences of which He wanted to exist in that entire succession of fathers.

Therefore God's voice from time to time repeats and renews the promise which in the beginning was heard in Paradise and later on was repeated and elucidated to Abraham. Nevertheless, God speaks less frequently with Isaac and Jacob than he did with Abraham; for they knew that it was necessary for them to keep His promise and Abraham's faith in mind. Yet as often as the faith of the most saintly patriarchs is in danger in their trials, God encourages and strengthens them again, in order that they may not succumb in the perils and difficulties they encounter. For we shall see astonishing conflicts and very severe tribulations in the life of both patriarchs — conflicts and tribulations through which they are led and preserved by God without any human help.

Irreligious people have no understanding of these matters, and when they read that Isaac or Jacob roamed about like vagabonds without fixed abodes, that they were men in private life, and that they busied themselves with household and mental activities, they laugh inordinately at these matters and give vent to contempt. For in keeping with the judgment, the wisdom, or the diligence of reason, they see no extraordinary or heroic accomplishment at all like the many things they read about with admiration in the historical accounts of the heathen. But they disdain these accounts of the fathers because they do not see the true adornments of these stories. They do not see the outstanding gift of the Word of God. Nor do they see the faith, the prayer, and the patience in misfortunes through which the saints overcame the world and the snares of Satan. These conflicts and victories surpass to the highest degree all the deeds and triumphs of all heroes.

Therefore he who wants to read about these matters with profit should be convinced that Holy Scripture is divine wisdom, not the wisdom of men. Then he will feel his heart being kindled by a marvelous love and desire for the things Scripture contains. For it is a well of such a kind that the more one draws and drinks from it, the more one thirsts for it, as Ecclesiasticus says (24:21, 20): "Those who eat me will hunger for more, and those who drink me will thirst for more. For my spirit is sweeter than honey, and my inheritance sweeter than the honeycomb"; for in that book are treated "things into which angels long to look," as 1 Peter 1:12 states.

But these things are hidden from the eyes of those who are wise according to the flesh; they are manifest only to the spirit.

At this point we shall begin the fourth book; for even though the Hebrews joined this little section about Ishmael and Isaac to the history of Abraham, it is readily apparent that after Ishmael and Isaac had buried their father Abraham, Moses then wanted to begin a new book about the patriarch Isaac.

The Second Part of Chapter Twenty-Five

11. *After the death of Abraham, God blessed Isaac his son. And Isaac dwelt at Beer-lahai-roi.*

Moses begins a brief narrative about Isaac. He says that God blessed Isaac after the death of his father. But he soon breaks off, and in few words he completes what there is still to say about Ishmael. But he does not speak of the blessing until the proper time for this has come. For it was delayed 20 years, during which Isaac lived with his wife Rebecca without offspring. Nor was he able to become a father through his natural powers, but he obtained progeny from God through his entreaties and his humble prayer.

But this is an amazing situation if you compare it with what precedes. The servant made use of a great display when he obtained the girl for Isaac, and by divine dispensation Isaac was united with her in such great hope and expectation that it seemed that she would be the mother of countless sons. For why would Isaac not entertain this hope when his wife was led to him by God's predestination, by a most saintly father, by a most faithful helper, and finally with the assistance of an angel? Nevertheless, he has a childless Rebecca for 20 years. Furthermore, his father was still living, and undoubtedly both sighed and prayed anxiously for offspring. And I am not sure whether this was not the reason why Abraham married Keturah, since he saw that in Isaac's case the seed was being delayed. But I shall make no positive statement. Those men, who were so saintly and were trained by various trials, were accustomed by long experience to wait for the hand of the Lord. They have been presented to us by God as an example of the true worship of God, which consists mainly and really, not in outward sacrifices or works but in faith, hope, and love of God.

Reason dreams that God has to be worshiped and appeased with physical sacrifices or other exercises devised by men. But the examples of the fathers show that the foremost and best worship is to wait for God. And this is the real benefit and the most appropriate exercise of faith. For faith first carries us away into things that are invisible when it points out that things that are not apparent to the eye must be accepted. This we can somehow bear and put up with. The heart, however, is not only led into what is invisible; but it is also kept in suspense and is put off for a long time, just as Abraham, as has been stated above, waited for 25 years before a son was born to him, and Isaac is without offspring for 20 years. But the third and by far the most serious thing is experienced when delay and postponement are followed by a disposition to the opposite effect. It is then that he who is able to endure and wait, to hope for the things that are being delayed, and to be pleased with what is contrary, will eventually learn from experience that God is truthful and keeps His promises.

But these are not works of the flesh, of human reason, or of monks and hypocrites, for whom every delay is too long and irksome. For they desire to get at once what they are asking for. They trust God only with regard to things that are at hand, not with regard to those things for which one still waits with uncertainty. But God wants His promises to be invisible and contradictory, in order that we may be put to the test and exercised, and may learn that waiting is true worship and is most pleasing to God. Consequently, those well-known admonitions in the psalms are so common, such as "Wait for the Lord; be strong" (27:14), etc. And the prophets constantly impress the same thing: "Wait, believe." But these words are laughed at by the irreligious. Thus their mockery is mentioned in Is. 28:13: "Command, command again; wait, wait again; here a little, there a little." In this way they derided the doctrine and the comforts pertaining to faith and patience as vain and uncertain. Nevertheless, it is certain that when we begin to pray and to be confident, at that very time that which is asked for or promised is actually and immediately prepared and at hand, in accord with the statement (Is. 65:24): "Before they call, I will answer; while they are yet speaking, I will hear."

This is indeed most certain and true. But when the human heart is in a trial and in danger, it finds it difficult to be satisfied with this comfort; for it is in the habit of constantly torturing itself and complaining: "What will happen? When will it happen? Where will it happen?" Therefore my answer is: "Wait, wait." But if the waiting continues to be prolonged and the heart again asks when it will finally happen, you should say: "I have no other advice to give than that you bear it and continue to wait one, two, or three years. He will surely come and will not tarry."

For this is true, and it is customary for God to tarry, to delay and defer His help, but in such a way that He comes when it is necessary, and comes quickly, as is evident in the wonderful deliverance of the people of Israel when they were led out of Egypt. The people had waited for a long time while they were oppressed by burdensome servitude and while the Lord tarried. But after they had been brought into the utmost danger — into danger involving life and death — and the prospect of immediate destruction was apparent on one side and on the other, the Lord then said to Moses (Ex. 14:15): "Why do you cry this way?" And suddenly the deliverance and the great deeds of the Lord are shown. But as long as an extreme need and a difficulty beyond human counsel are not insistent in their demands, He delays His action and help.

These very noble examples are presented to us in the saintly men in order that we may learn that the main and spiritual worship of God does not consist in building temples and proliferating ceremonies. All these are childish amusements through which God attracts and invites us to Himself, as He used to exercise the Jews by means of various rites and by a kind of pedagogy, as it were. But the worship of the fathers is a waiting. Thus Job says: "Though He slays me, yet will I trust in Him." And below (Gen. 32:26 ff.), when Jacob wrestles with the angel, he firmly and with a steadfast heart holds fast to the promise; but it is delayed, and his faith is shaken in a variety of ways. Nevertheless, his sentiment is this: "I believe that the promise is true. If it is not fulfilled at once, I nevertheless have hope. Even if He wrestles with me, I shall nevertheless love Him." Sacrifices of this kind give off a very pleasant odor in the sight of God, and they eventually gladden the heart of man with lasting happiness and joy. On the other hand, those who lose courage because of despair and fall away deprive themselves of eternal welfare, as Sirach says (Ecclus. 2:16): "Woe to those who have lost patience." But he who endures and retains his trust and expectation overcomes and triumphs. Thus Noah waited 120 years and meanwhile endured the jibes and the ridicule of the ungodly. Eventually, however, the entire world was submerged; but he himself and his house were miraculously preserved, and he became a father of righteousness.

Consequently, God must be worshiped with faith, hope, and love. Outward ceremonies are merely exercises for the unlearned by means of which they are accustomed to the far loftier duties of godliness, just as infants are first nourished with milk and softer food. But we who govern and teach others should learn that the true worship of God does not consist in sacrificing cattle, etc., but in holding fast to His promise and believing that it is true and unfailing. This trust is followed by the hope which reminds me that I should wait and that I have a gracious God. But if I endure in trouble, then Pharaoh and his troops are plunged into the deep, and the way out I have hoped for is opened to me.

Accordingly, Moses breaks off the narrative he had begun concerning the blessing of Isaac. For when he says that God blessed Isaac, one must understand this in faith and hope, since so far the opposite was evident, and Isaac was waiting for offspring during the entire 20 years. Indeed, the vigor of his age, of his nature, and of his strength was not lacking. Rebecca was a beautiful young girl. Because of her age she was able to be fruitful and to bear children. Nevertheless, the promise continued to be delayed; it remained invisible until they were almost 60 years old and definite danger of infertility was now threatening. Then Isaac undoubtedly recalled the anxiety of his own parents in the same danger of infertility and thought: "Behold, my Rebecca and I are experiencing the same trial and misfortune that previously afflicted my parents Abraham and Sarah, because everything seems to be opposed to and in conflict with the promise." Nevertheless, he decided that he should cling to it firmly, in accordance with his father's example. But this happens in order that God may call into existence the things that do not exist (Rom. 4:17). Thus today the Turk and the pope are raging against us with inhuman hatred and ferocity. Inside, however their consciences are disturbed in various ways; they are wrestling with fear, a lack of confidence, and the terrors of sin. Against all this, of course, we have most powerful consolations: the promise of the Word, Baptism, and the Eucharist, which should be apprehended and held fast with strong faith. But I do not see the forgiveness of sins, eternal salvation, and life. Yet I believe, and I am sustained by hope. And if faith is shaken and weakened either by temptation or by a fall and human frailty, nevertheless I hold fast to the Keys and cling to the promise of God, even if heaven falls. This is worshiping God and fulfilling the First Commandment, the usefulness of which is not perceived until there are trials, when the promise is invisible. I am put off for a long time, and eventually the situation is turned into the opposite.

The devil operates with another rule — a rule that is the opposite of this one. For he is in the habit of being at hand immediately when his priests and prophets want him, and he does not delay what they ask for. Thus sudden storms and thunderclaps are frequently caused by sorcerers.[21] In this manner the devil deludes and ensnares people. Consequently, they serve him gladly, because he helps and listens to them promptly; and, what is worse, it is decided that this is done by God. Therefore this difference in the ways in which God and Satan operate should be carefully noted. God wants us to wait, as Ps. 130:5 says: "My soul waits, and in His Word I hope." If you want to serve God, you must believe things that are invisible, hope for things that are delayed, and love God — even if He shows Himself unfriendly and opposed to you — and thus persevere until the end. This is what Moses means when he calls giving a wife to Isaac and not giving children a blessing. Isaac prayed for a wife in order to beget offspring. He got his wish, but he waits for 20 years without offspring, as his father Abraham waited just as many years until Ishmael was born. Yet this was not the promised offspring, and the son from Sarah had to be hoped for and waited for much longer.

The Well of the Living and the Seeing has been spoken of above.[22] When Hagar fled from her mistress Sarah, she wandered about in the wilderness of Beer-sheba toward Egypt, and there she gave the name to the well, in order that among all succeeding generations Hagar might be praised as an outstanding lady and matron, from whom the well had received its name; for she said (Gen. 16:13): "Surely, here I have seen the back parts of Him who sees me." Isaac regarded this as conferring glory upon himself, even though Hagar was his stepmother; and for this reason he dwelt near the Well of the Living and the Seeing. But now Moses will bring the account of Ishmael to a conclusion.

---

[21] This idea is the source of a name Luther uses for a witch, *wetermecherin* (*Luther's Works*, 37, p. 210).

[22] Cf. *Luther's Works*, 3, pp. 69—74.

12. *These are the descendants of Ishmael, Abraham's son, whom Hagar the Egyptian, Sarah's maid, bore to Abraham.*

13. *These are the names of the sons of Ishmael, named in the order of their birth: Nebaioth, the first-born of Ishmael; and Kedar, Adbeel, Mibsam,*

14. *Mishma, Dumah, Massa,*

15. *Hadad, Tema, Jetur, Naphish, and Kedemah.*

16. *These are the sons of Ishmael, and these are their names, by their villages and by their encampments, twelve princes according to their tribes.*

Moses' description of Ishmael is altogether different from the one he gives of Isaac, of whom he said that God blessed him. Yet he did not express the blessing. But above (Gen. 21:11 ff.) we heard the very sad decision concerning Ishmael, namely, that in spite of the grief and the reluctance of his father he was cast out of the house, not only in accord with his mother's will but also in accord with the will of God, and was called an offspring of the flesh and not of the promise. These are very hard and bitter facts. But in this passage he is being praised not only because of the carnal blessing but also because of the blessing that is spiritual. In the carnal blessing, of course, he was superior to his brother Isaac. This situation made the trial and anxiety of Isaac worse. For as yet he has no offspring. For many years he has been waiting for the blessing, but sons are not born to him until he is 80 years old. Meanwhile 12 princes are bestowed on Ishmael long before Isaac begets children. Yet neither Isaac nor Abraham begot so many princes. But Ishmael, who is the brother born of a slave woman, is honored by a blessing so great and glorious that in a short time he begets 12 princes, and both Abraham and Isaac saw that all these were living and flourishing. For Ishmael died 48 years after Abraham, and the sons of Ishmael developed at once into great men and princes before the blessing promised to Abraham and Isaac even began.

This was surely a severe trial for faith, hope, and love. Would these things not try a heart, no matter how godly and saintly it might be? Above all, however, they try the heart of Isaac, who believed God and heard himself preferred to all nations and to his brother Ishmael.

For it was stated: "In Isaac, not in Ishmael, shall your Seed be named —
the Seed in whom the entire world will be blessed." God also blessed
Ishmael when He said (Gen. 17:20): "He will become a great nation
and will be the father of 12 princes." But this is nothing in comparison
with the promised Seed. Here, however, everything seems to be
changed and turned around. Isaac, who has the true promise, is put
after Ishmael; and although the latter has only a carnal promise, he
goes very far ahead and becomes a lord of lords. He has 12 princes,
while Isaac lives alone and without offspring at Beer-sheba like a block
of wood and a log. Consequently, he thought: "O God, is this Thy
promise? Is this Thy truth?" Thoughts of this kind were very sharp
incentives for doubt and mistrust. Thus Job's wife reproaches her
husband. "Where is your godliness now?" she asks. "Do you still
hold fast your integrity? Curse God, and die." (Job 2:9.) Surely
the same thing could have been said to Isaac. For he who was previously despised and cast out of the house gets a far richer blessing
from God than either Isaac or Jacob obtained.

Therefore these are strange accounts and the cause of very great
offenses to carnal-minded people; for all the works of God are in
conflict with His promise, which nevertheless remains completely
true and unshaken. But what offends is the fact that it is invisible,
delayed, and turned into its opposite.

The marvelous counsels of God in governing His saints must be
learned, and the hearts of the godly must become accustomed to
them. When you have a promise of God, it will happen that the
more you are loved by God, the more you will have it hidden, delayed, and turned into its opposite. For if God did not love you so
exceedingly, He would not play with you in this manner; that is, He
would not delay His promise and help and turn it into its opposite.
These are the surest signs of a heart that is fatherly and burns with
love for you. Thus a father according to the flesh who loves his son
plays with him and promises him a small present, but he defers and
pretends that he will refuse to do what he has promised. He does
this because [23] he loves his son very much and wants to give richly,
provided that his son perseveres and swallows and overcomes the
delay. In this way God plays with us too. But we grumble and are
displeased at a delay, no matter how short it is. What is being prom-

[23] We have read *quia* with the Erlangen editors rather than *qui* in the Weimar text.

ised us we want to get either now or in another manner and in another way, whatever that way may be. Therefore the examples of the fathers teach us what the true forms of worship are, namely, genuine faith, perfect hope, and unwavering love. These virtues lead us to the realization that God is present and beneficent, no matter how He seems to be against us.

Besides, it is apparent that Ishmael was a great theologian who carefully unfolded the force and grandeur of the promises, which are certainly great and magnificent; and it is apparent above all that his mother Hagar was worthy of hearing the angel call her back to her mistress Sarah. All this he published abroad and praised richly. Thus any nation or house wants to be superior to the rest and to be the sole ruler of the world but despises the rest in comparison with itself. Therefore Ishmael carefully impressed the promises made to him and was able to say: "I see that the Lord is with me and He has blessed me even spiritually." At the same time he also retained and enriched the outward worship he saw in his father's house, and through ceremonies of that kind some of his domestics and sons came to the knowledge of godliness, just as many of the family and descendants of Cain were joined to the true church of Adam, and in our day very many are gathered into our little church.

In the same way many from the house of Ishmael joined the church in the house of Abraham, especially Ishmael himself, who, I believe, after repenting, returned and became a member of the true church — not from the flesh but from the spirit, because according to the flesh he was rejected. But in the text he is also praised spiritually. Furthermore, Moses has related above (v. 9) that he buried his father Abraham with reverence. This proves that he was not estranged from the church in the house of Isaac. Therefore I hold that he was a good and godly man, even though he was a warrior. He also gave striking names to his sons. For קֵדָר means "sad," "gloomy," "morose" — like the monks — as one about to die in sorrow; and perhaps the saintly man was in some sorrow when he gave this name to his son. At the same time it also denotes "homage" or "one to whom homage is paid."

I am passing over the nonsense of the Jews concerning these names.[24] To me it seems that one can conclude from this that Ishmael carefully preached the God of Abraham and accustomed his domestics

[24] Cf. Lyra *ad* Gen. 25:12-16.

to the true worship which he himself had previously seen. But because it usually happens that the true worship produces superstition, so his descendants, after they had lost the true forms of worship, retained only some outward show and hypocrisy. For when the First Commandment has been discarded, useless chaff and husks remain. Thus when people saw at first that Abraham offered sacrifices in one way or another, blessed, and gave thanks, they adopted that outward worship, but without the First Commandment. Thus people become apes of their fathers, because they imitate outward works and disregard faith.

This is the origin of all forms of idolatry. The heathen saw that Abraham and the other fathers worshiped the Creator of the most beautiful light with their faces turned toward the rising sun. This they imitated. But they retained only the shell. They lost the kernel.[25] Thus the sectarians receive the Word from us; but they do not do so in the proper manner, because they misuse it for vainglory and popular applause. Thus the Ishmaelites called themselves sons of God. Today they do not want to be called Hagarenes; they want to be called Saracens,[26] solely on account of the imitation and show of the outward worship and because of the physical blessing which the Arabs, who are Ishmaelites, still have, as was stated above in the promise (Gen. 16:12): "His hand against every man." They hold dominion over the world and boast that the spoils and booty are due them. They live on what they seize. Even though the Turks, who are Scythians, have taken possession of Arabia and are the masters there, they nevertheless retain the Arabic language, and its principal use is at the Turkish court. But before this they were never completely conquered either by the Romans or by the Persians. The Turk has humbled them. Nevertheless, they administer the rule jointly. Accordingly, Ishmael was first blessed carnally, since 12 princes were born to him. Now the spiritual blessing will follow.

17. *(These are the years of the life of Ishmael, a hundred and thirty-seven years; he breathed his last and died, and was gathered to his kindred.)*

Ishmael lived 137 years. He was born when Abraham was 86 years old, 14 years before the birth of Isaac; he died 48 years after Abra-

---

25 "I've lost the kernel and kept the shell for surety," Plautus, *The Captives*, line 655 (Paul Nixon translation).

26 Cf. p. 70, note 59.

ham. But Isaac long outlived Ishmael. Yet Ishmael saw Jacob and Esau, the sons of Isaac. This text clearly points out the spiritual blessing of Ishmael, because Moses employs the same words that he employed above in his description of Abraham's death. Not even a tittle has been changed. Consequently, he is bearing witness that Ishmael lived in the true faith and in godliness, since he states that Ishmael was gathered to the people of the saints.

גָּוַע means "to expire peacefully," when someone lies down, as Abraham did above (v. 8). When the hour of death draws near to him, he breathes his last without terrors but as the body is usually destroyed, in order that the soul may be freed from the workhouse of the body. In this manner Ishmael, too, died. The Lord granted him a saintly and peaceful end of his life. His strength left him, and by breathing his last he finally brought his life to a close and was carried into the bosom of the sainted fathers, where Abraham and the other fathers went shortly before. This is the spiritual blessing. Moreover, it is a beautiful and pleasing description of immortality when Moses says (Gen. 25:8): "He was gathered to his people." We are now living among the rude people of the world who are estranged from God and in the kingdom of the devil. But when we depart from this wretched life, we shall have a pleasant struggle and shall be gathered to our people, where there is no misfortune, no tribulation, and no affliction, but peace and rest and a quiet sleep in the Lord. But if there is another people besides the one with which we are now living, there must be a resurrection of the dead. This is most certain proof that there is a God and that the world was not created without purpose. For to live after death is not the work of man; it is the work of God.

Pliny and the Epicureans laugh at these things and do not agree that there is a passing from a turbulent kind of life to rest. For this reason the Epicureans bandy these sayings: "After death there is no pleasure," "Perish the fellow who bothers about what the future holds," "Neither fear nor wish for your last day." [27] In this manner they strengthen themselves for the purpose of despising death; and they completely remove the fear, that is, the hope of immortality. "Of what should I be afraid? Or what should I hope for?" they say. "Because there is no God, let us eat, drink, be merry, etc." But if reason were to grant that there is a departure from an afflicted people

[27] Martial, *Epigrams*, X, 47, 13; cf. *Luther's Works*, 13, p. 76, note 2.

to a people of peace, it would necessarily also have to admit that there is a life after this life; for to go to a people is not to go to nothing, especially when one speaks of going to one's own people, who had the same faith, hope, and affliction, and had the same language, to our fellow citizens and fellow countrymen, who surely are something. We do not go to enemies or to evil spirits. Indeed, we withdraw from them and are gathered to our fathers.

These are the testimonies of the fathers concerning the resurrection, immortality, and life eternal, namely, because in that place there are peoples. Consequently, it is inevitable that we live and rise again. Those who believe this Word will never be influenced by the nonsense of Epicurus. But reason neither understands nor accepts this. Indeed, what is more, it sees before its eyes that procreation takes place from nothing; yet it does not reach the conclusion that this is the work of God. I see that Isaac is born of a barren mother and of a dead womb as hard as the bones in the skull. I see no hair, no body, and no soul. Nevertheless, from the loins of Abraham and from the womb of his mother Sarah comes forth a son who has all these things. Do they not originate from nothing? Surely the semen and the womb are dead things, and more dead than a seed that falls into the soil. Therefore reason should not think that this is a natural operation, as it dreams. But it is blindness and the wickedness of the devil that we do not look at or consider these things. Therefore if we follow the lead of reason, we understand neither the future resurrection nor procreation. For he who does not believe the resurrection of the dead does not believe or perceive the miracle of procreation either, namely, that a human being is born from a human being, a beast from a beast.

Indeed, the entire world is full of evidences of resurrection.[28] From a tree and its very hard wood springs forth a most beautiful little flower; leaves, branches, and most delightful fruits are produced. But because this is a frequent and common occurrence, it becomes commonplace. So great is the stupor of human minds that if Lazarus were raised daily, unbelievers would nevertheless not be affected at all. Yet it does not follow from this that one should not hope for another kind of life — a life that is better and is blessed. But the experience and manifestation of that eternal joy are delayed until the hostile people pass away and our people remain — the people

---

[28] Cf. *Luther's Works*, 1, Introduction, pp. x—xii.

who, together with us, have believed the resurrection of the dead. On account of this testimony of Holy Scripture concerning Ishmael, therefore, we make him a saint and a great patriarch, although his descendants degenerated and were not like their father.

18. *They dwelt from Havilah to Shur, which is opposite Egypt in the direction of Assyria; he died in the presence of all his brothers.*

Even today, or at least at the time of Jerome, the children of Ishmael had possession of these places.[29] Nebaioth, the first-born, occupied a large part of Arabia, but not all of it. From him the region called Nabatea got its name. It is celebrated in the books of Greek and Latin writers especially for the one reason that among the inhabitants of that nation ingratitude toward parents and teachers was punishable by death.[30] This outstanding discipline and theology existed in that region. With such severity did those nations punish what many are permitted to do with impunity today.

The other part of Arabia is Kedar. It is no less celebrated and is the name of all Arabia Petraea. The Edomites appropriated part of it. In Ps. 120:5 we read: "Woe is me, that I dwell among the tents of Kedar!" That is, I am a foreigner among the Muscovites and the Tartars. The stretch from Havilah to Shur is in Arabia, or is the desert between Egypt and the Holy Land. But of Shur it is said that it faces Egypt because it has a common boundary with Egypt. Accordingly, the children of Ishmael inhabited that region from the Red Sea as far as the Euphrates. They had possession of almost the whole of Arabia except that part which the Idumaeans occupied.

About the last clause — "he died in the presence of all his brothers" — the expounders argue in various ways.[31] The usual explanation holds that Ishmael died in the presence of his brothers, that is, his sons, who, having been summoned by their father, assembled to hear and comfort their father, so that he expired in the sight and presence of his brothers. It is my own opinion — although I shall make no positive statement — that Moses is not speaking about

[29] Jerome, *Liber hebraicarum quaestionum in Genesin, Patrologia, Series Latina,* XXIII, 1027: "until this very day."

[30] Cf. Josephus, *The Antiquities of the Jews,* Book XII, par. 335; Book XIII, par. 11; Pliny, *Natural History,* Book V, par. 65; Book VI, par. 144, 157; Book XII, par. 73; Ovid, *Metamorphoses,* Book I, line 61.

[31] Cf. Lyra *ad* Gen. 25:18.

Ishmael personally, because Ishmael had already died. Furthermore, he did not say previously that *he* dwelt, but that *they* dwelt — namely, the 12 sons — in that stretch from the Red Sea toward Egypt. Or if you should say that after Ishmael died, he dwelt, this would be understood of his descendants, just as below there is a similar expression, namely, that Jacob went down into Egypt and went up from [32] Egypt. And in Ps. 114:2 we read: "Judah became his sanctuary." In those instances proper nouns become appellatives and names of nations. This is common in Holy Scripture. Therefore I think that the meaning is the same as in the earlier passage (Gen. 16:12): "He shall dwell over against all his kinsmen." This is expressed in our passage by "he died," or "he fell down," or "he pitched his tent." That is, after their father had died and had left his testament, in which he urged the sons and brothers to love and worship God, they raged cruelly after the fashion of wild beasts, with violence and the sword and occupied the land. They became נְפִלִים, as is stated elsewhere (Num. 13:33).

19. *These are the descendants of Isaac, Abraham's son: Abraham was the father of Isaac,*

20. *and Isaac was forty years old when he took to wife Rebecca, the daughter of Bethuel the Aramean of Paddan-aram, the sister of Laban the Aramean.*

I have frequently pointed out — and it must be impressed frequently — that in the accounts of the fathers it is most delightful to see how they are described as true human beings, weak and altogether like us. On the other hand, under that human weakness there were most saintly angels and sons of God. For, what is most surprising, in the kind of life involving the management of a household they had absolutely no unusual or special semblance of saintliness; and when the flesh, that is, the wise men of this world and the monks, sees this weakness, it is greatly offended and has profound contempt for the saintly patriarchs. Thus Augustine confesses about himself that he laughed at the accounts of Isaac and the other patriarchs when he was still a Manichean, because he kept in mind nothing else than that most ordinary kind of life, namely, having a wife, begetting children, having a few sheep and cattle, and living with one's fellow

---

[32] Reading *ex Aegypto* rather than *in Aegypto*.

citizens and neighbors.[33] What could one learn from this that is uncommon or unique? Or why are these seemingly unimportant and unprofitable facts read and presented?

It is indeed a misfortune of the flesh that [34] in this manner it must remain attached to the common weakness in respect to which the fathers are like other people and must therefore be offended and find fault with the ordinary life and invent another, extraordinary kind of life, such as celibacy, monasticism, the priesthood, etc. For an ungodly person must not see the glory of God; he must see only the weak and foolish things and, if I may use this expression, the nullity of God. But he must not see the glory and majesty, the power and wisdom of God, even if they are set before his eyes. Thus here Moses relates in a very simple manner that when Isaac was 40 years old, he married a weak little woman from Mesopotamia in Syria. What is this? Do not other people contract marriages that are similar to this one or sometimes more splendid? Why, then, do we read about these things? I answer that the flesh is permitted to see the human nature and weakness in the saints but by no means to see the divine nature and the saintliness of the angels, in order that it may be offended and seem to have found a reason for inventing new forms of worship in which to put saintliness.

Moreover, it is not without purpose and beside the point when Holy Scripture states that Isaac married Rebecca when he was 40 years old. For it points out that he did not take a wife in the well-known first passion of youth but stood firm for a considerable time in his battle against and victory over the flesh and the devil. For the accounts and the experience of individuals attest how great the impatience of lust is in youth, when the urgent sensation of the flesh begins and the one sex has an ardent desire for the other. This is a malady common to the entire human race, and those who do not resist its first flames and do not suppose that there is something for them to endure, plunge into fornication, adultery, and horrible lusts; or if they take wives rashly and ill-advisedly, they involve themselves in perpetual torture. Accordingly, Isaac endured that conflict and contended most valiantly with the flame and his flesh, because he was a true and complete human being just as we are. Moreover, our nature has been created in such a way that it feels the passions

---

[33] Augustine, *Confessions*, Book III, chs. 5, 6, pars. 9, 10.

[34] Reading *ut* rather than *et*.

of the flesh at about the twentieth year. To endure and overcome those passions up to the fortieth year is surely a heavy and difficult burden. In this last age our young people refuse to assume this burden; they are unwilling to have patience for a moderate period of time. Therefore if they take wives during those first manifestations of passion, the devil, who earlier inflamed them with lust, later on cools them down with a breath to the opposite effect and causes them to go to extremes in their hatred of the woman. Those things are truly diabolical. Therefore the heart should first be instructed by the examples of the fathers, in order that it may be able to undertake and keep up that first battle against the flesh. The maturer age, which has arrived at the years of manhood, has its own battles — battles that are greater. During adolescence love begins to learn, just as it is described in adolescents in the works of the comic poets.[35] But the sacred accounts present examples in which the victory, and at the same time the battles against the flesh, are set forth. Thus Isaac, too, felt the flames of lust just as other adolescents do. But he was taught by his father that one must contend against these flames, first by reading Holy Scripture and praying, and then by working, being temperate, and fasting. These should be the exercises of adolescents, at least for one year or two, in order that those who are no longer able to be continent may learn nevertheless what the endurance of lust means. For this, too, is endurance and martyrdom, just as some assume several kinds of martyrdom, among which they count a rich, generous, and chaste young man.[36] Indeed, this man is surely a martyr, because he is crucified every day by the passions of his flesh.

Young people should avoid promiscuity. In order to be able to protect their chastity, they should strengthen their hearts against the raging desire of the flesh by reading and meditating on the psalms and the Word of God. If you feel the flame, take a psalm or one or two chapters of the Bible, and read. When the flame has subsided, then pray. If it is not immediately checked, you should bear it patiently and courageously for one, two, or more years and persist in prayer. But if you can no longer endure and overcome the burning desires of the flesh, ask the Lord to give you a wife with whom you may live in a pleasing manner and in true love. I myself have seen

[35] Cf., for example, Crates in The Greek Anthology, Book IX, epigram 497.

[36] Cf. Luther's Works, 23, pp. 202—204.

many people who gave free rein to their passions and fell into detestable lusts. But in the end they had to endure woeful punishments; or if on a blind impulse they were fixing their minds on marriage, they got wives who were not at all suited and obedient. This, of course, served them right.

All people should know that they have been called to war against the flesh. This is one battle. The second is against the devil. The third is against the world. Therefore one should not yield immediately to those first impulses, especially in this era, when the hope of marriage has reappeared. We did not have it in the papacy, for he who wanted to become a priest was compelled to vow perpetual celibacy. That papal tyranny has now been brought to light, and true freedom has been restored. Consequently, you should learn to pray and to wage war against the flesh. But then ask God to give you a Rebecca and not a Hagar or someone worse. For a good wife does not come by chance and without God's guidance; she is a gift and not the result of our own plan or will, as the heathen think.

Isaac was not brought up in this heathen manner. He undoubtedly did not escape the vexation and the flame of his flesh during the 40 years he lived before his marriage, for the flesh contends against the spirit no less in the household than in the government or in the church. But he obeyed his father Abraham, who instructed him to meditate on the commandments of God and by means of sacred studies to arm himself for the first battle. This is why God later on gave him Rebecca, with whom he led a quiet and peaceful life. Holy Scripture points this out in a concealed manner, and in the matter of the weakness that has been mentioned it presents Isaac to us as a most excellent example of a young man's chastity, which is important because it is a war in which young people are involved. And the chastity of Isaac includes the upbringing and instruction through which he learned to avoid bad company; and evidence is given that he was diligent, meditated, prayed, and engaged in work. Here all this is discernible in a concealed manner in those 40 years during which he lived without a wife.

Moreover, it seems to have been customary at that time for young men not to take wives before they were 40 years old, but for girls to marry when they were 10 years younger, as we saw above in the case of Sarah. I think that Rebecca, too, was 30 years old. After the Flood nearly all the fathers took wives when they were about

30 or 40 years old. Before the Flood they married later; they waited until they were 100, 80, or 90 years of age. After the Flood God accelerated the multiplication of the human race. Therefore the time was shortened, so that men married when they were 40 years old, and the women when they were 30. Consequently, that age was far better and far more excellent than ours. We think that this evil is mitigated by satisfying lust through acts of fornication and adultery, but in this way human beings degenerate altogether into beasts and become unsuited for all good works. If they rush into marriage rashly and without the definite procedure prescribed by God, they do not take wives but incur punishment and perpetual annoyance, because they were without prayer and the fear of God. God forbids this when He says (Ex. 20:7): "You shall not take the name of the Lord your God in vain," and also (Ps. 50:15): "Call upon Me in the day of trouble."

"But," someone will say, "such delaying is very annoying and unbearable." Right indeed. This is why I stated above that it is on a par with the other exercises in patience by the saints, like the suffering and annoyance of fasting, imprisonment, cold, sicknesses, and tortures. In the same way lust is a serious sickness and burden. But one must resist it and fight against it. Thus later on, when you hold a position in the government, you will be annoyed by other difficulties, such as thefts, robberies, and various kinds of human wickedness. In the church you will have to contend with heretics and with the devil, who assails faith, hope, and the love of God. But you have the Word; you have Holy Scripture, your studies, exercises, and labors. From these your faith will grow and be strengthened. Thus lust, too, when it has been overcome by prayer, will serve to increase faith and prayer. Therefore in these seemingly useless words Holy Scripture presents an outstanding example of Isaac's chastity and of the very fine discipline that existed in the church and in the house of Abraham.

21. *And Isaac prayed to the Lord for his wife, because she was barren; and the Lord granted his prayer, and Rebecca, his wife, conceived.*

This is another trial. After the flame of lust has ceased and Isaac has become a husband and has had Rebecca as his wife for 20 years (for so long does God delay the promise in which He had promised his father Abraham: "Through Isaac shall your descendants be named"), another affliction now follows, and indeed one that is far more burdensome than the previous trial. The victor over lust overcame the devil by his chastity up to the time of his marriage. In the marriage state he longs for offspring, in accordance with the promise; and he certainly has no slight hope, since he knows that his wife was prepared for him and brought to him in accordance with God's plan. But Rebecca does not bear a child; nor does she have a promise that she will be a mother, just as Sarah, too, did not have a promise at first. This undoubtedly troubled his heart, and to this trial were added fear of and worry about perpetual barrenness, which they considered to be a curse. For the fathers laid very great stress on this statement (Gen. 1:28): "Be fruitful and multiply." They felt that a special blessing of God rested on this statement; and because they did not multiply, they supposed that they were cursed and under God's wrath.

Therefore one can easily conclude how severely Rebecca was tortured and how great Isaac's grief was when he saw that his wife almost despaired of having offspring; for at that time she was about 50 years old. Then she thought: "Now I shall be exhausted and unable to bear children." Isaac still had some hope. If Rebecca did not bear a child, he would take another wife, just as his father Abraham had done.

Rebecca was deprived of this hope, and she anxiously counted every year and day that had elapsed since she had married Isaac. She wondered whether her years and her age still left her any hope. Therefore this was a far more burdensome trial than the earlier one, for poor Rebecca suspects that she is numbered among those women who have been deprived of the blessing of God. What, then, shall she do, since she sees that she has so anxiously desired offspring in vain? She has been barren for 20 years, and now she is becoming a woman as good as dead; for the year and the time when her womb would be dead were at hand. She undoubtedly asked her husband to pray for her. This one last help she found. She does not want to give him another wife and deprive herself of the glory of motherhood, as Sarah had given her maid Hagar to her husband (Gen. 16:3). Therefore Moses says: "And Isaac prayed to the Lord for his wife." [37]

But once again the flesh will be offended and will look down on this as ordinary and trivial. For of what importance is it that a hus-

---

[37] We have used italics where the original has capitals.

band prays for his barren wife? After all, there are many women who become pregnant without prayer, yes, even contrary to the wish and will of many of them who do not desire to have offspring. But observe that most excellent perseverance, endurance, and expectancy of faith which the flesh does not perceive, and you will find something you will marvel at. For Rebecca could not think about the promise without grief and deep emotion — the promise that descendants should be born from Isaac. While all other women, who neither prayed nor had a promise from God, had been blessed, she alone was living without any hope of offspring and was passing the time of her marriage in great sorrow and tears. Nevertheless, she keeps her faith and with great perseverance urges her husband to intercede for her with the Lord.

If one of us is distressed for so many years by the same kind of affliction or by other misfortunes, by diseases, by exile, and by imprisonment, and does not murmur and does not cast aside his endurance but perseveres firmly in faith and hope, he will see what Rebecca suffered. The flesh considers only the outward things and the things that pertain to the management of the home, namely, that she is engaged in domestic and daily tasks and sleeps with her husband. But it does not see that she has been patient, has sighed, and has wept throughout those entire 20 years; for those most excellent virtues, such as patience, faith, and waiting when the promise of God is delayed, are hidden from the eyes of the world. The flesh gives thought and marvels when it sees a monk in a gray garment, girt with a rope, refraining from eating meat, and yet having none of the faith, the endurance, the affliction, and the things that Rebecca has. Why? Because the world is blind.

But we should accustom ourselves to those conflicts which from time to time, one after another, are usually in store for the godly; and we should learn to believe and persevere, in order that we may not waver and abandon the promise but may be strong and fight against impatience and the fiery darts of the devil (Eph. 6:16), who impels our hearts to grumble and to be angry with God in order that he may destroy our faith and endurance in misfortunes. Let us set before ourselves the example of Isaac and Rebecca. Both waited 20 years, and meanwhile they saw the happiness and the fecundity of the ungodly, who ridiculed them and assailed them with abuse. They said: "Why did he marry that woman and woo a foreigner?

Why did he not marry some respectable girl of our own families? Rebecca is done for and is rejected by God." She undoubtedly heard this sort of abuse, not without great grief in her heart and not without tears, just as Sarah deplored her barrenness and as Hannah mourns pitiably for the same reason (1 Sam. 1:11). Nevertheless she has overcome through patience and the strength of her faith.

We should praise these virtues, and in the accounts of the fathers we should carefully ponder those examples of patience. For this battle against the promise of God is very difficult. Through it ill will, murmuring, and impatience with God's delaying are overcome. This is characteristic of God, and He is very correctly called "the Expected One." But we are called "the expectant ones." These designations should be perpetually observed by our eyes and hearts, in order that we may learn to crush the first impulses, lest we immediately murmur if He delays for one or two or more years what we are looking for. But let us remember that we must persevere and boldly overcome everything that puts our patience to the test, just as Rebecca learned to disdain the insults of other women and of her own domestics until eventually she prevailed over God through her own prayers and those of her husband.

The Hebrew verb עָתַר is very emphatic; for it is a special verb of praying and means "to pray importunately and beyond measure," in such a way that by knocking and importuning in a vexatious manner we annoy God. We call it "to prevail upon." First one must ask; in the second place, one must seek; in the third place, one must knock (Matt. 7:7). If we have cried: "Lord, God, help me in this misfortune; deliver me from this evil or from another one," and immediate deliverance does not follow, then one should look for all the examples of the fathers. "Look, O heavenly Father, how Thou hast aided Thy people at all times." If He still delays, you should nevertheless not stop praying but should say: "I shall not cease, and I shall not stop knocking; but I shall cry out and knock until the end of my life." Rebecca exhorted her husband in this manner: "Dear Isaac, do not become weary, and do not give up." And Isaac saw her tears and sighs, and he prevailed upon the Lord.

Consequently, one should learn from this that when we pray, we are most certainly being heard, just as so far the church has certainly procured peace through prayer and has restrained the Turk together with the pope. Only let us be on our guard lest after we have once begun to pray, we immediately grow weary. But let us seek and let

[W, XLIII, 381]

us cast all our care, misfortune, and affliction on God (1 Peter 5:7) and set before Him the examples of every kind of deliverance. Finally let us knock at the door with confidence and with incessant raps. Then we shall experience what James says (5:16): "The prayer of a righteous man has great power"; for it penetrates heaven and earth. God can no longer endure our cries, as is stated in Luke 18:5 about the unjust judge and the widow. But one should not pray only one hour. No, one must cry out and knock. Then you will compel Him to come. Thus I fully believe that if we devote ourselves to prayer earnestly and fervently, we shall prevail upon God to make the Last Day come.

In the same way Rebecca took refuge in earnest and persistent prayer and sighed anxiously night and day. Isaac, too, prayed for her and placed before God nothing else than that one trouble, namely, his wife's barrenness. We should learn from this that all our troubles, even those that are physical, should be placed before God, but above all the spiritual needs. Isaac prayed in this way: "If it means the hallowing of Thy name, and if it tends to preserve Thy kingdom, give Rebecca offspring." Where a promise is lacking, as Rebecca lacked it, prayer should supply this and should come to the rescue. But it is a difficult thing and requires great exertion. It is far more difficult than the preaching of the Word or other duties in the church. When we teach, we experience more than we do; for God speaks through us, and it is a work of God. But to pray is a most difficult work. Therefore it is also very rare.

Hence it is something great for Isaac to have the courage to lift up his eyes and hands to the Divine Majesty and to beg, seek, and knock; for it is something very great to speak with God. It is also something great when God speaks with us. But this is more difficult; for our weakness and unworthiness come along and draw us back, so that we think: "Who am I that I should have the courage to lift up my eyes and raise my hands to the Divine Majesty, where the angels are and at whose nod the entire world trembles? Shall I, wretched little man that I am, say to Him: 'This is what I want, and I beg Thee to give it to me?'" The great crowd of the monks and the priests has no knowledge of this; nor do they know what praying is, although some of the godly overcome these thoughts more easily. But really efficacious and powerful prayers, which must penetrate the clouds, are certainly difficult. For I, who am ashes, dust, and full of sins, am addressing the living, eternal, and true God. Therefore it is no wonder that he who prays trembles and shrinks back. Thus long ago, when I was still a monk and for the first time read these words in the Canon of the Mass: "Thou, therefore, most merciful Father," and also: "We offer to Thee, the living, the true, and the eternal God," I used to be completely stunned, and I shuddered at those words. For I used to think: "With what impudence I am addressing so great a Majesty, when everybody should be terrified when looking at or conversing with some prince or king!" [38]

But faith, which relies on the mercy and the Word of God, overcomes and prevails over that fear, just as it conquered it in Isaac, who despaired of all human help; for no one is able to help his barren wife. Therefore he takes heart and directs a fervent and powerful prayer to God. Such outstanding boldness and greatness of faith the flesh does not see. But this is written for our sakes, in order that we may be bold and confident, and may learn to pray; for the prayers of believers cannot be in vain. Thus Isaac does not pray in vain either; but, just as Moses says: "And the Lord granted his prayer," so the Lord will not disregard our sighs and cries either. Only let us be stirred up to pray.

At this point the Jews raise a question about the word נֹכַח. To the Jews it really means "straightforward" or "directly," *stracks für sich,* as in Is. 57:2: "Who walks נְכֹחוֹ," that is who has turned aside neither to the left nor to the right. Accordingly, the Jews maintain that Isaac prayed directly in front of his wife.[39] If it was the common custom to pray in this manner, Rebecca stood directly before him or fell down on her knees, and he placed his hands on her as she wept and sighed. And in this manner they implored the Lord together. If there had been such a rite of praying, the proper meaning of the word could be retained; but if it was not an accepted custom, it has to be explained in a spiritual manner, namely, that he prayed with his whole heart and with concentration on his wife's misfortune, just as when I pray for someone, I present him to myself in the sight of my heart and see, or think of, nothing else but look upon him alone in my heart.

[38] Luther referred to this incident of May 2, 1507, frequently, especially in his *Table Talk;* it seems to have been on his mind about this time, for he discussed it at table in the summer of 1540 (W, *Tischreden,* V, Nr. 5357).

[39] Cf. Lyra *ad* Gen. 25:21: *contra uxorem suam.*

Thus Isaac prayed while he had his wife before his eyes. In this way Moses wants to point out that it was a fervent and earnest prayer, in which he was not hesitant and did not roam about in his heart and thoughts. A prayer of this kind is praised in the case of the man who had made a bet with Bernard that he would say the Lord's Prayer without any wandering thoughts. But since they had staked a horse and, in accordance with their agreement, he was forced to confess the truth after finishing his prayer, he confessed that while he was praying, he had been concerned about the saddle and the bridle, whether these had to be added to the horse or not.[40] The prayer of the godly should not be like this, because this prayer is not spoken in a straightforward manner. Instead, the heart wanders now to the right and now to the left. But a true and fervent prayer presents the case to God and with great zeal and fervor directs its attention to this matter alone. It is not disturbed either by any presumption or by any doubt; it says: "Lord God, consider this afflicted little woman and Thy promise." It neither thinks of nor is concerned about anything else. And this is that unremitting, that is, earnest and straightforward, prayer of a righteous man of which the Epistle of James (5:16) speaks.

And Rebecca, his wife, conceived.

This passage is outstanding and noteworthy to the highest degree. Paul discusses it in an excellent manner in the Epistle to the Romans (9:10-13): "And not only so, but also when Rebecca had conceived children by one man, our forefather Isaac, though they were not yet born and had done nothing either good or bad, in order that God's purpose of election might continue, not because of works but because of His call, she was told: 'The elder will serve the younger.' As it is written: 'Jacob I loved, but Esau I hated.'"

Here indeed we shall gladly stand up before St. Paul and grant him tutorship and the honor that he alone was able to explain this passage as it deserves; for we are unable to present any other or better explanation. Nevertheless, because something has to be said, we, as imperfect pupils, want to follow the most perfect teacher. I surely would never have looked at these words in this manner. Moses says:

---

[40] Bernard speaks of impediments to praying the Lord's Prayer, but not of the wager to which Luther refers here, in his *Sermones de tempore,* VI, *Patrologia, Series Latina,* CLXXXIII, 181—183.

"Rebecca conceived." But how? Not only physically or by the strength of nature, but the saintly patriarch Isaac procured this conception through his prayer. And this is no ordinary glory for Isaac. Although so many patriarchs were still living and saw those little boys, namely, Abraham, Shem, Shelah, and Eber, yet no mention is made of the praying of all these. To Isaac alone, as the heir of the promise, the glory is assigned that he prayed; that is, that he performed a priestly duty by placing his hands on Rebecca in accordance with the rite that was customary for priests. Consequently, this conception is not the result of the flesh or of nature; God wanted it to take place through the prayer of the saintly patriarch as the result of his faith, hope, and love.

Consequently, this passage teaches the same thing that Paul teaches in his Epistle to the Romans, where he distinguishes birth as a result of the flesh, that is, as the result of creation, from spiritual birth. For God preserved the former after Adam's fall, even though nature had become corrupted through sin and the devil, who had told Adam to become equal to God through the same fall through which Lucifer fell from heaven. Nevertheless, God did not deprive nature of procreation but permitted the godly as well as the ungodly to procreate. The only thing He wanted to point out was that it is not enough to be born into this world of the flesh, but that over and above the birth that remained in nature the rebirth and renewal of regeneration through the Holy Spirit is necessary. To prove this, St. Paul made use of this passage concerning Esau and Jacob and of the earlier one concerning Isaac and Ishmael. Both were born according to the flesh and the first birth, but neither would have come into the kingdom of heaven from the kingdom of man if Isaac had not been appointed the heir through the new birth. The same thing is true in the case of Jacob.

And God made use of these illustrious persons in order to present outstanding examples to the exceedingly arrogant nation destined to be the descendants of Abraham. For He knew their ungovernable pride, and their necks, which were harder than iron on account of the glory of being the children and descendants of Abraham. Therefore He wanted to put this warning in the text to stop the arrogant mouths of the Jews and to dispose of their argument concerning their birth according to the flesh. For this birth is in no wise adequate. No, regeneration is necessary over and above that birth. No matter how saintly the fathers Abraham, Isaac, etc., are, they nevertheless do not beget children of the kingdom by means of the first birth, which was instituted at the beginning of the world and was corrupted by the devil. But over and above the creation the call must be added. For thus says Paul (Rom. 9:11-12): "Although they had done nothing either good or bad, because of His call she was told," not because of the man who created, because both were conceived and created alike. But in order that the world, and especially that stiff-necked people, might know that over and above the creation the call, which elsewhere is called the promise, is required, Paul adds the words "not because of works, but because of His call, she was told: 'The elder will serve the younger.'"

This subject matter has been debated and discussed without interruption since the beginning of the world, just as the conflict between the brothers began in the womb of their mother. And the end of this war is not yet, because it is the same strife that took place between Cain and Abel and between the descendants of the serpent and the Seed of the woman. The first birth is arrogant and puffed up beyond measure, especially if the prestige of the parents is added, that is, that they have descended from the blood of the fathers. Then one must consider wealth, power, dominion over the world, wisdom, righteousness, and religion. This is the source of the hatred between Cain and Abel, between Ishmael and Isaac, between Esau and Jacob, and between the church of God and that of the devil. And the church of the devil is continually eager to have dominion, first on account of blood and the fathers, as the cause nearest at hand; in the second place, on account of the temporal blessing. "We are the children of the fathers," they say. "We have been blessed with royal authority, religion, wealth, most brilliant victories, and miracles. Finally we have been exalted to such an extent that all nations are the tail, as it were, but we are the head." This argument seems to be irrefutable and incontrovertible. But Scripture says the opposite. Not those who are born of the flesh, not those who are the children of the fathers, are for this reason children of God; for, as John says, the children of God are born, "not of blood nor of the will of the flesh nor of the will of man but of God" (John 1:13).

Therefore the strongest argument that can be opposed to the previous one is to be found in the fact that God made a distinction between Isaac and Ishmael and between Jacob and Esau, who were born in the same way of Abraham and Isaac. Nevertheless, Ishmael, no matter how much he desires it, cannot be the heir. No, the seed of the promise, which has the call and, over and above the first birth, has the second [41] and regeneration, is given the preference.

But this is the source of perpetual war from the beginning of the world to the end, not about trivialities [42] but about that glorious title "church," the people of God, the kingdom of heaven, and eternal life. Thus today we are at variance with the church of the pope, which wants to be the people of God and to have possession of the kingdom and the priesthood. They boast that they alone are the church of God which acknowledges God as the Father and worships Him properly. They condemn and persecute us as heretics and the church of the devil. This is what it means that the infants are at variance before they were born; for from the beginning there is a twofold church in the world, just as the seed is twofold: the seed of the serpent and the seed of the woman, which contend and are at variance with each other because of the title "church."

Paul certainly handed down an exceedingly clear and powerful dialectic when he pointed out the difference between the birth and the call. Where there is the birth alone, there is condemnation; for, as John says, "That which is born of the flesh is flesh" (John 3:6) and "not of blood, etc." (John 1:13). Paul says something else. "Because of His call she was told," he writes (Rom. 9:11-12); that is, the Word of God and the promise are necessary. Over and above the creature, he who wants to rule and be a son of God must hear Him, not as the God who creates but as the God who calls. But if the first birth were sufficient, why would we need God? The Turks are most honorable people, very wise and very religious. By means of the strictest discipline they are preserving the kingdom which they have acquired through great exertions. Therefore if the people of God were like the Turkish people, nothing more would have to be required. Besides, they are adorned by God with wealth, wisdom, glory, reason, and very brilliant victories. But what else is there among the Turks than the first birth? For reason is born of a woman; and to reason belong wisdom, civil rights, discipline, and laws. About all these people Holy Scripture says that they are lost and condemned before God.

[41] Reading *secundam* rather than *secundum*.

[42] The phrase *de lana caprina* is from Horace, *Epistles*, I, 18, 15, and had become proverbial; cf. *Luther's Works*, 26, p. 106, note 26.

In their time the Jews had both the blood and the glory of the flesh. The Turk has only the glory of the flesh. But the Jews gloried in the blood; that is, that they were born of the fathers and the prophets. In addition, they had the glory of the flesh, namely, a kingdom, power, religion, and hypocrisy. Therefore they were vainglorious in every way, not only because of the cause but also because of the effect. The cause was that they were born of most saintly parents; the effect was that they had a kingdom, glory, and wealth. The Turk does not have the glory of blood, for he is not descended from the fathers. But he has a kingdom, wisdom, and glory; and on the basis of these very important effects he tries to prove that his people is the people of God. But one asks: "Where is the call?" "There is no need for it," they say; "the first birth suffices. If man does what he can of himself, he will be saved." [43] This is by no means the case; but the call is required, that is, the Word. If the first birth were enough, why would we have need of the Word? Why does God call from the east to the west? Are we not righteous, saintly, and sensible men? But in opposition to all this God says: "This is what I want. All flesh is grass, and all its beauty is like the flower of the field" (Is. 40:6) — so that no one may glory in his flesh and blood but may acquire the renewal which takes place when God calls. Otherwise all glory, both of the cause and of the effect, will be vain and worthless, and a people that trusts in this glory alone will be condemned eternally.

But when there is teaching of this kind, the Jews rage and almost go crazy; for in the matter of the first birth they have lost their reason and do not advance to the thought of the second birth. Thus they perish. In like manner, the Turk takes pride simply in the first birth and does not concern himself about the call. The pope has been wholly absorbed in the same birth to such an extent that he has accommodated all godliness and religion to it, as when he taught that the Sacrament of the Altar is a mere work that is performed [44] — a work by which the godly manifest their obedience toward the church. Nothing is there except the nature resulting from the first birth, which can understand the work that is performed, that is, obedience to the church. Later on he filled the world with laws which are the fruits of an evil tree, although they have a very respectable

---

[43] Cf. *Luther's Works,* 26, p. 173, note 89.

[44] On *opus operatum* see *Luther's Works,* 26, p. 122, note 38.

and beautiful outward appearance; but there I do not hear the God who calls and promises. No, there I hear a human being who is performing a work as the result of the first birth.

Consequently, we are at variance, just as has happened in the entire world from the beginning to the end. We say that they are not the church, for they glory only in the first birth. They, on the other hand, condemn us, who believe the God who calls and promises. We look for salvation from that source. Who will be the arbiter and judge here? This text: "Not those who are of the flesh, but those who are of faith." The call and the promise are required to obtain salvation. If the question is asked whether a Turk will be saved, the answer is: "He will not." "Yet here there are wisdom, a most respectable life, a manifold worship, respect and obedience toward the government, and outstanding military discipline." "Indeed, they are here." "But to what do all these things pertain?" "To the first birth." Therefore he must be condemned and cannot be a child of the kingdom; for the call and the rebirth are lacking, and he wants to be saved through his first birth, which is corrupt unless it is restored through regeneration. Therefore it is sure that the Turk is not the church. Nor are the Jews; for they do not have the call, although neither the cause nor the effect is lacking, as has been stated above. Thus the church of the pope is not the true church, because they walk in the first birth and presume to obtain salvation as the result of works. But where, over and above the first birth, God adds the call, as Paul says (Rom. 9:11-12): "Because of His call she was told," there you will find the church. The Romans were the authors of very fine rights and laws, as the poet praises them: "Remember, O Roman, to rule the peoples." [45] But they are nothing else than reason which is born of the flesh through a woman and a man. This is altogether unprofitable and dead before God. Consequently, no papist or Turk or monk or jurist or physician will save himself; [46] for whatever there is in the entire world in the way of very fine and useful things is all condemned by one name, namely, because it is flesh and the glory of the flesh (cf. Is. 40:6).

Therefore this is the teaching of the true church: We are not only created and born of flesh, but God sent His Word and calls us;

[45] Vergil, *Aeneid*, VI, 851.

[46] The passive *salvabitur* may be meant in a reflexive sense here, or the phrase "of himself" may be implied.

that is, He proclaims the remission of sins and the adoption of sons through Jesus Christ. If we believe this, we are the church. Thus Isaac is the son of the promise and does not have that sonship from Abraham and Sarah, because this is a birth of the flesh. No, he has that sonship as the result of the words "Isaac shall be the seed." The same thing is true of Jacob. He is part of the church, not because he was born of Isaac but because the voice of Him who calls says: "Jacob is the younger. Nevertheless, he must be the master." Thus Abraham was a very wise and honorable man in Babylon. He had one legitimate wife and lived chastely with her, but he would have perished with all this if God had not called him out of Ur of the Chaldeans.

Therefore the true church must be distinguished in this manner from the false church, which is presumptuous either on account of blood — that is, because of birth — or on account of the effect. Ishmael reasons from the cause: "I was born from Abraham and am indeed the first-born. Consequently, I shall be the people of God." The cause and the blood are there; but unless he has the call, his presumptions on account of blood and birth will all be in vain. Thus all the papists and Turks boast that they are the people of God, and although they cannot glory on account of the blood of the fathers as on account of the cause, they nevertheless glory on account of the effect, that is, on account of their power, righteousness, and religion, which are all of the flesh. But if you ask them whether in addition to this they have the other call — that they are the sons of God — they have no answer but vaunt only those great blessings of God, which is an empty glory and is poured out over those who are good as well as over those who are evil.

If you ask the pope why he is the people of God, he answers: "Because I am sitting in the seat of the apostles Peter and Paul and am their successor. Furthermore, I have a reason in Scripture (Matt. 16:18): 'You are Peter, and on this rock I will build My church.'" Even a dog or a swine, however, can sit in the place of St. Peter; but to have the call — that is, the Word which you believe over and above that succession — that, of course, establishes the church and the children of God. This the pope does not have, but he persecutes it in a hostile manner. Therefore he is not a son of God but is God's enemy and an adversary of Christ. We, however, have no doubt whatever that we are the church; for we have the Gospel, Baptism, the Keys, and Holy Scripture, which teaches that mankind is lost and condemned in original sin and that it must be born again through Christ.

Therefore this doctrine, which distinguishes between the true and the false church, is necessary. God presented it to the Jews first, in order to destroy the pride they had in the glory of their blood by means of these outstanding examples in both houses, namely, that of Abraham and that of Isaac. For both Ishmael and Isaac were born of the same blood of Abraham. Nevertheless, Ishmael is not the heir; for he wants to be saved through the first birth, and through it alone. But Isaac is the heir because he has the Word and the promise. Thus Esau and Jacob were descendants not only of one father but also of the same mother, and this is a stronger argument than the preceding one. For the father is the same, the mother is the same, and the blood is the same. But why is Jacob preferred to Esau? I answer that the call came to Jacob. On the basis of the first birth Esau presumes that the inheritance of the kingdom falls to him. God is displeased with that presumption and wants the renewal of his nature, apart from which no right to the kingdom or inheritance is left to be added. And on the basis of these passages we can powerfully and most effectively refute even our Jews, who still dream of that glory of the blood today. For two are begotten from the same blood, the one being the heir, the other not; and they are distinguished by the call. They are equals in regard to all glory of the flesh; but the one has the Word and hears it, the other despises it.

We have an altogether similar example in the pope's church and in ours; for we have the same Baptism, the same Sacrament of the Altar, the same Keys, and the same Scripture and Word. Finally we have our origin from the same apostles and the same church, as though from one mother Rebecca. Why, then, do we disagree? We apprehend the Word in the Sacrament, follow the call, and discuss the Word in accordance with faith; but they do so in accordance with what is seen on the outside. We declare that when making use of the sacraments one must pay attention to the Word and accept it in faith; they make it a mere work that is performed. Therefore the true church is the one that holds fast to the Word and faith and does not rely on works but hears and follows God when He calls. But the call is the Word through which our nature, which has been corrupted by the devil and sin, is regenerated.

This is not an unimportant disagreement and struggle. And it is

not without cause that our adversaries are angry with us in such
a hostile manner, for we are debating about the most important matters in the entire world — not about the empire and not about wealth,
prestige, or power but about eternal damnation and eternal life.
This is the reason why the hatreds are so bitter. And nowhere are
they bitterer than in disagreements in the matter of religion, for it
is a most important and most serious cause. Are we children of God
or children of the devil? They do not want to be children of the
devil, but they usurp the glory and the name of true church and
therefore condemn and kill us. On the other hand, we condemn
them on the basis of the Word, and because of true evidences we
are sure of our own salvation. We keep a firm hold on the difference which God established between Abraham and the Babylonians,
between Ishmael and Isaac, and between Jacob and Esau, namely,
the call by which Abraham was told (Gen. 12:1): "Go from, etc.";
"Through Isaac shall your descendants be named" (Gen. 21:12); and
(Gen. 25:23): "The elder shall serve the younger."

Apart from this consideration the first birth is completely useless
not only for Abraham, or for Isaac and Jacob, but for all human
beings. Then indeed it is the source and origin of all evils. One can
discern this in the example of the 12 patriarchs who descended from
Jacob. They become murderers. Indeed, they murder near relatives,
and betray and slay their own father, because they sadden the very
pious old man to such an extent that he wants to die (Gen. 37:35).
And if someone wanted to exaggerate, this sin of theirs could very
correctly be called patricide. Naturally, these are fruits and works
of the flesh and blood. They show that by his nature man is completely like Cain and inclined to murder. God could surely also have
made an example of the sons of Jacob; but he did not want to reject
them and was content with these two proofs: Ishmael and Isaac,
Esau and Jacob. And it is my opinion that they were saved, just as
I also think that Ishmael and Esau repented and gave their assent
to the call. Nevertheless, God wanted this proof to be there, that
the first birth is nothing before God and that the flesh is altogether
condemned together with everything it has and is able to do, no
matter how great and excellent it may be, such as empires, laws, and
justice. In this respect the reign of Augustus was by far the most
glorious. Then wisdom, justice, riches, quiet, and magnificent victories flourished. But all these belong to the first birth, or to reason,
creation, and the flesh. Therefore they are condemned.

Consequently, one must look to see whether there is anything over and above those natural gifts, no matter whether the heathen, the Turk, or the pope possess them. If the call is not there, you must maintain that all is completely lost and condemned. For God Himself judged in this manner and pointed out especially to this people in the instance of their own foremost fathers that apart from and over and above the first birth they had to be called. And the horrible crimes of the foremost patriarchs, who defiled themselves with patricide and incest, reveal what the first birth could do without the call. The historical accounts of the kings and of the judges and finally that frightful crime when they crucified the Son of God and their Messiah bear witness to the same thing. This striking and astounding example of the conception of the two infants who struggled with each other in their mother's womb teaches these facts about the distinction between the true and the false church.

For the sake of those who at some time or other will read the commentaries of the rabbis let us next add something of the Jewish nonsense.[47] At this point they raise the question why Isaac did not marry another wife after he had discovered in the course of almost 20 years that his wife was barren, while in the example of Sarah they conclude that 10 years should be allowed for discovering barrenness or fecundity. Their answer is that in Isaac's case the situation is different from what it is in the case of Abraham. They say that because Isaac was sacrificed to God and became a burnt offering by the direction of God, he was not permitted to marry another wife. Thus Paul wants a bishop to be the husband of one wife (1 Tim. 3:2). Everybody sees how absurd and worthless these ideas are. Nevertheless, they must be touched on at times, in order to advise those who are students of the Hebrew language to read the sayings and writings of the Jews with discretion. We acknowledge, of course, that it is a great benefit that we have received the language from them; but we must beware of the dung of the rabbis, who have made of Holy Scripture a sort of privy in which they deposited their foulness and their exceedingly foolish opinions. I am advising this because even among our own theologians many give too much credit to the rabbis in explaining the meaning of Scripture. In the matter of grammar I readily bear with them; but they lack the true sense and understanding, in accordance with the well-known words in Is.

---

[47] Cf. also *Luther's Works,* 1, p. 296 and passim.

29:14: "The wisdom of their wise men shall perish, and the discernment of their discerning men shall be hid." This statement declares that there will be no understanding of Scripture among the Jews. No, this book of Holy Scripture has been closed for them and sealed. "With an alien tongue the Lord will speak to this people" (Is. 28:11). And they know nothing else than sheer blasphemies against the Christian religion.

Therefore there is no connection between the statement that Isaac was sacrificed and the statement that for this reason he cannot take a second wife. Abraham was dedicated to God just as much as Isaac was, yes, even more so; for he was called out of Ur of the Chaldeans and was immolated not once but often. Nevertheless, this sanctification does not prevent him from taking another wife. Thus Isaac would certainly have been permitted to take another wife if he had wanted to do so, but he preferred to bear everything and to suffer the worst in order to present himself as an example of patience and waiting. For there was also the great and sure hope that Rebecca would become a mother, since God had chosen her to be his wife, angels fetched her and were the bridesmaids, and his father appointed and sent the servant. But he is put off until the twentieth year because God wanted to try this saintly man and this saintly woman as an example and as instruction for all the churches.

22. *The children struggled together within her; and she said: If it is thus, why do I live?*

These accounts of the saintly fathers speak of procreation, of cohabitation, and of uniting man and woman. Nothing in the world seems more trivial and more laughable than this. Nevertheless, in these trivial matters most excellent examples of faith and of other virtues are presented. Rebecca, this pious and saintly woman who was flesh and blood just as we are, has been tried most severely for so many years. For in the first place, she was most certainly the mother chosen by God who was sought. She was found and was brought to her bridegroom by the angels in order that she might become a mother. But absolutely nothing happens, and she is tried by God with a long cross and suffering. There indeed lust and pleasure were followed by sorrow, bitterness, tears, and distress. These, of course, are the joys of wedlock. Hence she prays and wishes to an extraordinary degree and ardently to become the mother of this seed. Later on, when she is heard and God is overcome by force, as it were, to make the barren Rebecca fecund, another difficulty follows. It was hard to lose the hope she used to have as the result of being chosen and called by God, and to become the reproach of her neighbors and her domestics. She has now obtained offspring and has become pregnant beyond, and contrary to, nature; her barrenness has been overcome, and she has conceived through a new miracle. But far greater difficulties remain to be borne. When she has the fetuses in her womb and congratulates herself that after such deep despair she is being cheered up by a hope so glorious that she will become the mother of twins, she, who formerly had been rejected and disdained and was already about to yield the glory of motherhood to another, as Sarah did (Gen. 16:2), is then at last driven to the limits of the most mournful despair. For although the children within her are struggling, she does not know for sure whether they are children or not. Therefore she says: "If it is thus, why am I?" This is Rebecca's elliptical way of speaking, since she is agitated and regrets her earlier prayer, in which she had wished to become pregnant. She thinks: "Would that I had never prayed! Why did I not have patience and give the right of motherhood to another woman, since I am being compelled to experience and bear much greater sorrows than before?"

This is a twofold, yes, a sevenfold trial; for Rebecca now feels that it would have been better to remain barren forever than to be so woefully afflicted and at the same time to have doubts about becoming a mother. This she is now compelled to give up a second time because at present she is feeling death and is beginning to be in peril of her life. For she does not know what evil there is, what sort of commotion there is in her womb. She feels only the struggling, and she cannot avoid accusing herself and finding herself guilty of folly for having so earnestly demanded offspring from God. She realizes that she will have to die in greater disgrace than if she had remained barren. Thus her hope of becoming a mother dwindles a second time. Indeed, the mother is destroyed with the unborn child. For whenever God lets our hope and prayer become weak, reason cannot feel or think otherwise than to say: "The longer I pray, the more severely I am afflicted and tormented."

Therefore will it be unnecessary to pray, to trust, and to hope? Must we be like the Epicureans, who now declare that they leave everything to God's will and direction, for the things God has decreed are bound to come to pass? Prayer should by no means be discontinued; for God has commanded us to pray, to believe, to call upon Him, to hallow His name, and to hope. God could gather a church without the Word, manage the state without a government, produce children without parents, and create fish without water; but He commands us and wants us to preach and to pray, and everyone to do his duty in his station. But if the outcome does not always come up to what we have determined in advance, we must nevertheless continue in our calling and leave the result and the issue to Him.

This is the kind of trial Rebecca underwent. For she thought: "Behold, you prayed God to give you offspring; it would have been better not to pray." When she feels the struggling, she does not think as yet that she is carrying children in her womb but supposes that it is some kind of monster. This is why she says: "If it is thus, why am I?" The common translation is "If this was going to happen to me, why was it necessary for me to conceive?" But the very saintly woman is indicating that she regrets and finds fault with her earlier prayer. It is as though she were saying: "If it was to be thus, it would have been better not to pray. If it was to be thus, why did I pray? Why did I wish to become a mother contrary to God's will?" These are the words of a woman who repents of her earlier prayer and is now despairing. People in very great despair make half-complete statements, and in their speech there are more interjections than nouns and verbs. The ellipses indicate the greatness of the grief in their afflicted and almost despairing hearts, as the heart of Rebecca was. For the main concern and anxiety of those saints concerned the promise of the Seed. Hence she despairs and thinks: "I shall not be a mother in that church; another woman, who is worthier, will be chosen after my death." In this way she gives up the thought of becoming a mother, as Sarah did above (Gen. 16:2) and as Rachel does below (Gen. 30:3). Rachel really was Jacob's wife. Nevertheless, she is compelled [48] to yield the right of motherhood to another. "Go in to the maid," she says to Jacob.

Few people, however, give consideration to this in these accounts, just as the papists imagine that the only thing the fathers did was to satisfy their pleasures and lusts, as they themselves, who live without trials and hardships, do. But those saintly men felt very great emotions and afflictions, which readily removed every thought

[48] Reading *cogitur* rather than *igitur*.

and feeling of pleasure. Numerous domestics had to be ruled, and meanwhile severe trials had to be borne, as though the fathers had been bereft of all divine help.

But these facts are presented to show and teach us, in the first place, that this physical procreation, no matter how vile and corrupt it is, nevertheless does not belong to nature but is a gift of God. This should be learned in the case of the fathers. To be sure, God scatters this gift among a large number of the worst human beings; but the godly realize that it is truly a gift of God, as Ps. 128:3-4 states: "Your children will be like olive shoots around your table. Lo, thus shall the man be blessed who fears the Lord." Therefore he who is godly should learn that it is a very great gift and a creation of God to beget and give birth to sons or daughters. For this reason we call God our Creator and our father. Nor should the ugliness of sin and punishment with which procreation has been covered prevent us from realizing that it is a blessing of God and a work that is acceptable and pleasing to God.

The ungodly do not understand this. They also use the rest of the creatures in vain, just as they use the Creator Himself in vain — to such an extent that not only the creature but also the Creator has been subjected to futility (cf. Rom. 8:20). But one must distinguish this distortion from the creature that God wants to be glorious and highly esteemed. Thus the saintly fathers learned from these trials that procreation is a work of God, and of God alone. And it is surely true that if it were not tainted with such loathsome lust and depravity, we could not help being amazed at the value and the miraculous quality of such a great work. For what is more marvelous than that a human being is born of a human being? But this is obscured and concealed by the loathsome sin of lust. Therefore it should be praised and made much of, in order that people may recognize the excellence of the work and of the divine blessing.

In the second place, these examples set forth faith, hope, and love, that is, the manner in which God customarily works with us; for thus He deals with the saintly patriarch, as is stated in Rom. 11:33: "Unsearchable are His judgments and inscrutable His ways," not only in His works but also in His words and promises. For this reason nothing in the world seems more uncertain than the Word of God and faith, nothing more delusive than hope in the promise. In short, nothing seems to be more nothing than God Himself. Consequently, this is the knowledge of the saints and a mystery hidden from the wise and revealed to babes (Matt. 11:25). The pope and the Turk believe easily; because among them there are such great successes, and because they are flourishing with such great power, with wisdom, with the outward appearance of saintliness, and with their religion, to the point that there is nothing beyond this. The Turk maintains with such assurance that he is the people of God that he does not hesitate to give his life and head as a pledge. For he has the situation and God in his hands. God adorns him with the finest and highest gifts, and deals in the opposite manner with Christians. These He subjects to the cross and hands over to their adversaries to be killed like sheep for the slaughter (Rom. 8:36). On this account the Turk taunts us in the most insolent manner. This happened in the case of a defeat of the Christians. When the Turks saw corpses lying here and there with the noses cut off, they laughed at the misery of those who had been slain, and with virulent sarcasm they repeated these words: "Jesus Mary!" It is as though they were saying: "Where is their God now?" [49]

Hence we find those mournful laments in the psalms, such as "Arise!" in Ps. 7:6 and "Why dost Thou stand afar off?" in Ps. 10:1. Similar words are spoken by hearts that are in doubt as to whether we have a God and ask: "Where is your God?" (Ps. 42:10.) "We do not have to believe in Him who conceals and withdraws Himself from us, do we?" But the Turk does not know what he himself is doing or what is in store for us. He thinks that the Christians have been rejected and cast aside by God, and he takes God's favor and His election for granted and is hardened and obdurate to a greater extent than the devil himself. But when we are delivered into his hands and succumb, heaven is filled with martyrs, and the godly are spurred on to groan and sigh for the Last Day. But he hastens eternal destruction for himself. At the time of the Assyrians and the Babylonians God dealt no differently with the Israelites; no success, no victory, and no God was in sight. Then indeed God had hidden Himself, the God of Israel, the Savior, as is stated in Is. 45:15. Thus today heaven and earth, the pope and the Turk, and all things are against us; and God, in whom we believe, is altogether nothing. But the prince of the world and its god is god. On this account many among the Christians who have not been properly instructed and

[49] During these years Luther was giving considerable attention to the Turkish menace; in August 1541 he wrote his *Exhortation to Prayer Against the Turks*.

do not have the Word desert from us to the Turk. They see that everything is flourishing there, and from this they conclude that God gives them life but slays us and delivers us into the hands of the cruel enemy.

But we have nothing from God except the pure Word, namely, that the Lord Jesus sits at the right hand of the Father and is the Judge of the living and the dead, and that through Him we are kings and priests (Rev. 1:6). But where can this be discerned? Not in the indicative mood, but in the imperative and in the optative. Why He hides Himself in this way we shall see on that Day, when all enemies will have been put under His feet (1 Cor. 15:25). Meanwhile we should believe and hope. For if one could see it now before one's eyes, there would be no need of faith. But no matter how false our faith seems and how vain our hope, I know in spite of this that we shall tread the Turk under our feet and that those who now lie buried and whose blood he shed will tread him underfoot and thrust him down into hell. All the rest of the martyrs who were burnt by the emperor, the pope, the French, and others will do the same thing.[50] For it is the wisdom of the saints to believe in the truth in opposition to the lie, in the hidden truth in opposition to the manifest truth, and in hope in opposition to hope.

This wisdom is set forth in this example of Rebecca. She has been heard and has been chosen to be a mother; but she is anything but a mother, even now, when she has obtained fecundity, and when abundant hope of becoming a mother has been given. In these circumstances all her hope and expectation collapses suddenly. Is this, then, the fulfillment of the Word of God? My answer is that one must simply cling to that knowledge of the saints and to the marvelous manner in which they are led. Thus when Christ Himself is about to enter into the glory of the Father, He dies and descends into hell. There all glory disappears. He says to His disciples (John 14:12): "I go to the Father," and He goes to the grave. Let us constantly meditate on such examples and place them before our eyes. For when we are killed by the Turk with much abuse and blasphemy, and when infants, old men, and girls are slaughtered with inhuman cruelty, we cry out: "Where is Christ? Where is our God?" They also taunt us: "Go now, and believe in Jesus." But even though they do not listen, we should answer them with confidence: "Behold, this infant which

[50] Cf. *Luther's Works*, 1, p. 288, note 45.

you have cut to pieces or impaled will be adorned in the other, better life with such great glory that you will wish for the happiness of being able to see the wounds you inflicted on it." For the Turk accomplishes nothing else than filling heaven with martyrs, because they are all being slain on account of the name of Christ. On the other hand, he is filling hell with his own body and with the bodies of his people.

Thus the pope (although he is worse than the Turk, because he believes nothing) imagines that those whom he has killed have been utterly annihilated and that he may rage with impunity against anybody he pleases. He spurs the sovereigns on to like cruelty. Meanwhile we complain [51] that we are being killed and oppressed, and we cry (Ps. 44:23): "Why sleepest Thou, O Lord?" For God hides Himself for a time, and, as is stated in the Song of Solomon (2:9): "He stands behind our wall, gazing in at the windows, looking through the lattice." Consequently He is not far away but is present and sees everything. Both the pope and the Turk, by the very fact that they are killing us, are compelled willy-nilly to serve us, so that we may "obtain the unfading crown of glory" (1 Peter 5:4), just as Herod also would never, by doing good, have been able to oblige the infants as much as he benefitted them by killing them. Thus He seems to have forsaken us too, because He ascended into heaven, is sitting at the right hand of the Father, and nevertheless leaves behind the Word and the sacraments. The flesh will object: "But what is this? I do not see anything; it is merely a word." Indeed, it is the Word; but in it there is an extraordinary and divine power, which you will experience if you cling to it with a firm faith. Even if your life must be endangered, this matters little; for you are not far from rising again from the dead and being made alive. "Unsearchable are His judgments, and inscrutable are His ways" (Rom. 11:33) toward His saints, as His only-begotten Son, who is the most perfect example of all sons, bears witness.

In this manner, then, Moses treats of most important matters in human procreation and in the physical work. Rebecca loses her glory of motherhood and God Himself, who had heard her and had made her pregnant. He withdraws His hand and hides His face, so that she no longer sees God's work of conception but sees some mockery of Satan. She has no other thought than that she has been cast aside

---

[51] Reading *querimur* rather than *quaerimur*.

and rejected. But He does not delay or keep aloof forever. Indeed, He manages all things in such a manner that the Word seems to be altogether of no account and nothing. But out of this nothing and out of what is of no account He makes everything through a very great and amazing change, so that what previously appeared to be *everything* perishes and is reduced to nothing. Thus the downfall of the pope has already begun, and through the Spirit of the mouth of Christ he will daily be done away with more and more. And in a short time it will happen that the Turk, too, will meet with the destruction he deserves.

So she went to inquire of the Lord.

Poor Rebecca feels that everything is lost and beyond hope. What, then, should she do? She goes to inquire of the Lord. So far it has seemed that she has been cast away from the face of the Lord, and her hope and faith are now in the greatest distress. But that very day is decisive. She comes to life again and goes to seek the advice of the Lord when she seemed to be in the uttermost distress and danger; for the string breaks most easily when it is stretched most tightly.[52]

The Jews argue about where Rebecca went to seek the advice of the Lord.[53] The rabbis are too much like the monks when they say that she withdrew to a solitary place. Therefore we hold fast to the opinion of those who maintain that she went to the saintly patriarch Shem, who, together with Shelah and Eber, was still living. Those fathers governed the church and constantly held fast to the Word and the true forms of worship. Undoubtedly, however, she did not go to Shem of her own accord in such great distress but went at the advice and bidding of Isaac and Abraham, who were in the clutches of the same trial. She was sent to him as to a public place and to a public person, where they knew that the main church was. For Shem was a most saintly man who had in his charge the church, the Word, and the worship during so many centuries after the Flood. Hence his words were regarded as oracles. But Rebecca inquired not only about her unborn child but also about her salvation and whether this was

---

[52] Apparently a proverbial saying: *Tum enim facillime rumpitur nervus, cum intenditur vehementissime.*

[53] According to the rabbis, Rebecca went "not to some prophet, but to a consecrated and secret place, where she could pray more quietly," Lyra *ad* 22; cf. p. 303, note 7.

a sign of God's wrath or of His favor. For any misfortune, even if it is physical, brings with it despair or doubt concerning the will of God toward us. Therefore in every trial the heart must be fortified in advance and must be strengthened, lest it feel that it is being afflicted by an angry God who wants us to be destroyed eternally. For example, when the Turk and pope rage so savagely against us, we all have reason to be worried and in a state of trepidation. But if you have the Word and the sacraments, then, close your eyes and safely despise their cruelty to the extent that you say: "Rage and rave as much as you please! Even tear me in pieces bit by bit. In spite of this I know that Christ, my Deliverer, lives and sits at the right hand of the Father. Therefore I, too, shall live; and I, in turn, shall trample you underfoot."

But that confident pride has its origin in the future state of affairs, not in what is happening at the present time. Reason follows only the things that are visible. But in this instance it must be killed, in order that the Word and faith may have room. Yet reason cannot be killed except through despair, mistrust, hatred, and murmuring against God, with the result that eventually the heart, after everything external has been removed, clings to and finds rest in the Word and the sacraments alone; for God is utterly incomprehensible and is nobody in all His works and miracles, because, according to our understanding, He forsakes us in suffering and afflictions and gives only the Word, by means of which He leads us through that sea of perils and trials to the port, just as a fish is pulled along by means of a hook.

23. *And the Lord said to her: Two nations are in your womb, and two peoples, born of you, shall be divided; the one shall be stronger than the other, the elder shall serve the younger.*

Up to this point it has been related how God was hidden, yes, even lost, for this most saintly little woman and even for Isaac and Abraham and also for all who were in that church, so that it was necessary to have recourse to the church and the patriarch Shem, and to seek help and advice there. But now Moses records how that lost God is found again and appears — as an example for us, in order that we may not despair in our trials if our prayer relies on a definite promise but may be sure that it is impossible for God not to appear and answer, even if heaven and all creation were to threaten ruin and destruction.

But although that waiting is difficult, we should nevertheless have been taught and trained by the Holy Spirit in such a way that we know that God is forced to hear our prayers, because it is impossible for Him to lie. He had promised Isaac the blessing; but many difficulties and hindrances were put in the way of that promise, so that a weak heart could doubt that the promise was true. Although Rebecca did not have a promise, she nevertheless kept on praying. And if it is a true prayer — as Rebecca's prayer undoubtedly was — it must rely on the promise of God. For who would be bold enough in his own right to lift up his hands and eyes to God unless he were sure about the will of God? Accordingly, all prayer relies on the command and promise of God, because in the Second Commandment there is the Word of God, which teaches us to pray: "You shall not take the name of the Lord your God in vain" (Ex. 20:7). Likewise: "Call upon Me in the day of trouble" (Ps. 50:15). But after you have prayed, you should know that just as you can have no doubts about the promise, so you should have no doubts about its being heard; for the foundation of the prayer is the promise — and not our will, not our worthiness, and not our merits. An outstanding example of this teaching is Rebecca's prayer, which, after so many hindrances, is finally heard in a wonderful way.

For at first, after she has become pregnant, Rebecca has no doubts whatever that she had been heard and helped by God. But that confidence is immediately disturbed by a new and unexpected danger. For the fetuses struggle with each other in her womb, so that she is again driven to despair. But when her trepidation is at its greatest, God buoys her up once more with the Word and indicates that she has been truly heard. He does so to bear witness that He loves those who pray in faith and wait in prayer, that is, when praying is difficult.

Of such examples the papists have no knowledge or understanding, for their prayer is nothing else than mockery of God. But an earnest and fervent prayer, which does not cease and does not become tired but keeps on waiting up to the last moment, eventually forces its way through heaven and earth, and it is impossible for it not to be heard. For it is a sacrifice most pleasing to God when we pray in such a way that the prayer surpasses our comprehension and understanding, as is stated in the Epistle to the Ephesians: "Who is able to do far more abundantly than all that we ask or think" (3:20). When the situation is hopeless and all plans and efforts are in vain, then be courageous, and beware of giving up; for God calls all things from the dead and from nothing. When no resource or hope at all is left, then at last God's help begins. And so these are perfect prayers. Meanwhile weak prayers and those of weak people should nevertheless not be despised. But the former are presented to us in their highest grade and by a perfect example, in order that we may try to imitate them. For at first — just as children learn the alphabet and Donatus [54] — we stammer in imperfect praying. This should by no means be despised; for just as he who does not learn the alphabet and Donatus will never learn to read Vergil or to speak Latin, so he who does not pray weakly will never achieve a perfect prayer. Consequently, the teaching of this passage should be carefully noted. It points out how great the power of prayer is and how perseverance in prayer is a sacrifice pleasing to God, just as Rebecca perseveres to the end when no counsel is left except to seek the advice of the church.

Moreover, Moses describes at very great length how Rebecca was heard. *"The Lord said,"* namely, through Shem. Above we stated that God also spoke through Adam,[55] just as Christ explains in Matt. 19:4-5: "Have you not read that He who made them from the beginning made them male and female, and said: 'For this reason he shall leave, etc.'?" God spoke these words. Nevertheless, in Gen. 2:23-24 Moses writes that Adam spoke them. Consequently, Adam was full of the Holy Spirit and of God, who spoke through Adam. Therefore the words of Adam are the words of God. Similarly, to this day whatever the church, full of God, says should not be received any differently from the way one should receive it if it had been spoken by God Himself. Thus God commands that we should obey our parents and the government, and that we should listen to His Word from them. In the same manner the Lord spoke to this most saintly matriarch through Shem, who, over and above the usual discernment of faith, was full of prophecy.

But the greatest and richest comfort is presented in these words: *"Two nations,"* etc. For this is what Shem wants to say: "You have prayed, and your husband and Abraham have prayed with you. But you think that your entreaties have not been heard and that you are about to die. But you should not fear this at all." And Shem quickly goes to the heart of the matter and to words of comfort. "For far

[54] On the grammar of Donatus cf. *Luther's Works,* 45, p. 370, note 45.

[55] *Luther's Works,* 1, p. 136.

from being in danger of your life," he says, "two nations will come from your womb. You have only been afflicted, and your prayer has been a test whether you are willing to persevere. Consequently, you should know that more has been granted than was prayed for, that more has been given than was asked for or understood. For you were not able to understand what or how much God would grant. He understood your prayer better than you did."

This example should be well noted and imitated by us; for we, too, pray against Antichrist, the Turk and the sects. And we surely have very important and desperate causes — so much so that we are unable to think of or to understand any relief or help apart from imploring God's mercy to hasten the coming of the Last Day. Therefore one must not cease praying, but those who are strong must cry out boldly, and those who are weak must cry out weakly, as Christ Himself says in Luke 18:7 about the godly, who cry out to Him day and night.

But our need and cause is greater and more difficult than it ever was in the church at any time. For we have against us the dregs and the end of the world, and that extreme rage of the pope and the Turk, who want to, and will, devour us. Therefore we must pray, and we must pray in such a manner that we rely on Christ's command and promise. Although it seems that in a short time everything will go to ruin, what of it? Let it indeed go to ruin! In spite of this your prayers will obtain more than you ask for. For He Himself has given us the promise, and our prayer asks that the name of God be hallowed and that the kingdom of God be preserved in preference to everything, even in preference to help in our misfortunes. Therefore although everything is hopeless and here, too, we would all be killed, I nevertheless know that our adversaries must perish; they shall be brought down,[56] because the prayer has been heard.

Accordingly, Shem comforts Rebecca in this manner: "Rebecca, your prayer has been heard richly and beyond all understanding. You asked the Lord for one child, and now, in this peril, you merely desire a successful childbirth without detriment to your life. Indeed, you would be satisfied if you knew that your prayer has been heard. But be of good cheer and unconcerned about the birth, for God has heard you and has an excellent understanding of your prayer. You asked for one little son or daughter, but He Himself will enlarge that prayer and make a very rich addition to it. How? 'Two nations are

[56] Here the text breaks into German again.

in your womb, etc.' This surely means that your prayer has been heard; for those to whom you will give birth are not two sons but two very great patriarchs. Therefore not only the prayer concerning the birth of a son has been heard but also your prayer concerning the descendants of your two sons, concerning two great nations. Therefore do not argue, and do not despair. You are not carrying a monstrosity or a devil, which you could have been afraid of as the result of the struggling in your womb. No, you are already the mother of two very great peoples."

Thus Rebecca prayed only for her own life and that of her son, and she obtains the life of two patriarchs and of their descendants. She asks for a trifle and obtains a mountain of gold. This she had not had the courage either to hope for or to believe. For she wanted her prayer to be modest and satisfied with a modicum, just as we usually press for small and trivial things and do not consider with what a great Majesty we are speaking when we pray. For if God wanted to give only small and trivial things, He would not have prescribed such a great and magnificent form of prayer (Matt. 6:9 ff.): "Our Father who art in heaven, hallowed be Thy name. Thy kingdom come, etc." God is not a Euclio or some Irus,[57] but He puts before us and offers us immense riches and the best gifts in heaven and on earth. These He wants us to ask for and to expect; for in every petition — "Hallowed be Thy name. Thy kingdom come. Thy will be done. Give us this day our daily bread, etc." — heaven and earth and everything that is in them are comprised. For what does it mean that His name is hallowed, that His kingdom comes, and that His will is done? It means to overthrow countless devils and to swallow the entire world with one prayer. But our courage is small, and our faith is weak. Therefore we should carefully note this example and learn how God is not content with a little, even though we ask for very little; but He gives more than we understand or have the courage to ask for (Eph. 3:20).

But let us look at the words of the patriarch Shem. They comprise four statements, which we shall first take only in their legal sense. In the first place, he says: "Two nations are in your womb." And before God they are already as great as they are destined to be. But when they have been born and have grown up, then they will

[57] Euclio is the miser in the *Aulularia* of Plautus; Irus is the beggar in Book XVIII of the *Odyssey*.

be divided. The second part is the promise that Edom and Jacob will be two peoples divided according to the flesh, the Edomites and the Israelites, as Holy Scripture attests. Yet, they will not be under one head, but each will have his own glory as the ruler of his own people. They will also have established households, governments, and churches; but there will be some difference. For they will be divided into diverse religions, governments, rights, and laws. It is believable that Esau brought with him from Abraham's house circumcision and some sacrificial rites. Thus his people had its own government, rights, and church. But Jacob received a special arrangement of the government and the church — there was nothing like it in the world — and at the same time the succession and the inheritance of the promise. Consequently, those nations will be separated politically and so far as the church is concerned, this was also fulfilled physically. But Paul has the spiritual interpretation in the Epistle to the Romans. About this, however, something is said elsewhere. The last two clauses are: *"The one shall be stronger than the other, the elder shall serve the younger."*

Edom, or Esau, increased very much, as we shall see later on when he meets his brother Jacob with 400 men and Jacob had no one with him except his four wives. And in the thirty-sixth chapter the 11 chiefs who possessed the land of Edom are enumerated. From this one can conclude that the power of Esau was very great. But Jacob was still wandering about in the land of Canaan and was sojourning in Egypt, while meanwhile 11 grandchildren and great chiefs had been born to his brother. Therefore that prophecy was also fulfilled literally. But at the time of David, Israel, the younger, increased, occupied kingdoms, and also subjected Edom to himself, as is stated in Ps. 60:8: "Upon Edom I cast My shoe." But below, in the blessing of Esau, Isaac will explain and mitigate this promise by stating that this bondage will last up to a definite time; for this is what he says (Gen. 27:40): "The time will come when you will throw off and break his yoke from your neck." This happened at the time of Ahab, when Edom revolted and chose its own king.

This, then, is the essence of the promise and the bountiful manner in which Rebecca's prayer is heard; for this is how Shem comforted her: "Behold, my dear Rebecca, you have prayed for yourself, and the only thing you longed for was the safety of your child. But I am promising you far greater things. You will have not only one child, but you will have two sons and the princes of two peoples. Besides,

God is indicating to you the rank and condition of each, in order that you may know what kind of descendants you will have even after your death. The one will be stronger in the matter of government and religion, and the other will be weaker; but the smaller people will remain the heir and lord. The stronger will not altogether suppress the weaker. Indeed, the latter will rule over the former. Consequently, you are not only keeping your person and your sons safe and unharmed, but you also have a description of the history of both parts to all their descendants without end."

Thus this is written for our instruction and comfort, in order that we may learn to pray with full confidence and not to despair or have any doubt about being heard. Although prayer is offered contrary to and beyond understanding, yet it is not unavailing; for God does not want us to insult Him by thinking that He is not truthful. And this is why He has told us to pray. He has not only commanded us to do so; but He has also promised that He will hear, in order that we might maintain with assurance that He wants to grant what we are asking for. Therefore it is the highest type of religion and worship to believe that God is truthful. Besides, we have a simple and definite form in which He has prescribed what we should pray for and how this should be done. Therefore if you pray: "Our Father, etc.," think: "Thou, O Lord, hast told me to pray and hast promised that Thou wilt hear him who prays." Nor should you have any doubts about God's truth and promises. Even if the devil were to overturn the entire world in a single moment, the name of God will nevertheless be hallowed. And even if we all had to die, yet we are undoubtedly preserved and watched over for the future resurrection. Indeed, we see the manifest power and efficacy of our prayer; for the government of the world is surely preserved through prayer, our life is preserved, and all the good things we enjoy in this world are preserved.

Furthermore, in Rom. 9:10 ff. St. Paul treats this passage in a rather sublime manner and relates it to the spiritual and true account. There he quotes from the prophet Malachi (1:2-3): "I have loved Jacob, but I have hated Esau." In Rom. 9:12-13 he says: "Because of His call she was told: 'The elder will serve the younger.'" There Paul is not dealing with the temporal promises. No, he is dealing with the true promises. The Jews understand these words only according to the flesh, as when they occupied the land of Canaan after they had been led out of Egypt. But in those physical promises those that are spiritual are included. For from that weak part the Son of God had to be born, in order that salvation might not be from the Gentiles and from the Edomites but might be from the Jews, as is stated in John 4:22. Everything has been written on account of Christ, who came from that line of the smaller people. Accordingly, Paul treats this passage by establishing a twofold birth, namely, of the flesh and of the promise. Esau, too, was a son of the promise. But there a separation and division into a larger people and a smaller people takes place. There Paul, in accordance with his great and apostolic spirit, gives the interpretation that the smaller will be the heir, namely, Jacob, not the greater. Thus all the others who adhere to the promise also become heirs, as has been stated above at greater length. Accordingly, the promise that pertains to the body belongs to Esau; but that which pertains to the spirit belongs to Jacob, who was Rebecca's smaller son according to the flesh but the lord and the greater son according to the spirit.

I have stated about the church of Cain and the church of Ishmael that they were rejected, but in such a way that the rejection would lead to their humiliation, in order that they might relinquish the inheritance which they presumed they would have as a result of their flesh. Yet they were saved through repentance and through faith in the promise. Thus the text gives evidence that many descendants of Edom were saved, not because they were the children of Edom — for that line was rejected — but because they took hold of the promise by faith, in accord with Paul's statement (Rom. 9:8): "It is not the children of the flesh who are the children of God, but the children of the promise." Accordingly, they joined the Ishmaelites and said: "Sarah is our grandmother, and Abraham is our ancestor. But this will not save me, for the carnal procreation is of no benefit at all. But I believe in the Seed promised to the fathers, just as Isaac and Jacob believed and were saved." All who had this faith obtained the inheritance of eternal life, but of those descendants who persisted in presuming that they were greater because of the flesh all perished.

We Gentiles cannot glory as the Turk glories in his kingdoms or the pope in the orderly succession and the supreme power in the church. No, we glory in what is written in John 1:12-13: "But to all who received Him, who believed in His name, He gave power to become children of God; who were born, not of blood nor of the will of the flesh nor of the will of man, but of God." We must all come to this knowledge, just as in Rom. 4:12 Paul calls Abraham the father of the circumcised, "who are not merely circumcised but also follow the example of the faith which our father Abraham had before he was circumcised." Thus Christ says in John 8:39: "If you were Abraham's children, you would do what Abraham did"; for he believed God, and through the promised Seed he obtained righteousness and salvation. Thus those who believe God become children of Abraham and children of God.

Hence we should learn from this passage that all glorying in the flesh has been rejected and condemned by God, and that we cannot be justified through it, just as the fathers were not justified because of the glory of the flesh or blood, as this example, which is altogether outstanding and deserves to be written in golden letters, demonstrates with power.

Furthermore, these two brothers struggled in the womb; and later on, after they had been born, they quarrel throughout the entire time of their life. Thus we continually contend with the pope and the Turk, and it is everlastingly impossible for us to have fellowship or peace with them. Ishmael and Edom — that is, those who are older and stronger, who surpass us in wealth, power, numbers, and wisdom — oppose us, who are younger and weaker. But this is our comfort. Since we have to struggle and wage a truceless [58] war with the Edomites, we are sure of victory; for without a doubt the Word, or the promise, will prevail. But if some of our adversaries are saved, they are not saved because they are papists, monks, or Turks, but because they come to us, that is, to Abraham, Isaac, and Jacob. And although they are not of our seed, yet they are grafted into it. Thus not the entire mass is rejected, but only the glory and pride of the mass, which glories in its fathers, in ceremonies, and in the Law. And if it wants to be engrafted together with us, it will be a holy mass together with us and with the entire generation of the godly, but as a result of grace, not as a result of the righteousness of the flesh and of works, in which the world seeks salvation and righteousness.

24. *When her days to be delivered were fulfilled, behold, there were twins in her womb.*

25. *The first came forth red, all his body like a hairy mantle; so they called his name Esau.*

[58] Here Luther uses the word ἄσπονδος from 2 Tim. 3:3.

26. *Afterward his brother came forth, and his hand had taken hold of Esau's heel; so his name was called Jacob.*

This is the description of the amazing and dangerous birth on account of which the mother undoubtedly was exceedingly frightened when the fetuses were struggling so in her womb. For the birth is described as such a one that if the promise had not preserved Rebecca, she would have died suddenly in childbirth. I surely had no understanding of this; nor have I ever read or heard of a similar example. This is what the text says: Twins were found when she began to give birth, for the women who were at hand were expecting only one child. But soon, as they are looking on, they realize that there are twins. It certainly is common that twins are born, even without danger to the mother. But here the danger is great, since Jacob comes out immediately after Esau is born, and comes out in such a way that he takes hold of his brother's heel with his hand. Moreover, we know that it is an unfortunate and difficult birth when an infant is not brought forth properly and the head comes out first. But when one hand or foot has been thrust out, the life of mother and child are endangered. Often, too, the fetus is torn to pieces and brought out bit by bit. Thus this passage describes a birth that is wonderful and full of danger to the mother and to Jacob. The first child comes out safely, but the life of the second is in danger. It was the promise, however, that preserved Rebecca — the promise in which she had heard that she would give birth to two peoples, or to the founders of two peoples. For this reason she does not despair in such great peril.

Furthermore, Moses describes each infant. The first came out אַדְמוֹנִי. From this word Adam gets his name, because he was formed from red earth, which Pliny and Josephus maintain is the best.[59] After it black earth is praised, but yellow and pale yellow earth are inferior. אָדֹם means red. In this case, however, there must have been an unusual redness; for all infants are usually born red and are also red after their birth. But Esau was especially red in comparison with his brother or other infants. Then he has another mark to distinguish him from his brother; for he is shaggy and hairy, not only on his head — just as other infants, and especially males,

---

[59] Pliny, *Natural History*, Book XVIII, ch. 3, reports that "red earth has been praised by many"; Josephus, *The Antiquities of the Jews*, Book I, par. 34, calls red "the color of true virgin soil."

have much hair — but in addition to the redness Esau also has a rough and completely hairy skin. On his hands and feet and on his entire body he is shaggy, for Moses adds the comparison "like an אַדֶּרֶת." This is surely an amazing description of the red and shaggy infant; and in spite of the fact that the accounts of the heathen have often commented on unusual births, they hardly have anything like it.

The Hebrew word denotes a shaggy skin or mantle like the garment of Elijah described in 2 Kings 2:8. This was a hairy mantle with which he struck the Jordan, so that the waters were divided. And in Joshua 7:21 we read: "I saw among the spoil אַדֶּרֶת שִׁנְעָר." Here this is called שֵׂעָר. I do not know, however, whether at that time people made garments from wool. This kind, I suppose, was a garment made of skin, beautiful and long like a mantle or toga, which was the dress of the prophets. It can also be understood as a hyperbole, just as in our language we have comparisons of this kind when we speak of those who have disheveled and shaggy hair as being similar to hedgehogs, *wie ein Igel oder ein hareul.* Thus the women, too, could have spoken about Esau in their customary way of resorting to exaggerations in the household.

After Esau has been born, the birth of Jacob is described. He is in danger both of his own and of his mother's life. For he follows his brother so quickly that he grasps him by the heel. And one may imagine that they were brought forth almost in one moment. Therefore these are wonderful things. One finds nothing like them in any historical accounts. For it is simply and truly a divine work which God is performing here. And for this reason Moses is so painstaking in these descriptions. He wants every happening to be carefully noted, in order that the reader may be spurred on to take the importance of these matters into consideration.

Here the foundations of the entire Christian doctrine are confirmed. Through the birth of these twins God wants to pass sentence in advance on the entire world, yes, even to anticipate and put an end to all righteousnesses of the flesh. He wants to teach that all wisdom and excellence of the flesh is lost and vain by reason of this one statement: "The elder shall serve the younger." Hence this is no discussion about kingdoms and empires of the world. Much less is it a discussion of mere trifles [60] or of old wives' tales. No, these words lay the foundations of our doctrine and powerfully support

[60] Cf. p. 345, note 42.

them, namely, that before God the flesh is dead and condemned, but the spirit is made alive. And sin and original depravity are hinted at, lest anyone trust in the flesh instead of in the Lord and His promises.

This cannot be stated and impressed enough; for those are most profound judgments of God, and they are God's unsearchable ways. I am not speaking about the judgments of God a priori, which He has with Himself in His innermost and secret counsels: why He deliberates, acts, rules, saves, destroys, etc., in this way or another. No, I am speaking about God a posteriori, as He calls, speaks, and manifests Himself, just as He says to Moses (Ex. 33:23): "You shall see My back." For here indeed we see such ways and such judgments as man does not comprehend, just as is stated in 1 Cor. 2:14: "The unspiritual man does not receive the gifts of the Spirit of God; for they are folly to him, and he is not able to understand them," so that even the saints do not understand what they are asking for. To this extent those judgments and ways of God are unsearchable for us a posteriori, that is, when He calls and manifests Himself by means of the Word and an outward work. But if those things are not comprehensible, how shall we comprehend these, when He is hidden for us within Himself and in His divinity? Thus you have enough trouble and pains to understand God when He is working and calling, and there is no need for you to search and explore secrets and things that are too high for your comprehension.

Is it not the utmost blindness of the human flesh that it is so deeply offended by this example of the judgment of God, namely, that Esau, the first-born, must not be the heir, but that Jacob, who is the younger and was born after him, must have the inheritance? This you will never comprehend with your human reason, although you hear Him calling and crying aloud those words of His, yes, even destroying kings and kingdoms of the world because of them. Nevertheless, such reasoning will lead to condemnation of this judgment of God, which says: "The elder shall serve the younger." You will never persuade the Turk that he is condemned before God; nor will you persuade the pope that the Roman See is the see of Satan; nor will you persuade Charles V, Ferdinand, and the king of France. For the flesh, that is, the older, is arrogant, prevails, and is everything, as it were, in the world. On the other hand, the spirit is sad, dead, and altogether nothing. Thus Esau thinks: "I am the first-born.

Therefore I am the church. I am the son and the people of God. But Jacob has been cast aside without honor and name." In like manner, we are finding out today that our adversaries arrogate the title "church" to themselves, even though they are anything but the church.

Esau, then, is the first-born, and Jacob is born later. But God inverts the order and says: "The flesh is proud, but the spirit is sad. Nevertheless, the flesh is falsehood; but the spirit is truth." For every human being is not only a liar but is also φίλαυτος (2 Tim. 3:2). He always convinces himself, takes for granted that he knows better, and despises and hates this doctrine. Begin from the beginning of the world, and consider in order the examples of all ages. Cain, the first-born, is the lord; Abel is the servant. The kingdom of Egypt is the flower of the world, and yet it is the dung of the devil. Next the kingdom of the Assyrians, of the Babylonians, of the Greeks, and of the Romans rules.[61] The Israelites and the people of God, even of the New Testament, are oppressed by a very harsh bondage. This is recorded in opposition to the invincible pride of the flesh, in order that we may know how we should conduct ourselves in such great diversity of fortune, and how we can retain firm judgment and steadfast and dauntless courage for bearing adversity. If I see the Turk or the pope in their greatest majesty, I shall say: "You are without the Word. The Word is not with you. Therefore you may glory as much as you can, and you may be more powerful than even all the angels. Nevertheless, you are condemned, because the flesh, or the elder, shall serve the younger."

But the Turk and the followers of the pope retort: "What does the Word matter? What do Elijah, Elisha, Luther, and Philip matter? I have kingdoms, riches, power, vigor, a fine appearance, and wisdom, things in which the entire world takes pride and by means of which it rules. Hence I am blessed and am the people of God. But you are wretched and afflicted. Therefore you are cast aside by God." In opposition to this very great stumbling block we say: "We hear God, who calls, manifests Himself, and declares: 'The elder must be the younger'; that is, the flesh, which rules, must become a servant; and the spirit, which serves, must become lord." This is our glory. Of course, it is laughed at by the world and by the powerful

61 A reference to the four monarchies of Dan. 2:36-45, traditionally taken to be a prophecy of the rise and fall of empires.

of this age, just as Cain dominated at the very beginning and Abel served. Yet Cain is cast aside, but Abel lives. Thus the Assyrians and the Babylonians dominated and devastated Judea, Jerusalem, and the temple. Thus the Persians ruled and the Jews were captives. Nevertheless, the Jews remained; but the others perished completely. Thus the Romans exercised sovereignty in an arrogant manner; but the apostles were exiles and fugitives. They hungered, thirsted, were naked, and were like men destined for death (1 Cor. 4:9 ff.). Today the Turk rules and the Christians serve, the pope is arrogant and the church mourns. Nevertheless, the pope will fall and be killed by the Spirit of the mouth of Christ. "It is indeed true," says God. "The world is the elder, and the church and my people are the younger; but I decree that the elder will be the younger, and, on the other hand, the younger will be the elder."

This is the doctrine of faith, hope, comfort, and of love toward God and men. There is no other difference except that here in the church God is calling, but there in the world and among the ungodly God is silent. The Turk does not have even one letter to prove that what he is doing is being done justly. No God is there who calls. Thus the pope and the emperor hear nothing but are in silence. But we have God, who calls because He has disclosed Himself to us, so that we have a visible, perceptible, and available God. We have the Word, Baptism, the Keys. Still we suffer. It is good. Let us suffer indeed. But the servants will be lords. On the other hand, we shall remain; but they will perish. Our descendants, who are truly ours, will also remain here on earth, just as some prophets have continually remained ever since the beginning of the world (Luke 1:70) and, as though by a hereditary right, have handed down to us the Word of God.

God wanted to present this evidence to the entire world, and He wanted to confirm it with this account. Therefore we should not read it listlessly, as though it were some secular account. Otherwise it is wholly trivial, bare, and dull, as though I were reading some story about the birth or the deeds of the Turkish emperor. By a special plan God wanted to point out His teaching in this example and to manifest His work in those two brothers, in order that we might see how the elder will serve the younger. Esau is the first-born, and on this account he proudly puts on airs. He is a Chaldean, Babylonian, Persian, Greek, and Roman emperor; in short, he is the pope and the lord of lords. But he does not have the God who calls. No, he has the God who condemns him with these words: "The elder will serve," even though he does not believe these words. But Jacob has Him who calls and assigns the rule over the elder. But he is not powerful, wise, and holy. Nevertheless, since he has been called, he will rule. Thus the prophets have carefully unfolded this and have derived manifold comfort from it, as Is. 41:14 states: "Fear not, you worm Jacob."

God wanted to point this out at the very moment of his birth. Esau comes out first; he is Edom, red and shaggy. The other has a smooth skin and is not unusually red. On him nothing stands out as extraordinary. But Esau, who is the first, must be extraordinary in comparison with his brother through two very great signs; and not only his parents but also the friends and neighbors who are present unanimously called him Esau, since they were impressed by these two signs. For human reason cannot conclude otherwise than that Esau will be the heir because he is the first-born and is distinguished by two very outstanding marks, namely, redness and hairiness. Moreover, he gets the name from working or doing, as though they were saying: "This will be the man who will do everything admirably and will be what is popularly called a factotum," just as Cain got his name from the fact that his mother thought that she had obtained the man whom God had promised as the Victor over sin and the serpent.[62] This is surely how the world is when it forms an opinion about those very important matters. Therefore let us judge better about the judgments of God, which are foolishness before the world; for the world itself is Esau and the factotum, just as the Turk and the pope are Esau. But we are spurned and despised. Yet in the Word and in the call these things can be separated.

Moreover, they have three reasons for praising Esau so highly. In the first place, he is the first-born. In the second place, he is the child that was waited for with a great longing during 20 years and was obtained through many prayers. In the third place, he is red and shaggy. All these things bring it about that they all promise themselves something extraordinary from that infant, contrary to the decree of God.

Thus we are wont to interpret the signs which are against us,

62 Cf. p. 195. In his translation of the Bible Luther rendered Gen. 4:1: "I have gotten a man, the Lord," namely, a man who is the Lord, the Messiah.

and by which God threatens the ungodly, in the opposite way, as though they were favorable to us. We flatter and comfort ourselves, as though no misfortune could happen to us. Thus the Jews understood it in the most favorable way when, before the destruction of Jerusalem, the temple was opened at night without a hand, which was a sign that the city would be destroyed together with the temple, and that the heathen would enter the temple without any hindrance.[63] They kept on saying: "The Lord will now be with us; He is coming to us of His own accord." To this extent our reason is fond of itself, and whatever good is said it applies to itself. For example, if anyone is praised, it assumes that this is being said most truthfully of itself. To this extent man is his own worst sycophant and a Gnatho.[64] From signs that portend evil we infer good things, and we assign the evil things to other people.

Thus these two signs, namely, being red and shaggy — which they suppose were given to glorify the first-born — are decidedly unfavorable. For in Holy Scripture redness denotes bloodthirsty justice, but shagginess denotes cruelty, just as, on the other hand, brightness, light, and whiteness have a good meaning. Here, therefore, the birth itself points out that all who are of the blood are relentlessly bloodthirsty and cruel without compassion. Furthermore, a shaggy skin is deceptive and denotes hypocrisy. These are surely very bad signs and contrary to reason. Therefore it interprets them to its own advantage and in a more favorable way.

Moreover, let us note that on the body of Satan there are shaggy and detestable hypocrites, because a shaggy skin is a mendacious skin. But a natural skin should not be rough. Furthermore, the red color pertains to homicides. These two portents — namely, falsehood and homicide — are in the church and on the body of the devil. Yet those people do not recognize these signs but glory in their righteousness and compassion. Thus Christ says in John 16:2: "Whoever kills you will think he is offering service to God." Therefore he who kills Christ and those who are His does not seem shaggy and red, does he? Indeed, he seems exceedingly white, like the sun, and more brilliant than all the stars. Nothing shaggy is apparent in the hypocrites. Indeed, here one sees righteousness at its best, religious de-

---

[63] This is reported by Josephus, *The Wars of the Jews*, Book VI, pars. 28—30.

[64] Gnatho was the attendant of Thraso in the *Eunuchus* of Terence, one of Luther's favorite plays; cf. *Luther's Works*, 13, p. 182; 23, p. 217.

votion, and truth. Therefore one should note carefully that Esau carries with him the true and characteristic signs of the church of the devil, as whose head he is described. But Jacob, the other child, is not red; he is smooth and white.

In this manner God has embellished this account not only with promises but also with signs, in order to strengthen this conviction that the flesh is subject to death and the devil, however powerful and grand it may be, and no matter if it is a thousand times greater than the Turk and all kingdoms. But Jacob and those who are really godly in the world are nothing. The others are everything. But the difference is this: Among us there is the Word; on the other side there is silence. Moreover, God calls into existence the things that do not exist (Rom. 4:17); and He destroys into nothingness the things that exist. For the Word of God is greater than countless worlds. Therefore it is not without a special plan that God has presented these two very clear signs to strike the eyes and ears of all people. Esau is the deed and work that God has done. We are not Esau; we are absolutely nothing. But this account teaches the opposite and gives us powerful confirmation that all the things of the world and of Esau are nothing, but that the Word of God alone is everything.

One should also note in this passage, when Isaac does not immediately understand the signs and the birth of his sons in accordance with the meaning of the promise, that the saints do not learn or understand everything at one time and suddenly. Thus above, too, we heard that Abraham and Sarah were compelled to make progress and advance, and did not immediately have a perfect understanding of God's promise. Accordingly, experience enables the saints to progress from clarity to clarity. Abraham kept thinking that he would have offspring from Sarah. But when he sees that she is exhausted and barren on account of her age, he marries Hagar; and he regards her as the mother of the Seed until, as a result of the Holy Spirit's interpretation, the promise is explained anew to the effect that Sarah will be the mother of the Promised Seed. Thus from day to day the fathers were trained and made progress more and more, as Peter admonishes in 2 Peter 3:18: "Grow in the grace, etc." They did not arrive immediately at perfect and complete understanding, but varied practice and experience, various trials and perils, instructed them. Thus here Isaac and Rebecca heard that there would be two peoples and that the elder would serve the younger. Then they reasoned in this manner: "He who is the first-born is undoubtedly the older." And they think that the war has already been brought to an end in the mother's womb. For this reason they name the first child Esau, that is, maker or doer of all things, as though they were saying: "Jacob should have been the elder, but in accordance with God's decree he was overcome in the womb by his brother, who came out first and was distinguished by these two signs." For this reason it is not stated about Jacob: "They called his name," as the first-born is called Esau in accordance with the common consent of all; but his father named him. And he has his name from the sole, as though you called him one who trips up another's heels or treads underfoot. Nevertheless, it is more the expression of a wish than a statement of fact.[65] The name Esau is a statement of fact and not the expression of a wish; he will do these things. But because Jacob, who was the elder in the womb, became the younger at the birth and was overcome by the elder, the father thought: "God grant that you may become one who trips up, just as it is apparent up to this time from your posture that you wanted to trip up the elder, since you took hold of his heel. But the voice of God has reversed this." Therefore it was the father's wish that Jacob be what he wanted, namely, one who treads underfoot, not his first-born brother and the victor, of course, but the heathen and other nations.

This, I believe, is how Isaac understood the promise and the birth of his two sons at first. For the fathers were not so holy and perfect as the monks dream about Augustine and other saints, who, as they imagine, were altogether perfect. And it is an example which proves that the saintly fathers grew in knowledge, just as all godly persons must continually grow. On this account God permitted them to fall and to go astray, in order that we might know that knowledge, faith, and love remained imperfect in them, just as later on the very serious fall of Isaac will be described.

Examples of this kind teach us that one should not believe any human being, no matter how saintly he may be, but must pay attention to Him who calls and to His Word. But one should not study the Word for only a year or two, for the Word of God is a boundless subject. Our adversaries exclaim: "Ambrose, Augustine taught this or that!" But they are of no importance to us unless they bring the voice of Christ. Whoever of them has the Word and that voice

---

[65] Luther uses the terms "indicative" and "optative."

in greater clarity, I would rather follow him than I would want to follow Augustine or anyone else. Thus Augustine teaches Holy Scripture more clearly and discusses it more skillfully than Ambrose. Therefore it is more profitable to read him than Ambrose. But in regard to all let us always hold fast to the following words: "Thy Word is a lamp to my feet and a light to my path" (Ps. 119:105); and 2 Peter 1:19 states: "We have the prophetic Word made more sure. You will do well to pay attention to this as to a lamp shining in a dark place, until the day dawns and the morning star rises in your hearts."

For nothing can be learned so perfectly and completely as it is perfect and pure in itself, for the carnal mind still clings to us. It must be purged by means of trials, in order that the light may become clearer and clearer.

Isaac was sixty years old when she bore them.

27. *When the boys grew up, Esau was a skillful hunter, a man of the field, while Jacob was a quiet man, dwelling in tents.*

Moses mentions Isaac's age in order to point out and commend the very pure chastity in which this man lived with Rebecca for 20 years. Then it is also pointed out how they waited for offspring for so long a time, to the point of despair. Thus the very saintly spouses were trained by many trials. They were not idle or in a frenzy in regard to lust, as the lazy race of men of this last age today usually is. They were also foreigners, and they had nothing of their own; but they wandered here and there in great patience and humility, as has been stated above about Abraham. All these matters belong here.

But at this time Abraham was still living. He lived in association with these grandsons for 15 years, but his life was far shorter than that of the rest of the patriarchs. Moreover, I have no doubt that the boys had outstanding natural qualities; for both were brought up and taught by Abraham himself to obey and respect not only their parents but also the patriarchs. Perhaps Abraham was also the interpreter of this promise and, together with the others, wanted Esau to become the elder on account of the victory given to him by God in the womb when he had been the younger. He did not understand or see more, because he died before becoming acquainted with the character and inclinations of the two boys.

Now, however, Holy Scripture begins to hasten to point out the difference between these two brothers and to make clear which one of these two is really the elder and the lord. It does so in order that this promise may be understood: "One nation shall be stronger than the other" and "The elder shall serve the younger." After they have grown up, that separation begins, and each of the two is known by his inclinations, as the ancient little line has it: "Just as the twig is bent the tree's inclined." [66] For at that time there was no doubt that Esau is the first-born, that the promise pertains to him because he is the elder, and that he should rule, but that Jacob, as the younger, should serve. But this is a description of the two brothers by antithesis. Esau is described in this manner because by his own fault and deserts he deprived himself of precedence and would soon be the younger. Jacob, on the other hand, would get possession of the rule and of precedence. For Esau is a skillful hunter and a man of the field. That lord, maker, and doer, you see, is smug and puffed up on account of his primogeniture, and little by little he falls away from the promise and the Spirit into the glory of the flesh. For he hears that he is the priest and lord. This leads immediately to contempt for his brother and the spiritual gifts, and the pride of the flesh follows. Jacob, on the other hand, is modest, humble, quiet, and forthright. He is not excessively proud and does not seek glory. He is the sack-bearer and the water carrier.[67] This is the beginning of Esau's horrible fall and a picture of the entire world, which in this manner falls from the Spirit into the flesh. For they despise what is moderate, humble, sorrowful, dangerous, and subject to annoyance and inconveniences; they seek glory, peace, riches, and the friendship of the mighty.

But at first Esau is not aware of his fall. He does not notice it until he is deprived of the blessing. Meanwhile he is arrogant, does not concern himself about or honor his father, takes a wife from the Canaanites, and takes for granted too confidently that he cannot lose such great blessings. All hypocrites and presumptuous persons always have this practice, as Ps. 10:11 states: "He thinks in his heart 'God has forgotten, He has hid His face, He will never see it.'" About the godly they say: "They are heretics and cursed; we are the

---

[66] The Latin hexameter is given here in the familiar rendering of Alexander Pope, *Moral Essays*, Epistle I, line 150.

[67] Several times in this and in the next paragraph the text breaks into German.

children of the kingdom; we are the church and the people of God."
Thus at all times all heretics and all adversaries of the Word are
completely sure and confident in God's favor. Indeed, this vice is
so widespread that it cannot be expressed in words. Thus at first
the Sacramentarians used to cry out: "It is the most certain truth."
For all those people are puffed up by the success of the flesh and
the things the flesh seeks, such as glory, greatness, and popular
applause. They are offended by the foolishness and weakness of
the Spirit. Therefore Esau also arrogated to himself the episcopate
and supreme government in the church of Abraham. But he did
not pay much attention to obeying his mother, as Jacob did; for it
seemed servile to obey his mother in the case of those trivial household activities that belonged to the servants and to Jacob. He thought:
"I am lord; Jacob must fetch water. I am lord in both estates of
society.[68] Jacob is my servant." Therefore he is completely smug
and chooses a kind of life that is not irksome or difficult but pleasant
and showy. "Esau," says Moses, "was a skillful hunter, a man of the
field" — not by being a farmer in the field, although he undoubtedly
had land and possessions; but this is an antithetical comparison of
the pursuits of each of the two brothers. Esau occupied himself in
the fields with hunting, riding horseback, and waging war. What
did Jacob do? He was forthright and irreproachable, and he lived
in the tents. *War ein mann, der sich fein still hielt.*

But it is impossible that Esau did not also lapse into many other
vices. Even if a hunter avoids other crimes and sins, he nevertheless often sins by becoming indignant and cursing in a wicked manner when everything does not go as he feels in his heart that it
should go; and when we are surrounded by the glory of the flesh,
we are in certain danger. Therefore the psalm (62:10) warns the
rich: "If riches increase, set not your heart on them." And Job declares about himself (31:24): "If I have made gold my trust, or
called fine gold my confidence, etc."; that is, I did not take pride in
the abundance of gold and riches, and I did not despise others.
Likewise (v. 17): "If I have eaten my morsel alone, and the father-
less has not eaten of it, etc." Consequently, riches are fraught with
danger. In the Gospel they are called thorns and the unrighteous
mammon (Luke 16:11); and if the Holy Spirit is not there, a rich
man is not among the number of those who mourn but goes along

---

[68] The estates of society are the church and the state (plus the family).

in his affluence and most certainly lapses into arrogance and into contempt for God and men, makes flesh his arm, and worships mammon instead of God. Thus wealth becomes an idol. Therefore Christ says: "You cannot serve God and mammon" (Matt. 6:24). And there is an old German saying: "Gold makes bold" (cf. Eccl. 41:26). But this is not the fault of riches; it is the fault of the flesh, which is arrogant and despises others.

In the second place, over and beyond that pride and idolatry, the flesh adds theft and rapine, namely, when it does not follow the example of Job and does not share its possessions with the poor, does not clothe the naked, and does not perform other duties of love. For the flesh loves and watches over its riches to such an extent that not even the rich themselves enjoy them. First, therefore, the rich become idolaters contrary to the First Table. Secondly, they become unrighteous toward their neighbor, robbers, and thieves; for they should give to the poor yet do not give. Some do give, but with the condition that they regard those who receive as under obligation to themselves; that is, they give grudgingly and haughtily, not with a guileless eye but in order that they may be honored and praised.

Hence it is exceedingly difficult for a rich person to be righteous and godly, because idolatry and contempt for one's brother are associated with wealth. Furthermore, the rich often do not refrain from manifest villainies; they plot against the property of others, do violence to orphans, and rob not only by omission but also by commission. Consequently, there are graspers and usurers. Their offenses are punishable even according to civil laws. But I am speaking only of those rich people who refrain from actual theft — that is, theft of commission — and commit theft of omission — that is, when they do not give to the poor, do not acknowledge that riches are gifts of God, and are not grateful. This is characteristic of all the rich if the Holy Spirit is not there, as He was in Job, in David, and in other godly kings, all of whom had an abundance of wealth. But David says (Ps. 62:10): "If riches increase, set not your heart on them."

Besides, the common danger for rich people is the sin of omission, when they do not come to the aid of the poor and needy, even though God has sternly commanded (Is. 58:7): "Share your bread with the hungry, and bring the homeless poor into your house." If you do not do this, you will hear that sad verdict (Luke 12:48): "Everyone to whom much is given, of him will much be required." Consequently it is very dangerous to be rich.

And in Is. 53:9 the rich are regarded as ungodly, because without the Holy Spirit, godliness, and faith there is no difference between a rich person and an ungodly one. The ungodly person robs God of His glory, does not give thanks to God, and then refuses aid to the poor. A rich person who is without faith does the same thing. Therefore he is ungodly.

Thus Esau's primogeniture causes him to strive eagerly for the glory of the flesh, for power, and for wisdom. He refuses to be satisfied with a menial state, as his brother Jacob is. He chooses the pursuit of hunting and riding, in which he could not engage without sin — even of commission — especially in the case of hunting, just as our princes sin not only by omission on their hunts but also most gravely by commission.[69] They ruin the crops and fields for the farmers, who are not permitted to drive the wild animals in any manner from their gardens or fields. But the animals run riot with impunity and destroy the fields that have been tilled with great toil. There not only help and defense cease, but damage is also inflicted on those who should be helped. Consequently, the Turk or another hunter will eventually come and wrest from the princes of Germany both their nets and their hunting spears.

I am saying this in order that we may know that hunting is not without great sins. In fact, many have debated the question whether hunting is proper or right. In itself, of course, it is not evil, and it can be pursued in a manner that is godly and good, as we see in the case of the most illustrious ruler of Saxony, Elector Frederick. He used to hunt in such a manner that he harmed nobody but rather benefited many. If at any time he noticed that even a little damage had been done, he paid doubly for it. He often even distributed to the peasants some measures of grain to compensate them for what the wild animals would consume. This is worthy of a good and estimable prince; for we do not want to deprive the princes of their royal prerogatives, as the peasants were attempting to do in the revolt that took place in the year 1525.

Besides, it is the purpose of hunting to keep the more ferocious animals — wolves, bears, boars — at a distance and to protect human beings and beasts of burden. Hunting should be done in such a manner that sheep and other harmless animals are protected; for a ruler's

---

[69] On the "sweet-sour" sport of hunting cf. Luther's letter to Spalatin, August 15, 1521, W, *Briefe*, II, 380, 381; and *Luther's Works*, 14, Introduction, p. xii.

duty obliges him to spare his subjects and to conquer the proud, as the poet says.[70] Furthermore, the pleasure and delight granted to those who engage in hunting without harm to and ruin for their subjects is even honorable. But if hunting is carried on in any other way, it is very bad and is a harmful pursuit.

I am afraid, however, that because Esau is supposed to have been completely carnal, he often forgot his duty and was guilty of many sins of commission and omission. But because he is the first-born and the specially beloved son of his father, he commits no sin whatever and does nothing wickedly or sinfully even when he does things that are sinful to the highest degree. But if he did sin to some extent, he undoubtedly concealed it from his father. He was able to do this, of course, since he was the ruler in the home and among the domestics.

Now let us also look at the second part of the antithesis: "While Jacob was a man תָּם, dwelling in tents." All have translated תָּם with "simple," "foolish," although the Hebrew text does not have this meaning. For תָּם does not denote one who is simple in mind and intellect, that is, without ingenuity and industry. No, it denotes one who is simple, upright, blameless, and sincere in regard to his will. The same word occurs in Ps. 119:1: "Blessed are the blameless." For, as is evident later on when he buys the birthright from his brother, Jacob is not dull. Lyra even explains it in this manner: "Without a trace of deceit, not simple on account of a lack of industry." [71] Esau was not such a man; but in regard to his will he was far more unstable and cunning, because he married heathen wives and mingled with the Canaanites. Hunters are not blameless, but they often adapt their pursuits to the difference in the times, the situations, and the persons. Jacob, however, is simple and stead-fast, is not influenced by persons and is not changed by events. Nevertheless, he is not foolish. This is a fine comparison.

In the second place, Jacob is not a man of the fields. He has no political and carnal pursuits — although affairs of state can be ad-ministered in a godly and proper manner — but he dwelt exclusively in tents; that is, he remained at home with his father and mother, and served them. Lyra tells what the Jews thought about the tents.

[70] Vergil, *Aeneid*, VI, 853.

[71] This is a verbatim quotation from Lyra *ad* Gen. 25:27, who reports that according to the rabbis Jacob frequented the tents of Melchizedek.

I am in complete accord with what he has to say, because it is taken from the fathers. They say that tents not only for the households but also for the churches are meant. Thus one speaks of the tent of Moses and means a sacred tent. We call them churches and schools. But at that time there was no difference between the sacred tents and those occupied by households. Abraham had in his tent a house of God and a church, just as today any godly and pious head of a household instructs his children and domestics in godliness. Therefore such a house is actually a school and church, and the head of the household is a bishop and priest in his house. Thus the tents in which Jacob dwelt were sacred, and there he sought first the kingdom of God (Matt. 6:33). Esau, on the other hand, sought the kingdom of the world. Therefore he lost both, namely, the worldly and the spiritual kingdom, because it is a general and perpetual rule that for those who seek first the kingdom of God the other things are added. On the other hand, to those who want to get their own advantages and their daily bread before being concerned about the kingdom of God the opposite will happen; they will lose the kingdom of God together with the physical kingdom.

For a time, therefore, Jacob was younger and lower than his brother. But his heart and trust clung completely to God, and he was a pious and godly young man. He went to the church and schools often and gladly, learned the Word and good manners, and heard the addresses of the patriarch Shem and the others, just as the Jews have commented — and they got this from the fathers — that this passage should be understood of the tents of Shem and Eber, who were contemporaries of Jacob for 80 years.

Moreover, they were most saintly men; they burned with wonderful zeal for the Word of God and had a far greater concern for religion and the worship of God than we have. Yet we, too, shall properly call our houses and churches tents when someone has a church in his home and in it instructs his children and domestics in godliness and virtue. But the more fervent and vigorous the spirit with which the Word is treated, the more fruit it brings. Therefore the gloss of the Jews pleases me, and this is an outstanding example of a pious and godly young man who does not involve himself above all in secular affairs and carnal pursuits. Of course, he did not disregard these completely; but his first concern was to cling to the fathers — Shem, Shelah, and Eber. And on the basis of a computation of the years [72] one concludes that Jacob was a contemporary of Eber for 80 years, of Shem for 46, and of Shelah for 23. With these fathers Jacob undoubtedly associated eagerly and reverently, especially with Eber; for Shem, who was exhausted by old age, commended the boy Jacob to the patriarch Eber. Shem, you see, was the father of all the churches, as was stated above in the tenth chapter: "Shem, the father of all the children of Eber" (v. 21). For this reason the entire people and the whole church looked up to him in his extreme old age. But Eber took care of and taught the church, because he was able to bear the burden of governing it. Consequently, I gladly agree with the words of the Jews, or rather of the fathers, that Jacob was not only in the tent at home but also in the tents of others, especially with Eber and Shem.

Jacob refrained from marrying for almost 70 years. Esau, as the lord and a man who was altogether worldly, took Canaanite wives when he was 40 years old. All these circumstances indicate that Esau was excessively proud on account of his primogeniture, despised his brother, disdained the tents, and devoted himself completely to those equestrian pursuits and to hunting.

But this is not to be understood as meaning that Esau was never in the tents. On the contrary, he sometimes visited them with his brother and others, just as the hypocrites studiously resort to something like this and want to appear even saintlier and more righteous than those who are truly saintly and godly. Thus he was a hearer in his father's church, and now and then, for the fun of it, he visited the other churches in which Eber and Shelah taught. Secretly, however, he did not regard them highly, just as among us Christians for the most part despise the ministry and divine worship. "Why should I go to church?" they say, "After all, I can read at home." And in this way they start gradually with a loathing of the Word until they are involved in civil affairs and become completely irreligious. But the godly should carefully remember that he who seeks the kingdom of God finds both, and that he who disdains the kingdom of God loses both. Therefore they should place Jacob's example before themselves for imitation and should diligently hear and learn the Word of God. Wherever this is taught, there one finds the tents of God; and everyone should be fully

[72] Cf. p. 300, note 1.

convinced that if first of all he has the Word of God, all things will then follow. For God existed before the founding of the world. He created everything through the Word. Therefore the Word of God makes and brings everything.

This, then, is the description of the two brothers. Holy Scripture praises and prefers Jacob in respect to religion and godliness; it praises and prefers Esau in respect to civil government, because he sought the rule of the world. And this is justly censured in him. There one can see how he turns aside and loses his primogeniture on account of his irreverence, but how Jacob gets it on account of his piety and godliness. From this we should learn first of all to seek the kingdom of God and not to disregard it in favor of the pursuits and desires of this world.

28. *Isaac loved Esau, because he ate of his game; but Rebecca loved Jacob.*

This part of the account is quite obscure, difficult, and involved; for Moses presents an amazing difference between the two brothers. Esau is loved by his father, but Jacob is loved by his mother; and this stems from the difference in the natures and interests of the brothers. For it is natural for all mothers to take pleasure in mild and unassuming dispositions and manners, because women who are pious and honorable are by nature timid and gentle. Thus Peter (1 Peter 3:6) comforts them as the weaker and exhorts them not to be greatly afraid of any disturbance. And there is a natural difference between the dispositions of sons and daughters. Men are endowed with rather impetuous dispositions. Daughters are more amiable and attach themselves to their parents in a gentle and pleasant manner. Therefore Rebecca loved Jacob by nature because he had mild and pleasant manners and a kind, modest, and shy disposition. For he honored his mother with all respect, heard the Word and the sermons, and honored the saintly fathers. All this is wonderfully pleasing in young people and delightful to mothers. On the other hand, Rebecca was offended by Esau's disposition and by his rather uncouth and rough manners.

But just as mothers love sons who have a mild disposition more than they love those who are somewhat impetuous and bold, so fathers love sons who are a little livelier and more spirited and for this reason, it seems, will be more suited and more eager to manage affairs. And it is certainly fitting for sons to be livelier than daughters. Such a man was Esau, and Isaac was aware that for governing an alert and active mind was needed. Therefore he favored Esau's disposition.

Furthermore, over and above their nature each had something worthy of special [73] commendation. Jacob had an upright and unspoiled will, was saintly and very zealously devoted to godliness, and was fervent in his desire for the kingdom of God. This pleases his mother Rebecca, for she is a saintly and godly woman. For this reason she wishes Jacob to be the first-born, and, what was most important, that the promise be fulfilled, in order that the elder may serve the younger. In addition to his energetic and active disposition, Esau has a special talent for shooting with arrows, as has been stated above about Ishmael (21:20). This pleases his father as an appropriate adornment of his first-born, who must uphold the government.

For natural law, which is known to all nations,[74] assigns the rule to the first-born. In civil law there is a different stipulation. But over and above the law of nature Esau also relied on the authority of the fathers and on the Law of God, according to which the first-born was the lord but the other brothers were servants. This is the difference in their pursuits and in the dissimilar love the parents had for the twins. Jacob's godliness commends him to the mother, but because of primogeniture the father has the reason for his favorable inclination from the Law of God. Yet the mother does not take primogeniture into consideration to the extent that she considers the line of descent and the inheritance of the promise (Gen. 22:18): "In your Seed shall all the nations be blessed." This she especially desires to transfer to Jacob.

At this point a difficult question arises. I have already touched on it briefly. The promise clearly states: "The elder shall serve the younger." But everybody is agreed that Esau is the older, just as in the opinion of all Jacob is the younger. Consequently, if Isaac knew the promise according to which Jacob must be the elder, then he clearly sinned deliberately, wittingly, and perversely against God's plain promise. What are we going to say here? Even if he has on his side the Law of God, which makes lords of all the first-born, nevertheless God, the author of the Law, has the power to

[73] Reading *singularis* rather than *singulari*.
[74] Cf. *Luther's Works*, 13, p. 160, note 27.

make exceptions from the Law. Therefore Isaac is not excused because he has the Law on his side; but he must give the primogeniture to Jacob and not to Esau, in accord with the promise. Thus he is terrified later on as though guilty of a sin when Jacob has snatched away the primogeniture.

Then another question arises. Did Isaac know about that promise or not? Nearly all treat this passage in such a manner that they seem to think that Rebecca kept this promise to herself and concealed it from her husband.[75] For it is on this account that Isaac so steadfastly and wholeheartedly assigns the primogeniture to his son Esau and not to Jacob.

But I shall not readily agree with this. For above we heard how Isaac prayed in Rebecca's behalf and sent her to Shem. Consequently, it is not likely that Rebecca concealed that declaration, especially since she did not know at that time which of the two would come out first. Therefore I have no doubt that she shared with her husband the answer of Shem, who said that the older should serve the younger. But after their birth Isaac transfers to wicked Esau the primogeniture and the blessing which rightly belongs to his son Jacob. This is a very troublesome and difficult matter. That question is still undecided, and I do not see how we may settle it. But I would readily accede to the opinion that after Isaac had heard the declaration about the struggle of the two infants in the womb, he thought that it had to be understood in such a way that he who would come out first overcame the elder in the womb, since he was the younger, that the struggle had been brought to an end in this way, and that the promise had been fulfilled. In the womb Jacob was the elder, but God's promise changed that order, so that Jacob, he who treads underfoot, became the younger and was born later.

These thoughts come to my mind about this question. Although I have neither the courage nor the desire to make a positive statement, yet it seems altogether probable and likely. I am influenced by the example of Ishmael, who, as Abraham believed, would be the heir when he still knew nothing about Isaac. He held fast to the statement made in the sixteenth chapter: "I will so greatly multiply your descendants that they cannot be numbered for multitude" (v. 10). At that time he did not understand the promise in any

75 By this means the exegetical tradition had sought to exonerate Isaac.

other way than that Ishmael would be the heir, because the promise
is completely general and no clear and sure meaning can be gathered
from it until God explained His statement. "The promise," He said,
"is not to be understood about Ishmael, as you think, but about Sarah
and her son."

Thus Isaac seems to have been wholly of the opinion that the
primogeniture rightly belonged to his son Esau. Nor was he disturbed
by the fierceness of manners and disposition for which his mother
was wont to find fault with Esau; he thought this was appropriate
for the first-born, and future lord and ruler. And if there were
some fault, he hoped that it would be corrected as Esau grew older
and changed his pursuits for the better, and that he could accustom
himself to some restraint. Indeed, I am pleased with this thought
or conjecture about what Isaac did. But if his purpose was different,
and if he intentionally and wittingly transferred the blessing to
Esau, he cannot easily be excused, just as Rebecca cannot be excused
either if she concealed that answer from her husband. Therefore
one must take a middle course.

But because both persist so strongly in their opinion — for the
husband's simply states the fact, while the mother's expresses a wish
and is truer — people argue further that Rebecca, by special divine
inspiration, had the understanding that the younger would be the
elder. This I grant. Thus above Sarah also had the inspiration of
the Spirit that her son Ishmael had to be cast out. For it is not
recorded or clearly commanded anywhere that he should be cast
out; but Sarah determines this on her own, because in Ishmael she
detects many things that conflicted with the primogeniture and sees
that he persecutes him who was born according to the promise. Thus
Rebecca must have had an extraordinary inspiration — an inspiration
which Isaac did not have.

But one should not accept any inspiration at all rashly and without a definite reason, for this is dangerous. The pope declares that
the inspiration of nature is sometimes like a favor of the devil, and
as an example of this he mentions the account of the temptations of
Christ in Matt. 4:1 ff.[76] But there is more truth in the statement
that the devil can disguise himself as an angel of light (2 Cor. 11:14)
and change himself into the majesty of God. Therefore the Word of

[76] On the *instinctus naturae* cf., for example, Thomas Aquinas, *Summa Theologica,* I, Q. 19, art. 10.

God must be added to that inspiration. Thus Sarah's inspiration originates from the fact that she knows that she has the promise according to which she is the mother of the true Seed. Ishmael did not have this promise. Then she judges the tree from its fruits, because Ishmael persecutes her son and the true heir, seeks carnal things, and teaches idolatry. That inspiration is trustworthy.

Thus it is possible that Rebecca heard from the fathers: "Your son Esau is unmanageable and headstrong. Therefore he will not be the heir of the blessing. To be sure, he visits the temple or the tent; but he is not seriously affected by any zeal for godliness. Jacob, however, is godly and pious. Therefore he is destined to become the elder." In this case there is added the example and the experience, for Esau is irreligious and becomes worse. Jacob, on the other hand, seeks the kingdom of heaven and grows in the fear of God and in other virtues. That inspiration is also good and sure.

Accordingly, we must always take pains to have a sure Word. Or even if the command of God does not always precede, one sees after the event what kind of inspiration there was. Thus David kills a lion, a bear, and Goliath; but the Spirit rushes upon him. This was an inspiration that was not seen until after the event. And such inspirations have the Word of God as their foundation; or even if they are without the Word at first, they are recognized later on and judged to have been from God. This is what has happened to us. We attacked the pope without a Word, but now we see that this was an inspiration of God without our knowledge and plan. But about this we shall speak elsewhere. Now Rebecca plans further how Jacob may acquire the primogeniture. Esau is completely smug and thinks he is out of all danger, since he is the first-born and the lord. But now follows the opportunity which causes him to lose the primogeniture altogether.

29. *Once when Jacob was boiling pottage, Esau came in from the field, and he was famished.*

30. *And Esau said to Jacob: Let me eat some of the pottage, that red pottage; for I am famished! (Therefore his name was called Edom.)*

Up to this point Moses has described the divergent pursuits the two brothers had. Esau was a man of the field and a hunter; that is,

he concerned himself little about the pursuits of godliness, the sermons
and teaching of the fathers who were still living. But what usually
happens to everybody happened to him. When people are indifferent
about small things, they gradually lose the greater things too. Esau
considered it a small and unimportant matter that he was more
indifferent in the pursuits of godliness than Jacob was, that he did
not glow with zeal for the divine services and the knowledge and
worship of God as Jacob did. But that indifference gradually grows
and progresses to the point that he even despises his birthright. Next
he falls into the smugness and arrogance which cause him to think
he can deceive his brother with impunity, as though he had not sold
his birthright in earnest. For he did not believe that the birthright
could be transferred to his brother; he believed that it belonged
rightfully to him, and he hopes that he will keep the blessing. He
makes sport of his brother and thus becomes completely ungodly in
his relation to God, to his fellowmen, and to his brother.

Such ungodliness and smugness follow when the Word of God is
despised and is not made use of. People become atheists, Epicureans,
and bereft of reason. The examples of even very excellent people
prove this. David was a very saintly man and most ardent in his
worship of God. But how quickly he is driven to adultery, murder,
and blasphemy! For to be asleep with regard to the Word of God
is to open the window to the devil. Therefore we have been commanded to be watchful, as is written in 1 Peter 5:8: "Be sober, be
watchful. Your adversary the devil prowls around like a roaring lion,
seeking someone to devour." And Eph. 5:15 says: "Look carefully,
then, how you walk, not as unwise men but as wise, making the
most of the time." Sluggishness and indifference in sacred matters
have often resulted in the greatest lapses and in horrible sins.

Yes, even in wordly matters it is of the utmost importance to
be vigilant and to pay heed to or neglect an opportunity. Thus the
Turks watch carefully for all opportunities. For this reason they have
won many victories over us in a short time. In the year 1532 our
emperor had an opportunity near Vienna to be brilliantly successful
against the Turks; but since he neglected it, we are now looking in
vain for other opportunities.[77]

Therefore let us accustom ourselves to wholehearted love for
the First Table. If it is necessary to take the field or to assume

[77] Cf. p. 28, note 33.

some other responsibility, in the household or in the government, the kingdom of God should be our first and foremost concern. If this is disregarded, we see Esau falling so wretchedly that he never rises again. Jacob, on the other hand, prospers and becomes the first-born because of a very favorable opportunity. Esau has the name and the glory of being the first-born, but meanwhile he falls suddenly and horribly and is deprived of all glory and honor. Therefore do not sleep; but be very attentive to all opportunities, lest you lose your gifts and the kingdom of God because of your negligence. For this reason Scripture has set this example before us, not as a cold and dead story but for our instruction and to remind us of the state of affairs and persons as it exists in all ages.

The Holy Spirit wants us to keep those two brothers before our eyes continually and to consider them a daily proverb, for at all times we are either Esauites or Jacobites. In outward appearance Esau is saintlier and more religious than all the others and seems to be the owner and heir of the kingdom of heaven; yet he is nothing else than Esau, that is, self-righteous, work-righteous, and a hypocrite who is not seriously concerned about religion. He is religious solely for the sake of gain and his belly. Nor can the name "church" be taken away from him, just as we do not have the name "church" before the world but are regarded as heretics and as born second. But the papists boast that they are the first-born. And even if we were to prevail over the pope and his followers and to achieve success with the doctrine which characterizes the true church, there would arise among us either papists or Turks who would arrogate to themselves the title "church," just as the Anabaptists and the Sacramentarians, etc., have already appeared. And it cannot happen otherwise. Thus the Arians arose when the heathen persecutors had been overcome. They usurped the name "church," and the true church was despised and spurned. Thus at all times Cain or Abel, Esau or Jacob certainly originate from the same stock and from the same Gospel of salvation.

And so Esau is the bishop, the factotum, and the church. Yet nothing is owed to him; for by divine authority the entire blessing has been transferred to Jacob, who is the true possessor of all honors and of the kingdom of heaven. But so far he has been deprived of the name and prestige owed to him until his brother Esau himself provides a wonderful opportunity to acquire it — an opportunity that surpasses Jacob's every hope and thought. One cannot get away from the pottage.[78] The intention to deceive his brother does not enter Jacob's mind; but everything happens in accordance with the arrangement and plan of God, contrary to the intention of each of the two, Jacob and Esau.

Jacob is attending to his usual tasks; he is in the tent with his mother Rebecca, and there he is cooking pottage. This simple matter God turns into a wonderful opportunity. Esau returns from the field. The exertion and activity of hunting — a pursuit which pleased his father Isaac — have made him tired, and it is apparent that he did not bring along anything to eat, because he is not only fatigued but also hungry and thirsty. This is why he asks so eagerly for some of that red pottage, for he employs a repetition: "Let me eat some of the red pottage, that red pottage." This indicates a great appetite and desire for food. It is as if some famished person were to say: "Let me eat with you of the carp, and of just that carp for which I have a desire." Moses wanted to indicate not only the hunger and weariness of Esau but also his pleasure and appetite, namely, that he looked at and longed for that red pottage with extraordinary pleasure.

I commend this passage to the Hebrew grammarians for more careful explanation, for it is impossible to translate any language in such a way that all the emphases and forms of all words and sentences are preserved. The verb Esau uses in speaking to Jacob is הַלְעִיטֵנִי. It occurs in this passage only, but what its meaning is neither the Jews nor I know.[79] The conjugation and the construction reveal the meaning to some extent: "I beg you; let me eat; feed me; give me to eat." It is not without a reason that Holy Scripture wanted to speak in this particular way; it could have used another expression to denote feeding, nourishing, or something of that kind. But it wanted to use a special verb. Rabbi Solomon imagines that Esau was so tired that he was unable to raise his hands to his mouth and put the food into himself. But I do not know whether this agrees properly with what follows, when the text says: "He ate and drank and went his way" (v. 34). But the meaning is that Esau wanted

[78] Here and in the next paragraph the text breaks into colloquial German, as Luther himself presumably did in his paraphrase of the conversation between Jacob and Esau.

[79] The source of this information is Johannes Reuchlin, *De rudimentis hebraicis* (Pforzheim, 1506), Book II, p. 271.

the pottage, which Jacob had cooked for himself, to be given to him. He said: "Feed or refresh me with that red pottage."

That the words "Therefore his name was called Edom" are added is not at all without a purpose, although the reason for the name, namely, the lentils or the red pottage, seems rather ridiculous and senseless. Undoubtedly, however, something more important is hinted at. For above (v. 25), when Esau was born completely red, he was not called Edom because of his red skin, which would be a weightier and more justifiable reason for this surname; but there his name is called Esau. Now, when he had his fill of the red pottage, he is called Edom.

But Esau has three names. Esau is his own name, which he received at birth or at his circumcision. His surname is Edom, from the red pottage. His third name is Seir. Above these two names, Edom and Seir, are combined; and yet he is called Esau. Furthermore, he got the name Seir either from the mountain on which he lived — previously it was called Seir — or from his shagginess, because he was red and hairy; perhaps even the region he occupied was rough and wild. Hence the Idumaean nation is called the nation of Seir, from Esau, who occupied Mt. Seir, or because in that land the שְׂעִירִים lived, that is, fauns and shaggy satyrs, whom we call wild, hairy men.[80] But I am not sure whether or not such fauns and satyrs lived in this region. Elsewhere in the Bible the שְׂעִירִים are taken to be demons who appear in the form of fauns.[81]

31. *Jacob said: First sell me your birthright.*

32. *Esau said: I am about to die; of what use is a birthright to me?*

33. *Jacob said: Swear to me first. So he swore to him, and sold his birthright to Jacob.*

34. *Then Jacob gave Esau bread and pottage of lentils, and he ate and drank, and rose and went his way. Thus Esau despised his birthright.*

At this point an important question about the purchase and sale of the birthright arises; for the birthright is something sacred, and one may neither purchase nor sell it. Consequently, one asks whether both did wrong: the one by selling his birthright, the other by buy-

---

80 The German phrase is *die wilden rauhen menner.*

81 Perhaps an allusion to Lev. 17:7 and similar passages.

ing it. Lyra maintains that Esau sinned by selling it; but he says that Jacob did not sin by purchasing it, because he was the first-born by divine decree in accordance with the statement: "The elder will serve the younger." [82] Esau was in possession of the primogeniture that did not belong to him. Although he appropriated it to himself on account of his birth, nevertheless he did not have it by God's will. But, as people are wont to say, possession is nine points of the law. For this reason Jacob was unable to confuse him. Esau had the support of human right, divine right, and birth; and among all nations all this gives the property and the lordship to the twin born first. Besides, the law grants him a double share in the father's possessions. Therefore if God had not changed and revoked that right, Esau's primogeniture would have remained unimpaired. But because Jacob knows by the voice of God that it belongs to him, he does not sin by buying his own right for himself. He did well by watching for all opportunities to obtain the primogeniture that belonged to him.

But this could not be done by any more convenient method than a sale. Even though that pottage or morsel is not a fair price for the birthright, nevertheless it serves to ward off a lawsuit or to obviate trouble, as the jurists say. For it often happens that someone is unjustly harassed by sycophants who resort to legal proceedings against him, and, either by producing false witnesses or by devising other tricks, try to deprive him of his possessions, as though they had been wrongfully acquired by him. Although they could protect their right, people who love peace nevertheless give money to the syco-phants in order to avoid their chicanery rather than see the lawsuits through. In this case, the common saying holds good: "One must light two candles to the devil." Thus Jacob gave Esau the red morsel and freed himself of any trouble from his brother, who kept boasting of the primogeniture. As a result, Jacob could keep his property and right in peace. This is approximately what Lyra, in a manner pious and godly enough for that time, says concerning this passage.

Above, in connection with the history of Abraham, who bought a field for a burial (Gen. 23), I spoke about simony, namely, whether on this account Abraham must be called a simonist, since a burial is one of the things that are sacred and the purchase or sale of

---

[82] Lyra *ad* Gen. 25:31-34 says that thereby Esau became guilty of both gluttony and simony.

sacred things is called simony.[83] But we heard that the field which was purchased was a worldly thing subject to a carnal-minded master. And the sale of a field is a completely civil transaction. Therefore Abraham did not sin when he bought the field and established a burial place there. Otherwise whatever a Christian purchases for his daily needs — bread, meat, wine, all of which are devoted to the need of the saints — would be an act of simony. This is absurd.

Furthermore, the laws and canons call it simony when spiritual things are sold for money. They call the sale of a cemetery simony, because a cemetery is sacred to Christians. They also call it simony to sell part of a parish or lands from benefices, which they call ecclesiastical things. This was that monstrous sin against which the theologians and canonists used to inveigh unanimously before these times. They condemned the bishops and the Roman courtiers who bought or sold bishoprics. But they accomplished nothing with their outcries, and now they are laughed at by the entire papacy, which is actually full of simony. And if you take simony out of the papacy, you have already taken the sun away from it. For the courtiers have no other business than to buy and sell sacerdotal offices.

Hence to rid the Roman Church of simony is to destroy it from the very bottom. Where will the splendor and pomp of the cardinals of the Roman Curia be if you do away with simony? Indeed, the entire Curia itself will perish from the very bottom. For the number of the cardinals who have already swallowed up all the church properties is too great. The cardinals plundered and devoured the monastery of Agnes in Rome — the monastery which supported 160 persons.[84] Thus as simony is defined in canon law everything is full of simony, and he who wants to take simony away from the papacy will be acting as if he wanted to put the devil in heaven. John Hus and others who taught at that time censured this vice severely. But they did so in vain. For the Roman Curia is a damnable institution which all people should beware of and abhor. What instructions, therefore, would it give concerning faith and good morals? The papacy is a congregation of demons and of the worst people. They themselves condemn simony, and yet they live and are supported by it. For this reason it is fitting that we are warned in Rev. 18:4:

[83] Cf. p. 199, note 13.

[84] The basilica of Santa Agnese on the Via Nomentana in Rome dates from the fourth century and was rebuilt in the sixth century.

"Come out of her, my people, lest you take part in her sins, lest you share in her plagues." All its assemblages are of the devil. Therefore let us shun them, lest we become sharers in their plague.

But we could excuse these thefts of theirs by means of some gloss to the effect that one should not call them simony, because they are nonecclesiastical depredations, and there is no difference between such simony and nonecclesiastical seizure. It is no different from what we see today, namely, that the nobles fight among themselves about the seizure of lands, estates, and villages. The benefices and salaries which we enjoy are also acquired in a simoniacal manner.[85] "From the hire of the harlot they have been gathered," as is stated in Micah 1:7. But if they plunder the possessions of the church, they devote them to luxury and pomp, not to the use of godly priests. We, on the other hand, devote them to their proper use, namely, to the support of ministers of the church and to the maintenance of schools. Therefore we are not at all concerned about this simony. But because they burden themselves with their canon law, we say to them: "I will condemn you out of your own mouth" (Luke 19:22).

True simony, however, is the sale and purchase of a spiritual thing for money, as, for example, if someone wanted to buy grace, faith, love, miracles, and the virtues of the Holy Spirit with which the church of God is adorned. Simon tried to do this (Acts 8:19). It is not that the thing itself can be handed over by buying or selling holy things. For the Holy Spirit does not bestow His gifts for money; nor does God accept gold and silver for the forgiveness of sins, for life, eyes, senses, and all blessings. No, God's munificence dispenses His gifts to the grateful and the ungrateful. The only thing it demands is thanksgiving, so that we say: "Blessed be the Lord God in His gifts," so that divinity is attributed to Him, that is, that we acknowledge Him as God, of whom we confess wholeheartedly, by mouth and by deed, that He is the Creator. For no other price can be paid for such great gifts.

But one should look at the intention and the desire that prompt the purchase or sale of sacred things. Simon's intention, for example, is [86] simoniacal, since it is his wish to be able to receive the Holy Spirit for cash. Such is also the meaning of these words when we pray that God may be glorified and that His kingdom may be pre-

---

[85] Cf. *Luther's Works*, 27, p. 122, note 16.

[86] We have read *est* rather than *et*.

served. God cannot be debased or disgraced, because He is in essence the very glory, power, and goodness. But our intention and desire is such that we wish that God did not exist and that His glory were profaned; and we manifest this toward the Word and the sacraments. If we were able to harm or debase God as we do His Word and sacraments, then indeed we would not refrain from doing even this. Hence true simony is the traffic which is carried on with the Word of God, the sacraments, the church, and the saints. This simony the pope has not understood; nor does he understand it today, although the entire papacy is engulfed in it, and has been long before it became simoniacal according to the laws; for they used to sell heaven, the forgiveness of sins, grace, and the Holy Spirit for works. This accounts for such a great number of churches, cloisters, Masses, indulgences, and holy orders. With these works we wanted to earn God's grace.

In this manner they made a peddler of God, who would not bestow the kingdom of heaven without pay but would do so for a price and for merits. Even though He offers it gratis, they nevertheless scorn the freely bestowed favor and contribute 100 or 1,000 guldens for building cloisters, churches, and the like, with which to buy grace and God's benefits. Is this not trafficking in grace and forgiveness of sins? And this is the kind of person the pope was when he was best, and with this kind of simony he filled the entire world, to the extent that the world is nothing else than a cesspool of true simony. For what else are the societies doing than to receive money and to regard profit as godliness?

Strictly speaking, however, it is impossible to buy grace; and if you were to attempt this, it would be like wanting to milk a he-goat.[87] The pope milks the he-goat; the people hold the sieve underneath, as the proverb says. Consequently, even if it were possible for the pope to be reformed and for crass simony to be purged away, they nevertheless cannot be purged of true simony, because this is the soul of the pope. Just as the soul is the essence of the body, so the pope is a simonist in body and soul. But when an end has been put to simony, whatever there is in the way of papal pomp, splendor, and prestige will be done away with, and only the Bishop of Rome will remain.

[87] A proverbial expression whose Latin version goes back to Vergil, *Eclogues*, III, 91.

Thus one can see what great dangers and evils there are in the papacy, how great an abyss it is, and how horribly the entire world has been swallowed up through the primacy of the pope. Therefore we should hate that beast with a perfect hate. Nevertheless, they are still fighting to keep his primacy safe and intact. But what else would this be than to restore simony to life? It is surely horrible blasphemy and a misuse of the name of God, and it will be punished with eternal condemnation. To such a point they have dragged the Word, the name of God, and the church. Yet nothing has been bought. They only imagine that God's nature is such that He wants to sell grace. The intention and desire are simoniacal. In reality, however, there is a sieve and a he-goat.

Yet by nature this evil is implanted in the hearts of all human beings. If God were willing to sell grace, we would accept it more quickly and more gladly than when He offers it gratis. Formerly, when simony prevailed, all people were exceedingly eager to build countless monasteries and churches, because it was a sale and purchase of the kingdom of heaven. Now, when it is offered gratis and the statement is made: "God has sent His Son into the flesh to bestow eternal life on all who believe. You have earned nothing, but deliverance from death and sins, the Holy Spirit, and the kingdom of heaven are given gratis" — now the world disdains this mercy and munificence of God. Formerly, when we were taught how we could earn grace by our works, all eagerly devoted all their efforts and means to this, just as this little town of Wittenberg gave 1,000 guldens to the monks every year.[88]

Everywhere there is praise of Ambrose's decidedly harmful statement that the kingdom of heaven belongs to the poor, which is based on what Christ says in Luke 16:9: "That they may receive you into the eternal habitations." [89] This statement, like a sharp knife, pierced the hearts of all. "If the rich want to be saved, they should buy from the poor," they would shout. "But the Franciscans and the other religious brothers are the poor; they have the kingdom of heaven, and from them you must buy."

What a monstrous, ominous, and amazing state of affairs it is that the world spurns deliverance from sin, death, and hell — deliverance offered gratis through Christ! If simony were to prevail again,

[88] Cf. also *Luther's Works*, 23, pp. 356, 357.

[89] Perhaps a reference to Ambrose, *De officiis*, Book III, chs. 134, 135.

all would generously pour out their wealth. But when we teach in accordance with the Word and commandment of Christ: "Receive gratis, and give gratis to preachers, ministers, and schoolmasters," it is like telling a story to the deaf.[90] Indeed, they even rob those whom they should honor and help. Are these not the horrible ragings of darkness? Thus every human being is a simonist, and yet no such sale can take place; for neither to any human being nor to the monks has God given anything else in return for their vows than the flames of hell and eternal tortures.

Moreover, one can see how pitiable and dangerous a matter it is to have fallen away from the proposition of primary importance — the proposition concerning justification by faith without works. When it has been obscured and obliterated, the entire world becomes addicted to simony. Thus the Turks also strive to placate God with their works and to buy spiritual things for money and for merits. Therefore it is simony in name, like that described in canon law. For they purchase and obtain nothing for a price and merits, but that intention and desire has taken root deep in the human heart. Because of this every human being is a simonist by nature and would want God to be so constituted that He would be appeased by human works and merits, and that one could point out to Him: "I have done much and have fasted much; these things Thou shouldst consider and shouldst sell me salvation and eternal life." But God neither knows nor hears such workers of iniquity. He sets forth His will in the apostolic teaching (Eph. 2:8-9): "By grace you have been saved, and not because of works." When that grace has been done away with, there is no longer any difference between the Turk and the pope, the heathen and the Jews; they are all simonists and milkers of he-goats.

The simony of the canonists is less serious and is only physical; it should be referred to as robbery in civil life. But when the pope receives crowns, cities, and regions from kings and monarchs in order that he may make mention of them in the Mass, when he puts forth a semblance of godliness and wants to appear most pious, then he is worst and a simonist through and through. For in the former instance he does harm only by his example and confesses to the simony of which he is guilty by resorting to robbery in civil life; in the latter

[90] An allusion to Terence, *Heautontimorumenos*, II, 1.10, which had become proverbial.

instance he does not confess his sin but extols and praises his righteousness and religion. I have wanted to call attention to these things in order that it may be understood what true simony is, and in order that we may continue in the pure doctrine, which teaches how God has given us His Son and through Him all heavenly and spiritual blessings, which the world wants to purchase for a price and does not want to accept gratis.

Let us now return to the account. It appears that Jacob insisted on the purchase. Therefore he cannot be excused and freed from the offense of simony; for he states plainly: "Sell me your birthright." By what right, then, does he make this demand and commit so great a sin that he tries to purchase the blessing, which is spiritual and pertains to Christ and to future events, all of which are sacred and concern the future life? In this life all things are unholy and polluted. But the sacraments and the sacred acts were not instituted for the sake of the present life but in order that they might be a sacred preparation for future things. For by the Gospel I am prepared, reborn, and renewed for the future life. It has not been delivered to me in order that I may become rich from it. But he who is a pastor and preaches it in order to acquire riches and the glory of this world is a simonist. Thus the benefit of Baptism is that I am transferred from the bosom of my mother and out of the grave and am put back into Paradise, out of death into life. Accordingly, I am not seeking there the joys and pleasures of the world; but I make use of the spiritual gifts in such a manner that when those that are physical come to an end, I am brought out of this life to eternal life and to immortality. Therefore he who serves as a pastor and absolves or administers the sacraments in order to obtain glory and power by doing so is a simonist according to that crude definition of the canonists. He is not one of those who are more subtle and want to earn eternal life with their works.

But why does Jacob demand that the birthright be sold to him? And since he wants to buy the birthright, it follows that this is a business transaction. I answer: Jacob saw the opportunity by which he could get possession of the birthright, and he wanted to take advantage of it.

Furthermore, his brother Esau is one of those who are simonists in a crude way; that is, in the spiritual blessing he sought nothing beyond the belly, since he did not visit the tent but despised the worship of God. First he was indifferent to little things. Then he came to despise the greater blessings, just as the first-born Cain did. Esau did not understand the greatness of the blessing. Therefore he sold it for the goods and pleasures of the present world, so that before God he was deprived in reality of his primogeniture and all his possessions. Therefore Jacob was waiting for the opportunity at hand and agreed with his brother on a definite price, lest in the future any troubles or any inconvenience be caused for him by his brother on account of the primogeniture.

Thus today the pope has the name "church." We do not have it. We know, however, that we really are the church because we have the Word, the sacraments, and the Keys, which Christ left behind, not in order that they may be of use to our power and to the lusts of this life, but that they may prepare us for the coming of the Son of God. Therefore we are the true church.

The pope, on the other hand, arrogates this name and title to himself; for he is in possession, and he boasts that he is the successor of Peter and Paul. Now if I wanted to make the following agreement with the pope: "I shall give you so many thousand guldens every year, in order that [91] you may let me preach the Gospel freely and in its purity" — would that be simony? No; for I am not buying what I have before this, namely, the proper use of the sacraments, the pure doctrine of the Gospel, of faith, and of hope by looking forward to the future life. All these things have already been granted to me even against the will of the pope and without his authority. In fact, by offering him 1,000 guldens I am merely seeking to rid myself of that annoyance by making payments. Consequently, I am not buying anything but am merely offering my opponent a morsel and red lentils in order to be able to deprive the pope of the word "church." I am not concerned about those bulls and indulgences of his. I would be willing to give the princes of our side the advice to pay him several thousand kronen every year, to the end that bloodshed and other offenses may cease and the Gospel may be spread in peace. This is not simony; it is ridding oneself of an annoyance by making payments.

For this reason it is not an actual sale when Jacob says to Esau: "Sell me your birthright"; for the birthright has already been in Jacob's possession, and Esau has been deprived of it. Possession is with Jacob, but without the name; the name is with Esau, but with-

[91] We have read *ut* rather than *et*.

out possession. Because Jacob now sees that Esau understands or seeks nothing in the blessing except the belly — just as the pope, under the pretext of the church, seeks only his own glory and power — he offers Cerberus a morsel to prevent him from being troublesome to him in the future.[92]

Thus I would surely wish that our princes would pay the emperor 20,000 guldens every year, so that the Gospel could be taught in peace and quiet. "But," someone will say, "will you in this way be paying money for sacred things?" Not at all; for we are not buying what we already have, and they cannot take it from us. But we are paying this money in order that they may let us alone and the pope and the emperor may grant us peace.

Besides, O pope and cardinals, those spiritual blessings are not yours; they are ours. Although the pope would never grant us both kinds in the sacrament, we nevertheless have them from God. Nor can they sell them; or, if they should want to do so, they will be milking the he-goat and holding a sieve underneath. We have both kinds. The pope objects to it; God allows it. But if they do not cease annoying us with their persecutions, killings, and robberies, we shall make an agreement with them to the effect that they devour the red pottage. But they must not get the glory of having given or presented anything to us, for this would be acquiescing in their authority. This is something divine and sacred which I cannot buy for money. Therefore we do not want it to be given or presented by the pope.

Thus Esau, like Ishmael (Gen. 21:9), undoubtedly annoyed his brother Jacob greatly and proudly gave him orders, because he [Esau] was the lord and the first-born; but Jacob was regarded as a servant and a fool. From this persecution and vexation on the part of his brother Jacob wanted to free himself, so that he could safely get possession of the spiritual blessing. Thus today many Christians leave cities on account of their confession of the Gospel, lest they be compelled to endure the tyranny of the papists.[93] And Paul says in Rom. 12:18: "If possible, so far as it depends on you, live peaceably

---

92 An allusion to Vergil, *Aeneid*, Book VI, lines 416—425, where the Cumaean Sibyl gives Cerberus a drugged honey cake.

93 Under the principle *cuius regio eius religio*, officially formulated in the Peace of Augsburg of 1555 but practiced earlier, the Protestant inhabitants of a territory with a Roman Catholic prince, as well as the Roman Catholic inhabitants of a territory with a Protestant prince, were to accept their prince's confession or emigrate.

with all." If the adversaries are unwilling to be peaceful, give them the red pottage, in order that they may give you peace, that is, let you enjoy in peace the blessings which you have before this.

Esau's answer to his brother's request follows: "Behold I am dying; and of what use is the birthright to me?" The scoundrel despairs [94] and by his own testimony betrays his irreligious heart. Should one act and feel this way about religion, godliness, and one's birthright? Now he confesses plainly that he does not understand his birthright and does not regard it as the inheritance of future life and as a sacred matter. But if the birthright is of no benefit except for the glory and riches of this life, what will become of faith, hope, and the expectation of eternal blessings? Hence we shall say with the ungodly and the Epicureans what they are wont to say when they hear heaven mentioned. Their response is: "What is heaven if we have flour here?" [95] The pope has a similar sentiment about the church and the Keys. "What are you saying about the Keys? I have to use them to accumulate riches and to hold kings in check." These are the Esauitic words of the ungodly, who regard gain as godliness and would long since have bidden Christ and His Gospel farewell if they would not be blessed temporally in this world.

Consequently, this is important evidence of Holy Scripture that Esau has already lost his birthright; for he is judged out of his own mouth. Yet he undoubtedly thought: "I am the lord; I shall indeed sell my birthright, but I shall only fool him. Even if I do sell it, still I can get it back." In this way he deluded and despised his brother, just as the pope and his masks have deluded the whole world by selling good works and indulgences. They thought that they would go unpunished or that eventually they could repent.

And today many misuse the doctrine of the Gospel and meanwhile flatter themselves by saying: "Even if I persist in sins and am a godless person, still I shall eventually recover and return to the way." Thus some say even about Duke George: "He could have been converted in the last moment of his life." [96] But all these people will

[94] Here again the text breaks into German.

[95] Both from Luther's use of colloquial German here and from his quotation of these words elsewhere (cf. *Luther's Works*, 23, p. 10) it seems reasonable to conclude that he is referring to an actual interview.

[96] Duke George had died on April 17, 1539; it was reported that his dying words were: "Help me, Thou dear Savior, Jesus Christ! Have mercy on me and save me through Thy bitter suffering and death!"

finally hear that sad verdict which appears in the Epistle to the Hebrews (12:17) concerning Esau: "For you know that afterward, when he desired to inherit the blessing, he was rejected; for he found no chance to repent though he sought it with tears."

Thus the antinomians enjoy the advantages of the world in order to be happy in this life. They say that they want to be converted in good time. They despise their blessing, the church, Baptism, the Keys, forgiveness of sins, and eternal life. They receive the grace of God in vain and disregard "the acceptable time" and "the day of salvation" (2 Cor. 6:2). But at some future time they will seek the neglected opportunity in vain and too late, as the bride in the Song of Solomon (5:6) laments: "I opened to my beloved, but my beloved had turned and gone."

Thus when Esau says: "I am about to die; of what use is the birthright to me?" he indicates that he is thinking only of his belly and that he is scorning the promise as worthless and unprofitable for the future life, precisely as the Epicureans say today: "Why is it necessary to hear the Gospel and to make use of the Keys or the Lord's Supper?" But Jacob thinks differently and knows that these sacred things are preparations for the life to come. Therefore he esteems them highly and burns with desire for them. But those who want to make use of them for this life only are deprived of them justly and by divine authority, for in that case they have the freedom of the will knowingly and willingly to sell or reject them.

After Jacob sees that the favorable opportunity is restricted to a moment and brief space of time, he follows up his request and wants the agreement made binding. He says: "Swear to me at this time," or in this hour, because the opportunity should not be missed. Then Esau swears, and thus he sells his birthright. This is the way we should deal with the papists too. If they gave an oath, hostages, and seals that they will not begin a war against us, we would at once set a red pottage before them.

But a question raised by others at this point remains.[97] We shall deal with it too, lest it prove troublesome to the reader. Was that red food the price of the sale and purchase? They reply that it was not, because the birthright was a very important and very precious thing. Therefore they say that it is not likely that Esau accepted this

[97] Cf. Jerome, *Liber hebraicarum quaestionum in Genesin, Patrologia, Series Latina,* XXIII, 1028.

insignificant food as the price. Consequently, they claim that this food was merely the pledge which confirmed the agreement which Esau accepted as a sign of having sold his birthright. Thus it is customary among us for one or two tankards of wine to be placed between the purchaser and seller as a sign of a sale. The Germans call it *gleichkauff*.

This opinion has come from the commentaries of the rabbis. We reject it. Thus all their opinions must be dealt with in such a manner that what is good in them is retained, but bad and false ideas are avoided. For this opinion conflicts with the clear text in the Epistle to the Hebrews (12:16), where it is plainly stated: "Esau sold his birthright for a single meal."

Holy Scripture wanted to portray the nature and ways of the wicked and hypocritical church, which must be recognized and understood from its ways, of which Esau is a type and figure. For it is in the habit of glorying very much in the name of God and wants to be and to be regarded as the church. And before the world it is the church. Similarly, Esau has the primogeniture; but he despises it. His contempt causes him to lose it; for he, in turn, is despised, rejected, and despoiled. Therefore his glorying is nothing, just as that of the papists, who boast that they are the church and the successors of the apostles, is nothing. He who wants to be the church must esteem his birthright highly, not only in this life but also after this life.

This conflict goes on and on in the world. Just as Esau struggled with Jacob, so we struggle against the papists, and before our time the Jewish people struggled against the apostles. The Jews maintained vehemently that they were the people of God, and Paul confesses that they are the church (cf. Rom. 2:17; 9:24). But because they retained only the name but despised the true church itself, they were rejected, and the Gentiles were called. Hos. 2:23: "And I will say to Not My people: 'You are My people'; and he shall say: 'Thou art my God.'" And in Deut. 32:21 we read: "I will stir them to jealousy with those who are no people; I will provoke them with a foolish nation."

Consequently, this is one mark, yes the worst color of the hypocritical church, that it is exceedingly proud and impudent in making use of the name of God, the church, the Keys, the ministry, and the sacraments, and can do nothing more than boast of God. Another mark is the fact that it actually despises and disregards the things that belong to the true church. It does not concern itself much about its birthright, just as the pope and the bishops do not teach, do not baptize, and do not perform any other duty in the church. They have only the name. But they show no fruit and result. Therefore Christ says (Matt. 7:16): "You will know them by their fruits." But because the pope despises the church, he loses the church, and that empty boast of his is of no importance: "We are the Christians, we are the church, and we are the bishops." If the real substance is not there, you will not keep the name for long. Indeed, you have already been rejected. What you have you do not have. Thus the heretics who will come after us will lose the church; for it is a pillar of truth (1 Tim. 3:15), which they will thrust aside; and the boast and name without the truth is of no benefit to them.

Therefore when they shout: "We are the church, we have the authority to give commands," and want to compel us to give assent to their ordinances, we shall answer: "The church is of two kinds: in number and worth, in outward appearance and truth, and in name and reality," as they themselves teach.[98] Without the reality Esau is the church only in name and outward appearance. So are all idolaters and heretics who arrogate to themselves the title "church." I can put up with it when someone is a Christian in number only and meanwhile still performs the outward duty. Even if he is secretly godless and vicious, there is nothing to prevent one from calling him a Christian or the church in number, but not worth — provided that he baptizes, takes care of the sick, and strengthens troubled consciences. This the pope and the bishops do not do. Therefore they should not even be compared to those who are secretly godless, for they do things that are contrary to their office in the church. They speak irreverently of the Word and persecute the godly, that is, the true church.

In our church there are many ministers in number only, but without worth. But the pope is an avowed adversary of the church; he suppresses the doctrine of faith, fills the world with idolatry, simony, and countless monstrosities. That is acting like a madman against the church in regard to number and worth, after the fashion of the Turks. Therefore the argument of the papists has no force at all. "We are the church in regard to number," they say. "Therefore you must put up with us." If they wanted to be such, they would have to

---

98 Cf. *Luther the Expositor*, p. 96.

agree with us in doctrine, teach, and govern. This is fitting [99] for true and godly bishops. But they are descendants of Esau, adversaries and destroyers of the church, as the heretics are.

Those however, who, like many who are mingled with the company of the godly, feign godliness and are hypocrites we tolerate among the number of the believers, provided that they do not teach anything contrary to the profession of the true doctrine.

Moses has also depicted the third mark of the hypocritical church in this type. After Esau very smugly and with great impudence slighted the spiritual blessings — faith, love, patience, and kindness, which are in the church — yes, even despised all these, there now follows the appetite and intense desire for that red pottage; that is, because he is not concerned about the knowledge of Christ or about the increase of spiritual gifts or about life eternal, he becomes greedily desirous of the pleasures, the glory, and the honors of this life.

This is undoubtedly because Esau prefers the pottage to his birthright; that is, he is the church in regard to number, but he follows his flesh and blood and seeks gain in godliness. Thus the false church feigns godliness merely in order to enjoy the pleasures and honors of this world. But the true church seeks eternal life through patience and faith. The others are beasts of the belly, and their god is the belly (cf. Phil. 3:19).

This is the mystery of the red pottage which Holy Scripture sets before us in this passage, where the conflict between the two brothers about the birthright is settled. But lentils are not red; they are yellow. Therefore I think that they were prepared with saffron or another condiment in order to stimulate the appetite. But such is the nature of the present good things of this world by which men are delighted in an astonishing manner, so that they prefer indulgence in reveling and gourmandizing to eating and drinking the flesh and blood of the Son of God, that is, to believing and seeking heavenly blessings. They look only for gain and the glory of the world, the pleasantness and delight of which is so great that it excites in people not only hunger but some concupiscence. Therefore Esau employs the repetition: "Let me eat, I beg you, of the red pottage, of that red pottage."

Hence Holy Scripture is pointing out that all people become greedier, prouder, and more carnal when they have lost the blessing

[99] We have read *decet* rather than *docet*, which is the reading of the Weimar text.

than they were before. For they all have flesh and blood and for this reason seek nothing except carnal things and long for the red pottage with horrible cupidity, but under the name of Christ and of God and under the title "church." Jacob, too, eats of the red pottage, but not so greedily. He does not repeat the word "red" twice, as Esau does. This means that the godly make use of the present things, not for their happiness but for their need.

Finally Moses adds that Esau attached little importance to the fact that he had sold his birthright. There, too, his exceedingly impudent pride is indicated, for he thought that with human help he could safely and easily uphold his right against his brother without any consideration to their agreement. Hypocrites and false brothers are in the habit of doing the same thing; they carry water on both shoulders.[100] They are wily. Now they pretend that they are yielding and making some concessions; now they seize again what by no right belongs to them. Nevertheless, they have their explanations with which they cover up and excuse their hypocrisy in order that they may keep the red pottage together with the birthright; for they want to serve God and the belly or mammon at the same time.

Thus Esau thought: "Even though I have sold my birthright, have sworn, and have consumed the morsel, and my most contemptible brother now seems to have taken away my birthright, I shall nevertheless retain it and not keep faith." For he did not sell it in earnest; but he wanted to fool his brother and deceive him, as though he had sold it. Nevertheless, he wanted to keep his right. But the Epistle to the Hebrews (12:17) bears witness that later on he was rejected, and although he tried to recover his birthright — because he repented of having sold it — yet that repentance did not accomplish anything at all, not that he was not saved, but that he was unable by means of any tears to obtain the blessing he had once lost. Consequently, it is my opinion that the morsel was the price of this sale; and I do not accept the gloss of the rabbis, because they are carnal people who understand nothing in the Holy Scriptures.

[100] The original expression is "a tree on both shoulders"; cf. *Luther's Works*, 21, p. 186, note 33.

Index

By WALTER A. HANSEN

INDEX TO SCRIPTURE PASSAGES